The Natural Disorder of Things

Other *Baby Blues*® Books from Andrews McMeel Publishing

Guess Who Didn't Take a Nap?
I Thought Labor Ended When the Baby Was Born
We Are Experiencing Parental Difficulties . . . Please Stand By
Night of the Living Dad
I Saw Elvis in My Ultrasound
One More and We're Outnumbered!
Check, Please . . .
threats, bribes & videotape
If I'm a Stay-at-Home Mom, Why Am I Always in the Car?
Lift and Separate
I Shouldn't Have to Scream More Than Once!
Motherhood Is Not for Wimps
Baby Blues®: Unplugged
Dad to the Bone
Never a Dry Moment
Two Plus One Is Enough
Playdate: Category 5
Our Server Is Down
Something Chocolate This Way Comes
Briefcase Full of Baby Blues®
Night Shift
The Day Phonics Kicked In
My Space

Treasuries

The Super-Absorbent Biodegradable Family-Size Baby Blues®
Baby Blues®: Ten Years and Still in Diapers
Butt-Naked Baby Blues®
Wall-to-Wall Baby Blues®
Driving Under the Influence of Children
Framed!
X-Treme Parenting

The Natural Disorder of Things

BABY BLUES® **25** SCRAPBOOK

BY RICK KIRKMAN AND JERRY SCOTT

Andrews McMeel
Publishing, LLC
Kansas City • Sydney • London

Baby Blues® is syndicated internationally by King Features Syndicate, Inc. For information, write King Features Syndicate, Inc., 300 West Fifty-Seventh Street, New York, New York 10019.

09 10 11 12 13 RR2 10 9 8 7 6 5 4 3 2 1

ISBN-13: 978-0-7407-8540-5
ISBN-10: 0-7407-8540-0
Library of Congress Catalog Card Number: 2009924138

www.andrewsmcmeel.com

Find *Baby Blues*® on the Web at
www.babyblues.com.

——— **ATTENTION: SCHOOLS AND BUSINESSES** ———

Andrews McMeel books are available at quantity discounts with bulk purchase for educational, business, or sales promotional use. For information, please write to: Special Sales Department, Andrews McMeel Publishing, LLC, 1130 Walnut Street, Kansas City, Missouri 64106.

For Sonia. Welcome to the world!

—J.S.

To "Monsewer" Paul Reeves. Thanks for your encouragement when I was
just a sprig of a cartoonist.

—R.K.

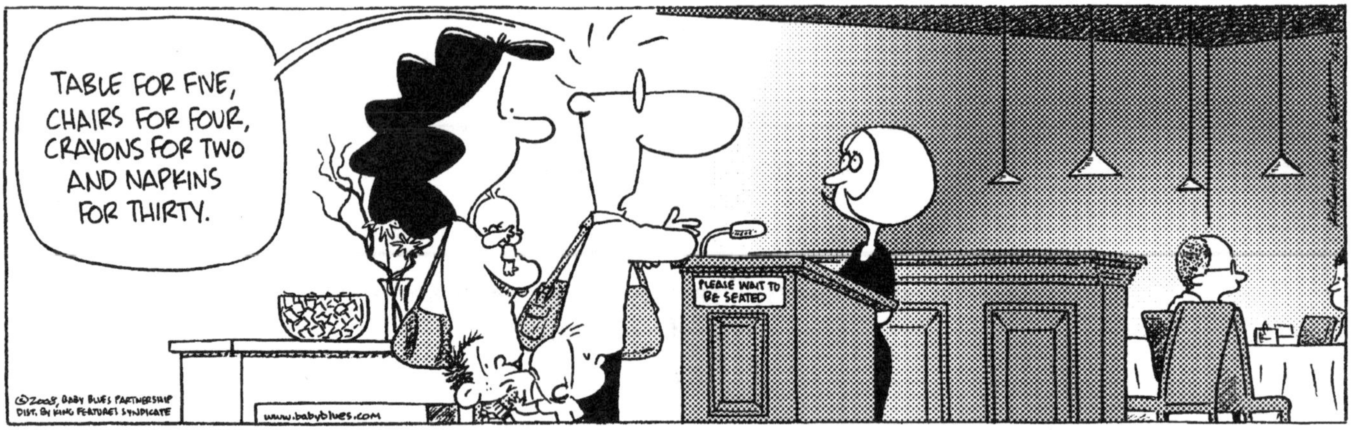
TABLE FOR FIVE, CHAIRS FOR FOUR, CRAYONS FOR TWO AND NAPKINS FOR THIRTY.
PLEASE WAIT TO BE SEATED
©2008, BABY BLUES PARTNERSHIP DIST. BY KING FEATURES SYNDICATE
www.babyblues.com

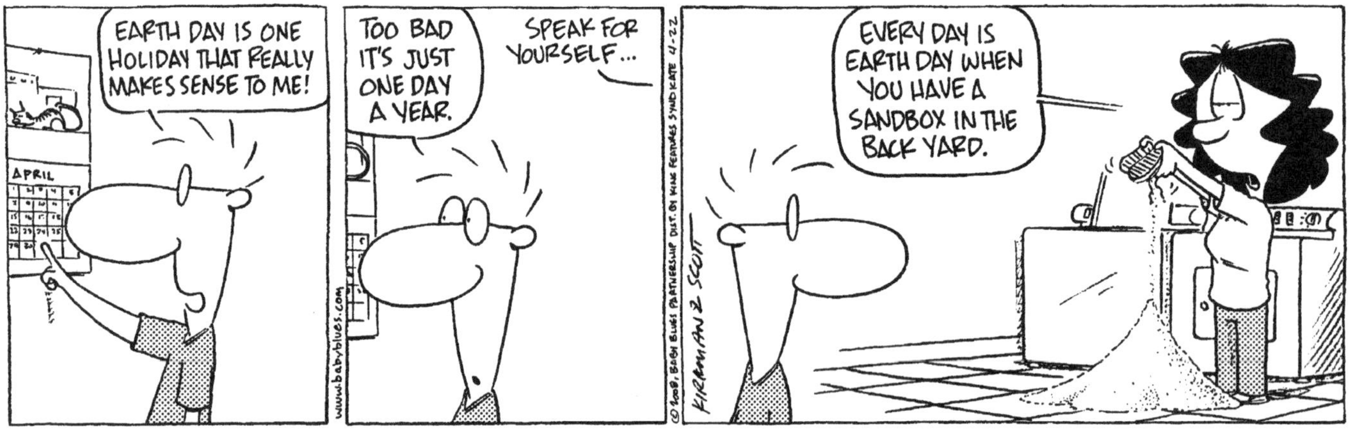
EARTH DAY IS ONE HOLIDAY THAT REALLY MAKES SENSE TO ME!
APRIL
TOO BAD IT'S JUST ONE DAY A YEAR.
SPEAK FOR YOURSELF...
www.babyblues.com
© 2008, BABY BLUES PARTNERSHIP DIST. BY KING FEATURES SYNDICATE 4-22
KIRKMAN & SCOTT
EVERY DAY IS EARTH DAY WHEN YOU HAVE A SANDBOX IN THE BACK YARD.

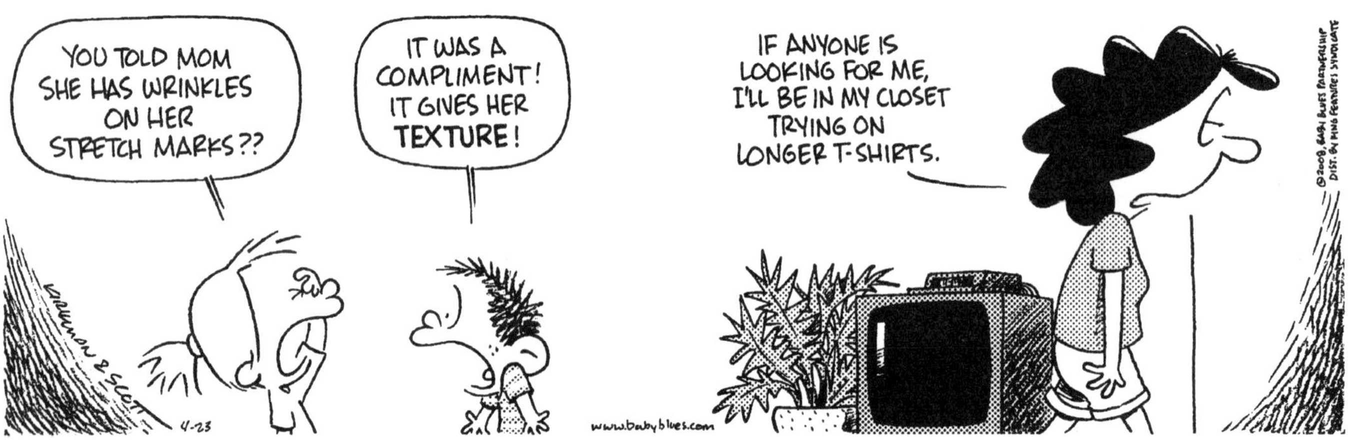
YOU TOLD MOM SHE HAS WRINKLES ON HER STRETCH MARKS??
KIRKMAN & SCOTT
4-23
IT WAS A COMPLIMENT! IT GIVES HER TEXTURE!
www.babyblues.com
IF ANYONE IS LOOKING FOR ME, I'LL BE IN MY CLOSET TRYING ON LONGER T-SHIRTS.
©2008, BABY BLUES PARTNERSHIP DIST. BY KING FEATURES SYNDICATE

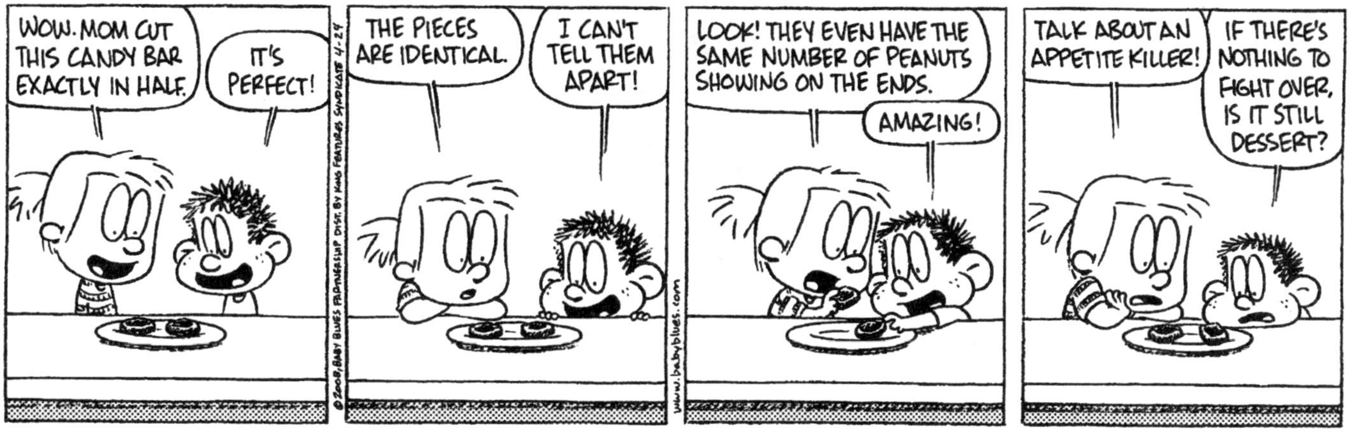
WOW. MOM CUT THIS CANDY BAR EXACTLY IN HALF.
IT'S PERFECT!
©2008, BABY BLUES PARTNERSHIP DIST. BY KING FEATURES SYNDICATE 4-24
THE PIECES ARE IDENTICAL.
I CAN'T TELL THEM APART!
www.babyblues.com
LOOK! THEY EVEN HAVE THE SAME NUMBER OF PEANUTS SHOWING ON THE ENDS.
AMAZING!
TALK ABOUT AN APPETITE KILLER!
IF THERE'S NOTHING TO FIGHT OVER, IS IT STILL DESSERT?

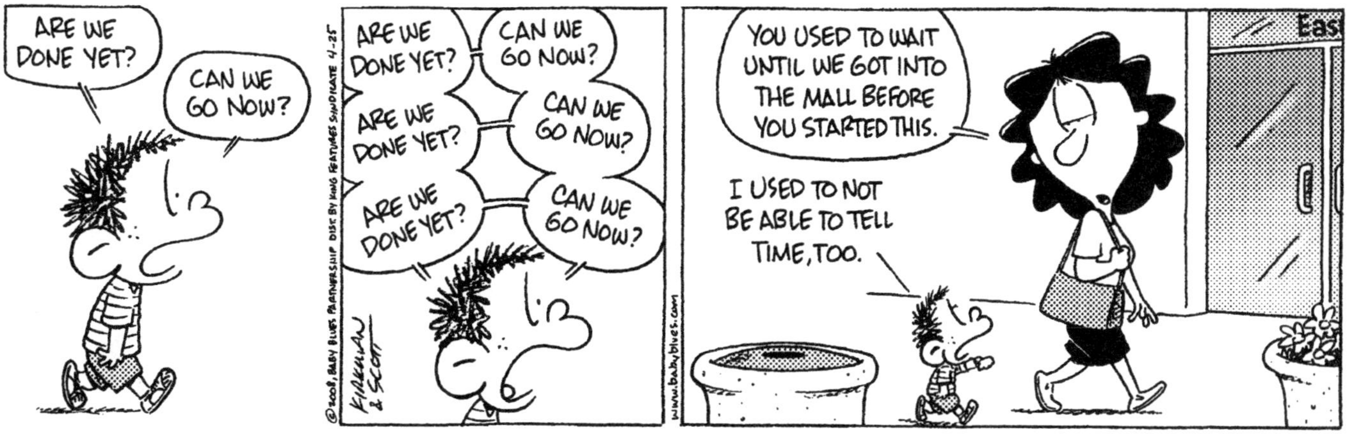
ARE WE DONE YET?
CAN WE GO NOW?
©2008, BABY BLUES PARTNERSHIP DIST. BY KING FEATURES SYNDICATE 4-25
ARE WE DONE YET?
CAN WE GO NOW?
ARE WE DONE YET?
CAN WE GO NOW?
ARE WE DONE YET?
CAN WE GO NOW?
KIRKMAN & SCOTT
www.babyblues.com
YOU USED TO WAIT UNTIL WE GOT INTO THE MALL BEFORE YOU STARTED THIS.
I USED TO NOT BE ABLE TO TELL TIME, TOO.

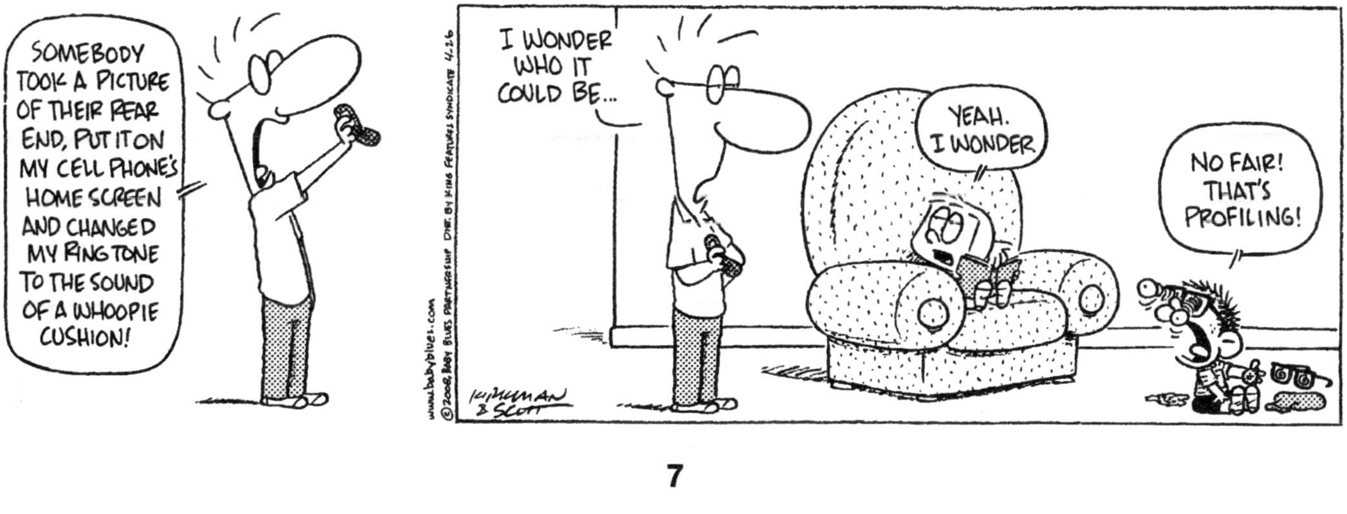
SOMEBODY TOOK A PICTURE OF THEIR REAR END, PUT IT ON MY CELL PHONE'S HOME SCREEN AND CHANGED MY RINGTONE TO THE SOUND OF A WHOOPIE CUSHION!
©2008, BABY BLUES PARTNERSHIP DIST. BY KING FEATURES SYNDICATE 4-26
www.babyblues.com
I WONDER WHO IT COULD BE...
YEAH. I WONDER.
NO FAIR! THAT'S PROFILING!
KIRKMAN & SCOTT

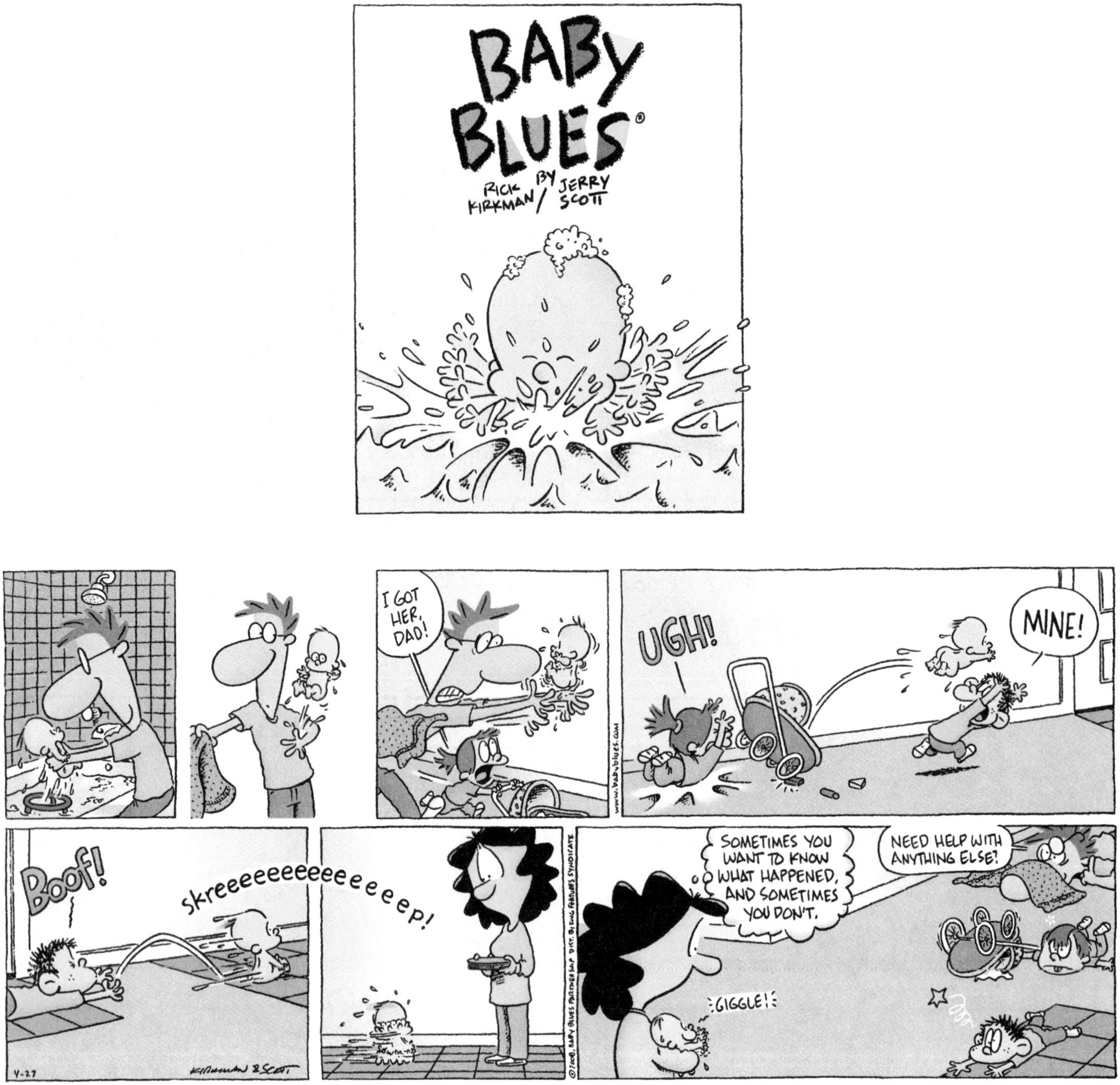
BABY BLUES®
BY RICK KIRKMAN / JERRY SCOTT
I GOT HER, DAD!
www.babyblues.com
UGH!
MINE!
BOOF!
skreeeeeeeeeeeeeeeep!
©2008, BABY BLUES PARTNERSHIP DIST. BY KING FEATURES SYNDICATE
SOMETIMES YOU WANT TO KNOW WHAT HAPPENED, AND SOMETIMES YOU DON'T.
NEED HELP WITH ANYTHING ELSE?
GIGGLE!
4-27

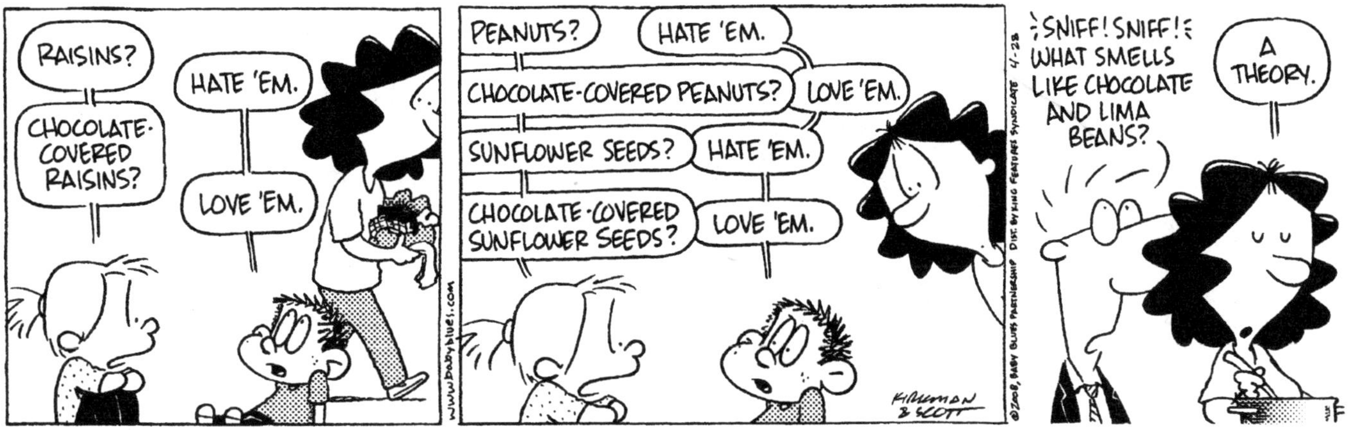
RAISINS?
HATE 'EM.
CHOCOLATE-COVERED RAISINS?
LOVE 'EM.
www.babyblues.com
PEANUTS?
HATE 'EM.
CHOCOLATE-COVERED PEANUTS?
LOVE 'EM.
SUNFLOWER SEEDS?
HATE 'EM.
CHOCOLATE-COVERED SUNFLOWER SEEDS?
LOVE 'EM.
KIRKMAN & SCOTT
©2008, BABY BLUES PARTNERSHIP DIST. BY KING FEATURES SYNDICATE 4-28
SNIFF! SNIFF! WHAT SMELLS LIKE CHOCOLATE AND LIMA BEANS?
A THEORY.

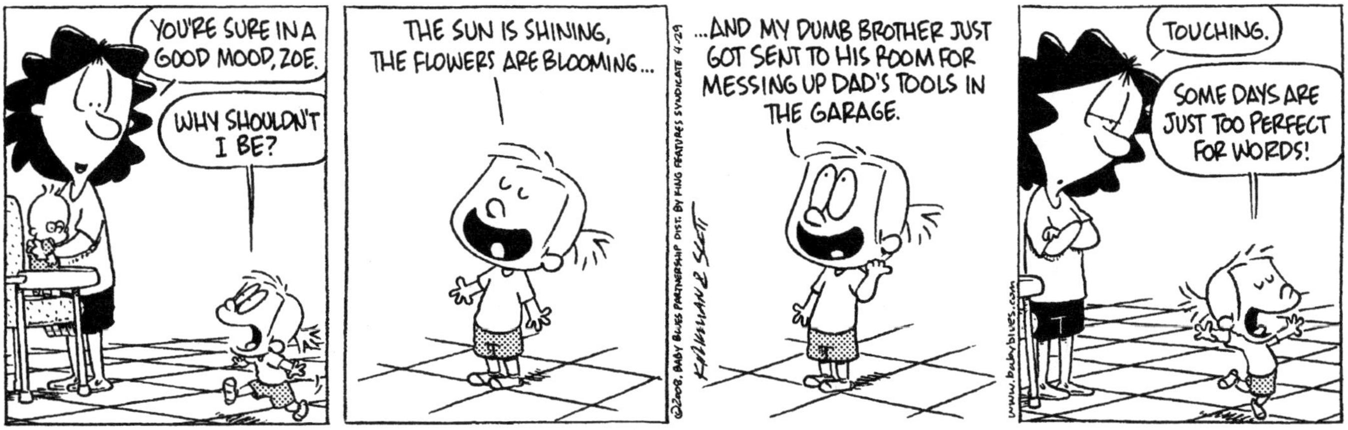
YOU'RE SURE IN A GOOD MOOD, ZOE.
WHY SHOULDN'T I BE?
THE SUN IS SHINING, THE FLOWERS ARE BLOOMING...
©2008, BABY BLUES PARTNERSHIP DIST. BY KING FEATURES SYNDICATE 4-29
KIRKMAN & SCOTT
...AND MY DUMB BROTHER JUST GOT SENT TO HIS ROOM FOR MESSING UP DAD'S TOOLS IN THE GARAGE.
www.babyblues.com
TOUCHING.
SOME DAYS ARE JUST TOO PERFECT FOR WORDS!

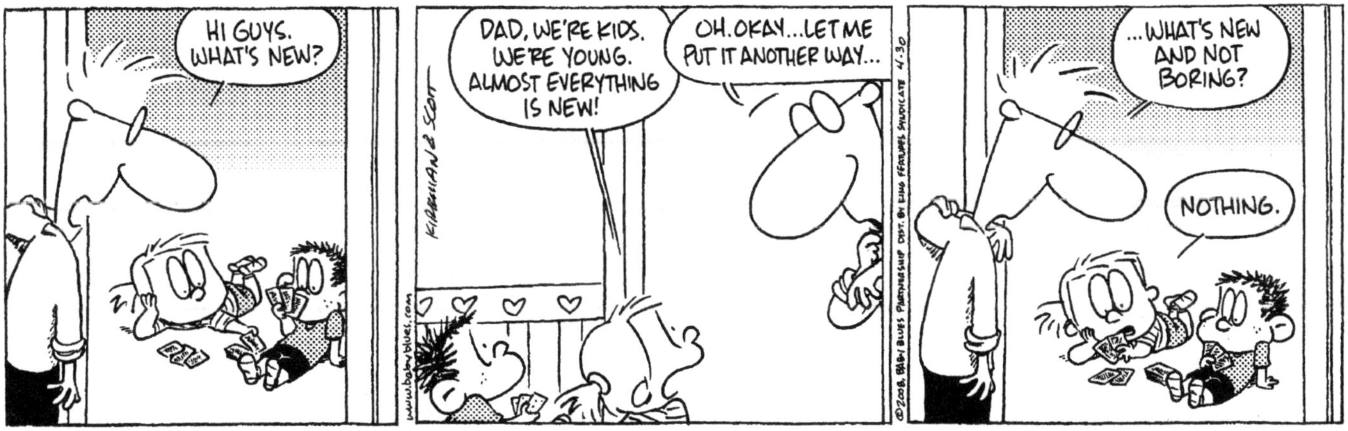
HI GUYS. WHAT'S NEW?
www.babyblues.com
KIRKMAN & SCOTT
DAD, WE'RE KIDS. WE'RE YOUNG. ALMOST EVERYTHING IS NEW!
OH. OKAY... LET ME PUT IT ANOTHER WAY...
©2008, BABY BLUES PARTNERSHIP DIST. BY KING FEATURES SYNDICATE 4-30
...WHAT'S NEW AND NOT BORING?
NOTHING.

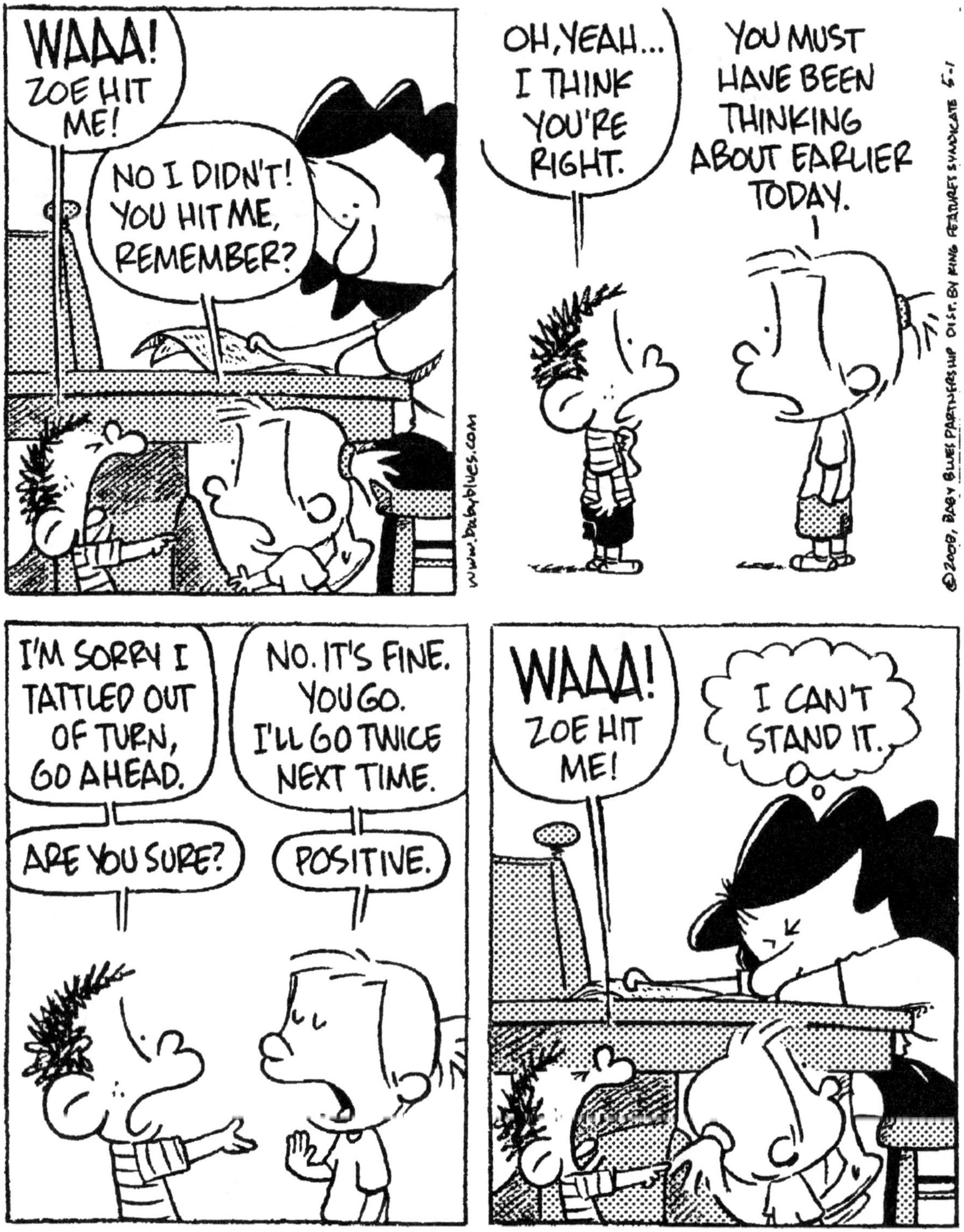
WAAA! ZOE HIT ME!
NO I DIDN'T! YOU HIT ME, REMEMBER?
www.babyblues.com
OH, YEAH... I THINK YOU'RE RIGHT.
YOU MUST HAVE BEEN THINKING ABOUT EARLIER TODAY.
©2008, BABY BLUES PARTNERSHIP DIST. BY KING FEATURES SYNDICATE 5-1
I'M SORRY I TATTLED OUT OF TURN, GO AHEAD.
NO. IT'S FINE. YOU GO. I'LL GO TWICE NEXT TIME.
ARE YOU SURE?
POSITIVE.
WAAA! ZOE HIT ME!
I CAN'T STAND IT.

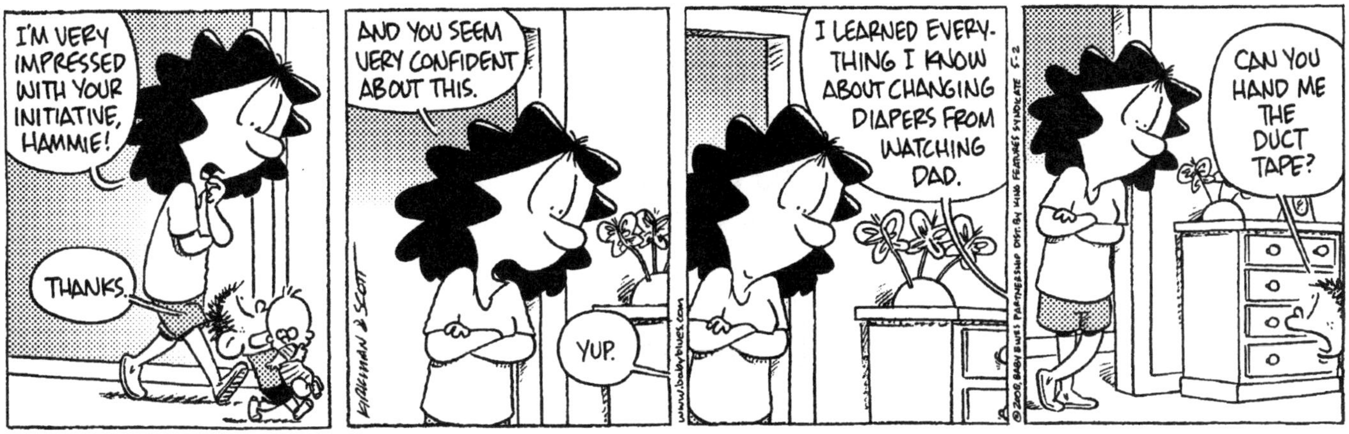
I'M VERY IMPRESSED WITH YOUR INITIATIVE, HAMMIE!
THANKS.
KIRKMAN & SCOTT
AND YOU SEEM VERY CONFIDENT ABOUT THIS.
YUP.
www.babyblues.com
I LEARNED EVERY-THING I KNOW ABOUT CHANGING DIAPERS FROM WATCHING DAD.
© 2008, BABY BLUES PARTNERSHIP DIST. BY KING FEATURES SYNDICATE 5-2
CAN YOU HAND ME THE DUCT TAPE?

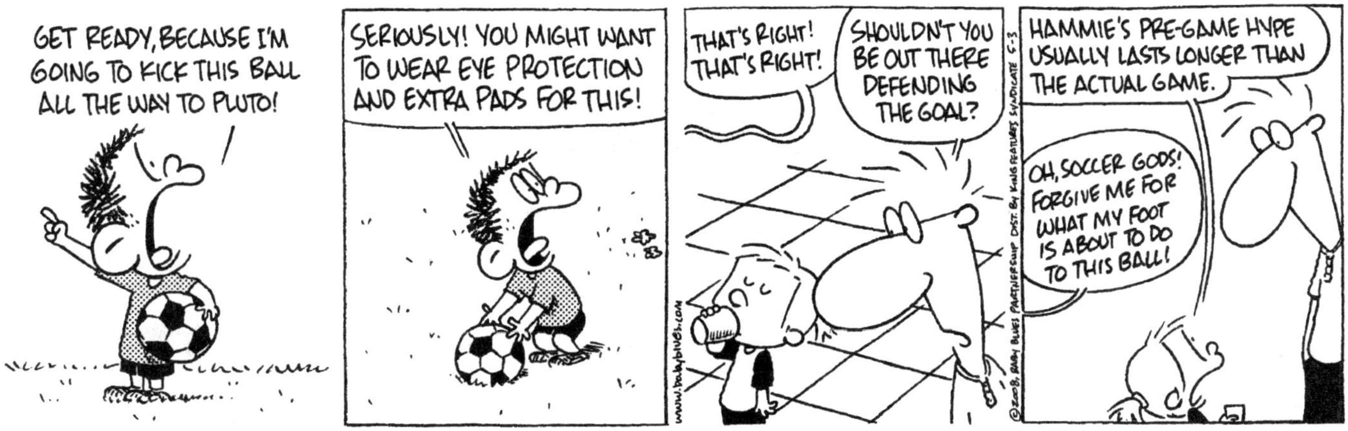
GET READY, BECAUSE I'M GOING TO KICK THIS BALL ALL THE WAY TO PLUTO!
SERIOUSLY! YOU MIGHT WANT TO WEAR EYE PROTECTION AND EXTRA PADS FOR THIS!
www.babyblues.com
THAT'S RIGHT! THAT'S RIGHT!
SHOULDN'T YOU BE OUT THERE DEFENDING THE GOAL?
© 2008, BABY BLUES PARTNERSHIP DIST. BY KING FEATURES SYNDICATE 5-3
HAMMIE'S PRE-GAME HYPE USUALLY LASTS LONGER THAN THE ACTUAL GAME.
OH, SOCCER GODS! FORGIVE ME FOR WHAT MY FOOT IS ABOUT TO DO TO THIS BALL!

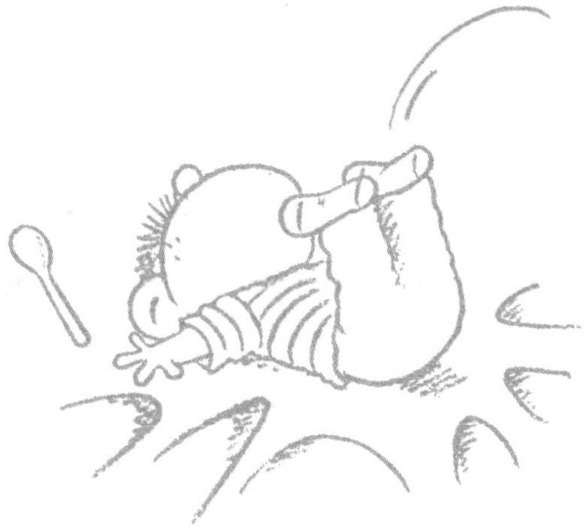

BABY BLUES®

RICK KIRKMAN / JERRY SCOTT

Draw Me

CHECK THIS OUT, HAMMIE.
FIRST YOU PUT YOUR HAND LIKE THIS ON THE PAPER...
UH-HUH...
...THEN YOU TRACE AROUND IT CAREFULLY...
RIGHT...
...ADD CERTAIN DETAILS, AND YOU HAVE...
...DAD!
WHOA!
KIRKMAN & SCOTT
©2008, BABY BLUES PARTNERSHIP DIST. BY KING FEATURES SYNDICATE 5-4
www.babyblues.com
IS IT JUST ME, OR DO YOU FIND THIS MILDLY INSULTING?
YOU HAVE JUST DOUBLED MY ARTISTIC ABILITIES!
FIND ME A LIGHT BULB TO TRACE, AND I'LL SHOW YOU HOW TO DRAW MOM'S HEAD!

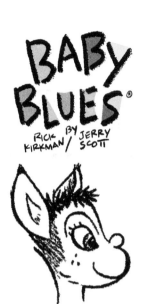

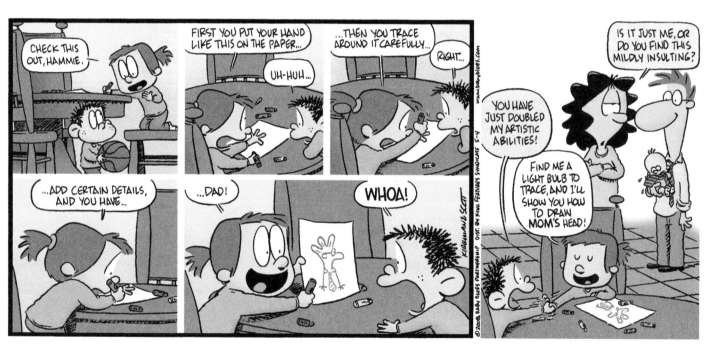

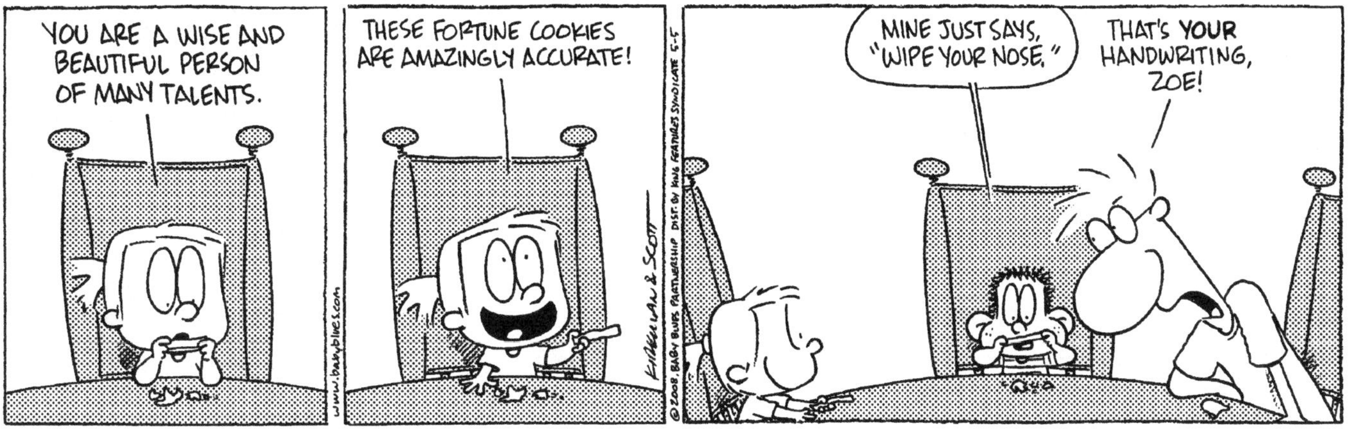
YOU ARE A WISE AND BEAUTIFUL PERSON OF MANY TALENTS.
THESE FORTUNE COOKIES ARE AMAZINGLY ACCURATE!
MINE JUST SAYS, "WIPE YOUR NOSE."
THAT'S **YOUR** HANDWRITING, ZOE!

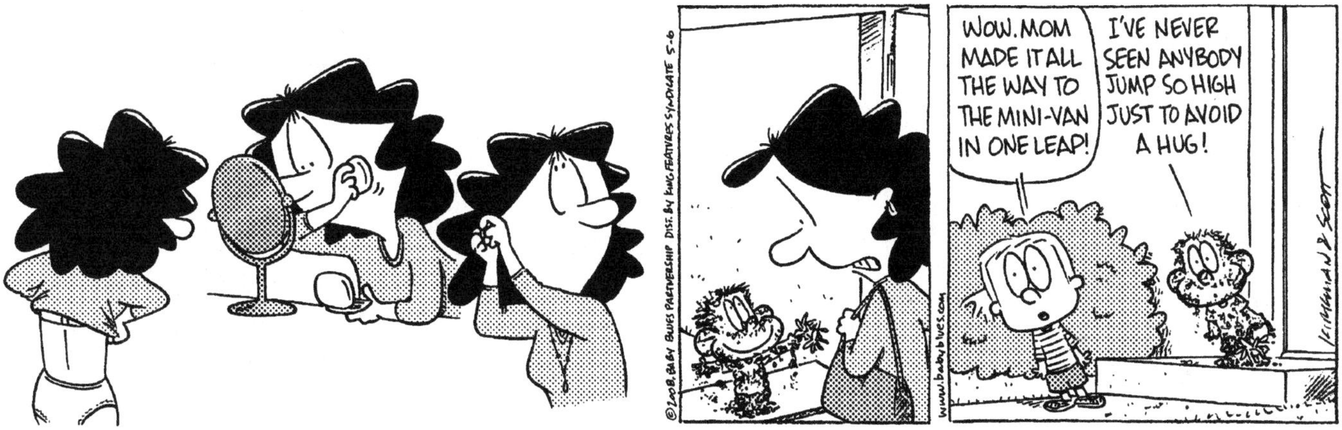
WOW. MOM MADE IT ALL THE WAY TO THE MINI-VAN IN ONE LEAP!
I'VE NEVER SEEN ANYBODY JUMP SO HIGH JUST TO AVOID A HUG!

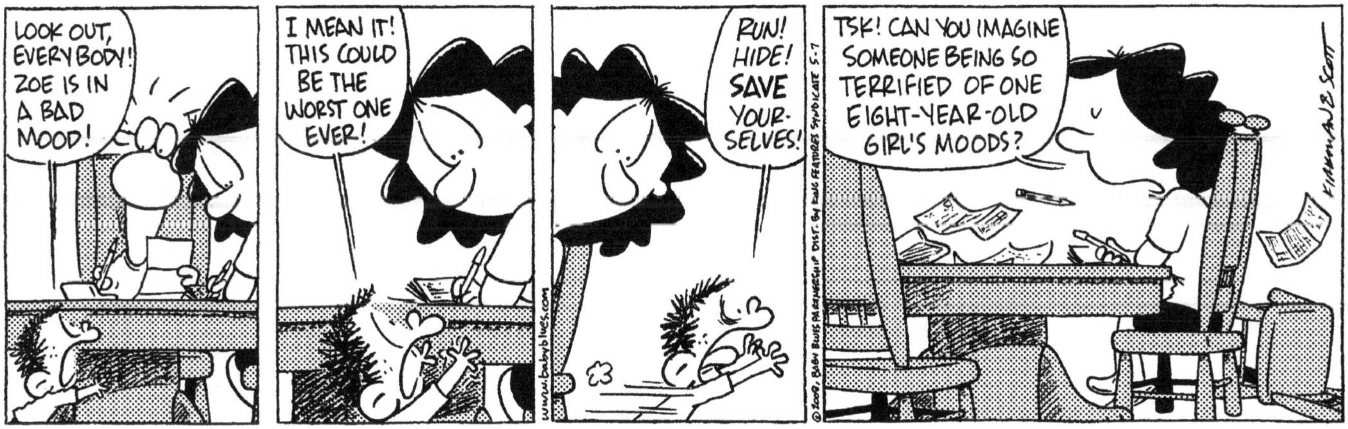
LOOK OUT, EVERYBODY! ZOE IS IN A BAD MOOD!
I MEAN IT! THIS COULD BE THE WORST ONE EVER!
RUN! HIDE! **SAVE** YOURSELVES!
TSK! CAN YOU IMAGINE SOMEONE BEING SO TERRIFIED OF ONE EIGHT-YEAR-OLD GIRL'S MOODS?

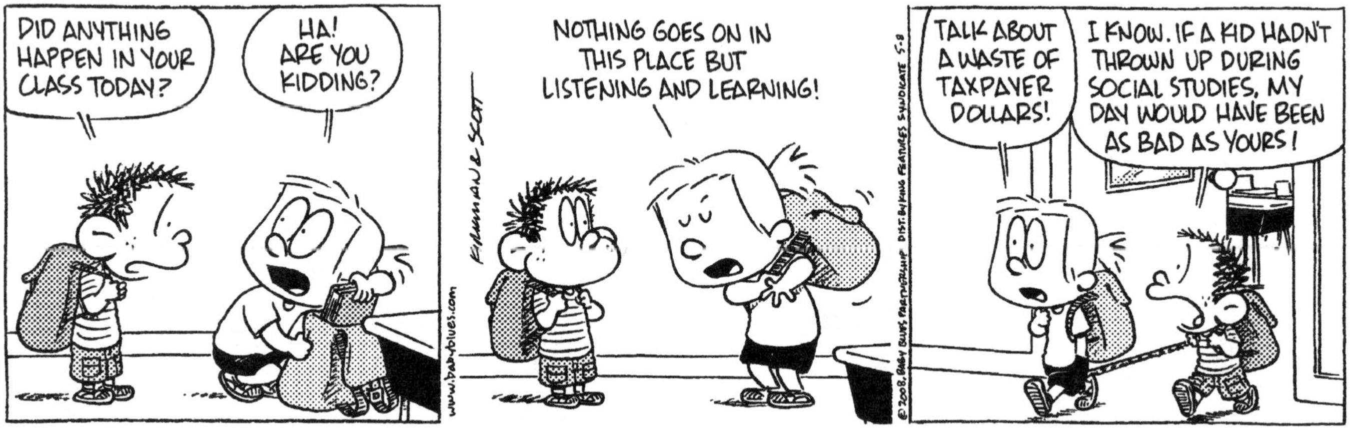
DID ANYTHING HAPPEN IN YOUR CLASS TODAY?
HA! ARE YOU KIDDING?
NOTHING GOES ON IN THIS PLACE BUT LISTENING AND LEARNING!
TALK ABOUT A WASTE OF TAXPAYER DOLLARS!
I KNOW. IF A KID HADN'T THROWN UP DURING SOCIAL STUDIES, MY DAY WOULD HAVE BEEN AS BAD AS YOURS!

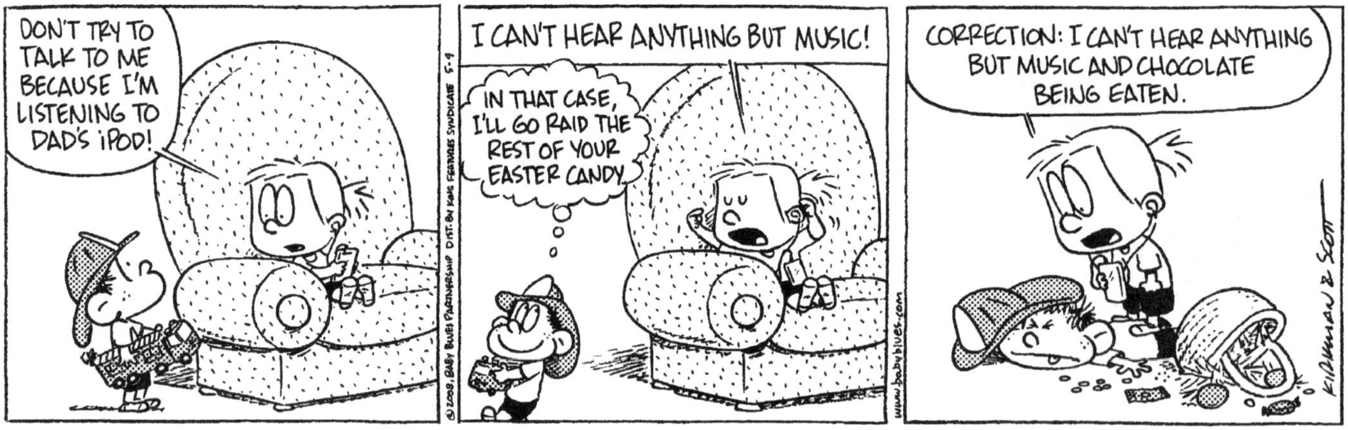
DON'T TRY TO TALK TO ME BECAUSE I'M LISTENING TO DAD'S iPOD!
I CAN'T HEAR ANYTHING BUT MUSIC!
IN THAT CASE, I'LL GO RAID THE REST OF YOUR EASTER CANDY.
CORRECTION: I CAN'T HEAR ANYTHING BUT MUSIC AND CHOCOLATE BEING EATEN.

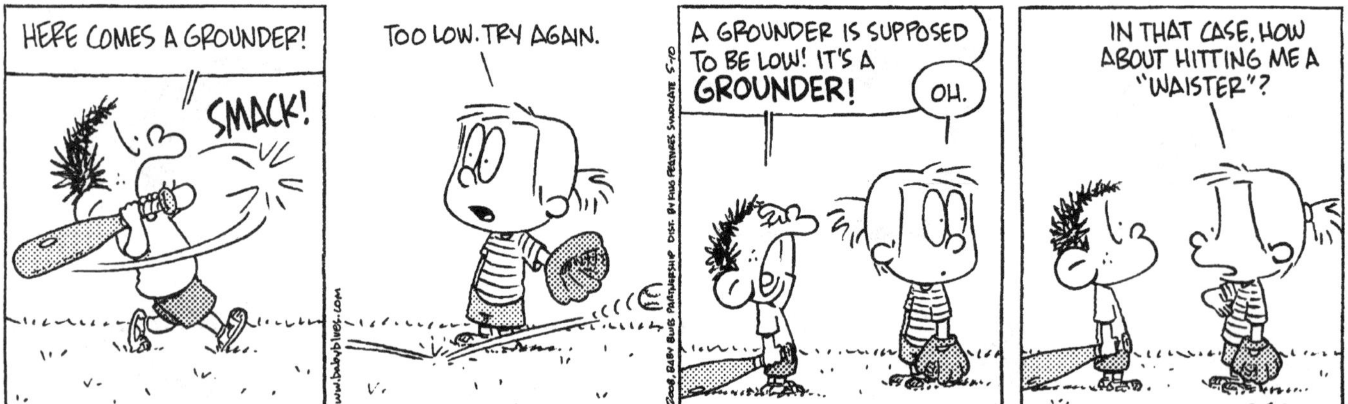
HERE COMES A GROUNDER!
SMACK!
TOO LOW. TRY AGAIN.
A GROUNDER IS SUPPOSED TO BE LOW! IT'S A GROUNDER!
OH.
IN THAT CASE, HOW ABOUT HITTING ME A "WAISTER"?

BABY BLUES®
BY
RICK KIRKMAN / JERRY SCOTT
TOOLS

WHO WANTS TO GO TO THE HARDWARE STORE WITH ME?
www.babyblues.com
FASTENERS!
LUMBER!
FLANGES!
I'M TALKING ABOUT HOURS OF POINTLESS MEANDERING UP AND DOWN ENDLESS WAREHOUSE AISLES AS I PONDER EVERY GADGET ON THE SHELF, TRYING TO FIGURE OUT WHAT IT'S FOR!
SO, WHO'S WITH ME?
© 2008, BABY BLUES PARTNERSHIP DIST. BY KING FEATURES SYNDICATE
IF YOU WANT TO SPEND THE MORNING ALONE, WHY DON'T YOU JUST SAY SO?
IT FEELS LESS SELFISH MY WAY.
KIRKMAN & SCOTT 5-11

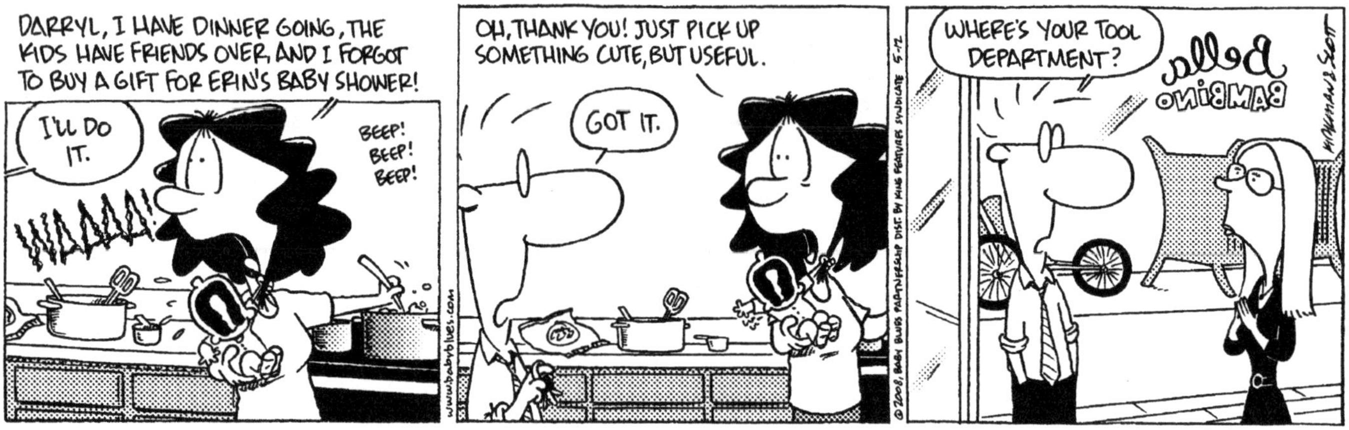
DARRYL, I HAVE DINNER GOING, THE KIDS HAVE FRIENDS OVER, AND I FORGOT TO BUY A GIFT FOR ERIN'S BABY SHOWER!
I'LL DO IT.
WAAAA!
BEEP! BEEP! BEEP!
www.babyblues.com
OH, THANK YOU! JUST PICK UP SOMETHING CUTE, BUT USEFUL.
GOT IT.
© 2008, BABY BLUES PARTNERSHIP DIST. BY KING FEATURES SYNDICATE 5-12
WHERE'S YOUR TOOL DEPARTMENT?
Bella BAMBINO
KIRKMAN & SCOTT

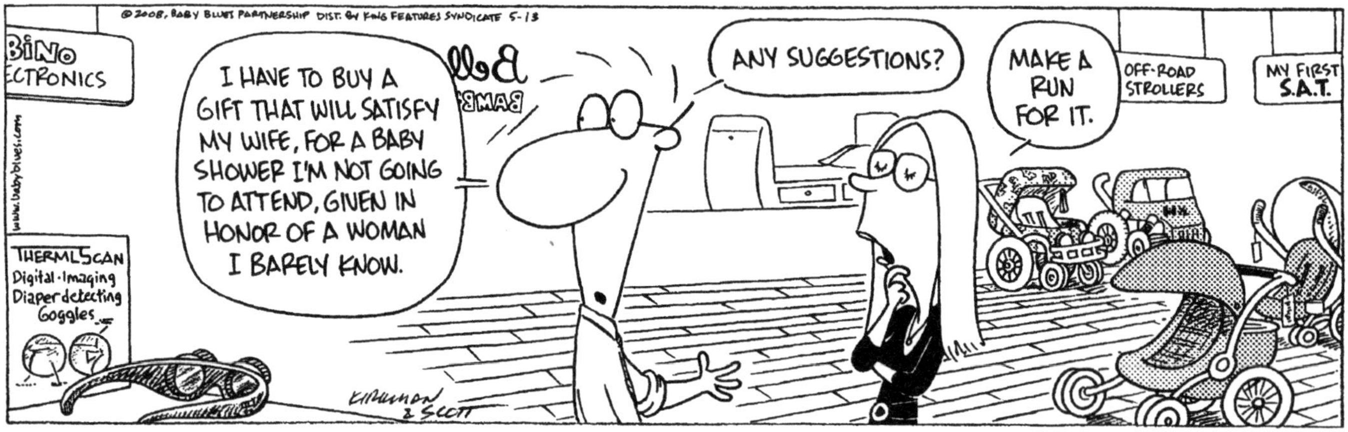
© 2008, BABY BLUES PARTNERSHIP DIST. BY KING FEATURES SYNDICATE 5-13
BINO ECTRONICS
www.babyblues.com
I HAVE TO BUY A GIFT THAT WILL SATISFY MY WIFE, FOR A BABY SHOWER I'M NOT GOING TO ATTEND, GIVEN IN HONOR OF A WOMAN I BARELY KNOW.
ANY SUGGESTIONS?
MAKE A RUN FOR IT.
OFF-ROAD STROLLERS
MY FIRST S.A.T.
THERML SCAN Digital-Imaging Diaper detecting Goggles
KIRKMAN & SCOTT

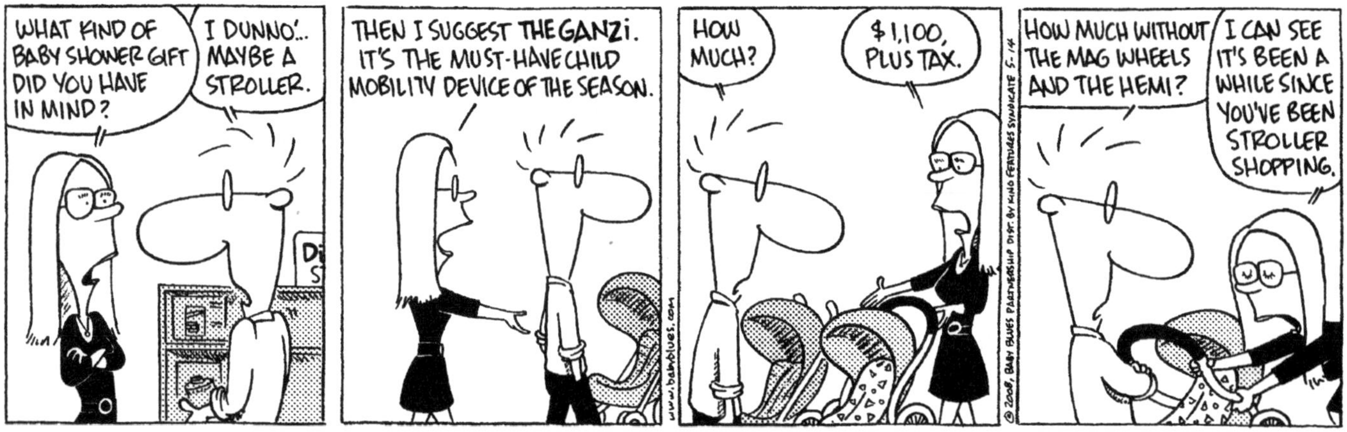
WHAT KIND OF BABY SHOWER GIFT DID YOU HAVE IN MIND?
I DUNNO!.. MAYBE A STROLLER.
THEN I SUGGEST THE GANZi. IT'S THE MUST-HAVE CHILD MOBILITY DEVICE OF THE SEASON.
www.babyblues.com
HOW MUCH?
$1,100, PLUS TAX.
© 2008, BABY BLUES PARTNERSHIP DIST. BY KING FEATURES SYNDICATE 5-14
HOW MUCH WITHOUT THE MAG WHEELS AND THE HEMI?
I CAN SEE IT'S BEEN A WHILE SINCE YOU'VE BEEN STROLLER SHOPPING.

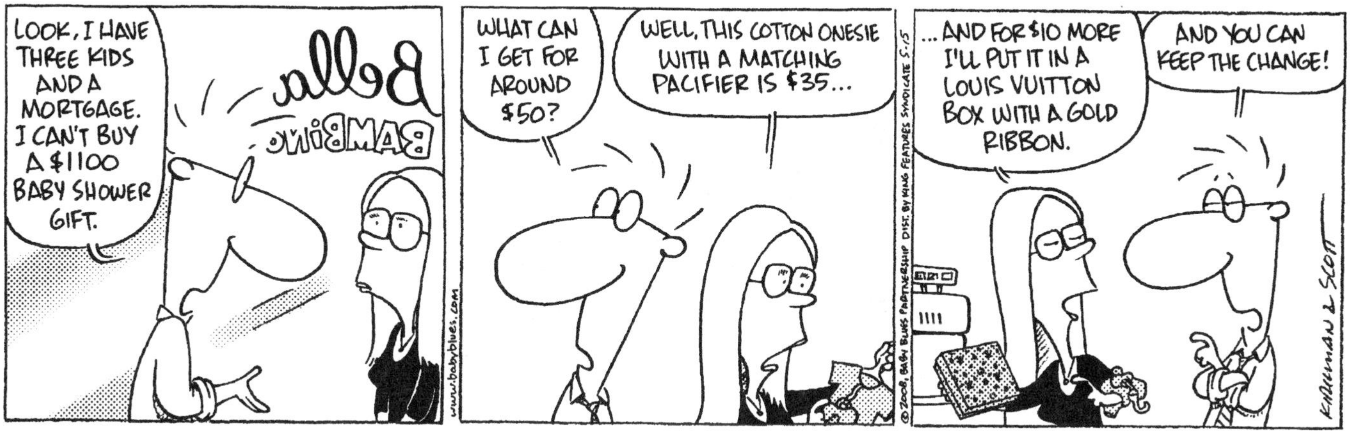
LOOK, I HAVE THREE KIDS AND A MORTGAGE. I CAN'T BUY A $1100 BABY SHOWER GIFT.
WHAT CAN I GET FOR AROUND $50?
WELL, THIS COTTON ONESIE WITH A MATCHING PACIFIER IS $35...
...AND FOR $10 MORE I'LL PUT IT IN A LOUIS VUITTON BOX WITH A GOLD RIBBON.
AND YOU CAN KEEP THE CHANGE!
www.babyblues.com
© 2008, BABY BLUES PARTNERSHIP DIST. BY KING FEATURES SYNDICATE 5-15
KIRKMAN & SCOTT

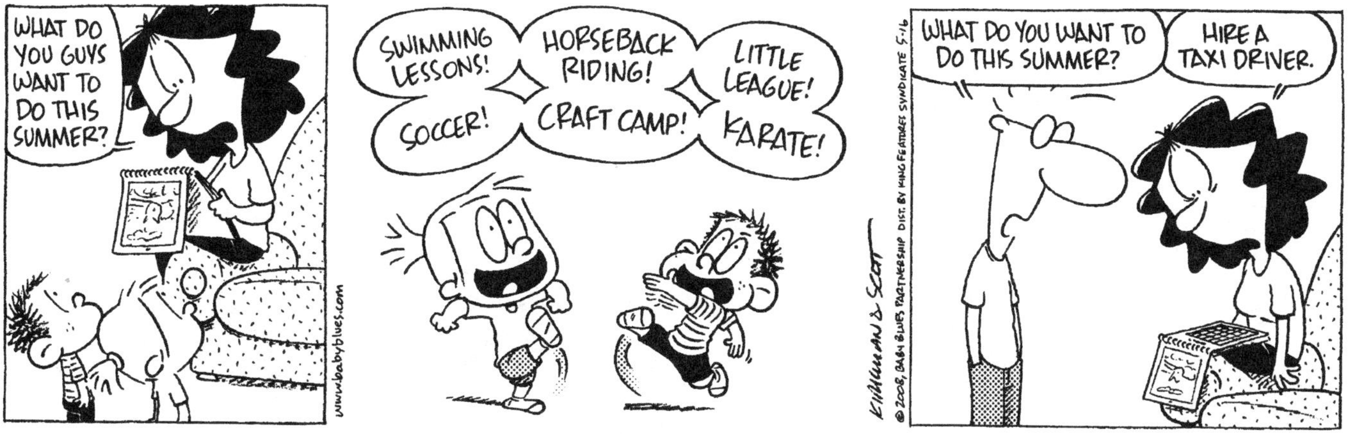
WHAT DO YOU GUYS WANT TO DO THIS SUMMER?
SWIMMING LESSONS!
HORSEBACK RIDING!
LITTLE LEAGUE!
SOCCER!
CRAFT CAMP!
KARATE!
WHAT DO YOU WANT TO DO THIS SUMMER?
HIRE A TAXI DRIVER.
www.babyblues.com
KIRKMAN & SCOTT
© 2008, BABY BLUES PARTNERSHIP DIST. BY KING FEATURES SYNDICATE 5-16

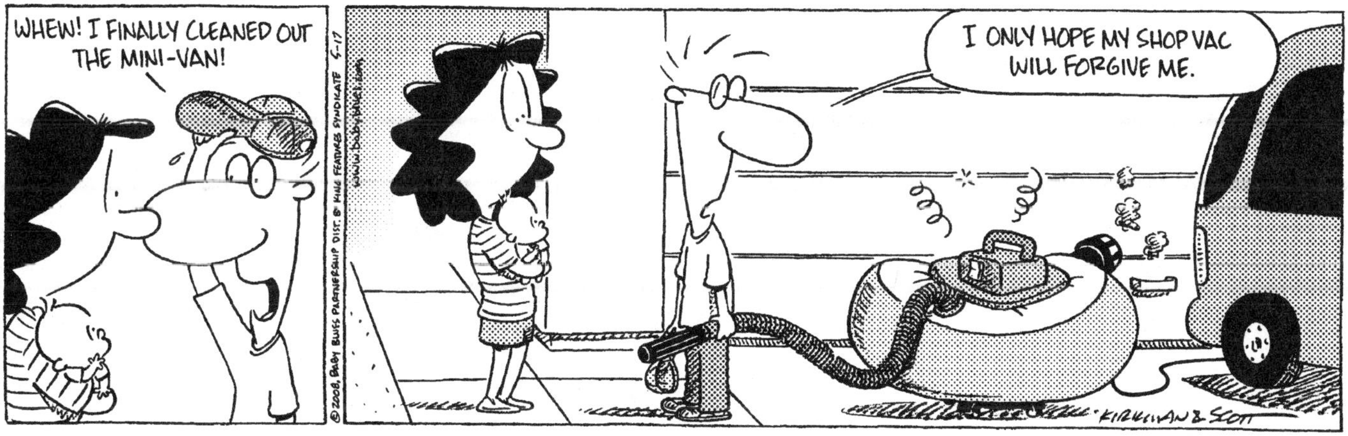
WHEW! I FINALLY CLEANED OUT THE MINI-VAN!
I ONLY HOPE MY SHOP VAC WILL FORGIVE ME.
© 2008, BABY BLUES PARTNERSHIP DIST. BY KING FEATURES SYNDICATE 5-17
www.babyblues.com
KIRKMAN & SCOTT

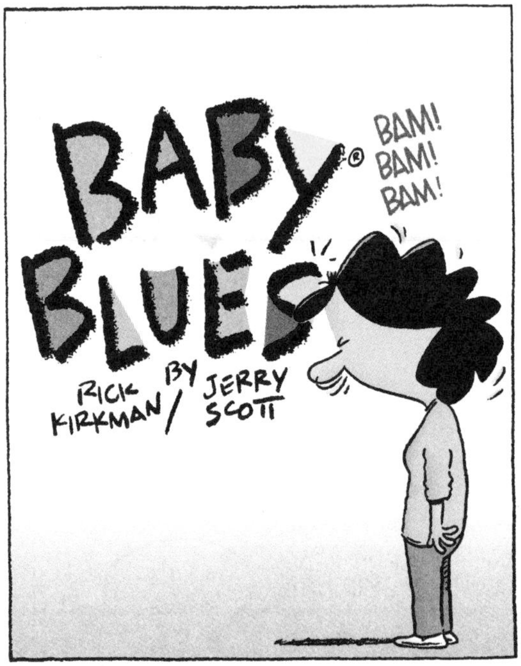
BABY BLUES®
BAM! BAM! BAM!
BY RICK KIRKMAN / JERRY SCOTT

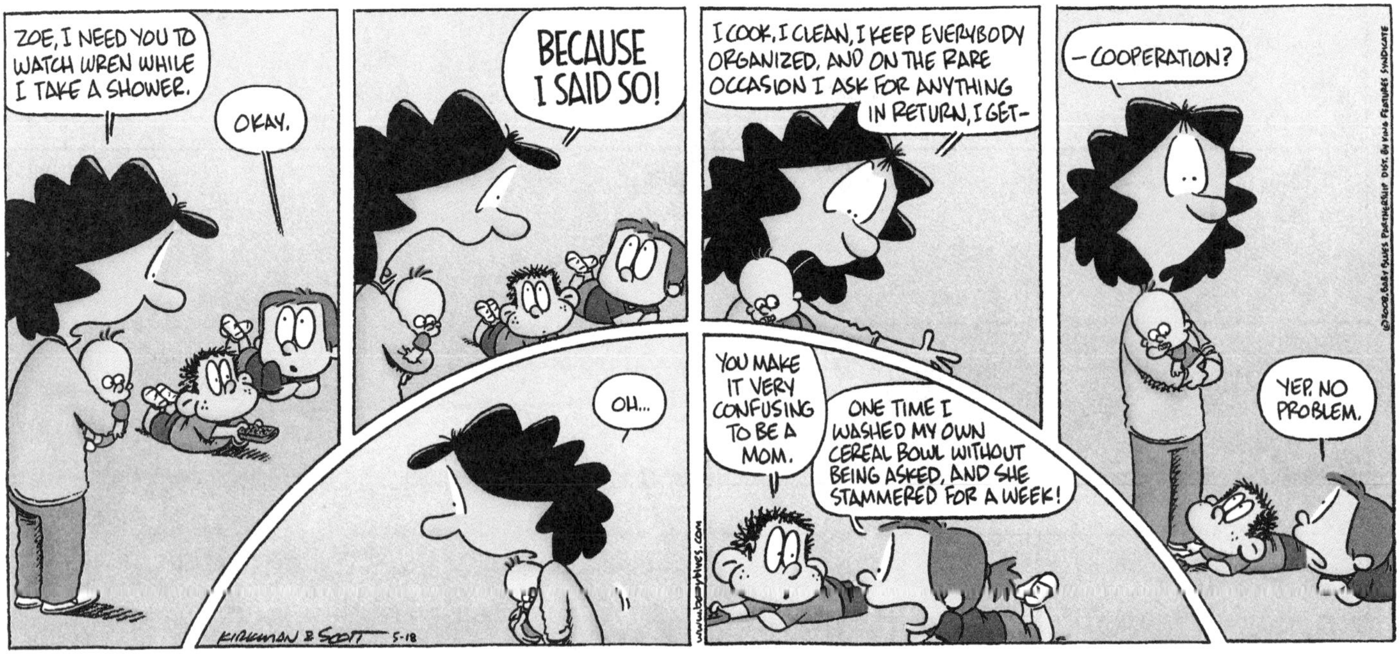
ZOE, I NEED YOU TO WATCH WREN WHILE I TAKE A SHOWER.
OKAY.
BECAUSE I SAID SO!
OH...
I COOK, I CLEAN, I KEEP EVERYBODY ORGANIZED, AND ON THE RARE OCCASION I ASK FOR ANYTHING IN RETURN, I GET-
YOU MAKE IT VERY CONFUSING TO BE A MOM.
ONE TIME I WASHED MY OWN CEREAL BOWL WITHOUT BEING ASKED, AND SHE STAMMERED FOR A WEEK!
-COOPERATION?
YEP. NO PROBLEM.
KIRKMAN & SCOTT 5-18
www.babyblues.com
©2008, BABY BLUES PARTNERSHIP DIST. BY KING FEATURES SYNDICATE

WREN?
MA.
DID YOU JUST SAY SOMETHING?
MA.
YOU DID! YOU SAID, "MA"!
©2008, BABY BLUES PARTNERSHIP DIST. BY KING FEATURES SYNDICATE 5-19
KIRKMAN & SCOTT
WAIT 'TIL I TELL DADDY! HE'S GOING TO BE SO—
BEEP! BEEP! BEEP!
www.babyblues.com
DA DA DA DA DA DA DA DA DA DA DA DA DA DA DA DA DA DA DA
—JEALOUS.
BEEP...

DA DA DA DA DA DA DA DA DA DA DA DA DA DA DA DA DA DA DA DA DA DA DA DA DA
ZOE, DO YOU THINK YOU CAN GO TEACH YOUR BABY SISTER ANOTHER WORD?
SURE! NO PROBLEM.
5 minutes LATER
©2008, BABY BLUES PARTNERSHIP DIST. BY KING FEATURES SYNDICATE
NO NO NO NO NO NO NO NO NO NO NO NO NO NO NO NO NO NO NO NO NO NO NO NO NO NO
HERE YOU GO.
www.babyblues.com 5-20
KIRKMAN & SCOTT

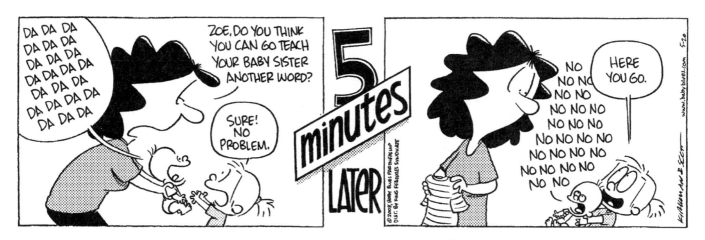

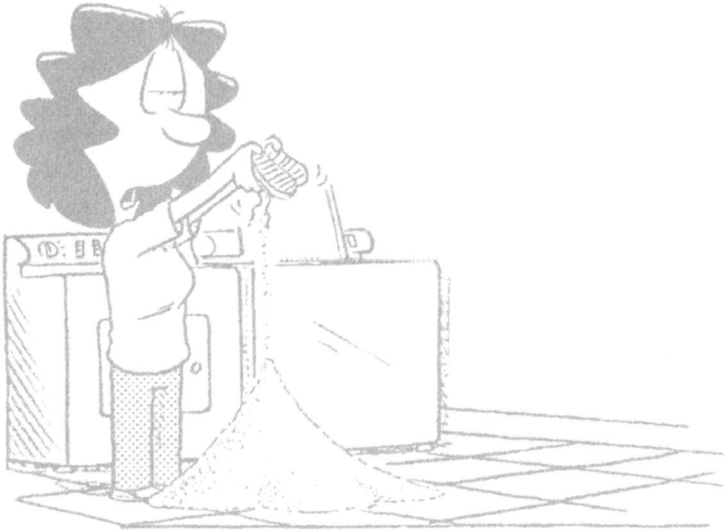

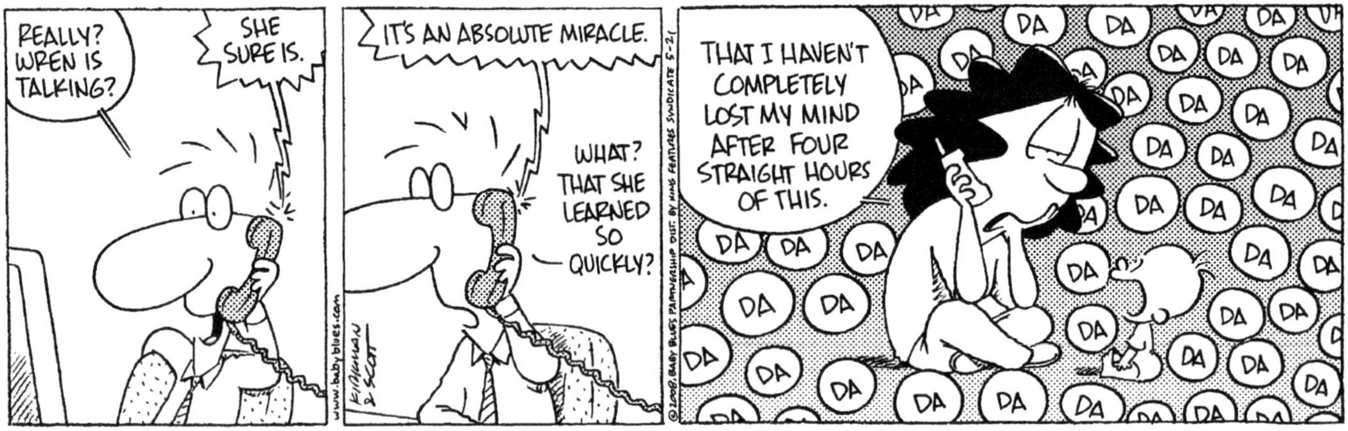
REALLY? WREN IS TALKING?
SHE SURE IS.
www.babyblues.com
IT'S AN ABSOLUTE MIRACLE.
WHAT? THAT SHE LEARNED SO QUICKLY?
KIRKMAN & SCOTT
© 2008, BABY BLUES PARTNERSHIP DIST. BY KING FEATURES SYNDICATE 5-21
THAT I HAVEN'T COMPLETELY LOST MY MIND AFTER FOUR STRAIGHT HOURS OF THIS.

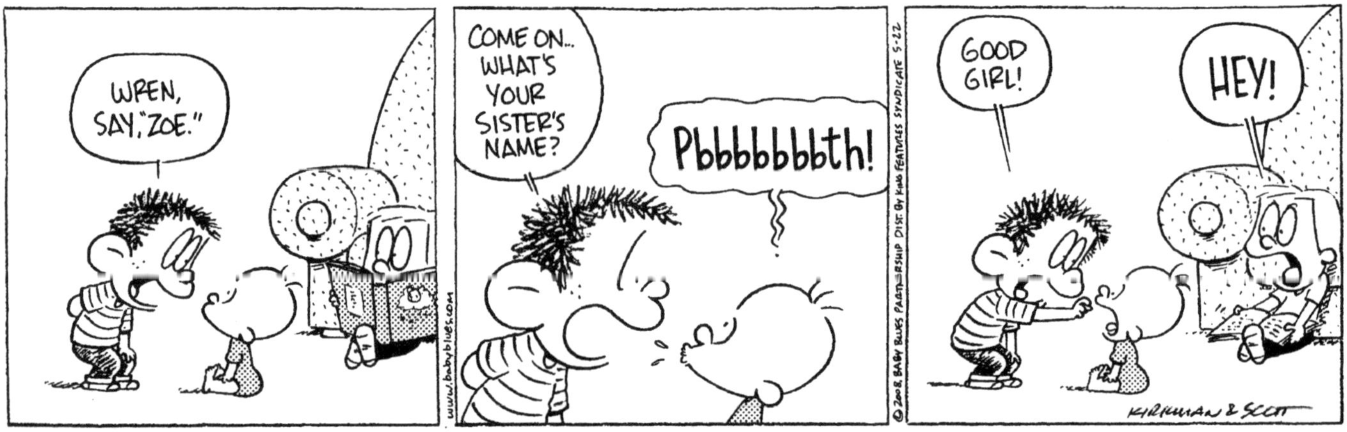
WREN, SAY, "ZOE."
www.babyblues.com
COME ON.. WHAT'S YOUR SISTER'S NAME?
Pbbbbbbbth!
© 2008 BABY BLUES PARTNERSHIP DIST. BY KING FEATURES SYNDICATE 5-22
GOOD GIRL!
HEY!
KIRKMAN & SCOTT

Library Books
Checkout Day
LIBRARY
www.babyblues.com
Library Books
Return Day
© 2008, Baby Blues Partnership Dist. by King Features Syndicate 5-23
REALLY? THIS IS ALL I COULD FIND.
KIRKMAN & SCOTT

WHO TRACKED MUD IN THE HOUSE??
I DID.
I DID.
www.babyblues.com
KIRKMAN & SCOTT
© 2008, Baby Blues Partnership Dist. by King Features Syndicate 5-24
HE DID.
SHE DID.

BABY BLUES®
BY RICK KIRKMAN / JERRY SCOTT

ZOE!
TCH! TCH! TCH!
YOU'RE CHEWING ON YOUR HAIR AGAIN!
OH.
IF YOU DON'T STOP THAT, IT'LL GET ALL WEIRD AND UNEVEN AND YOU'LL START COUGHING UP BIG, JUICY HAIRBALLS!
HAIRBALLS??
WOW.
YEAH.
I'LL GIVE YOU A DOLLAR IF YOU STOP TODAY.
I'LL GIVE YOU **TWO** DOLLARS IF YOU DON'T!
© 2008, BABY BLUES PARTNERSHIP DIST. BY KING FEATURES SYNDICATE 5-25
www.babyblues.com
KIRKMAN & SCOTT

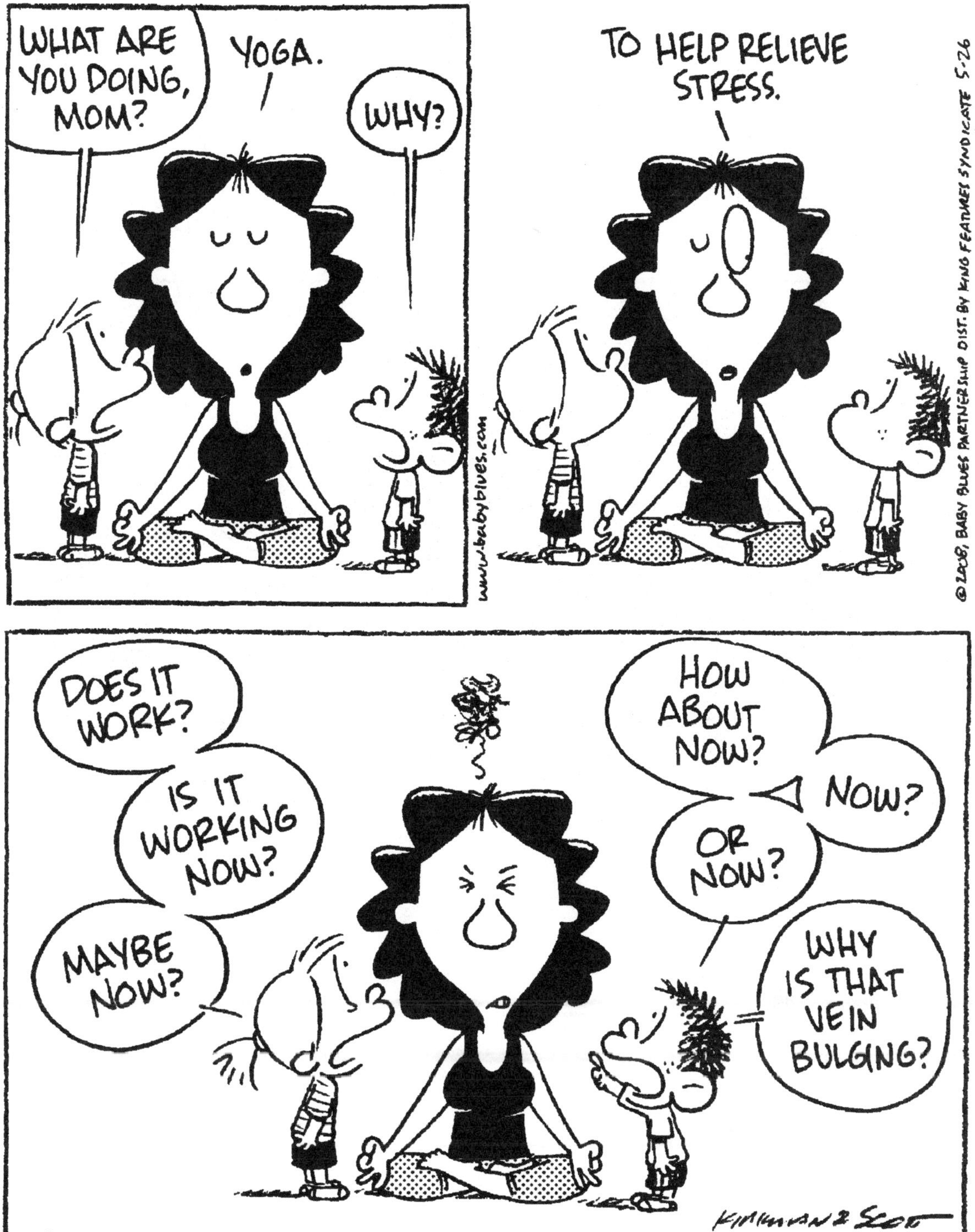
WHAT ARE YOU DOING, MOM?
YOGA.
WHY?
www.babyblues.com
TO HELP RELIEVE STRESS.
© 2008, BABY BLUES PARTNERSHIP DIST. BY KING FEATURES SYNDICATE 5-26
DOES IT WORK?
IS IT WORKING NOW?
MAYBE NOW?
HOW ABOUT NOW?
NOW?
OR NOW?
WHY IS THAT VEIN BULGING?
KIRKMAN & SCOTT

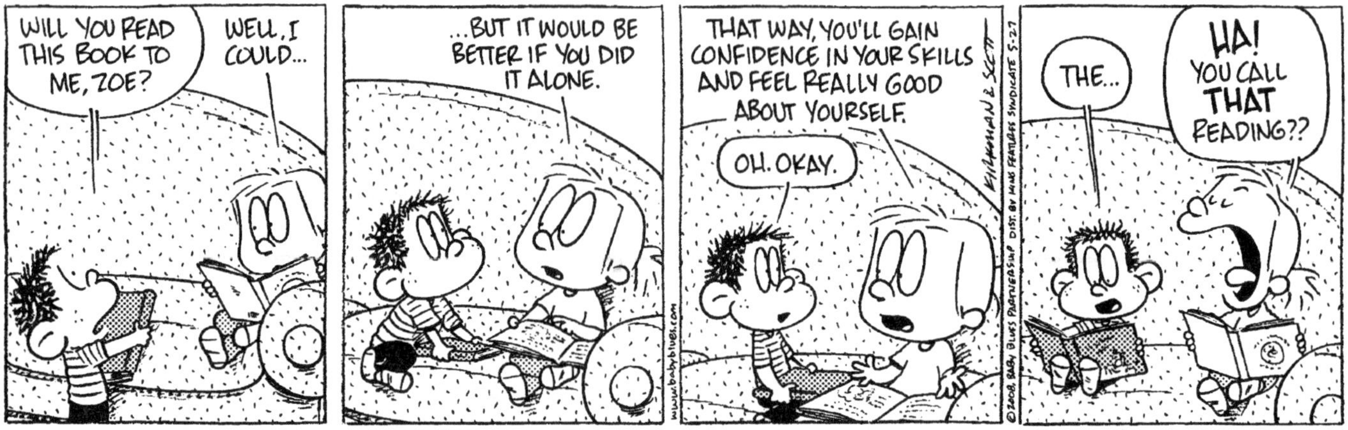
WILL YOU READ THIS BOOK TO ME, ZOE?
WELL, I COULD...
...BUT IT WOULD BE BETTER IF YOU DID IT ALONE.
THAT WAY, YOU'LL GAIN CONFIDENCE IN YOUR SKILLS AND FEEL REALLY GOOD ABOUT YOURSELF.
OH. OKAY.
THE...
HA! YOU CALL **THAT** READING??

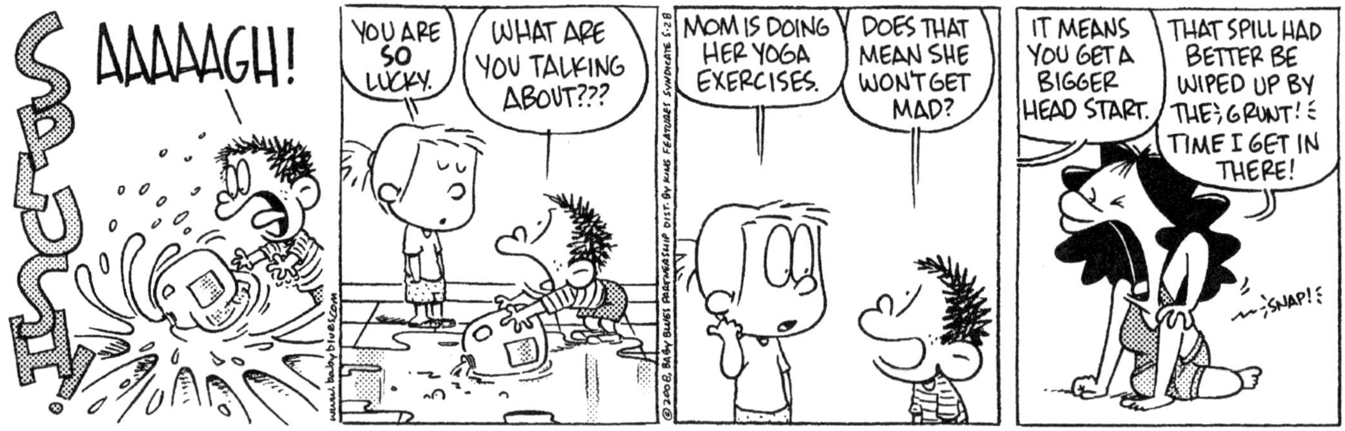
SPLUSH!
AAAAAGH!
YOU ARE **SO** LUCKY.
WHAT ARE YOU TALKING ABOUT???
MOM IS DOING HER YOGA EXERCISES.
DOES THAT MEAN SHE WON'T GET MAD?
IT MEANS YOU GET A BIGGER HEAD START.
THAT SPILL HAD BETTER BE WIPED UP BY THE GRUNT! TIME I GET IN THERE!
SNAP!

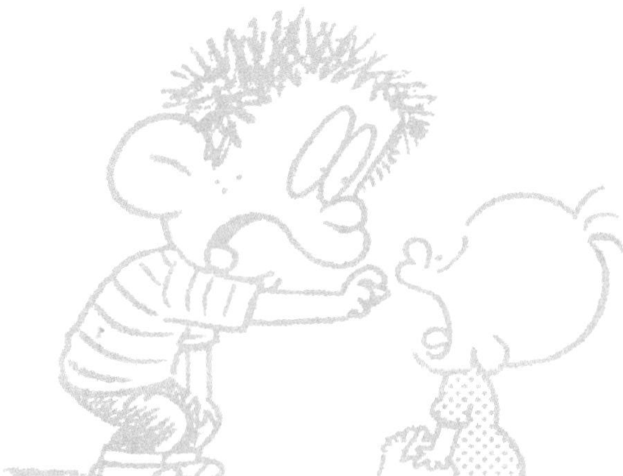

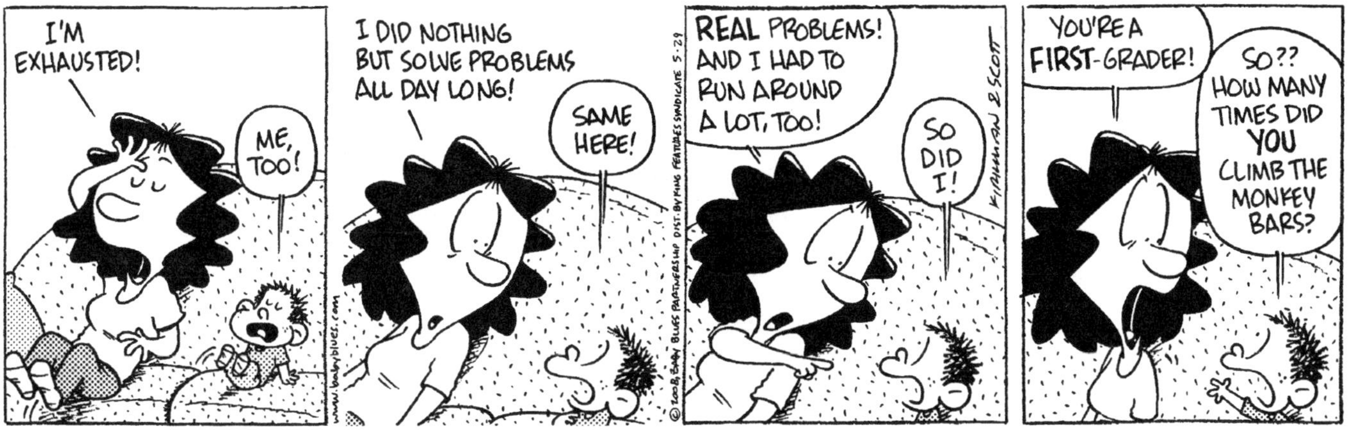
I'M EXHAUSTED!
ME, TOO!
I DID NOTHING BUT SOLVE PROBLEMS ALL DAY LONG!
SAME HERE!
REAL PROBLEMS! AND I HAD TO RUN AROUND A LOT, TOO!
SO DID I!
YOU'RE A FIRST-GRADER!
SO?? HOW MANY TIMES DID YOU CLIMB THE MONKEY BARS?

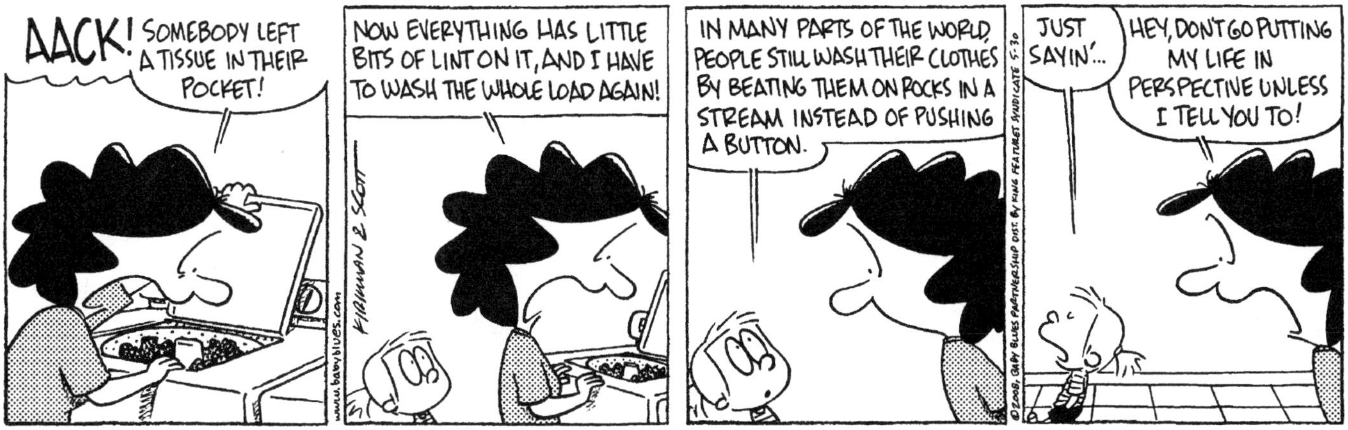
AACK! SOMEBODY LEFT A TISSUE IN THEIR POCKET!
NOW EVERYTHING HAS LITTLE BITS OF LINT ON IT, AND I HAVE TO WASH THE WHOLE LOAD AGAIN!
IN MANY PARTS OF THE WORLD, PEOPLE STILL WASH THEIR CLOTHES BY BEATING THEM ON ROCKS IN A STREAM INSTEAD OF PUSHING A BUTTON.
JUST SAYIN'...
HEY, DON'T GO PUTTING MY LIFE IN PERSPECTIVE UNLESS I TELL YOU TO!

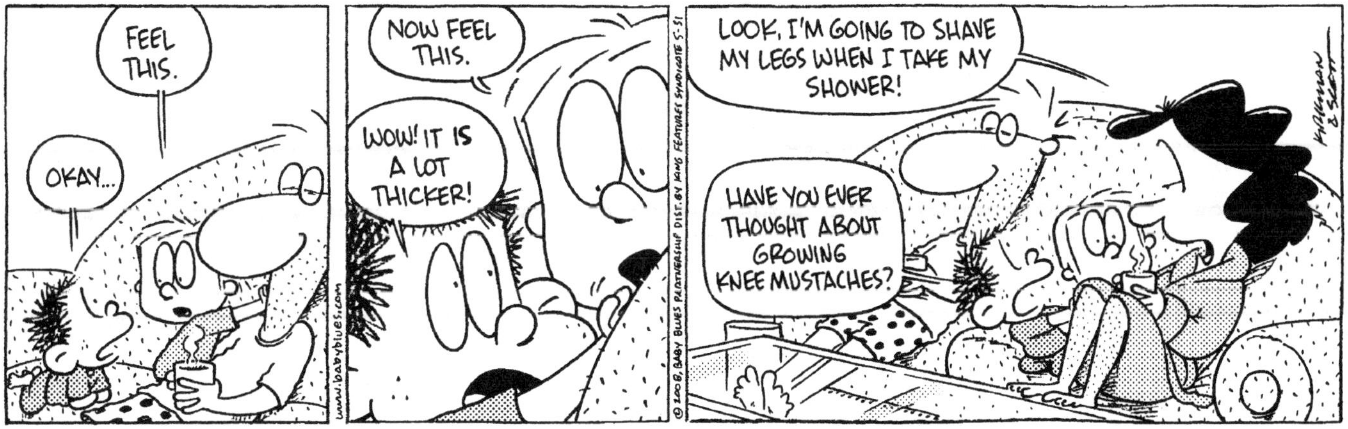
FEEL THIS.
OKAY...
NOW FEEL THIS.
WOW! IT IS A LOT THICKER!
LOOK, I'M GOING TO SHAVE MY LEGS WHEN I TAKE MY SHOWER!
HAVE YOU EVER THOUGHT ABOUT GROWING KNEE MUSTACHES?

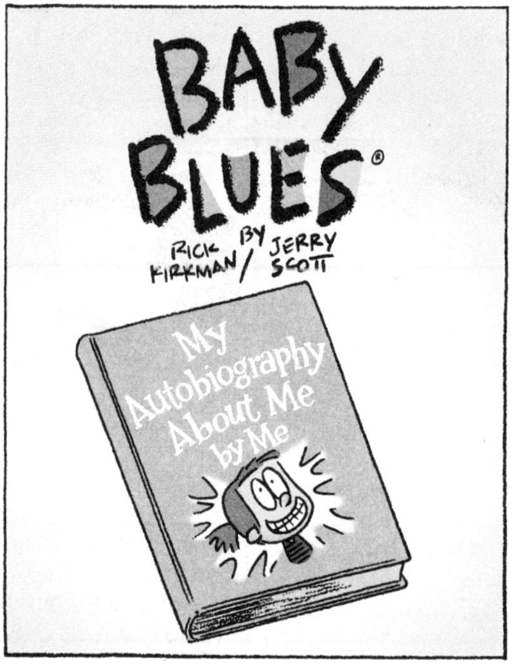
BABY BLUES®
BY RICK KIRKMAN / JERRY SCOTT
My Autobiography About Me by Me

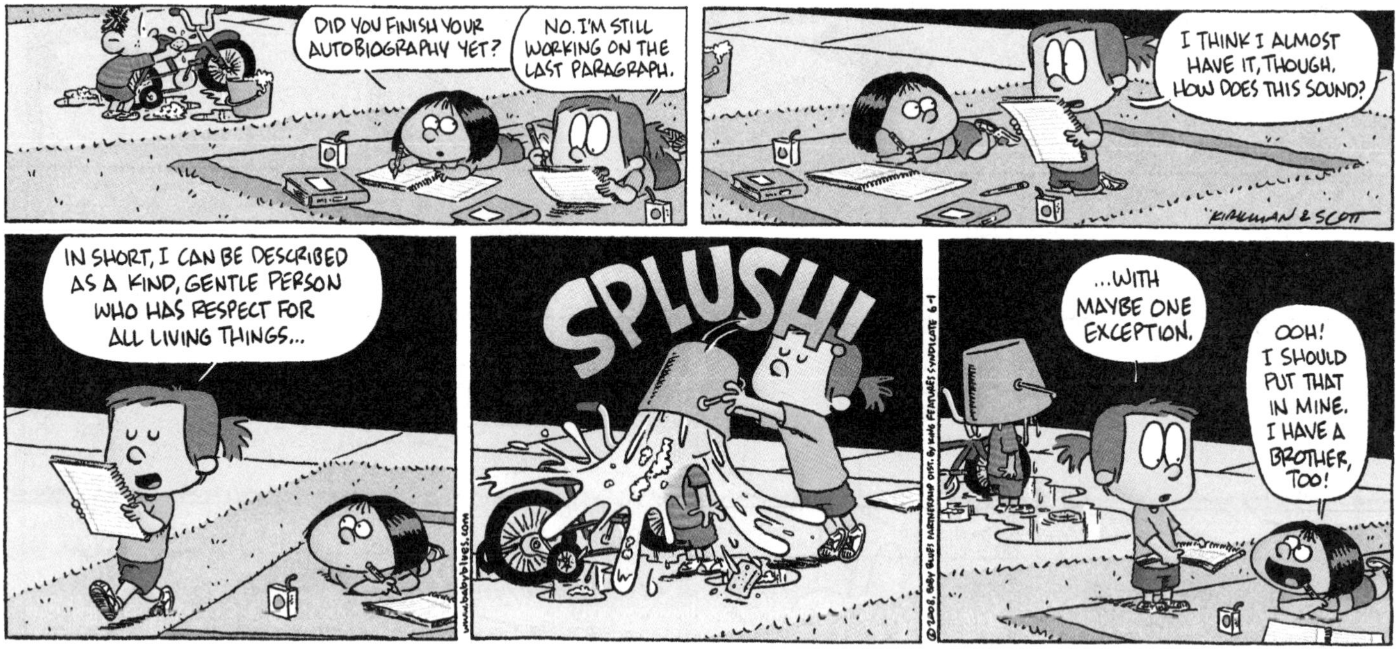
DID YOU FINISH YOUR AUTOBIOGRAPHY YET?
NO. I'M STILL WORKING ON THE LAST PARAGRAPH.
I THINK I ALMOST HAVE IT, THOUGH. HOW DOES THIS SOUND?
KIRKMAN & SCOTT
IN SHORT, I CAN BE DESCRIBED AS A KIND, GENTLE PERSON WHO HAS RESPECT FOR ALL LIVING THINGS...
SPLUSH!
...WITH MAYBE ONE EXCEPTION.
OOH! I SHOULD PUT THAT IN MINE. I HAVE A BROTHER, TOO!

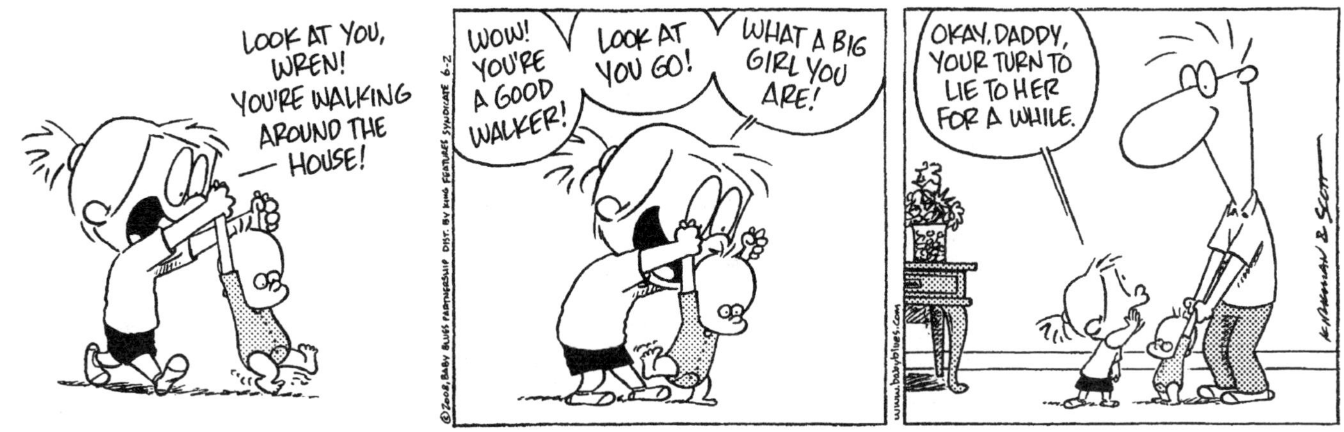
LOOK AT YOU, WREN! YOU'RE WALKING AROUND THE HOUSE!
WOW! YOU'RE A GOOD WALKER!
LOOK AT YOU GO!
WHAT A BIG GIRL YOU ARE!
OKAY, DADDY, YOUR TURN TO LIE TO HER FOR A WHILE.
©2008, BABY BLUES PARTNERSHIP DIST. BY KING FEATURES SYNDICATE 6-2
www.babyblues.com
KIRKMAN & SCOTT

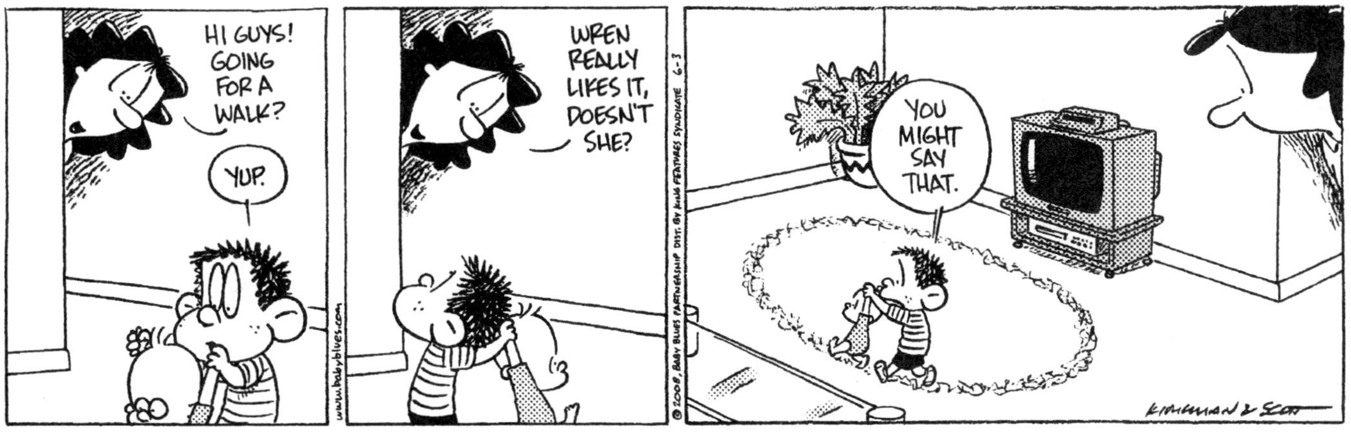
HI GUYS! GOING FOR A WALK?
YUP.
WREN REALLY LIKES IT, DOESN'T SHE?
YOU MIGHT SAY THAT.
www.babyblues.com
©2008, BABY BLUES PARTNERSHIP DIST. BY KING FEATURES SYNDICATE 6-3
KIRKMAN & SCOTT

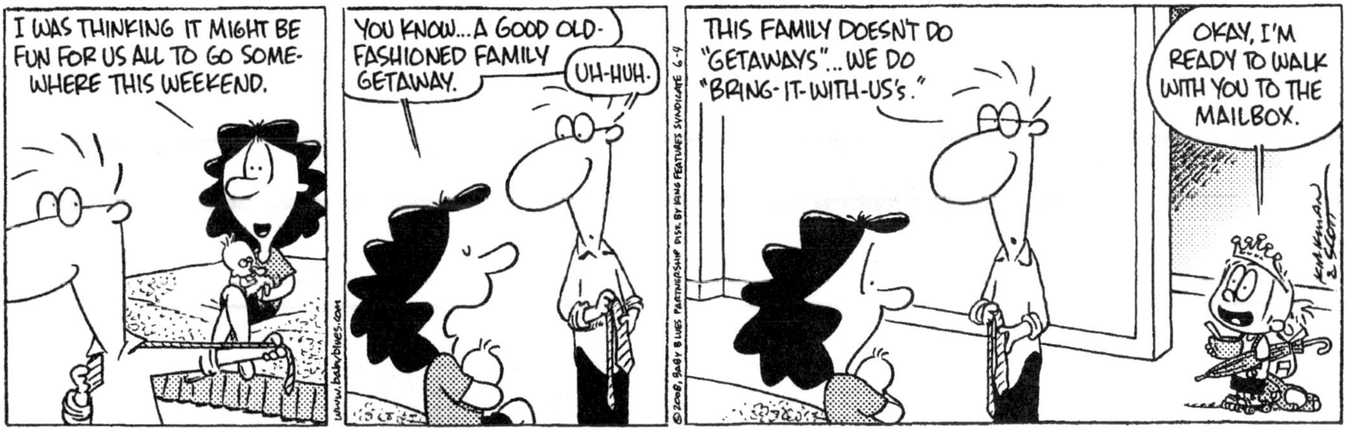
I WAS THINKING IT MIGHT BE FUN FOR US ALL TO GO SOMEWHERE THIS WEEKEND.
YOU KNOW... A GOOD OLD-FASHIONED FAMILY GETAWAY.
UH-HUH.
THIS FAMILY DOESN'T DO "GETAWAYS"... WE DO "BRING-IT-WITH-US's."
OKAY, I'M READY TO WALK WITH YOU TO THE MAILBOX.
www.babyblues.com
©2008, BABY BLUES PARTNERSHIP DIST. BY KING FEATURES SYNDICATE 6-4
KIRKMAN & SCOTT

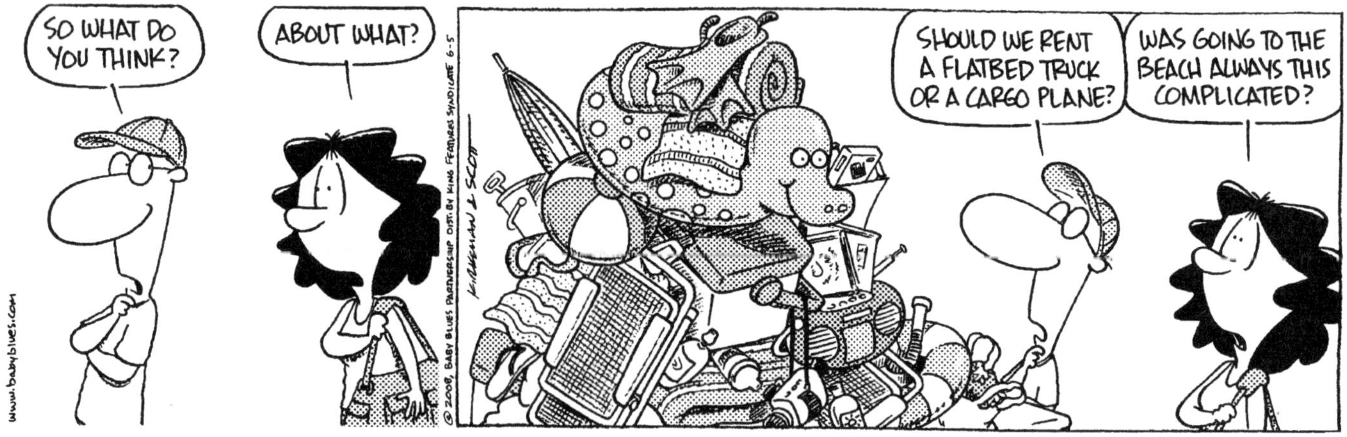
SO WHAT DO YOU THINK?
ABOUT WHAT?
SHOULD WE RENT A FLATBED TRUCK OR A CARGO PLANE?
WAS GOING TO THE BEACH ALWAYS THIS COMPLICATED?
www.babyblues.com
© 2008, Baby Blues Partnership Dist. by King Features Syndicate 6-5
Kirkman & Scott

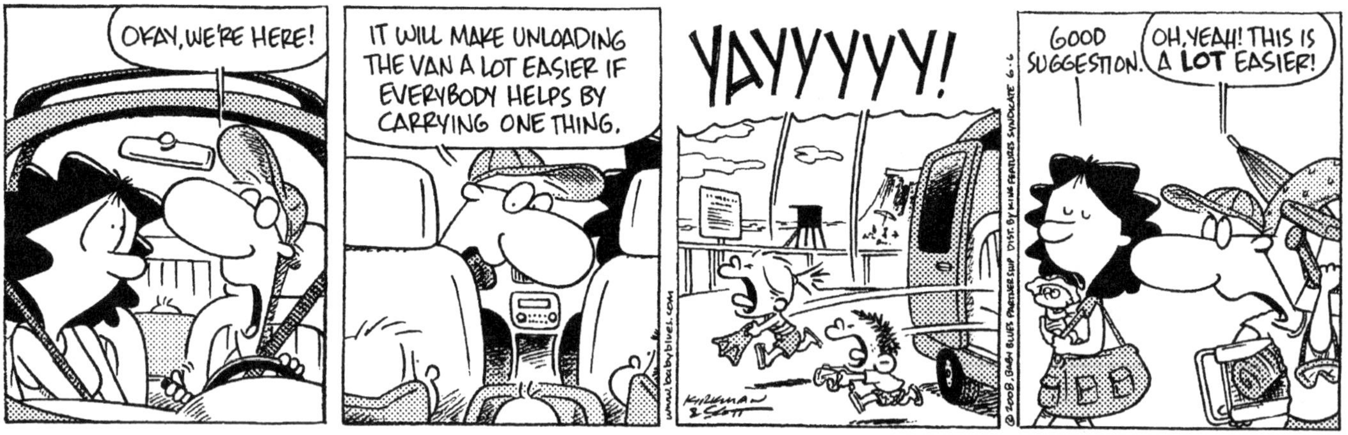
OKAY, WE'RE HERE!
IT WILL MAKE UNLOADING THE VAN A LOT EASIER IF EVERYBODY HELPS BY CARRYING ONE THING.
YAYYYYY!
GOOD SUGGESTION.
OH, YEAH! THIS IS A **LOT** EASIER!
www.babyblues.com
Kirkman & Scott
© 2008, Baby Blues Partnership Dist. by King Features Syndicate 6-6

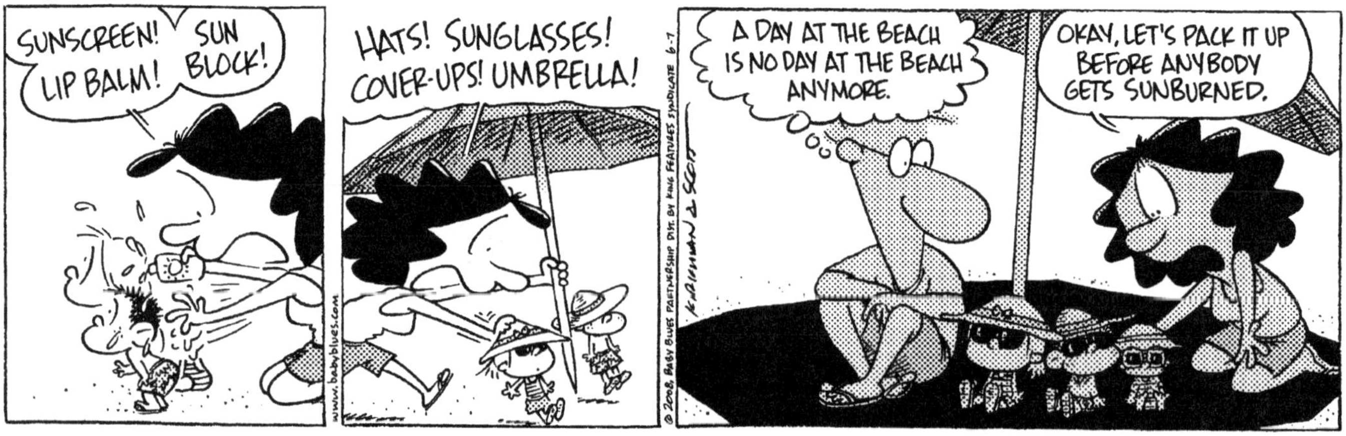
SUNSCREEN! LIP BALM!
SUN BLOCK!
HATS! SUNGLASSES! COVER-UPS! UMBRELLA!
A DAY AT THE BEACH IS NO DAY AT THE BEACH ANYMORE.
OKAY, LET'S PACK IT UP BEFORE ANYBODY GETS SUNBURNED.
www.babyblues.com
© 2008, Baby Blues Partnership Dist. by King Features Syndicate 6-7
Kirkman & Scott

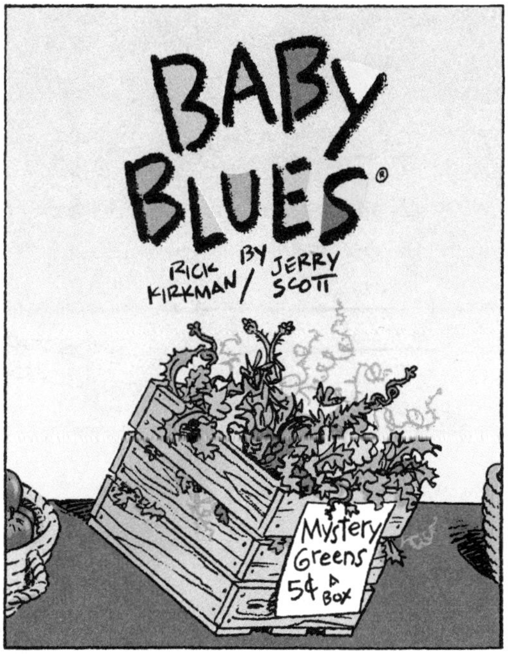
BABY BLUES®
BY RICK KIRKMAN / JERRY SCOTT
Mystery Greens 5¢ A BOX

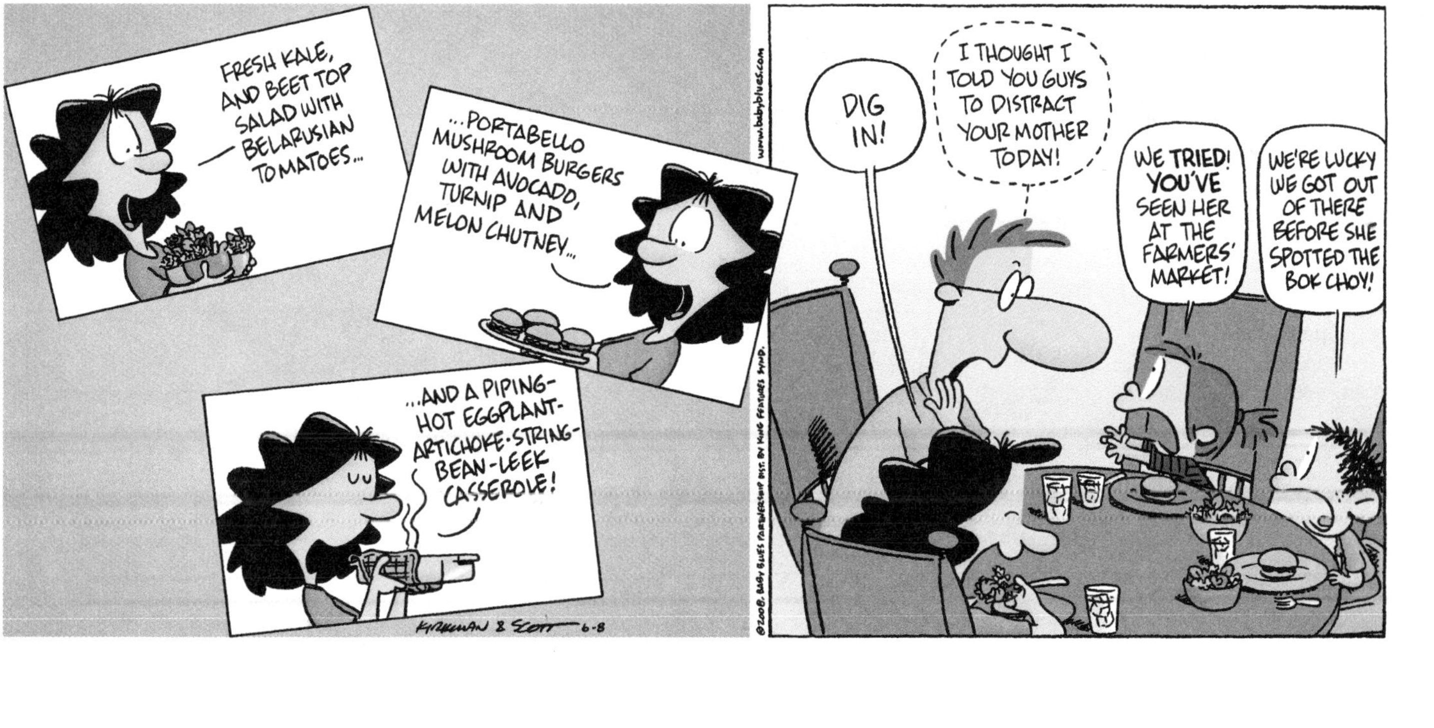
FRESH KALE, AND BEET TOP SALAD WITH BELARUSIAN TOMATOES...
...PORTABELLO MUSHROOM BURGERS WITH AVOCADO, TURNIP AND MELON CHUTNEY...
...AND A PIPING-HOT EGGPLANT-ARTICHOKE-STRING-BEAN-LEEK CASSEROLE!
KIRKMAN & SCOTT 6-8
DIG IN!
I THOUGHT I TOLD YOU GUYS TO DISTRACT YOUR MOTHER TODAY!
WE TRIED! YOU'VE SEEN HER AT THE FARMERS' MARKET!
WE'RE LUCKY WE GOT OUT OF THERE BEFORE SHE SPOTTED THE BOK CHOY!
www.babyblues.com

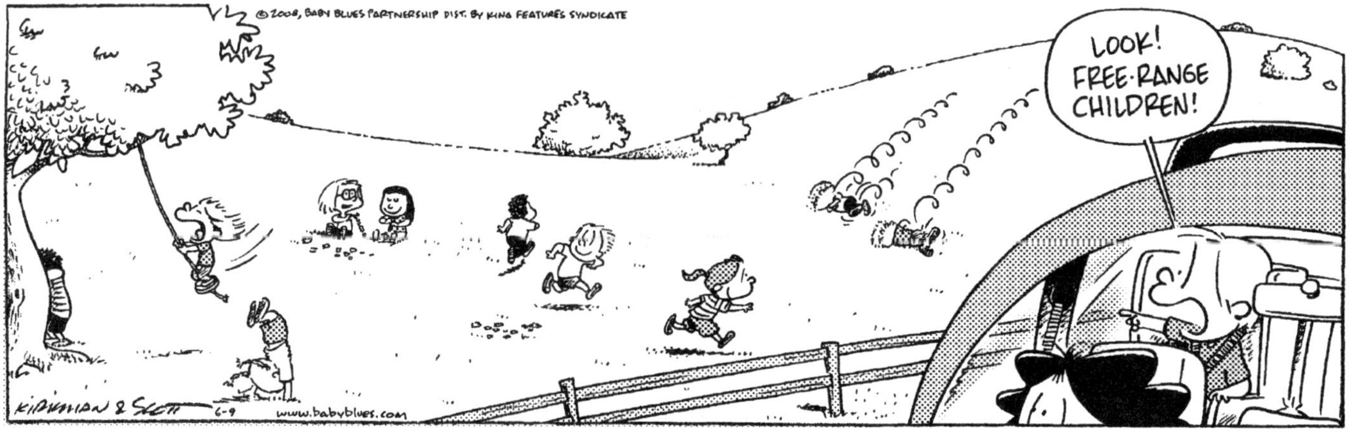
© 2008, BABY BLUES PARTNERSHIP DIST. BY KING FEATURES SYNDICATE
KIRKMAN & SCOTT 6-9
www.babyblues.com
LOOK! FREE-RANGE CHILDREN!

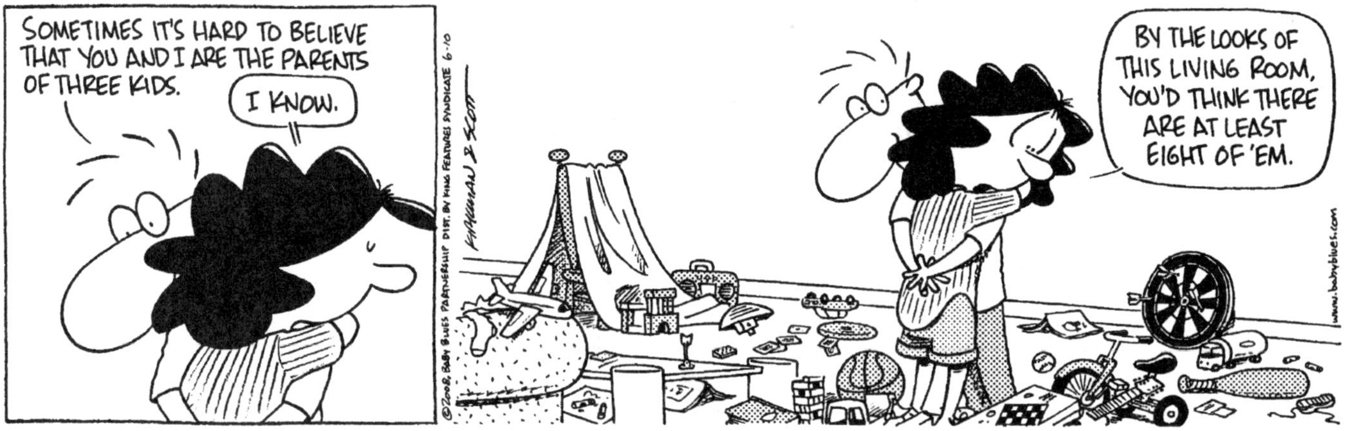
SOMETIMES IT'S HARD TO BELIEVE THAT YOU AND I ARE THE PARENTS OF THREE KIDS.
I KNOW.
©2008, BABY BLUES PARTNERSHIP DIST. BY KING FEATURES SYNDICATE 6-10
KIRKMAN & SCOTT
BY THE LOOKS OF THIS LIVING ROOM, YOU'D THINK THERE ARE AT LEAST EIGHT OF 'EM.
www.babyblues.com

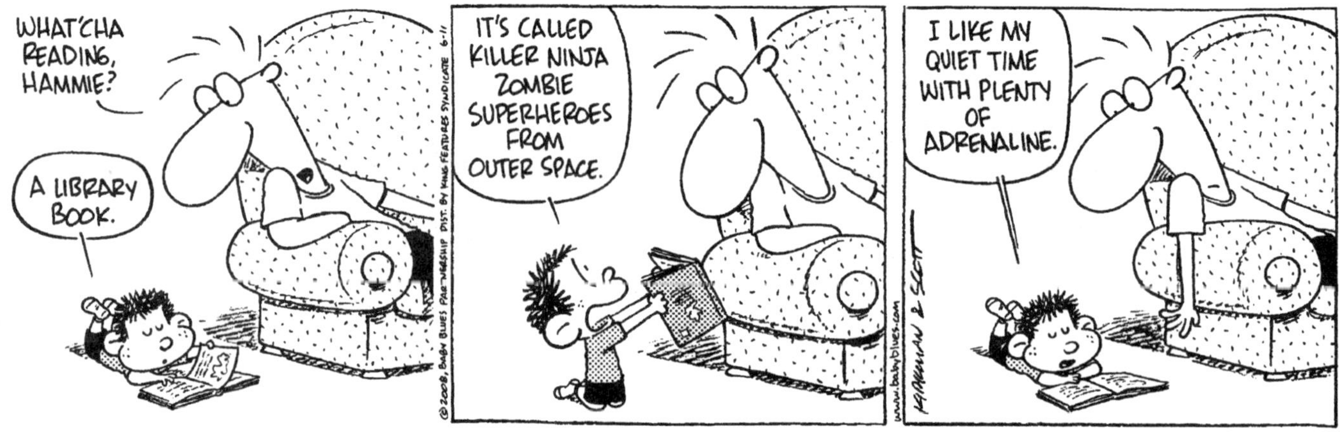
WHAT'CHA READING, HAMMIE?
A LIBRARY BOOK.
©2008, BABY BLUES PARTNERSHIP DIST. BY KING FEATURES SYNDICATE 6-11
IT'S CALLED KILLER NINJA ZOMBIE SUPERHEROES FROM OUTER SPACE.
www.babyblues.com
KIRKMAN & SCOTT
I LIKE MY QUIET TIME WITH PLENTY OF ADRENALINE.

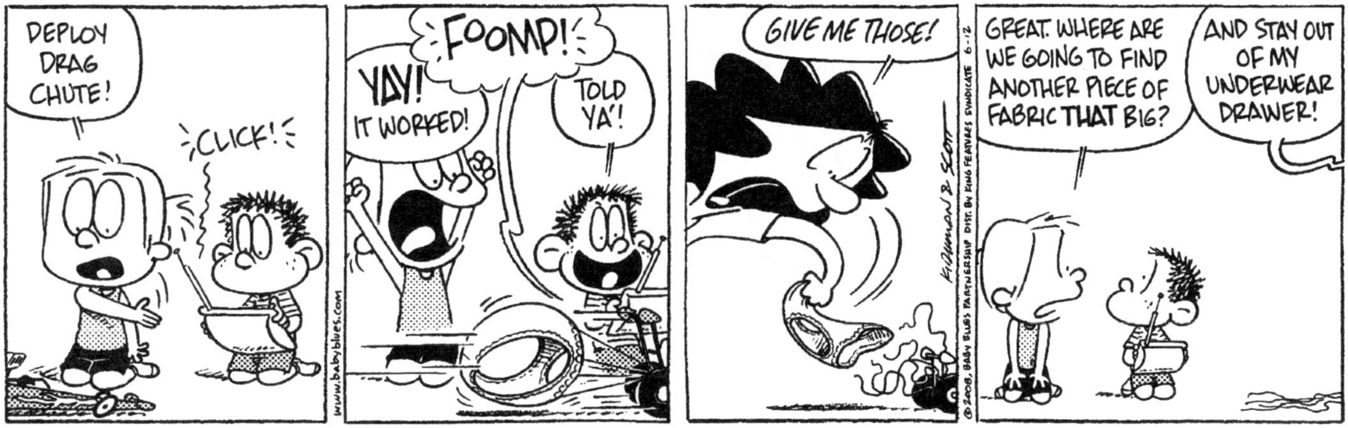
DEPLOY DRAG CHUTE!
CLICK!
www.babyblues.com
FOOMP!
YAY! IT WORKED!
TOLD YA'!
GIVE ME THOSE!
KIRKMAN & SCOTT
© 2008, BABY BLUES PARTNERSHIP DIST. BY KING FEATURES SYNDICATE 6-12
GREAT. WHERE ARE WE GOING TO FIND ANOTHER PIECE OF FABRIC THAT BIG?
AND STAY OUT OF MY UNDERWEAR DRAWER!

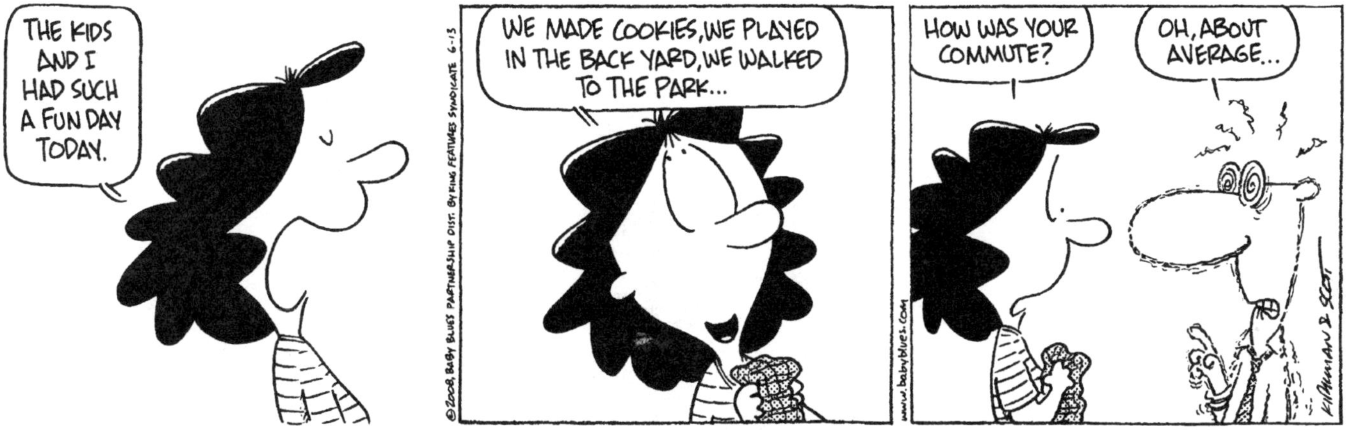
THE KIDS AND I HAD SUCH A FUN DAY TODAY.
© 2008, BABY BLUES PARTNERSHIP DIST. BY KING FEATURES SYNDICATE 6-13
WE MADE COOKIES, WE PLAYED IN THE BACK YARD, WE WALKED TO THE PARK...
www.babyblues.com
HOW WAS YOUR COMMUTE?
OH, ABOUT AVERAGE...
KIRKMAN & SCOTT

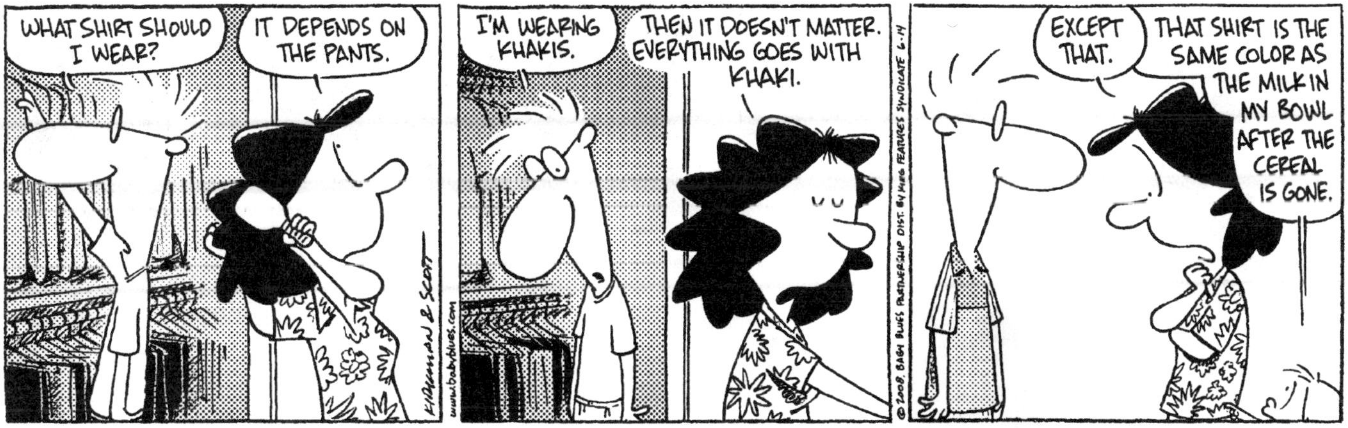
WHAT SHIRT SHOULD I WEAR?
IT DEPENDS ON THE PANTS.
KIRKMAN & SCOTT
www.babyblues.com
I'M WEARING KHAKIS.
THEN IT DOESN'T MATTER. EVERYTHING GOES WITH KHAKI.
© 2008, BABY BLUES PARTNERSHIP DIST. BY KING FEATURES SYNDICATE 6-14
EXCEPT THAT.
THAT SHIRT IS THE SAME COLOR AS THE MILK IN MY BOWL AFTER THE CEREAL IS GONE.

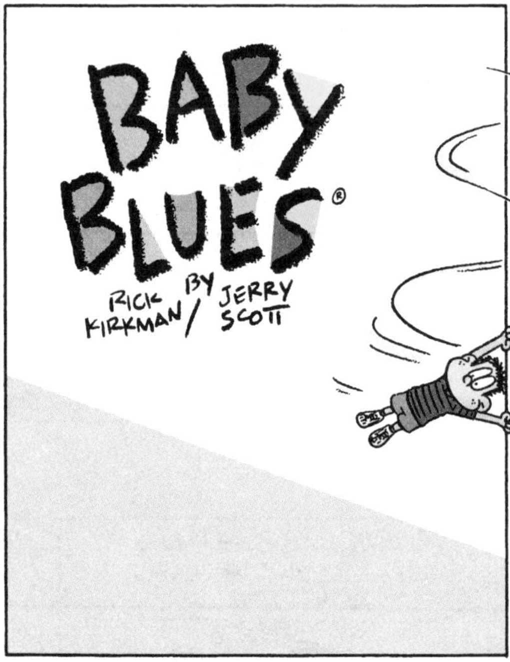
BABY BLUES®
BY RICK KIRKMAN / JERRY SCOTT

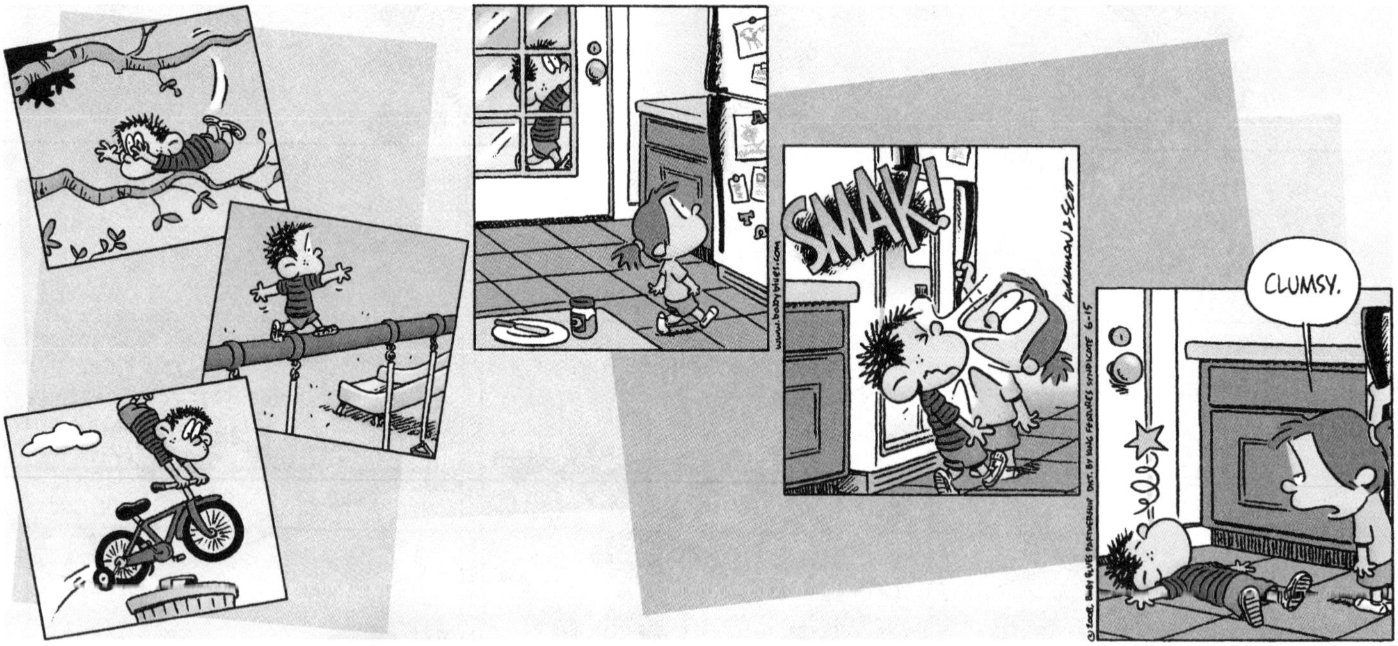
www.babyblues.com
SMAK!
KIRKMAN & SCOTT 6-15
CLUMSY.
© 2008, BABY BLUES PARTNERSHIP DIST. BY KING FEATURES SYNDICATE 6-15

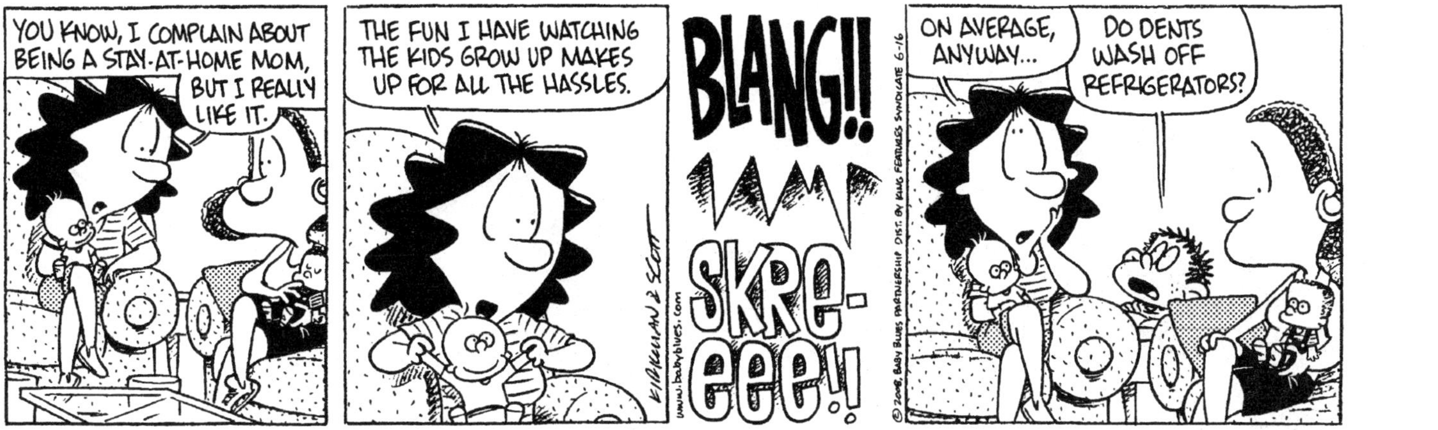
YOU KNOW, I COMPLAIN ABOUT BEING A STAY-AT-HOME MOM,
BUT I REALLY LIKE IT.
THE FUN I HAVE WATCHING THE KIDS GROW UP MAKES UP FOR ALL THE HASSLES.
KIRKMAN & SCOTT
www.babyblues.com
BLANG!!
SKRE-EEE!!
© 2008, BABY BLUES PARTNERSHIP DIST. BY KING FEATURES SYNDICATE 6-16
ON AVERAGE, ANYWAY...
DO DENTS WASH OFF REFRIGERATORS?

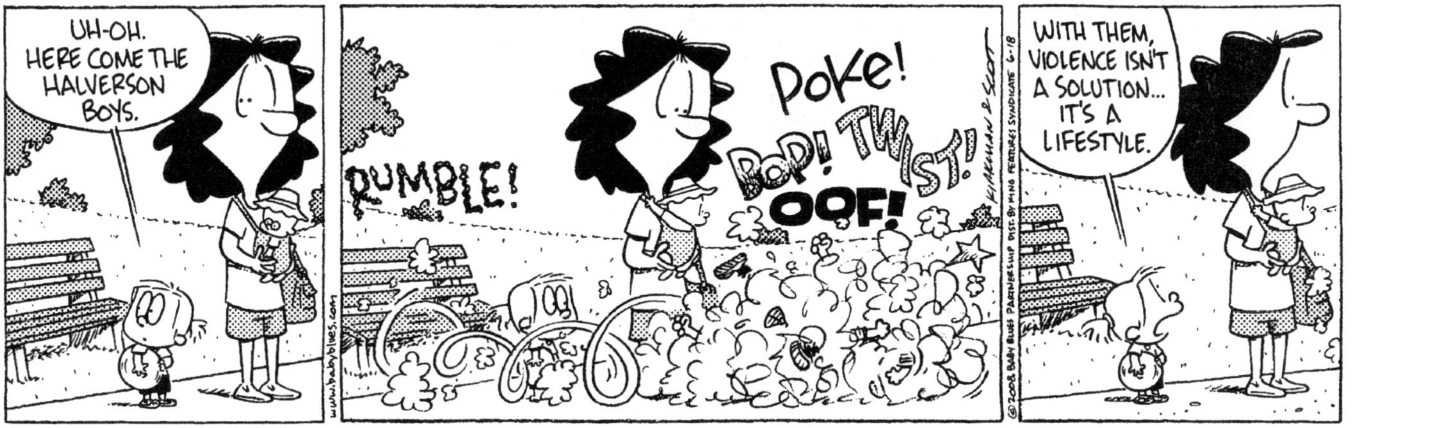
UH-OH. HERE COME THE HALVERSON BOYS.
www.babyblues.com
RUMBLE!
POKE!
BOP!
TWIST!
OOF!
KIRKMAN & SCOTT
© 2008 BABY BLUES PARTNERSHIP DIST. BY KING FEATURES SYNDICATE 6-18
WITH THEM, VIOLENCE ISN'T A SOLUTION... IT'S A LIFESTYLE.

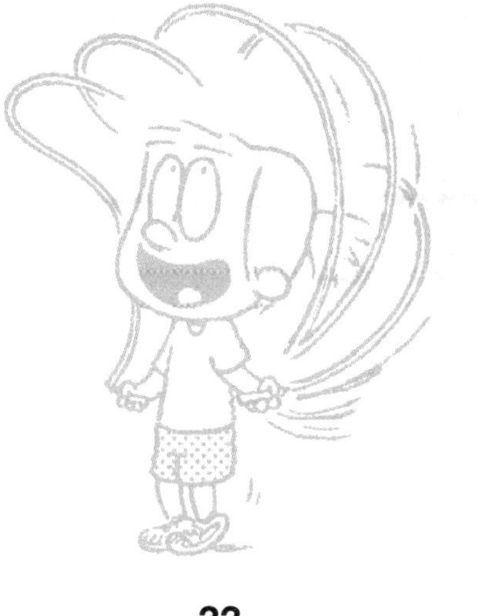

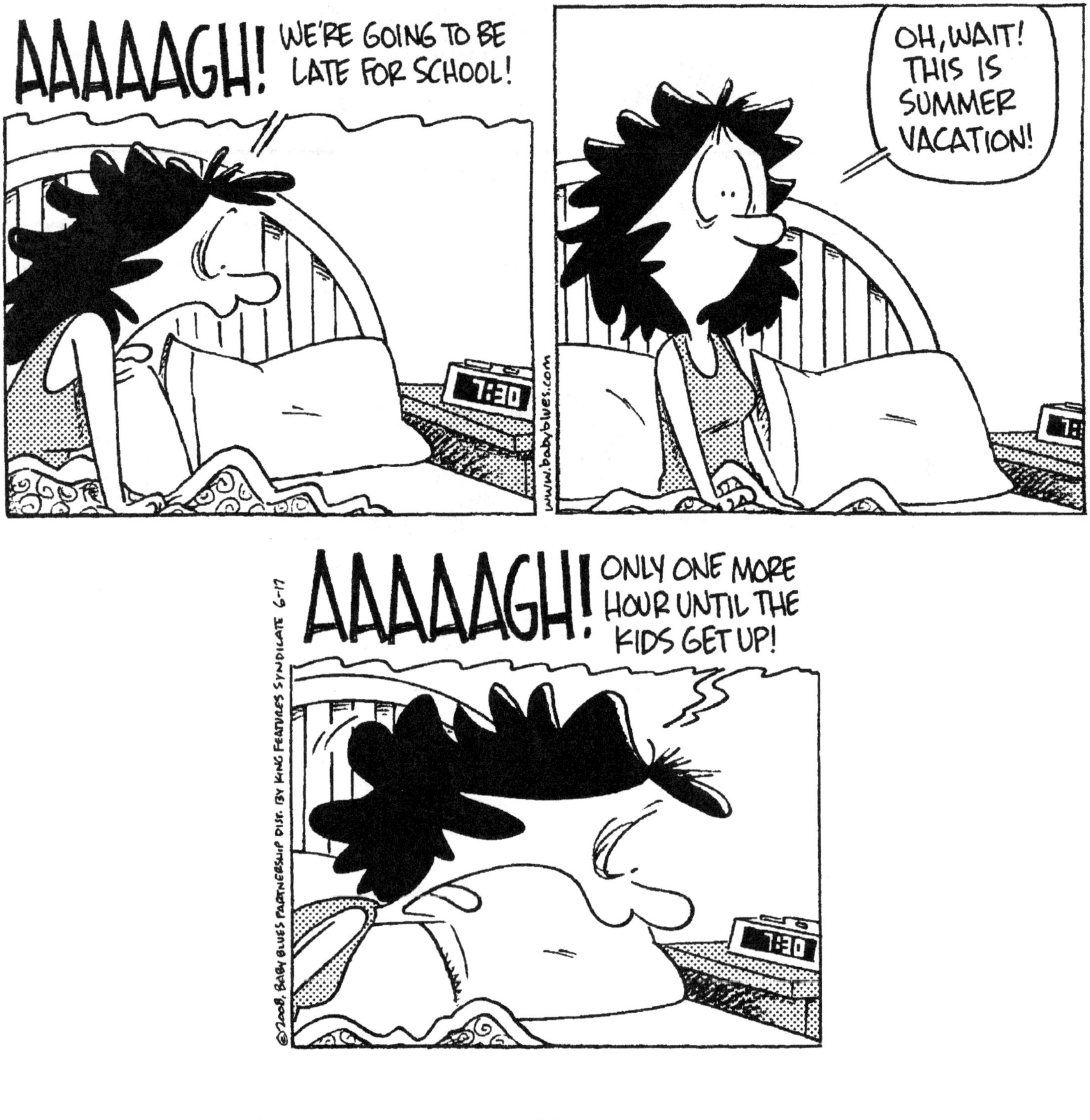
AAAAAGH!
WE'RE GOING TO BE LATE FOR SCHOOL!
www.babyblues.com
OH, WAIT! THIS IS SUMMER VACATION!
©2008, BABY BLUES PARTNERSHIP DIST. BY KING FEATURES SYNDICATE 6-17
AAAAAGH!
ONLY ONE MORE HOUR UNTIL THE KIDS GET UP!

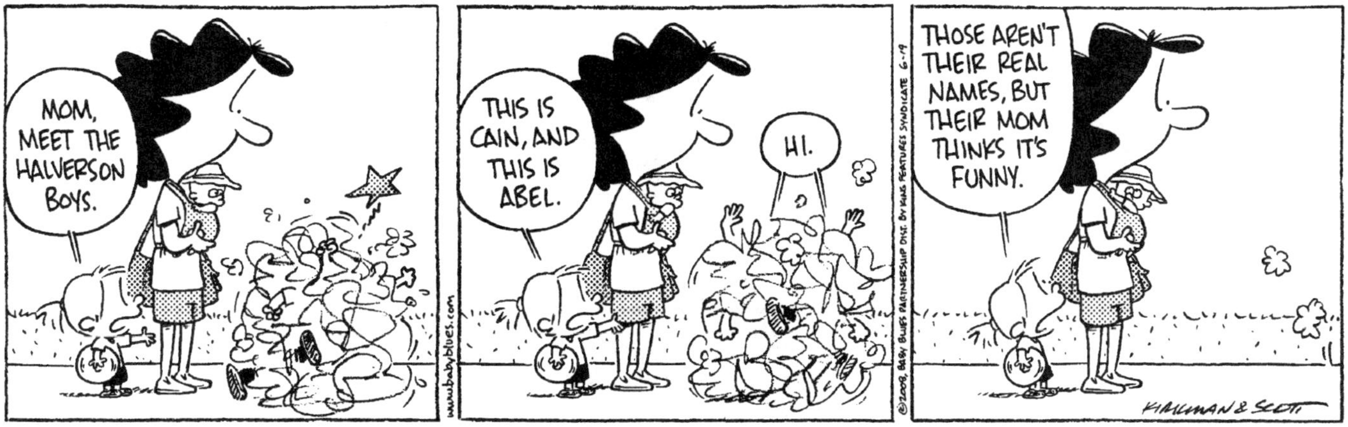
MOM, MEET THE HALVERSON BOYS.
THIS IS CAIN, AND THIS IS ABEL.
HI.
THOSE AREN'T THEIR REAL NAMES, BUT THEIR MOM THINKS IT'S FUNNY.
KIRKMAN & SCOTT

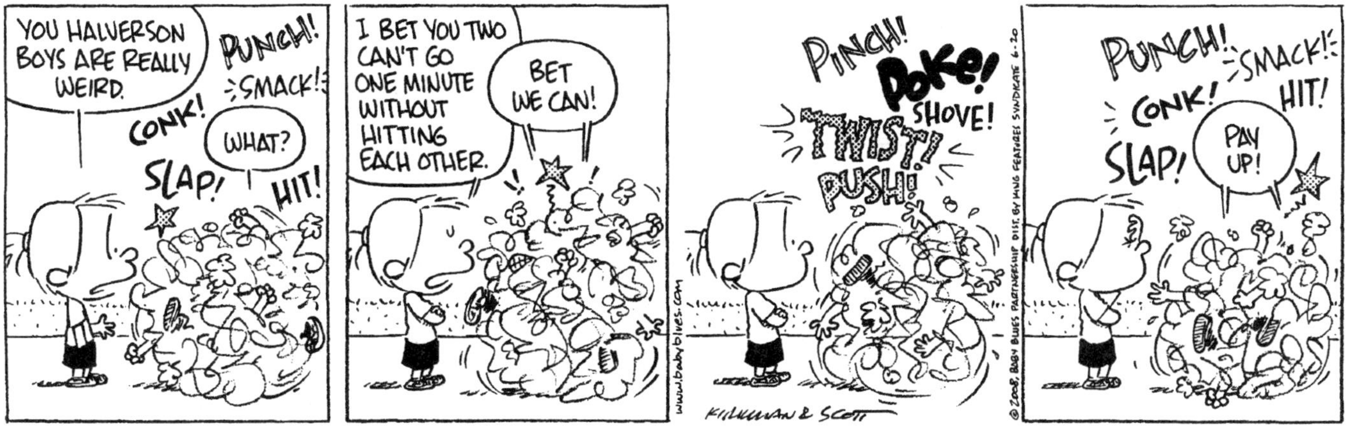
YOU HALVERSON BOYS ARE REALLY WEIRD.
PUNCH!
SMACK!
CONK!
WHAT?
SLAP!
HIT!
I BET YOU TWO CAN'T GO ONE MINUTE WITHOUT HITTING EACH OTHER.
BET WE CAN!
PINCH!
POKE!
SHOVE!
TWIST!
PUSH!
PUNCH!
SMACK!
CONK!
HIT!
SLAP!
PAY UP!
KIRKMAN & SCOTT

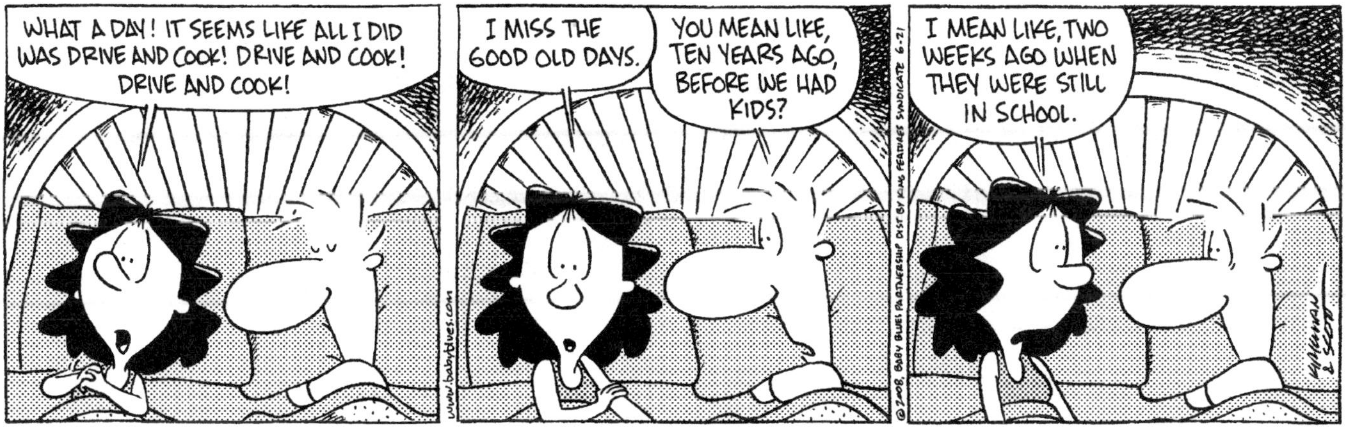
WHAT A DAY! IT SEEMS LIKE ALL I DID WAS DRIVE AND COOK! DRIVE AND COOK! DRIVE AND COOK!
I MISS THE GOOD OLD DAYS.
YOU MEAN LIKE, TEN YEARS AGO, BEFORE WE HAD KIDS?
I MEAN LIKE, TWO WEEKS AGO WHEN THEY WERE STILL IN SCHOOL.
KIRKMAN & SCOTT

BABY BLUES®
RICK KIRKMAN / BY JERRY SCOTT

My Day
Laundry Time
Kitchen Time
Cleaning Time
Me Time
Kid Time
©2008, BABY BLUES PARTNERSHIP DIST. BY KING FEATURES SYNDICATE www.babyblues.com
KIRKMAN & SCOTT 6-22

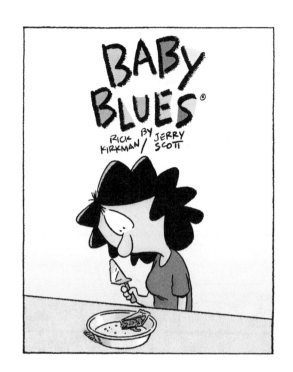

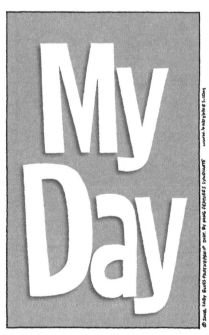

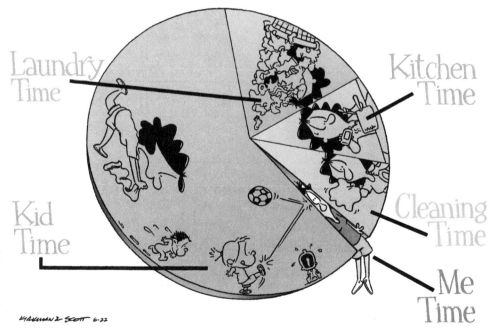

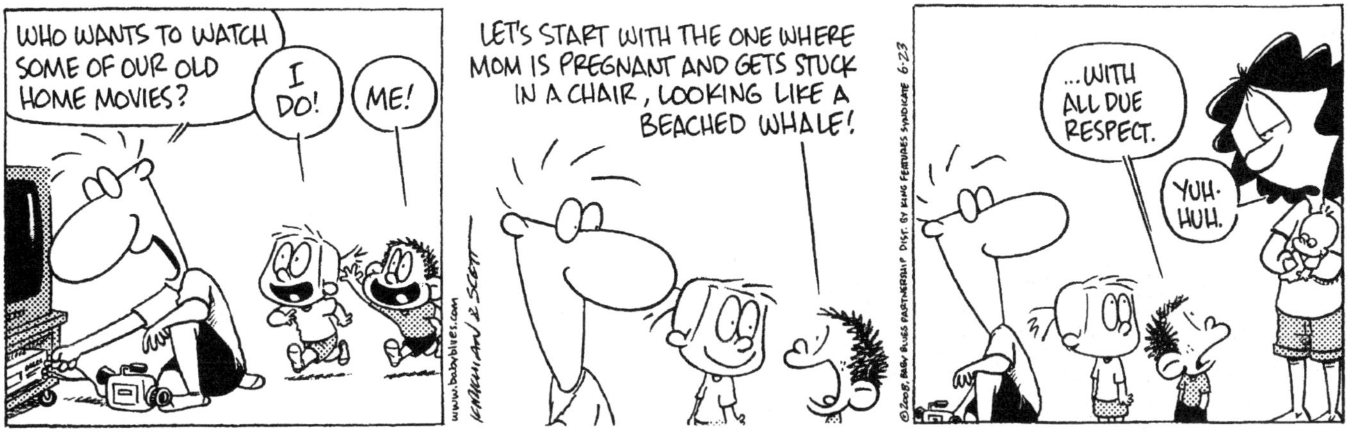
WHO WANTS TO WATCH SOME OF OUR OLD HOME MOVIES?
I DO!
ME!
LET'S START WITH THE ONE WHERE MOM IS PREGNANT AND GETS STUCK IN A CHAIR, LOOKING LIKE A BEACHED WHALE!
...WITH ALL DUE RESPECT.
YUH-HUH.
www.babyblues.com
KIRKMAN & SCOTT
©2008, BABY BLUES PARTNERSHIP DIST. BY KING FEATURES SYNDICATE 6-23

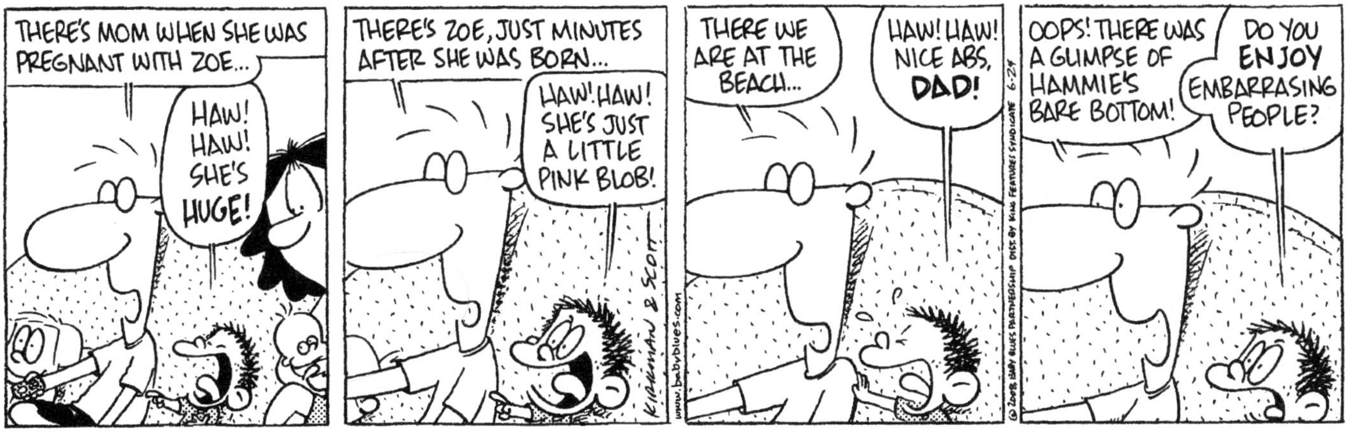
THERE'S MOM WHEN SHE WAS PREGNANT WITH ZOE...
HAW! HAW! SHE'S **HUGE**!
THERE'S ZOE, JUST MINUTES AFTER SHE WAS BORN...
HAW! HAW! SHE'S JUST A LITTLE PINK BLOB!
THERE WE ARE AT THE BEACH...
HAW! HAW! NICE ABS, **DAD**!
OOPS! THERE WAS A GLIMPSE OF HAMMIE'S BARE BOTTOM!
DO YOU **ENJOY** EMBARRASING PEOPLE?
KIRKMAN & SCOTT
www.babyblues.com
©2008 BABY BLUES PARTNERSHIP DIST. BY KING FEATURES SYNDICATE 6-24

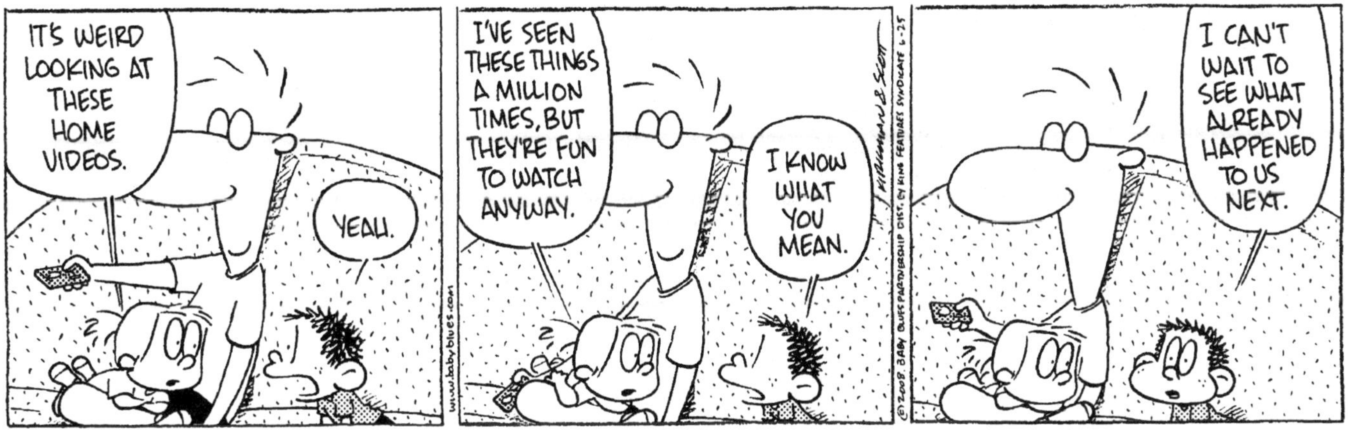
IT'S WEIRD LOOKING AT THESE HOME VIDEOS.
YEAH.
I'VE SEEN THESE THINGS A MILLION TIMES, BUT THEY'RE FUN TO WATCH ANYWAY.
I KNOW WHAT YOU MEAN.
I CAN'T WAIT TO SEE WHAT ALREADY HAPPENED TO US NEXT.
www.babyblues.com
KIRKMAN & SCOTT
©2008 BABY BLUES PARTNERSHIP DIST. BY KING FEATURES SYNDICATE 6-25

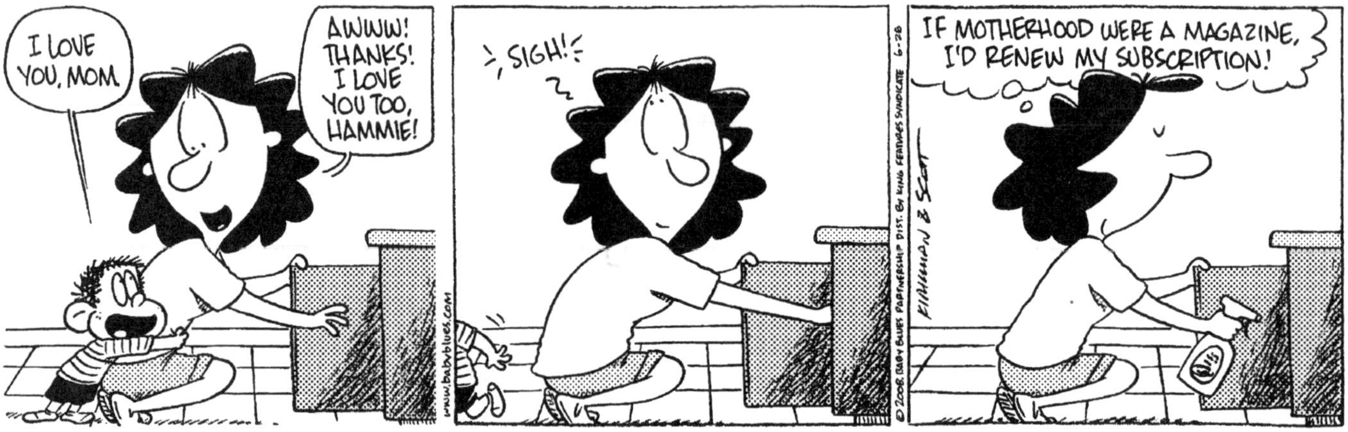
I LOVE YOU, MOM.
AWWW! THANKS! I LOVE YOU TOO, HAMMIE!
SIGH!
IF MOTHERHOOD WERE A MAGAZINE, I'D RENEW MY SUBSCRIPTION!
www.babyblues.com
©2008, BABY BLUES PARTNERSHIP DIST. BY KING FEATURES SYNDICATE 6-28
KIRKMAN & SCOTT

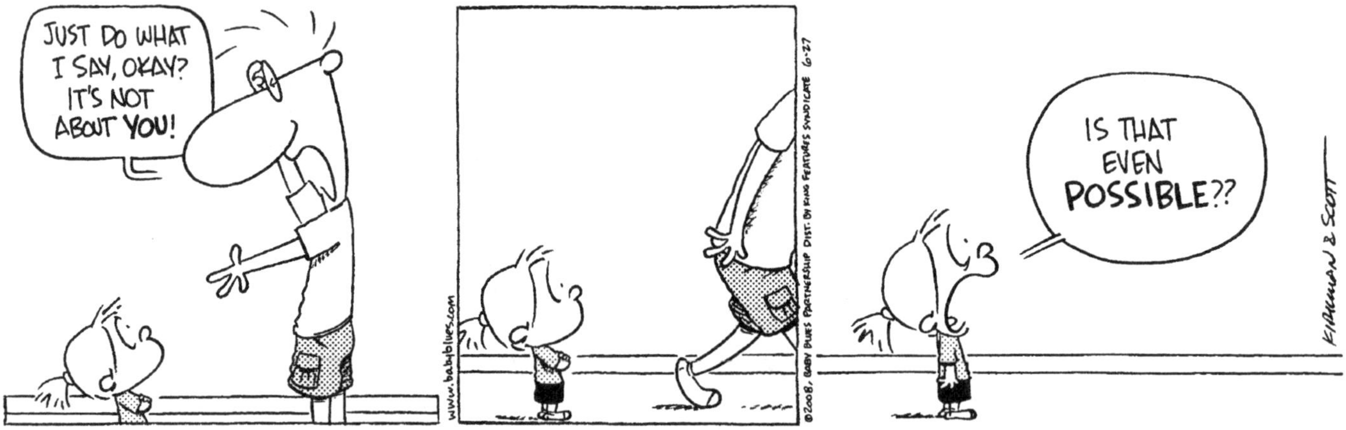
JUST DO WHAT I SAY, OKAY? IT'S NOT ABOUT YOU!
IS THAT EVEN POSSIBLE??
www.babyblues.com
©2008, BABY BLUES PARTNERSHIP DIST. BY KING FEATURES SYNDICATE 6-27
KIRKMAN & SCOTT

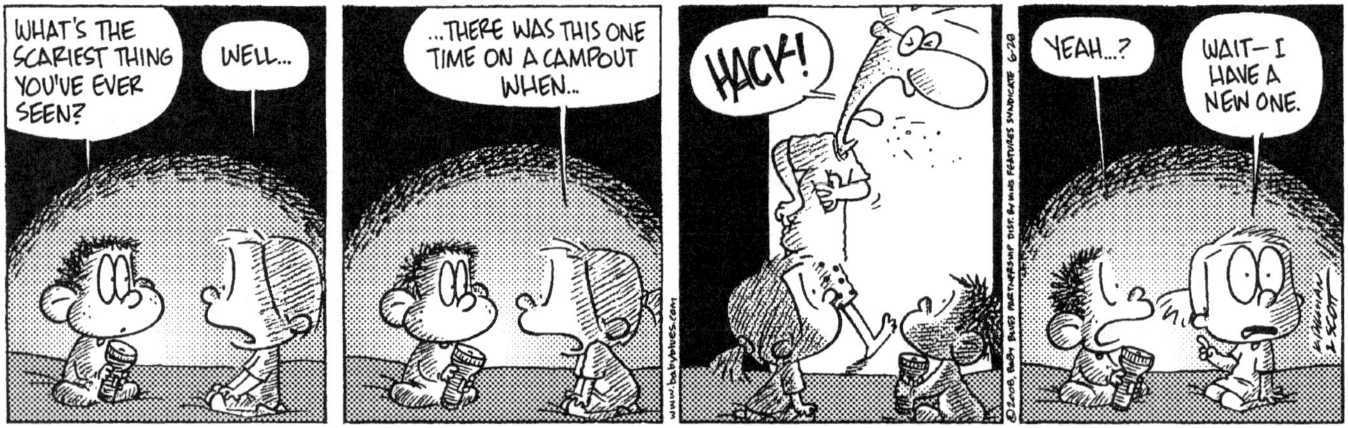
WHAT'S THE SCARIEST THING YOU'VE EVER SEEN?
WELL...
...THERE WAS THIS ONE TIME ON A CAMPOUT WHEN...
HACK!
YEAH...?
WAIT— I HAVE A NEW ONE.
www.babyblues.com
©2008, BABY BLUES PARTNERSHIP DIST. BY KING FEATURES SYNDICATE 6-28
KIRKMAN & SCOTT

BABY BLUES®
BY RICK KIRKMAN/ JERRY SCOTT

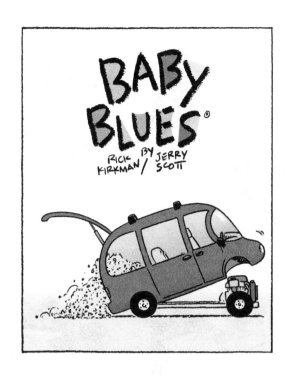

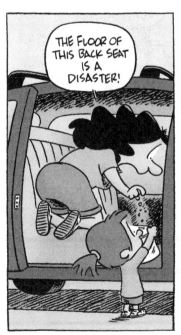

THE FLOOR OF THIS BACK SEAT IS A DISASTER!
CRUMBLED CHEERIOS...
...CRUSHED NUTS...
...STALE RAISINS...TEETHING BISCUIT CRUMBS... SUNFLOWER SEEDS...
CAN YOU HOLD THIS?
SURE.
6-29 KIRKMAN & SCOTT
© 2008 BABY BLUES PARTNERSHIP DIST. BY KING FEATURES SYNDICATE www.babyblues.com
WHERE'D WE GET THE TRAIL MIX?

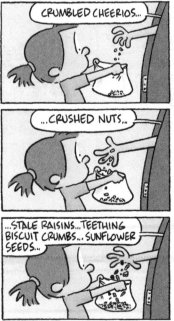

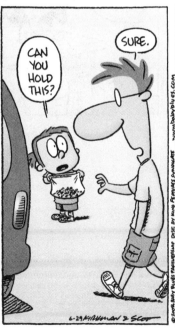

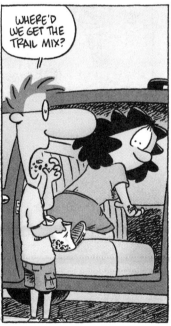

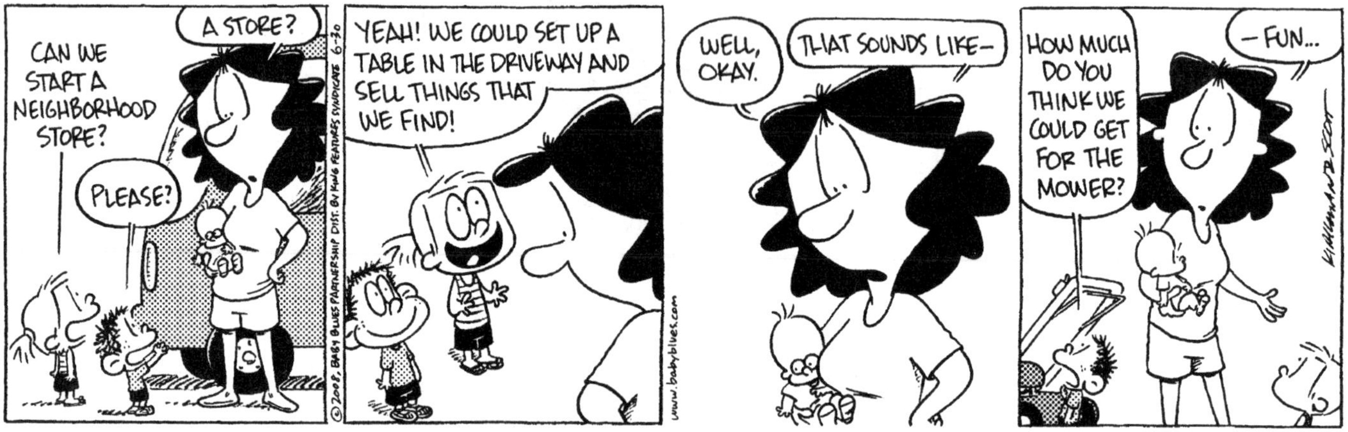
CAN WE START A NEIGHBORHOOD STORE?
A STORE?
PLEASE?
© 2008, BABY BLUES PARTNERSHIP DIST. BY KING FEATURES SYNDICATE 6-30
YEAH! WE COULD SET UP A TABLE IN THE DRIVEWAY AND SELL THINGS THAT WE FIND!
www.babyblues.com
WELL, OKAY.
THAT SOUNDS LIKE—
HOW MUCH DO YOU THINK WE COULD GET FOR THE MOWER?
—FUN...
KIRKMAN & SCOTT

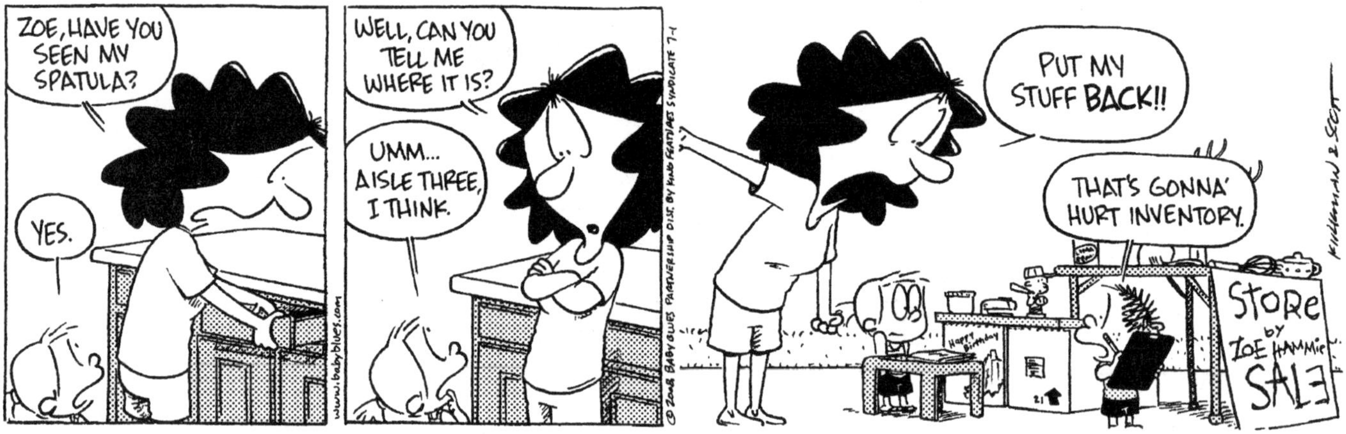
ZOE, HAVE YOU SEEN MY SPATULA?
YES.
www.babyblues.com
WELL, CAN YOU TELL ME WHERE IT IS?
UMM... AISLE THREE, I THINK.
© 2008 BABY BLUES PARTNERSHIP DIST. BY KING FEATURES SYNDICATE 7-1
PUT MY STUFF BACK!!
THAT'S GONNA' HURT INVENTORY.
STORE by ZOE HAMMIE SALE
KIRKMAN & SCOTT

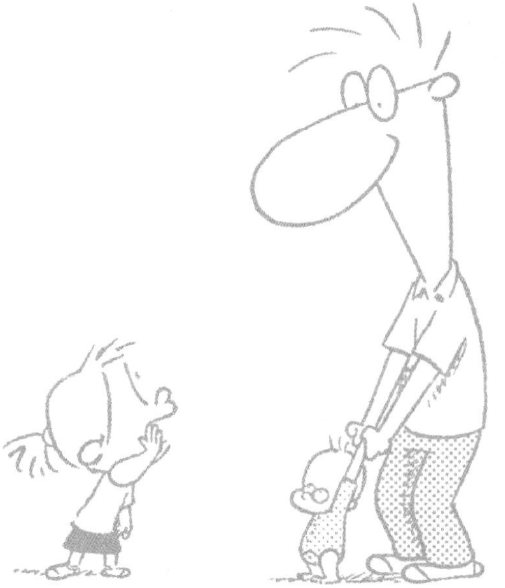

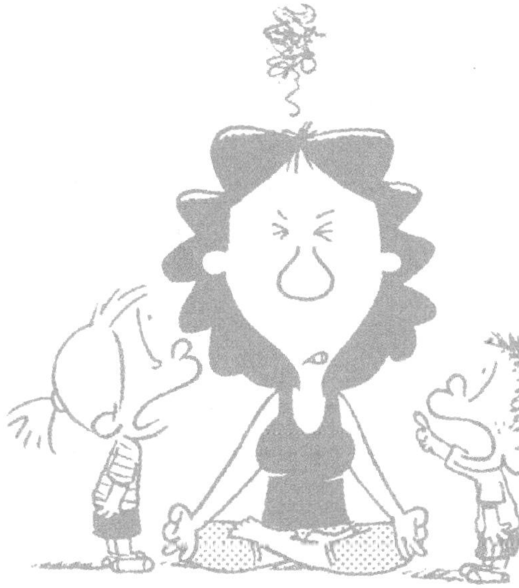

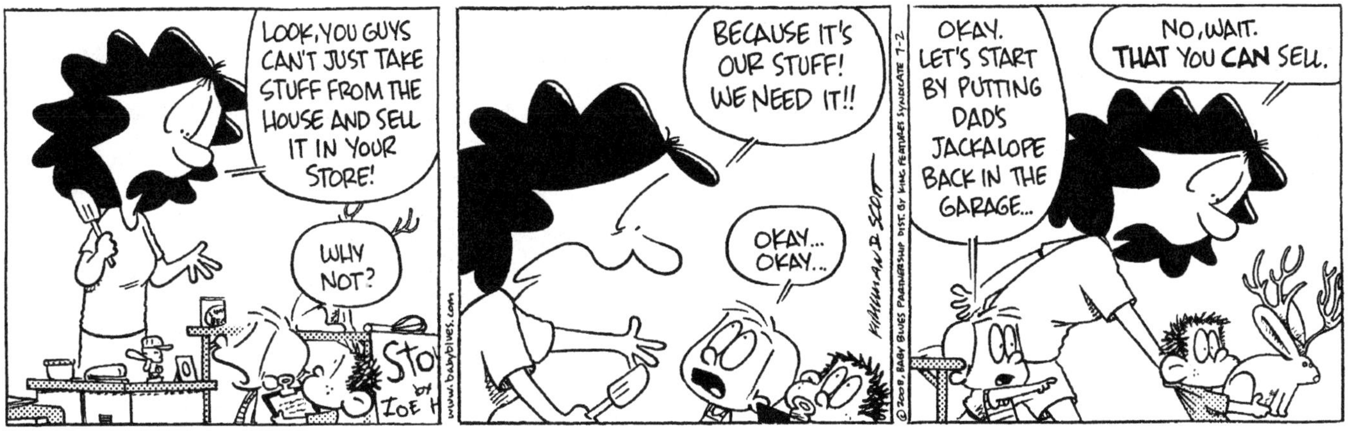
LOOK, YOU GUYS CAN'T JUST TAKE STUFF FROM THE HOUSE AND SELL IT IN YOUR STORE!
WHY NOT?
www.babyblues.com
BECAUSE IT'S OUR STUFF! WE NEED IT!!
OKAY... OKAY...
KIRKMAN & SCOTT
© 2008, BABY BLUES PARTNERSHIP DIST. BY KING FEATURES SYNDICATE 7-2
OKAY. LET'S START BY PUTTING DAD'S JACKALOPE BACK IN THE GARAGE...
NO, WAIT. THAT YOU CAN SELL.

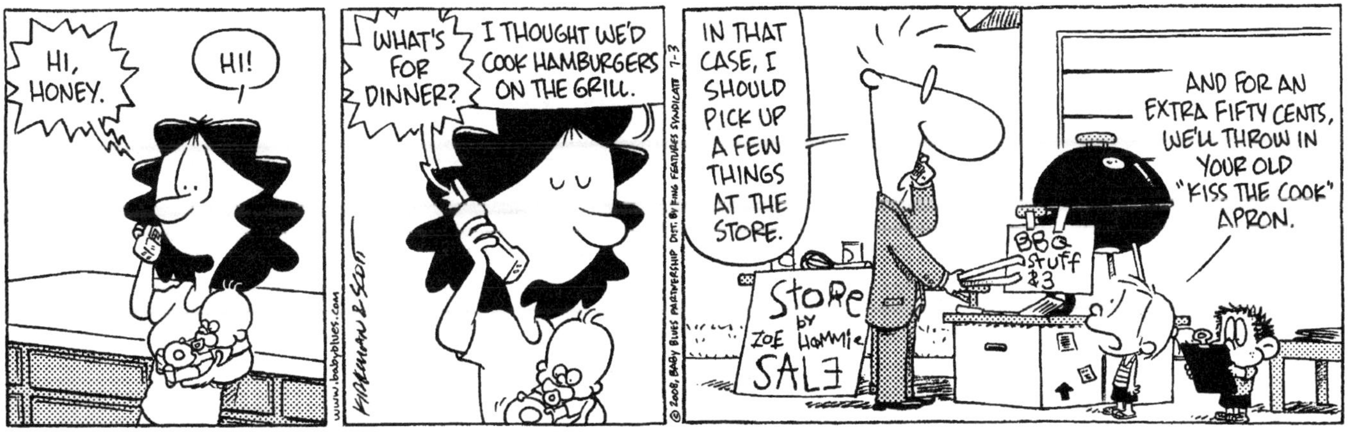
HI, HONEY.
HI!
www.babyblues.com
KIRKMAN & SCOTT
WHAT'S FOR DINNER?
I THOUGHT WE'D COOK HAMBURGERS ON THE GRILL.
© 2008, BABY BLUES PARTNERSHIP DIST. BY KING FEATURES SYNDICATE 7-3
IN THAT CASE, I SHOULD PICK UP A FEW THINGS AT THE STORE.
STORE by ZOE HAMMIE
SALE
BBQ STUFF $3
AND FOR AN EXTRA FIFTY CENTS, WE'LL THROW IN YOUR OLD "KISS THE COOK" APRON.

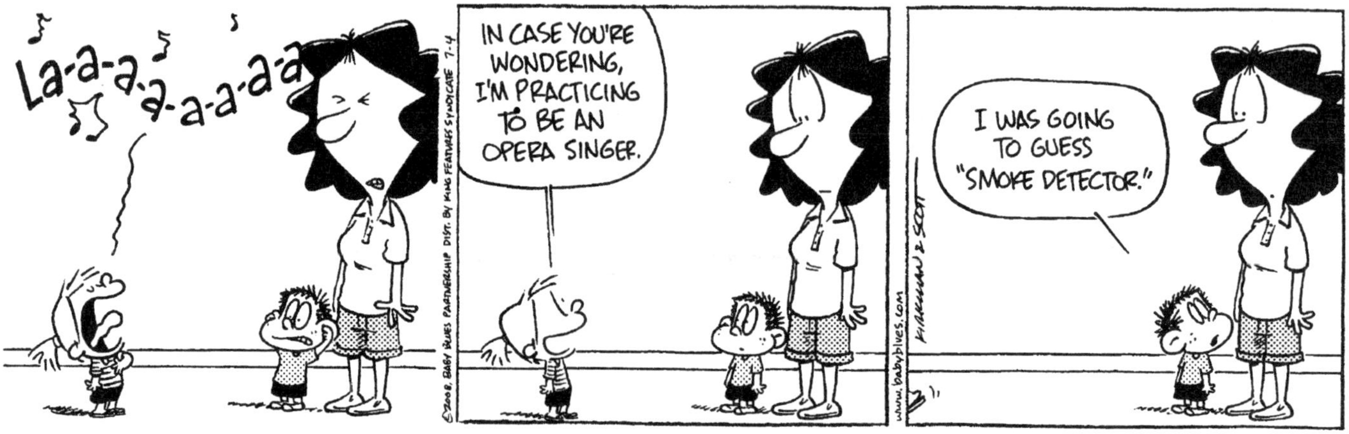
La-a-a-a-a-a-a-a
IN CASE YOU'RE WONDERING, I'M PRACTICING TO BE AN OPERA SINGER.
I WAS GOING TO GUESS "SMOKE DETECTOR."
©2008, BABY BLUES PARTNERSHIP DIST. BY KING FEATURES SYNDICATE 7-4
www.babyblues.com
KIRKMAN & SCOTT

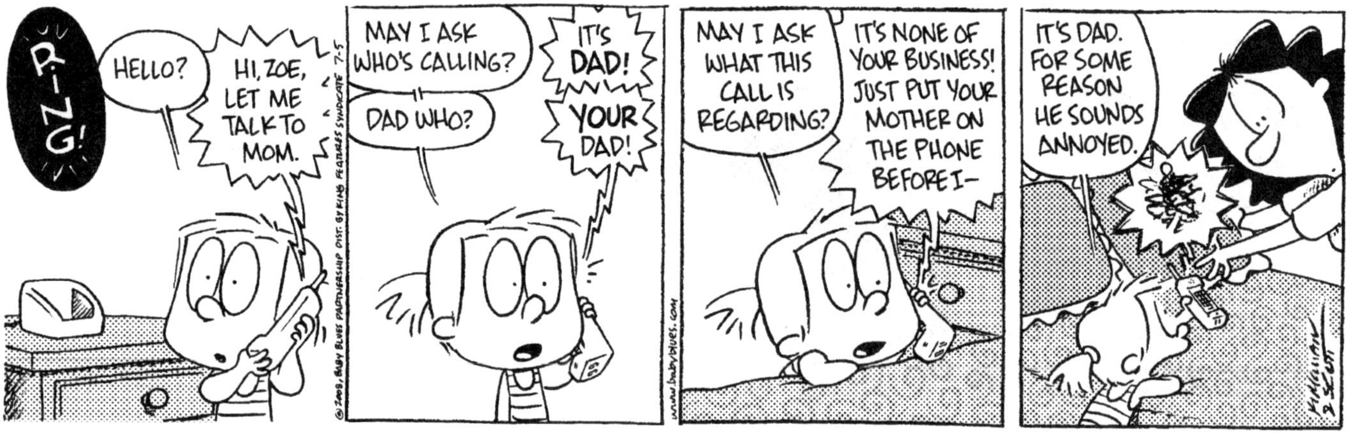
R-I-N-G!
HELLO?
HI, ZOE, LET ME TALK TO MOM.
MAY I ASK WHO'S CALLING?
IT'S DAD!
DAD WHO?
YOUR DAD!
MAY I ASK WHAT THIS CALL IS REGARDING?
IT'S NONE OF YOUR BUSINESS! JUST PUT YOUR MOTHER ON THE PHONE BEFORE I-
IT'S DAD. FOR SOME REASON HE SOUNDS ANNOYED.
©2008, BABY BLUES PARTNERSHIP DIST. BY KING FEATURES SYNDICATE 7-5
www.babyblues.com
KIRKMAN & SCOTT

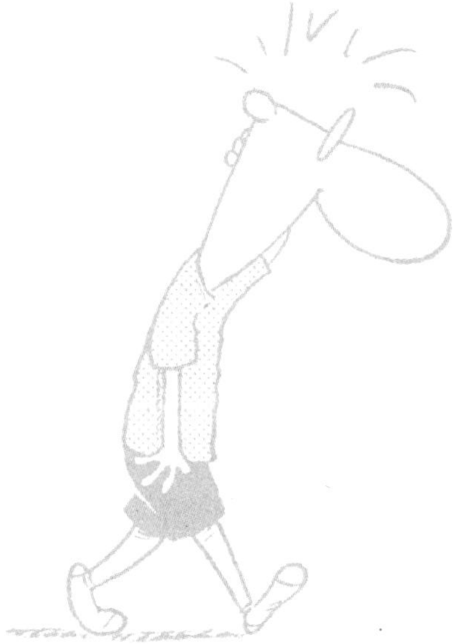

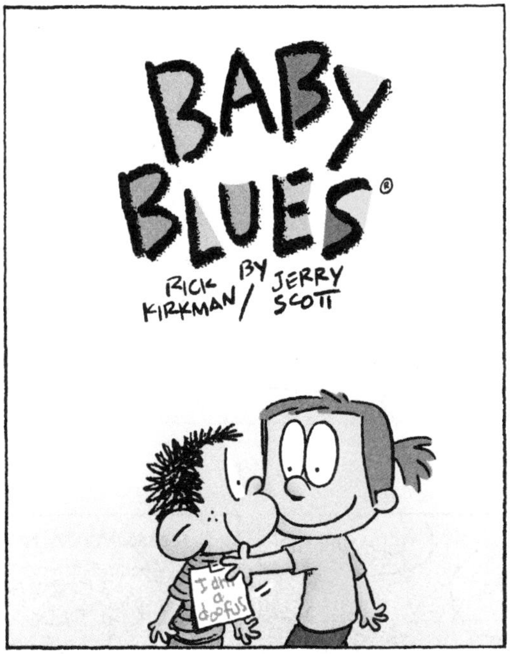
BABY BLUES®
BY RICK KIRKMAN / JERRY SCOTT
I am a doofus

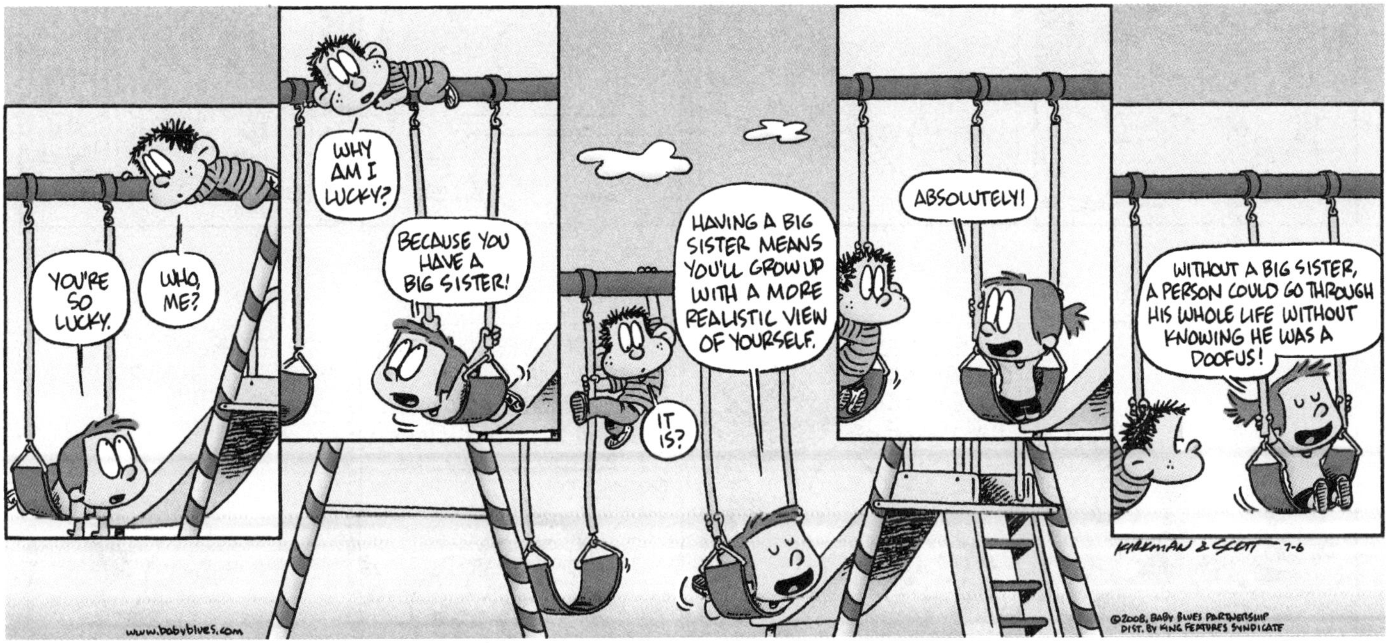
YOU'RE SO LUCKY.
WHO, ME?
WHY AM I LUCKY?
BECAUSE YOU HAVE A BIG SISTER!
HAVING A BIG SISTER MEANS YOU'LL GROW UP WITH A MORE REALISTIC VIEW OF YOURSELF.
IT IS?
ABSOLUTELY!
WITHOUT A BIG SISTER, A PERSON COULD GO THROUGH HIS WHOLE LIFE WITHOUT KNOWING HE WAS A DOOFUS!
KIRKMAN & SCOTT 7-6
www.babyblues.com
©2008, BABY BLUES PARTNERSHIP
DIST. BY KING FEATURES SYNDICATE

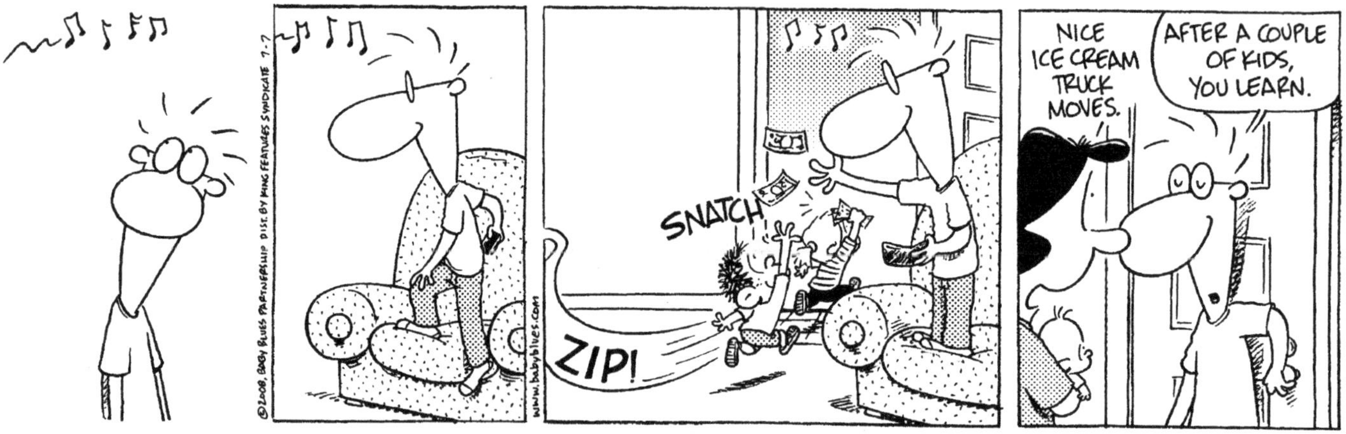
©2008, BABY BLUES PARTNERSHIP DIST. BY KING FEATURES SYNDICATE 7-7
www.babyblues.com
SNATCH
ZIP!
NICE ICE CREAM TRUCK MOVES.
AFTER A COUPLE OF KIDS, YOU LEARN.

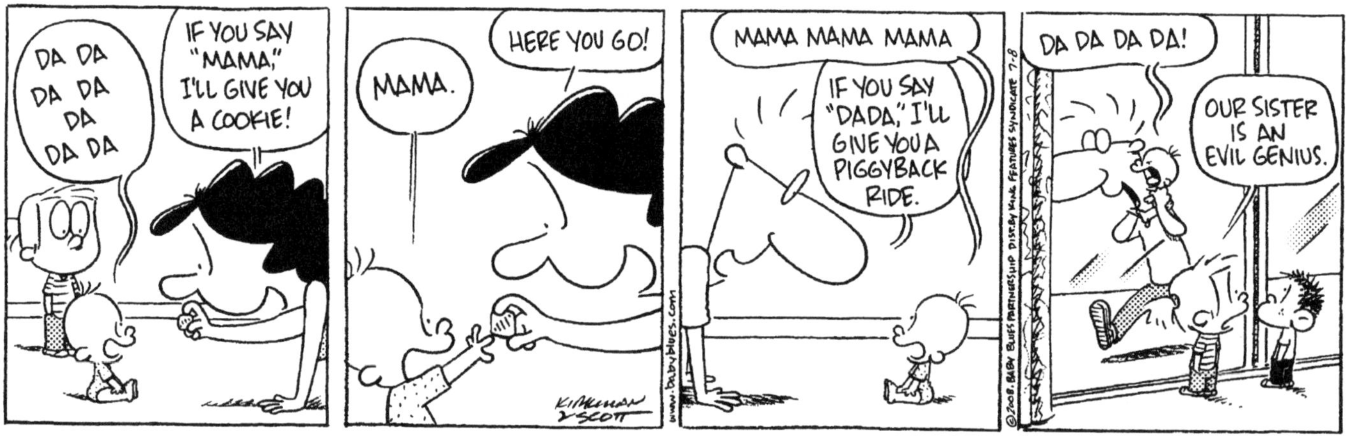
DA DA DA DA DA DA DA
IF YOU SAY "MAMA," I'LL GIVE YOU A COOKIE!
MAMA.
HERE YOU GO!
KIRKMAN & SCOTT
www.babyblues.com
MAMA MAMA MAMA
IF YOU SAY "DADA," I'LL GIVE YOU A PIGGYBACK RIDE.
©2008, BABY BLUES PARTNERSHIP DIST. BY KING FEATURES SYNDICATE 7-8
DA DA DA DA!
OUR SISTER IS AN EVIL GENIUS.

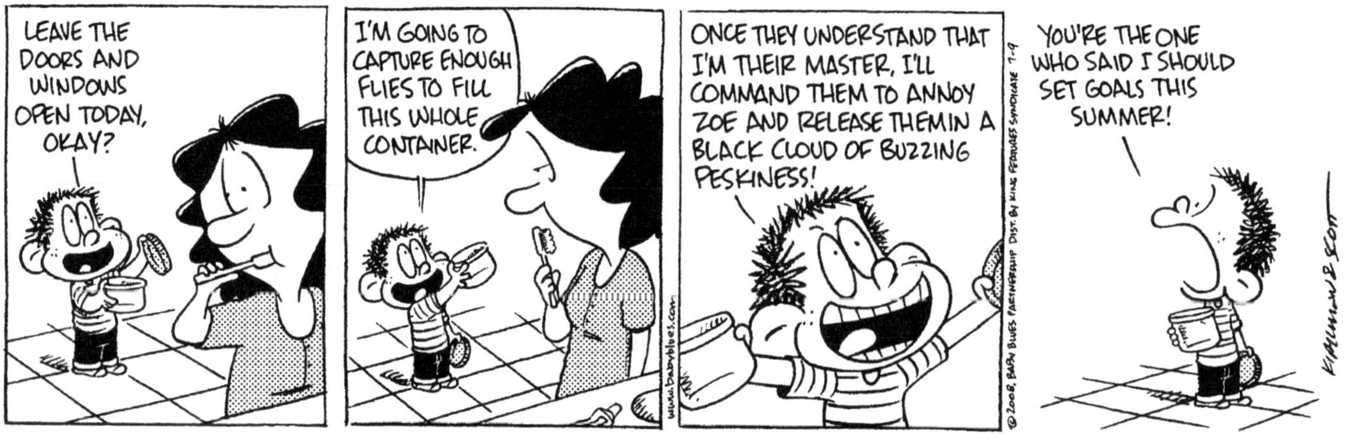
LEAVE THE DOORS AND WINDOWS OPEN TODAY, OKAY?
I'M GOING TO CAPTURE ENOUGH FLIES TO FILL THIS WHOLE CONTAINER.
www.babyblues.com
ONCE THEY UNDERSTAND THAT I'M THEIR MASTER, I'LL COMMAND THEM TO ANNOY ZOE AND RELEASE THEM IN A BLACK CLOUD OF BUZZING PESKINESS!
©2008, BABY BLUES PARTNERSHIP DIST. BY KING FEATURES SYNDICATE 7-9
YOU'RE THE ONE WHO SAID I SHOULD SET GOALS THIS SUMMER!
KIRKMAN & SCOTT

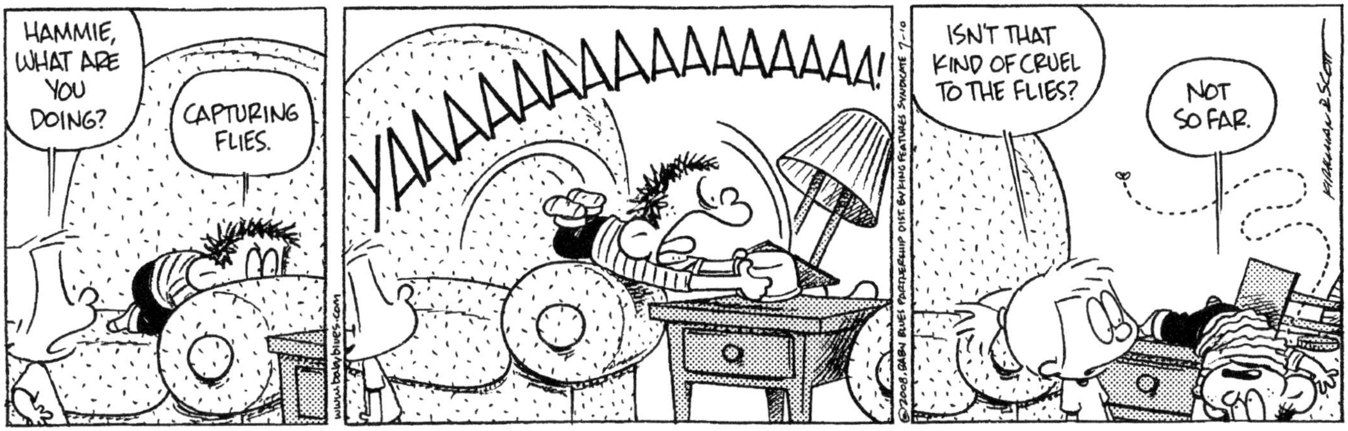
HAMMIE, WHAT ARE YOU DOING?
CAPTURING FLIES.
www.babyblues.com
YAAAAAAAAAAAAAAAAA!
© 2008, BABY BLUES PARTNERSHIP DIST. BY KING FEATURES SYNDICATE 7-10
ISN'T THAT KIND OF CRUEL TO THE FLIES?
NOT SO FAR.
KIRKMAN & SCOTT

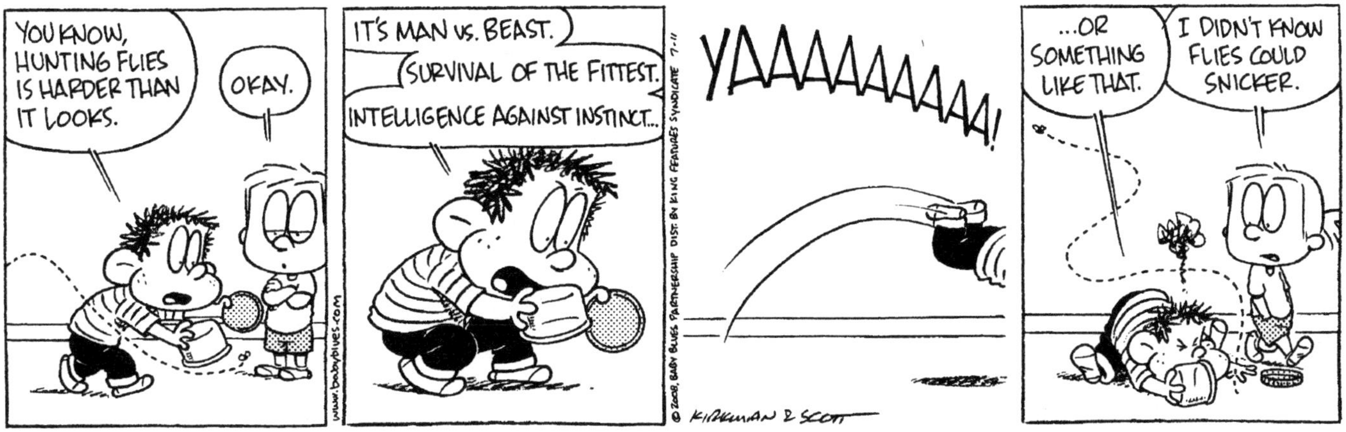
YOU KNOW, HUNTING FLIES IS HARDER THAN IT LOOKS.
OKAY.
www.babyblues.com
IT'S MAN vs. BEAST.
SURVIVAL OF THE FITTEST.
INTELLIGENCE AGAINST INSTINCT...
© 2008, BABY BLUES PARTNERSHIP DIST. BY KING FEATURES SYNDICATE 7-11
YAAAAAAAAAA!
KIRKMAN & SCOTT
...OR SOMETHING LIKE THAT.
I DIDN'T KNOW FLIES COULD SNICKER.

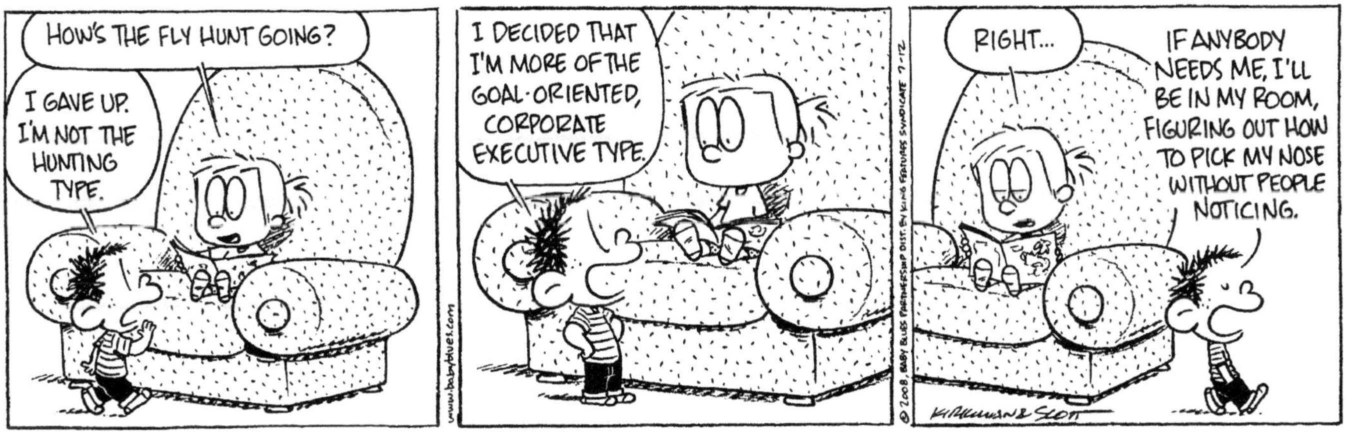
HOW'S THE FLY HUNT GOING?
I GAVE UP. I'M NOT THE HUNTING TYPE.
www.babyblues.com
I DECIDED THAT I'M MORE OF THE GOAL-ORIENTED, CORPORATE EXECUTIVE TYPE.
© 2008, BABY BLUES PARTNERSHIP DIST. BY KING FEATURES SYNDICATE 7-12
RIGHT...
IF ANYBODY NEEDS ME, I'LL BE IN MY ROOM, FIGURING OUT HOW TO PICK MY NOSE WITHOUT PEOPLE NOTICING.
KIRKMAN & SCOTT

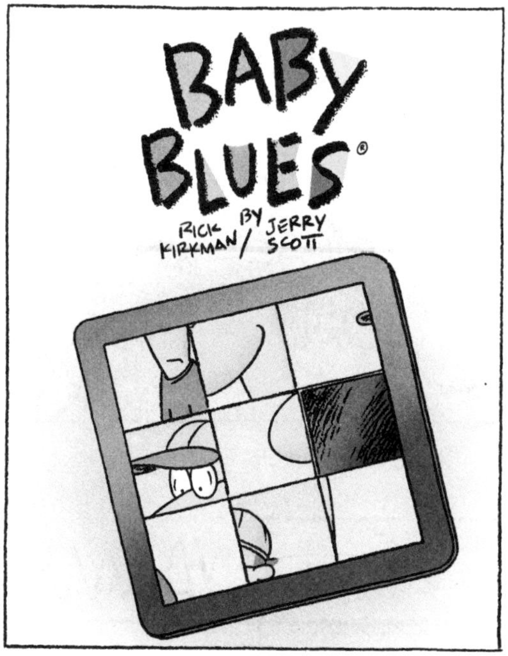
BABY BLUES®
BY RICK KIRKMAN / JERRY SCOTT

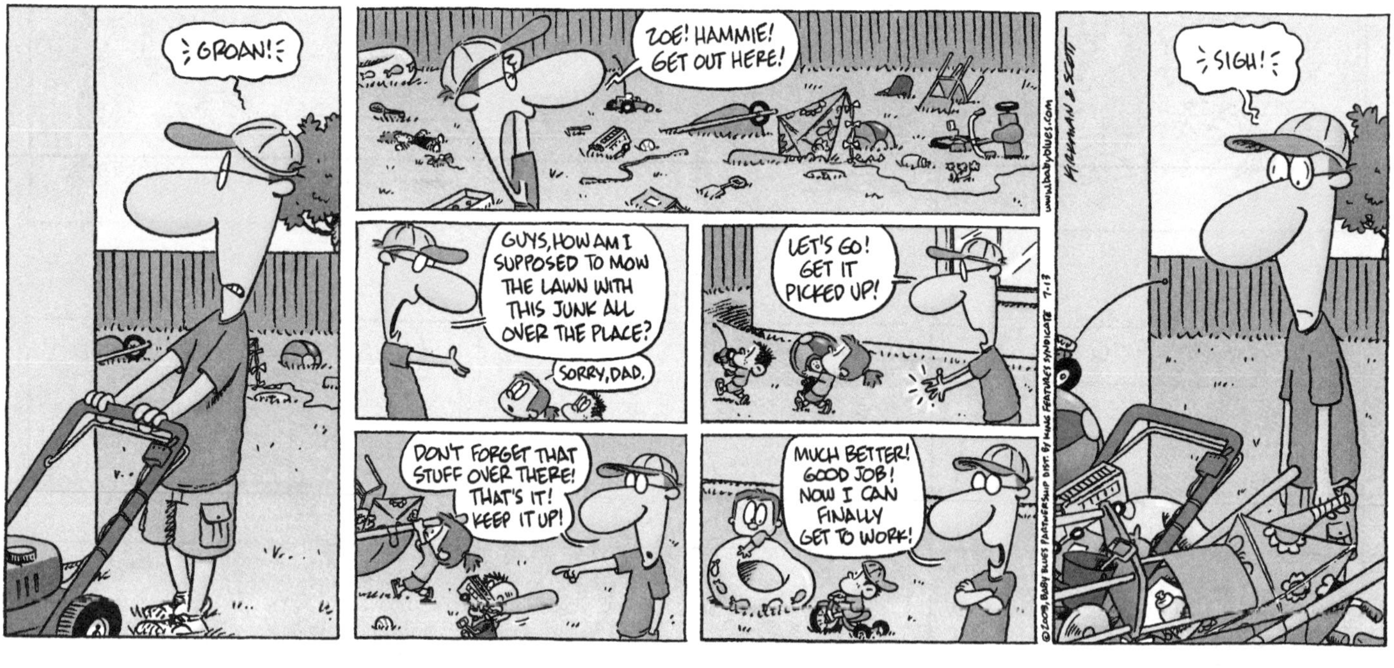
GROAN!
ZOE! HAMMIE! GET OUT HERE!
GUYS, HOW AM I SUPPOSED TO MOW THE LAWN WITH THIS JUNK ALL OVER THE PLACE?
SORRY, DAD.
LET'S GO! GET IT PICKED UP!
DON'T FORGET THAT STUFF OVER THERE! THAT'S IT! KEEP IT UP!
MUCH BETTER! GOOD JOB! NOW I CAN FINALLY GET TO WORK!
SIGH!
KIRKMAN & SCOTT
www.babyblues.com
©2009, BABY BLUES PARTNERSHIP DIST. BY KING FEATURES SYNDICATE 7-13

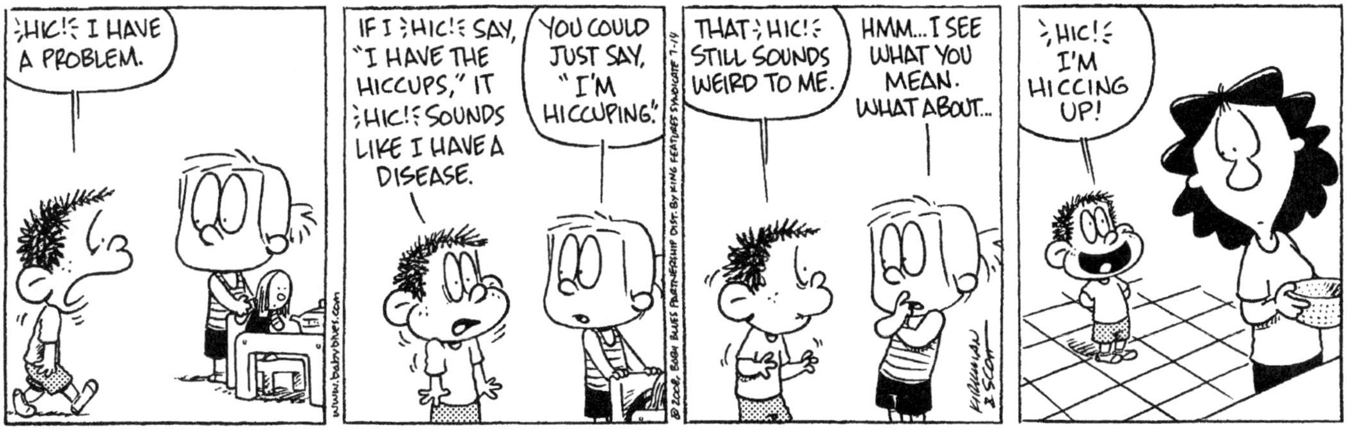
HIC! I HAVE A PROBLEM.
IF I HIC! SAY, "I HAVE THE HICCUPS," IT HIC! SOUNDS LIKE I HAVE A DISEASE.
YOU COULD JUST SAY, "I'M HICCUPING."
THAT HIC! STILL SOUNDS WEIRD TO ME.
HMM... I SEE WHAT YOU MEAN. WHAT ABOUT...
HIC! I'M HICCING UP!

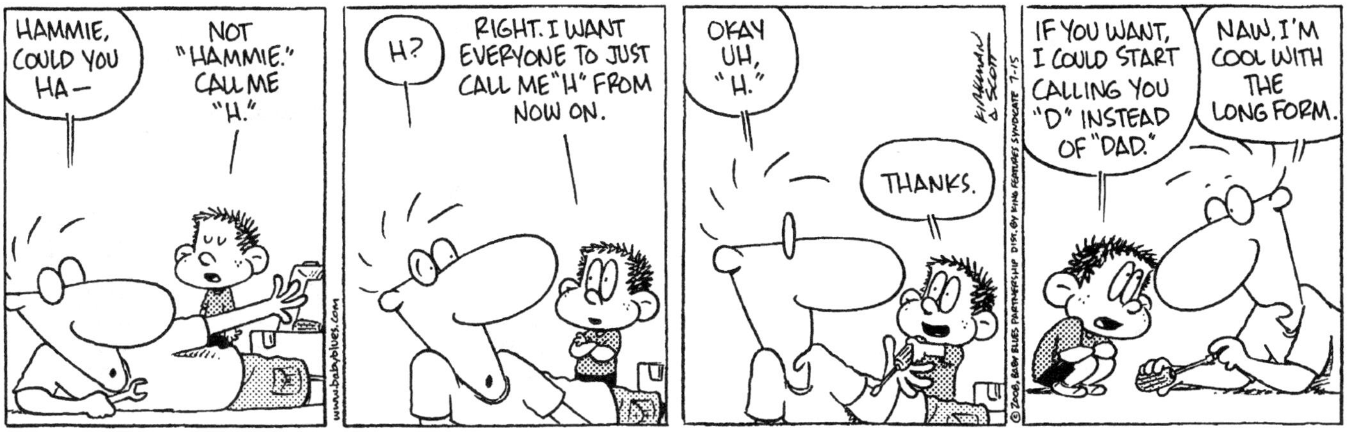
HAMMIE, COULD YOU HA—
NOT "HAMMIE." CALL ME "H."
H?
RIGHT. I WANT EVERYONE TO JUST CALL ME "H" FROM NOW ON.
OKAY UH, "H."
THANKS.
IF YOU WANT, I COULD START CALLING YOU "D" INSTEAD OF "DAD."
NAW, I'M COOL WITH THE LONG FORM.

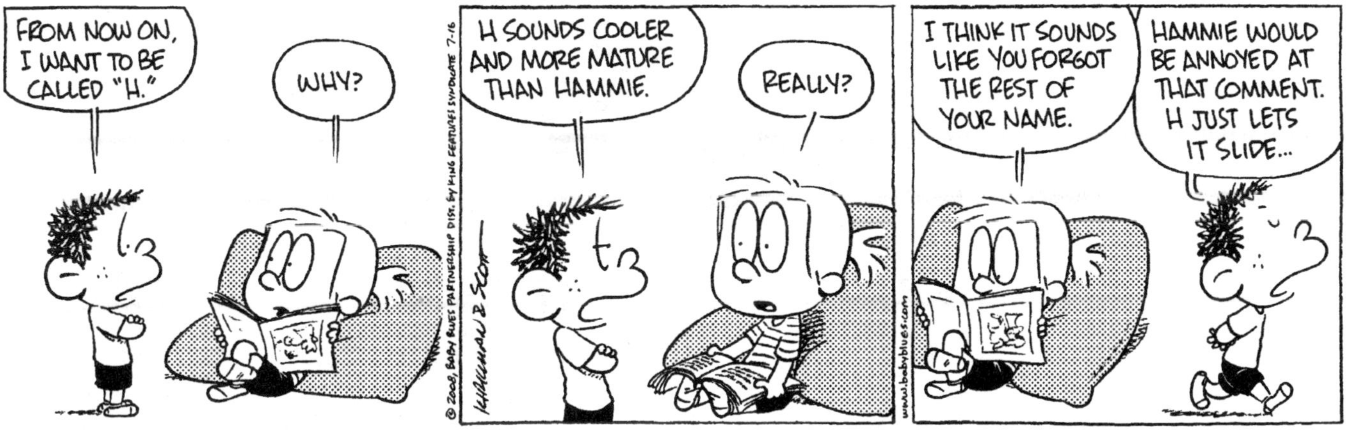
FROM NOW ON, I WANT TO BE CALLED "H."
WHY?
H SOUNDS COOLER AND MORE MATURE THAN HAMMIE.
REALLY?
I THINK IT SOUNDS LIKE YOU FORGOT THE REST OF YOUR NAME.
HAMMIE WOULD BE ANNOYED AT THAT COMMENT. H JUST LETS IT SLIDE...

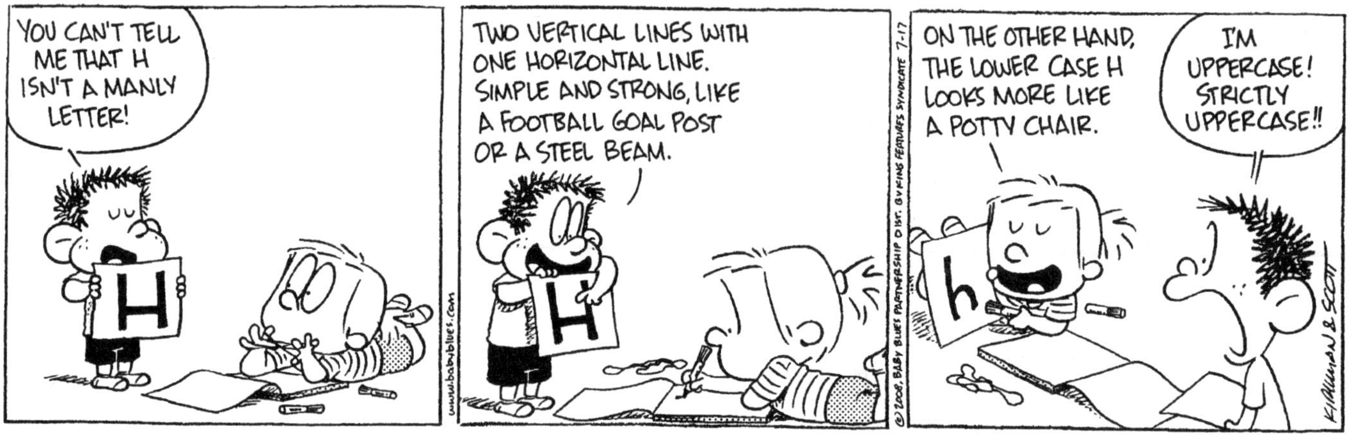
YOU CAN'T TELL ME THAT H ISN'T A MANLY LETTER!
H
TWO VERTICAL LINES WITH ONE HORIZONTAL LINE. SIMPLE AND STRONG, LIKE A FOOTBALL GOAL POST OR A STEEL BEAM.
H
ON THE OTHER HAND, THE LOWER CASE H LOOKS MORE LIKE A POTTY CHAIR.
h
I'M UPPERCASE! STRICTLY UPPERCASE!!
www.babyblues.com
© 2008, Baby Blues Partnership Dist. by King Features Syndicate 7-17
KIRKMAN & SCOTT

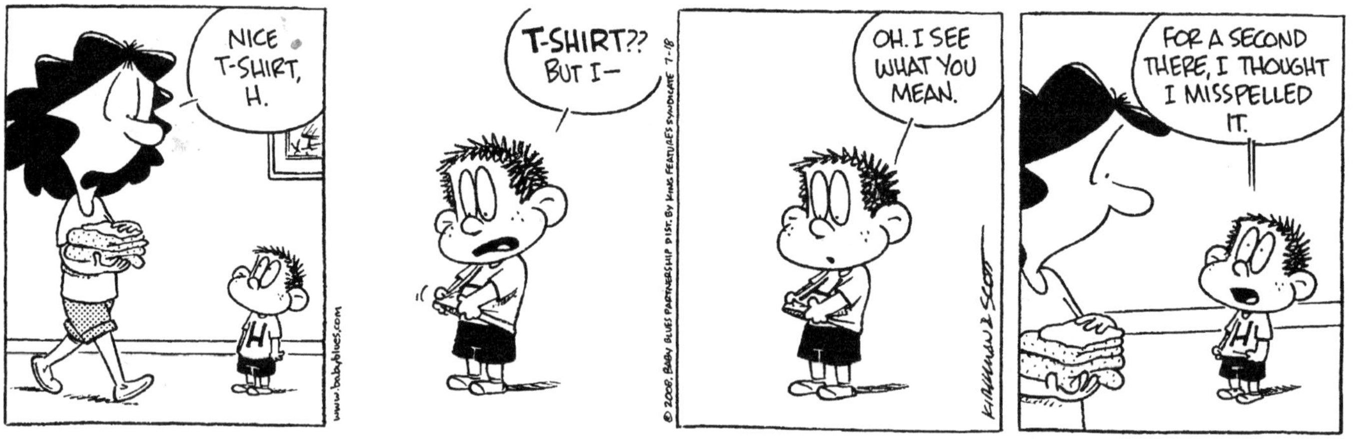
NICE T-SHIRT, H.
T-SHIRT?? BUT I—
OH. I SEE WHAT YOU MEAN.
FOR A SECOND THERE, I THOUGHT I MISSPELLED IT.
www.babyblues.com
© 2008, Baby Blues Partnership Dist. by King Features Syndicate 7-18
KIRKMAN & SCOTT

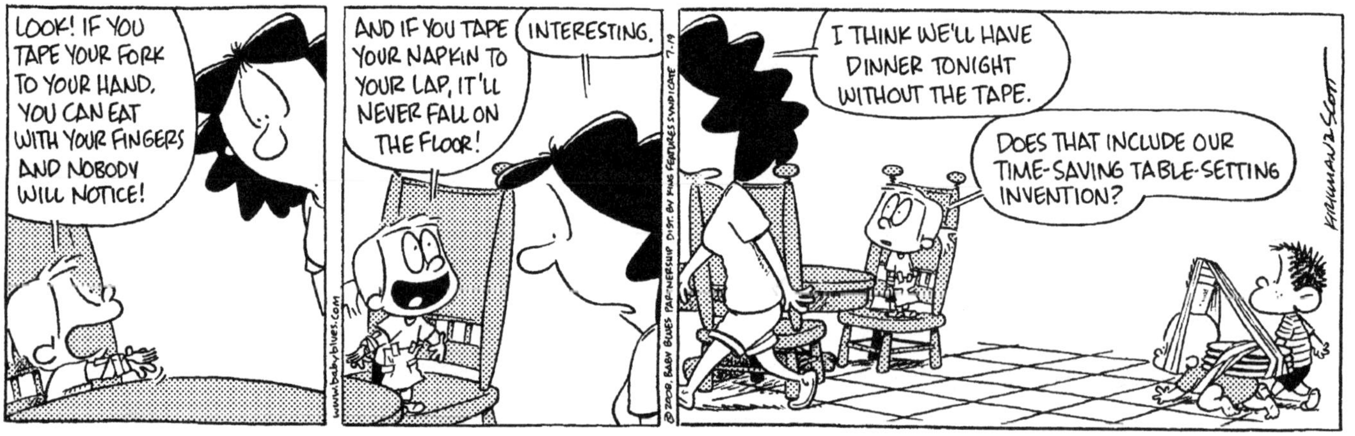
LOOK! IF YOU TAPE YOUR FORK TO YOUR HAND, YOU CAN EAT WITH YOUR FINGERS AND NOBODY WILL NOTICE!
AND IF YOU TAPE YOUR NAPKIN TO YOUR LAP, IT'LL NEVER FALL ON THE FLOOR!
INTERESTING.
I THINK WE'LL HAVE DINNER TONIGHT WITHOUT THE TAPE.
DOES THAT INCLUDE OUR TIME-SAVING TABLE-SETTING INVENTION?
www.babyblues.com
© 2008, Baby Blues Partnership Dist. by King Features Syndicate 7-19
KIRKMAN & SCOTT

BABY BLUES®
BY RICK KIRKMAN / JERRY SCOTT
SLOW AHEAD

THERE YOU GO!
CLICK!
SNIFF! SNIFF!
PEW!
THIS VAN REEKS OF OLD FRENCH FRIES, FRUIT PUNCH AND MICROWAVE POPCORN!
www.babyblues.com
GROSS!
SLAM!
© 2008, BABY BLUES PARTNERSHIP DIST. BY KING FEATURES SYNDICATE 7-20
KIRKMAN & SCOTT
DOESN'T EVERYBODY'S CAR SMELL LIKE THIS?
SNIIIIFF! ONLY THE GOOD ONES.

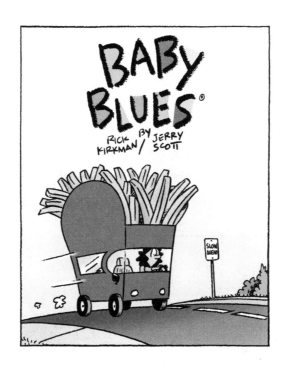

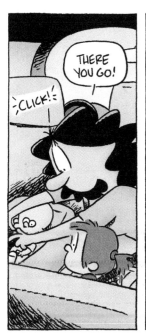

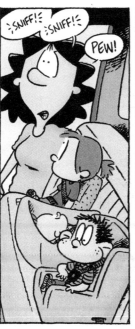

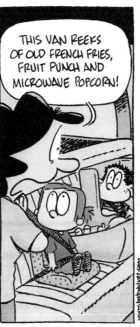

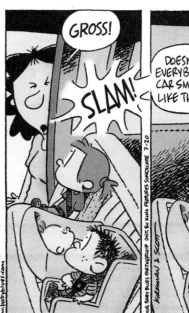

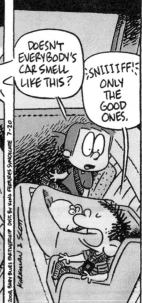

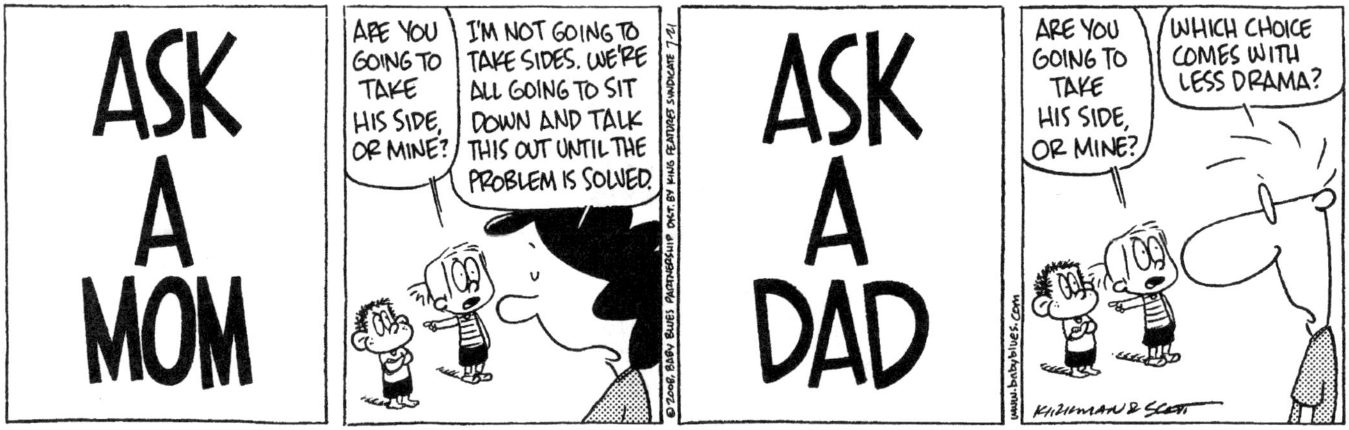
ASK A MOM
ARE YOU GOING TO TAKE HIS SIDE, OR MINE?
I'M NOT GOING TO TAKE SIDES. WE'RE ALL GOING TO SIT DOWN AND TALK THIS OUT UNTIL THE PROBLEM IS SOLVED.
© 2008, BABY BLUES PARTNERSHIP DIST. BY KING FEATURES SYNDICATE 7-21
ASK A DAD
ARE YOU GOING TO TAKE HIS SIDE, OR MINE?
WHICH CHOICE COMES WITH LESS DRAMA?
www.babyblues.com
KIRKMAN & SCOTT

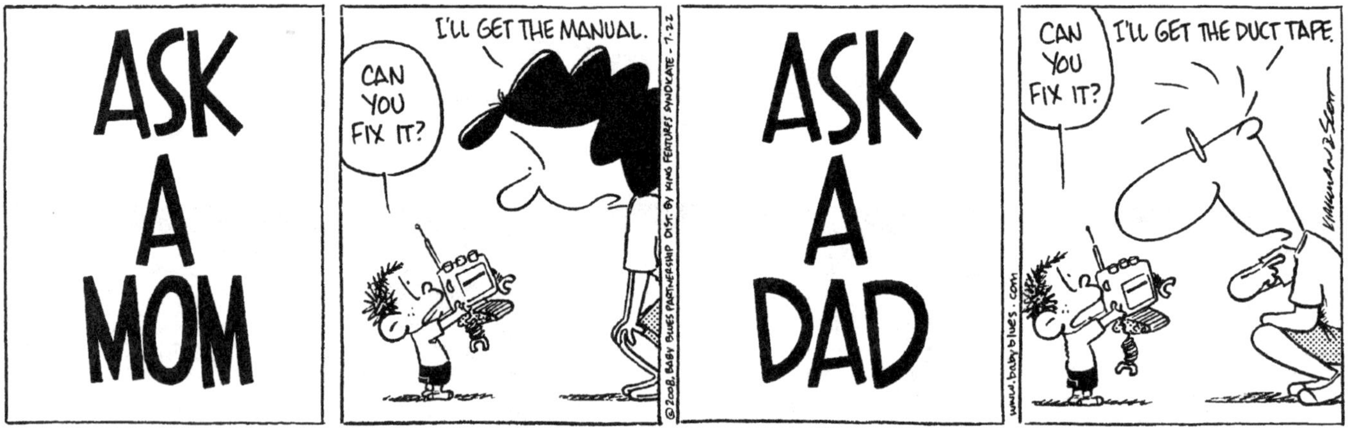
ASK A MOM
CAN YOU FIX IT?
I'LL GET THE MANUAL.
© 2008, BABY BLUES PARTNERSHIP DIST. BY KING FEATURES SYNDICATE 7-22
ASK A DAD
CAN YOU FIX IT?
I'LL GET THE DUCT TAPE.
www.babyblues.com
KIRKMAN & SCOTT

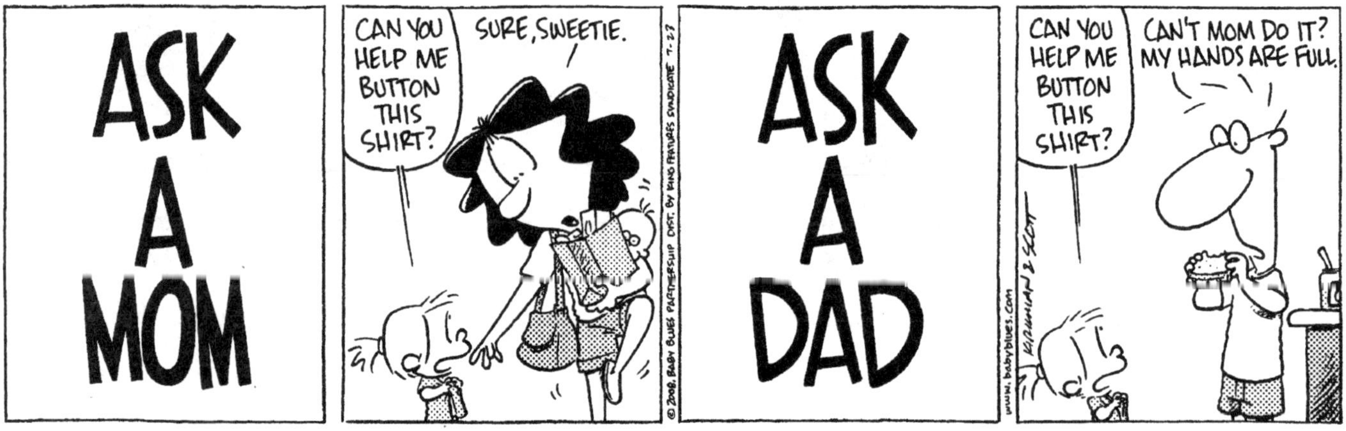
ASK A MOM
CAN YOU HELP ME BUTTON THIS SHIRT?
SURE, SWEETIE.
© 2008, BABY BLUES PARTNERSHIP DIST. BY KING FEATURES SYNDICATE 7-23
ASK A DAD
CAN YOU HELP ME BUTTON THIS SHIRT?
CAN'T MOM DO IT? MY HANDS ARE FULL.
www.babyblues.com
KIRKMAN & SCOTT

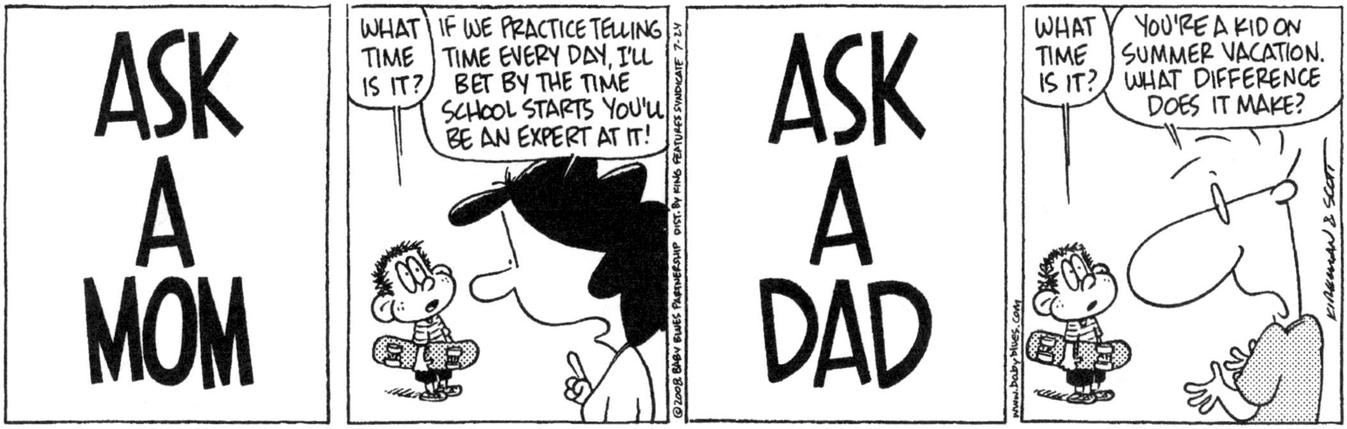
ASK A MOM
WHAT TIME IS IT?
IF WE PRACTICE TELLING TIME EVERY DAY, I'LL BET BY THE TIME SCHOOL STARTS YOU'LL BE AN EXPERT AT IT!
©2008 BABY BLUES PARTNERSHIP DIST. BY KING FEATURES SYNDICATE 7-24
ASK A DAD
www.babyblues.com
WHAT TIME IS IT?
YOU'RE A KID ON SUMMER VACATION. WHAT DIFFERENCE DOES IT MAKE?
KIRKMAN & SCOTT

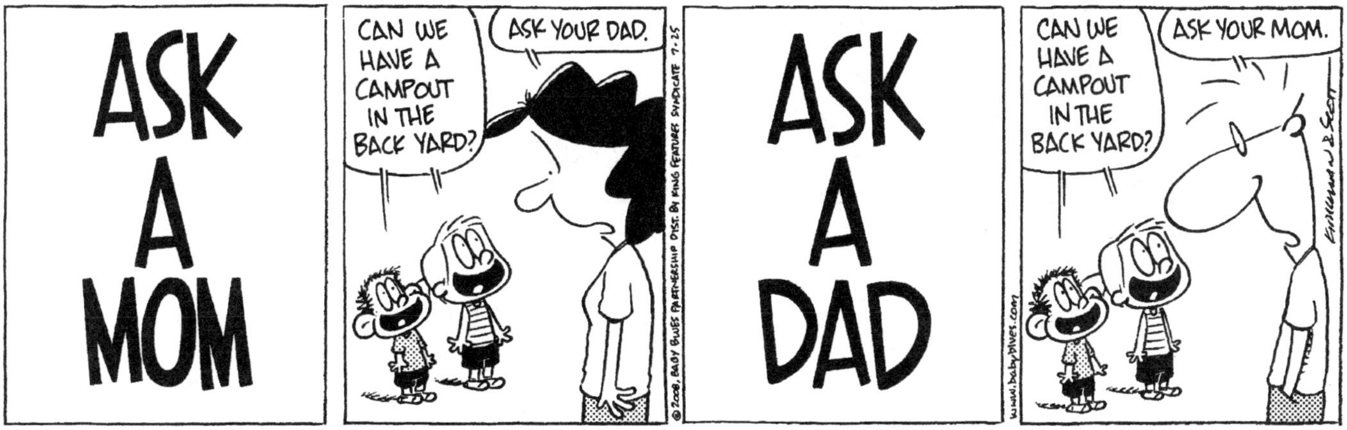
ASK A MOM
CAN WE HAVE A CAMPOUT IN THE BACK YARD?
ASK YOUR DAD.
©2008, BABY BLUES PARTNERSHIP DIST. BY KING FEATURES SYNDICATE 7-25
ASK A DAD
www.babyblues.com
CAN WE HAVE A CAMPOUT IN THE BACK YARD?
ASK YOUR MOM.
KIRKMAN & SCOTT

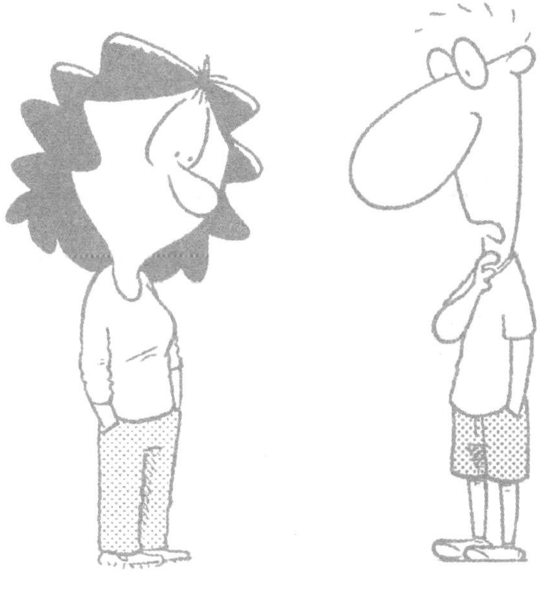

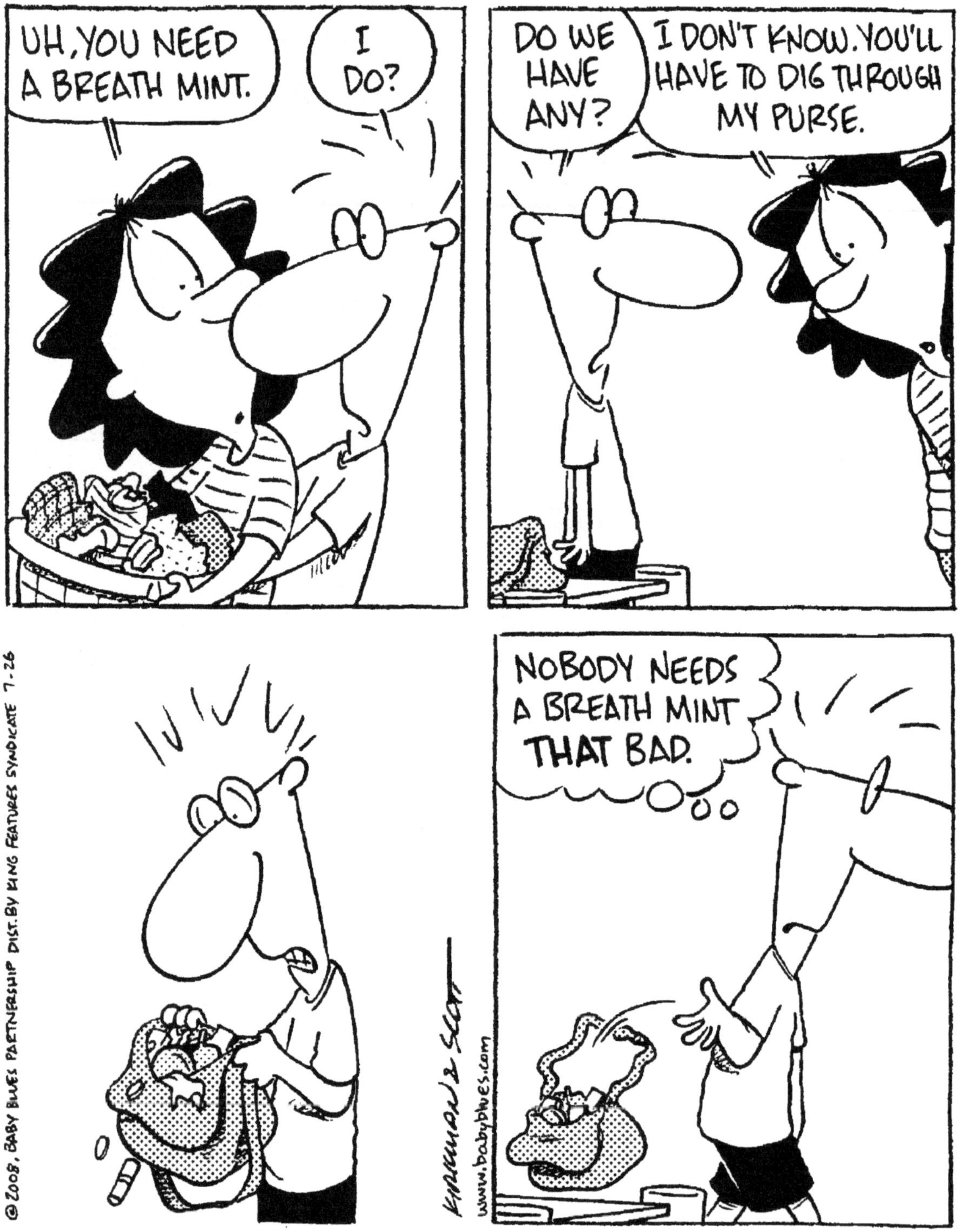
UH, YOU NEED A BREATH MINT.
I DO?
DO WE HAVE ANY?
I DON'T KNOW. YOU'LL HAVE TO DIG THROUGH MY PURSE.
NOBODY NEEDS A BREATH MINT THAT BAD.
©2008, BABY BLUES PARTNERSHIP DIST. BY KING FEATURES SYNDICATE 7-26
KIRKMAN & SCOTT
www.babyblues.com

BABY BLUES®
BY
RICK KIRKMAN / JERRY SCOTT

DAD! DAD! THROW ME!
OKAY.
YAAAAHHH!
MY TURN!
YAAAAHHH!
MY TURN!
YAAAAHHH!
MY TURN!
YAAAAHHH!
UNH!
MY TURN!
www.babyblues.com
YAAAAHHH!
OOF!
KIRKMAN & SCOTT
©2008, BABY BLUES PARTNERSHIP DIST. BY KING FEATURES SYNDICATE
MY TURN!
YAAAAH

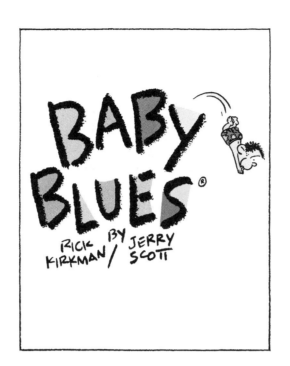

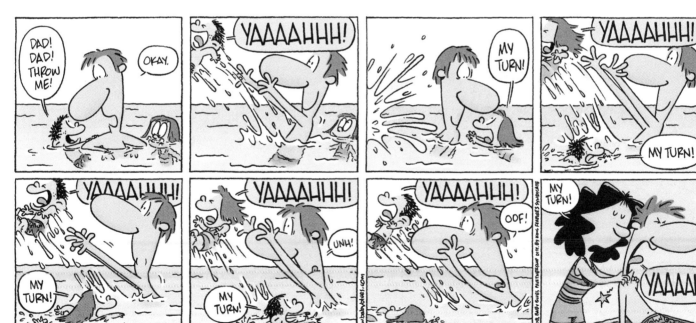

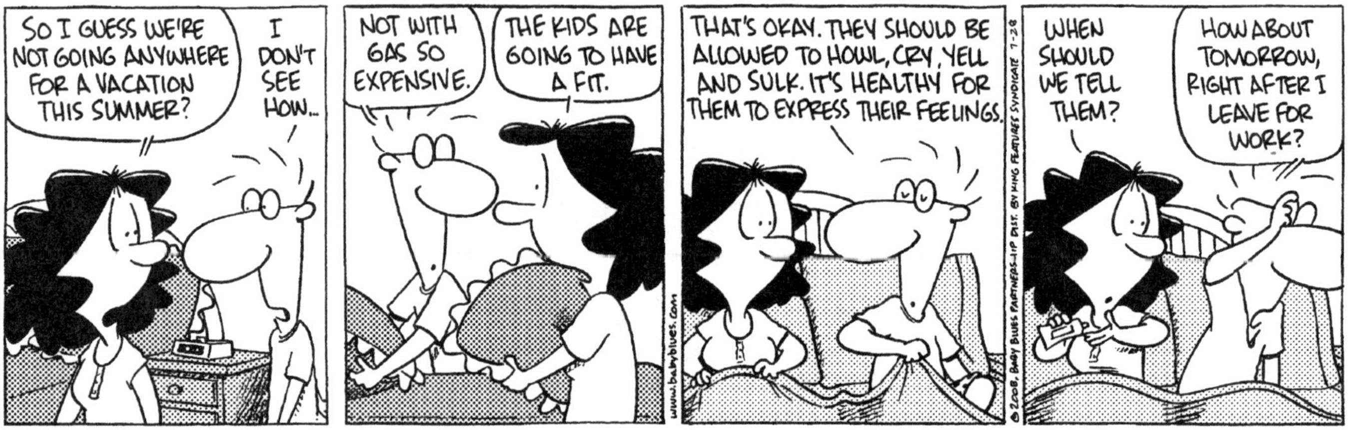
SO I GUESS WE'RE NOT GOING ANYWHERE FOR A VACATION THIS SUMMER?
I DON'T SEE HOW...
NOT WITH GAS SO EXPENSIVE.
THE KIDS ARE GOING TO HAVE A FIT.
THAT'S OKAY. THEY SHOULD BE ALLOWED TO HOWL, CRY, YELL AND SULK. IT'S HEALTHY FOR THEM TO EXPRESS THEIR FEELINGS.
WHEN SHOULD WE TELL THEM?
HOW ABOUT TOMORROW, RIGHT AFTER I LEAVE FOR WORK?
www.babyblues.com
© 2008, BABY BLUES PARTNERSHIP DIST. BY KING FEATURES SYNDICATE 7-28

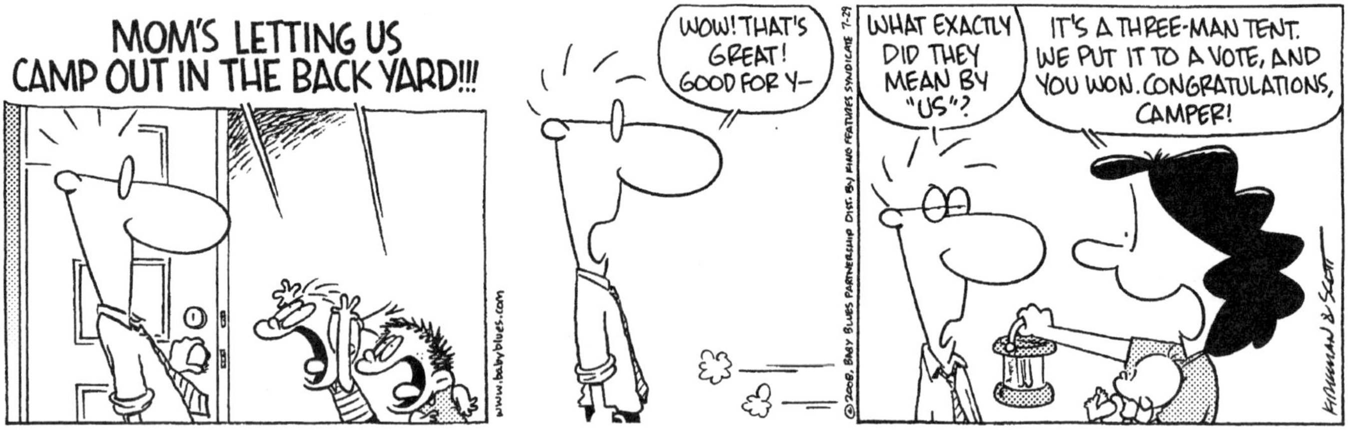
MOM'S LETTING US CAMP OUT IN THE BACK YARD!!!
WOW! THAT'S GREAT! GOOD FOR Y—
WHAT EXACTLY DID THEY MEAN BY "US"?
IT'S A THREE-MAN TENT. WE PUT IT TO A VOTE, AND YOU WON. CONGRATULATIONS, CAMPER!
www.babyblues.com
© 2008, BABY BLUES PARTNERSHIP DIST. BY KING FEATURES SYNDICATE 7-29
KIRKMAN & SCOTT

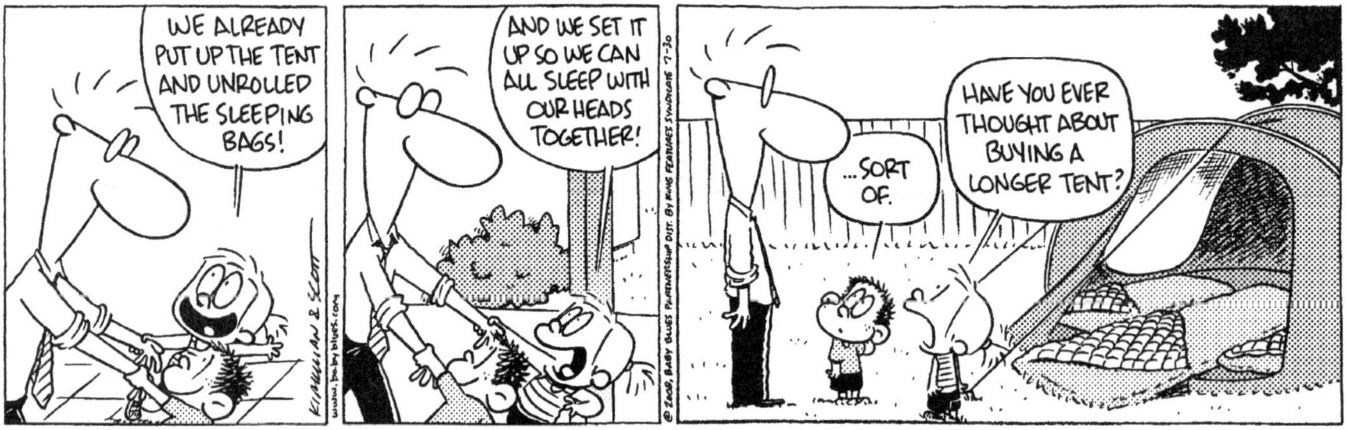
WE ALREADY PUT UP THE TENT AND UNROLLED THE SLEEPING BAGS!
AND WE SET IT UP SO WE CAN ALL SLEEP WITH OUR HEADS TOGETHER!
...SORT OF.
HAVE YOU EVER THOUGHT ABOUT BUYING A LONGER TENT?
KIRKMAN & SCOTT
www.babyblues.com
© 2008, BABY BLUES PARTNERSHIP DIST. BY KING FEATURES SYNDICATE 7-30

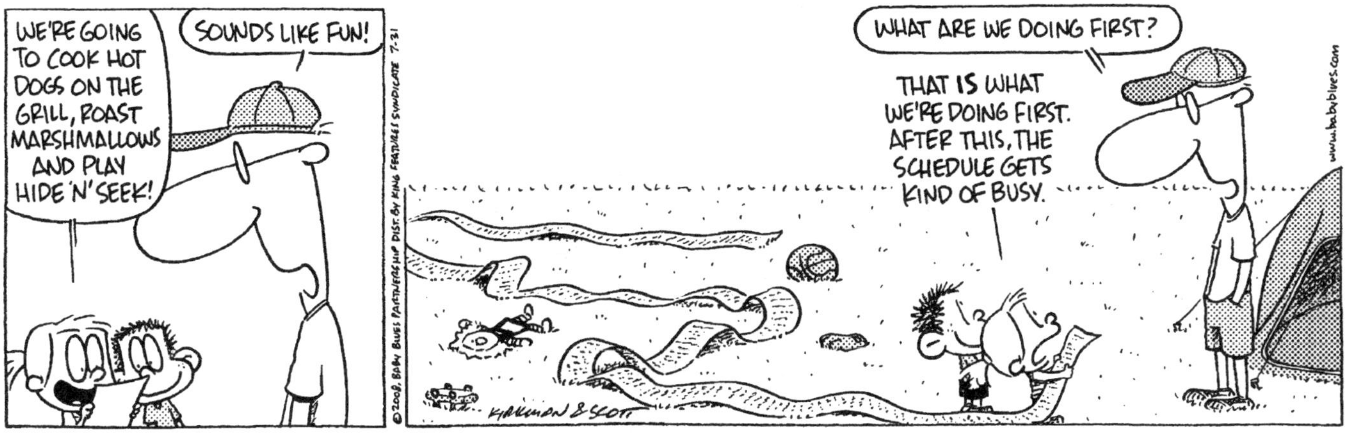
WE'RE GOING TO COOK HOT DOGS ON THE GRILL, ROAST MARSHMALLOWS AND PLAY HIDE 'N' SEEK!
SOUNDS LIKE FUN!
WHAT ARE WE DOING FIRST?
THAT IS WHAT WE'RE DOING FIRST. AFTER THIS, THE SCHEDULE GETS KIND OF BUSY.

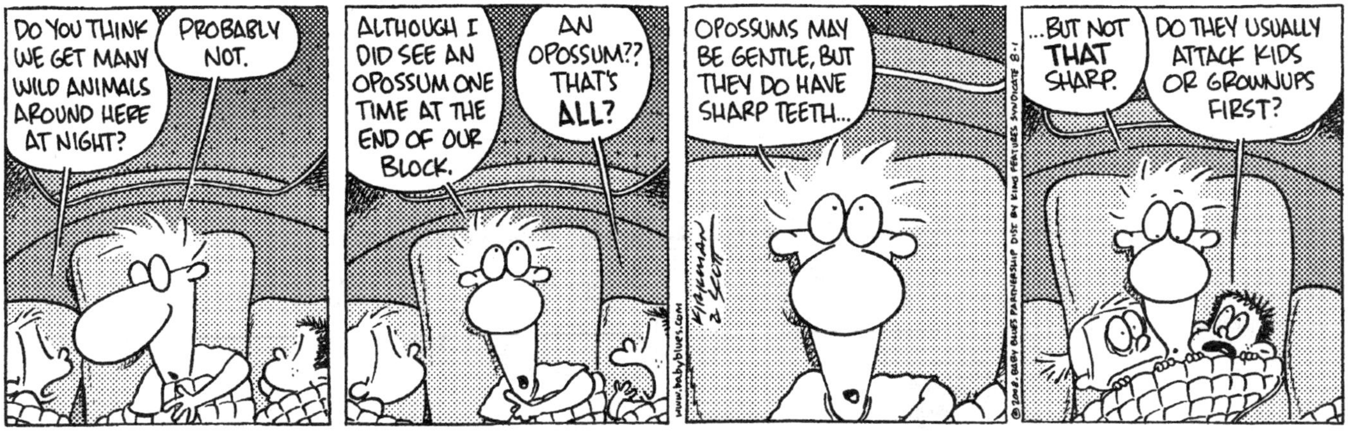
DO YOU THINK WE GET MANY WILD ANIMALS AROUND HERE AT NIGHT?
PROBABLY NOT.
ALTHOUGH I DID SEE AN OPOSSUM ONE TIME AT THE END OF OUR BLOCK.
AN OPOSSUM?? THAT'S ALL?
OPOSSUMS MAY BE GENTLE, BUT THEY DO HAVE SHARP TEETH...
...BUT NOT THAT SHARP.
DO THEY USUALLY ATTACK KIDS OR GROWNUPS FIRST?

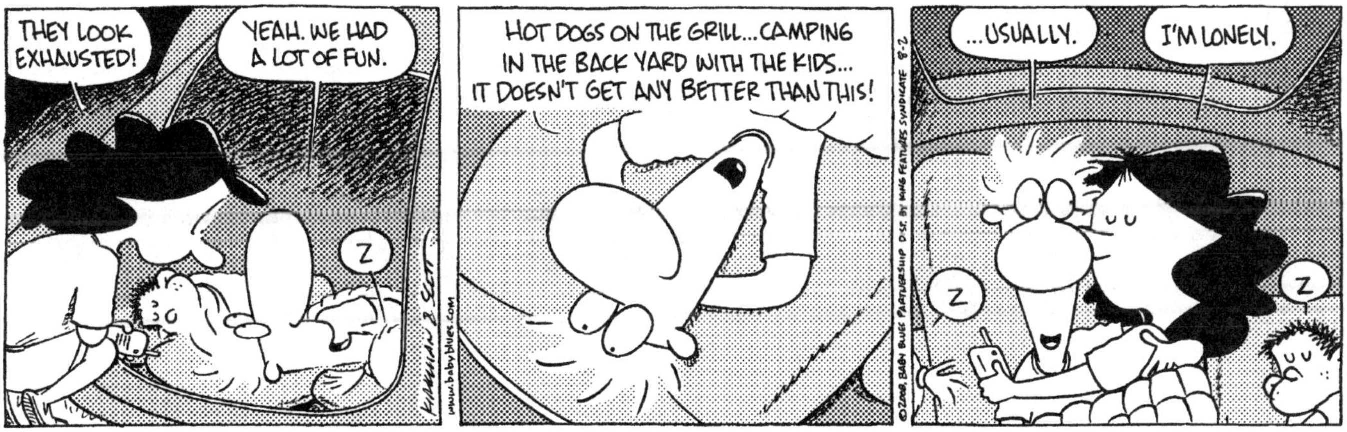
THEY LOOK EXHAUSTED!
YEAH. WE HAD A LOT OF FUN.
Z
HOT DOGS ON THE GRILL... CAMPING IN THE BACK YARD WITH THE KIDS... IT DOESN'T GET ANY BETTER THAN THIS!
...USUALLY.
I'M LONELY.
Z
Z

HOW to EAT DICED PEACHES

① Discover that you're out of diced peaches.

② Beg your mom to take you to the store to buy some.

③ Argue over which store to go to (if you talked her into it).

④ Argue over who gets to open the car door.

⑤ Argue over who gets to get in first.

⑥ Argue over who gets to open the car door when you get there.

⑦ Knock a bunch of stuff off the store shelves.

⑧ Buy the peaches.

⑨ Repeat steps 4, 5 & 6.

⑩ Make a huge discovery while your mom opens the peaches.

⑪ Change your mind about the peaches because you ate stale marshmallows instead.

⑫ Avoid your mom for a while.

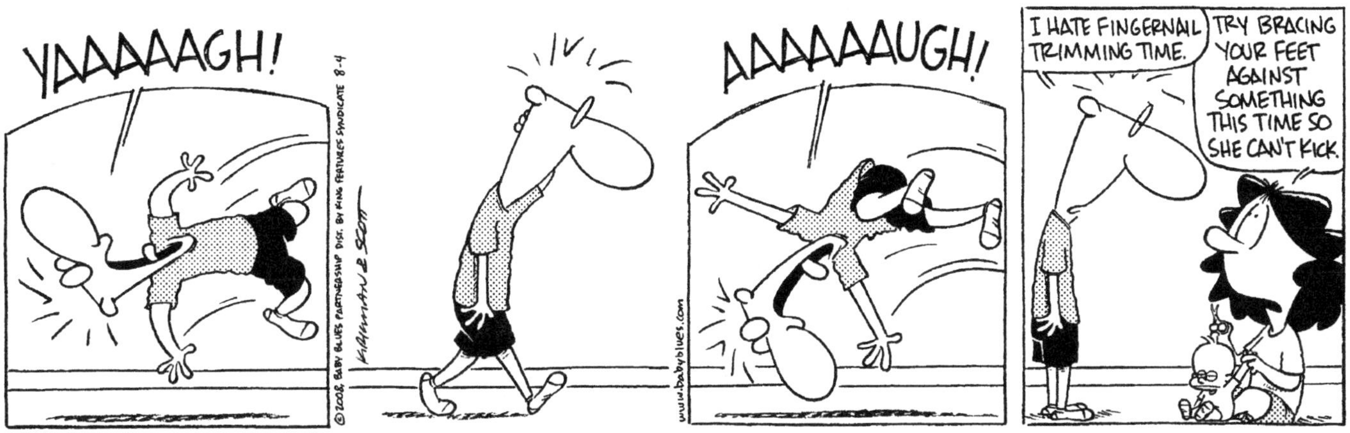
YAAAAAGH!
© 2008, Baby Blues Partnership Dist. by King Features Syndicate 8-4
KIRKMAN & SCOTT
AAAAAAUGH!
www.babyblues.com
I HATE FINGERNAIL TRIMMING TIME.
TRY BRACING YOUR FEET AGAINST SOMETHING THIS TIME SO SHE CAN'T KICK.

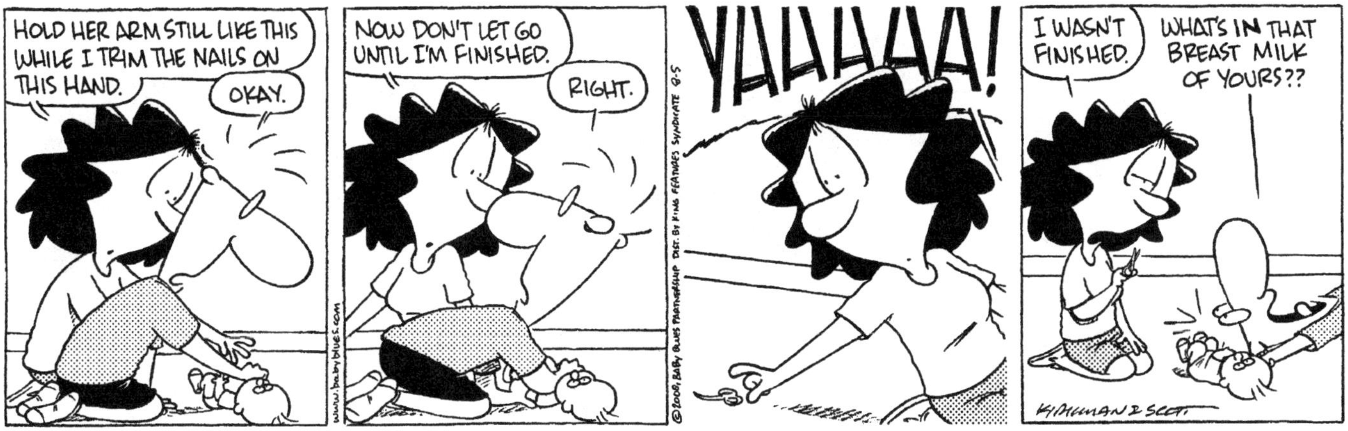
HOLD HER ARM STILL LIKE THIS WHILE I TRIM THE NAILS ON THIS HAND.
OKAY.
www.babyblues.com
NOW DON'T LET GO UNTIL I'M FINISHED.
RIGHT.
© 2008, Baby Blues Partnership Dist. by King Features Syndicate 8-5
YAAAAA!
I WASN'T FINISHED.
WHAT'S IN THAT BREAST MILK OF YOURS??
KIRKMAN & SCOTT

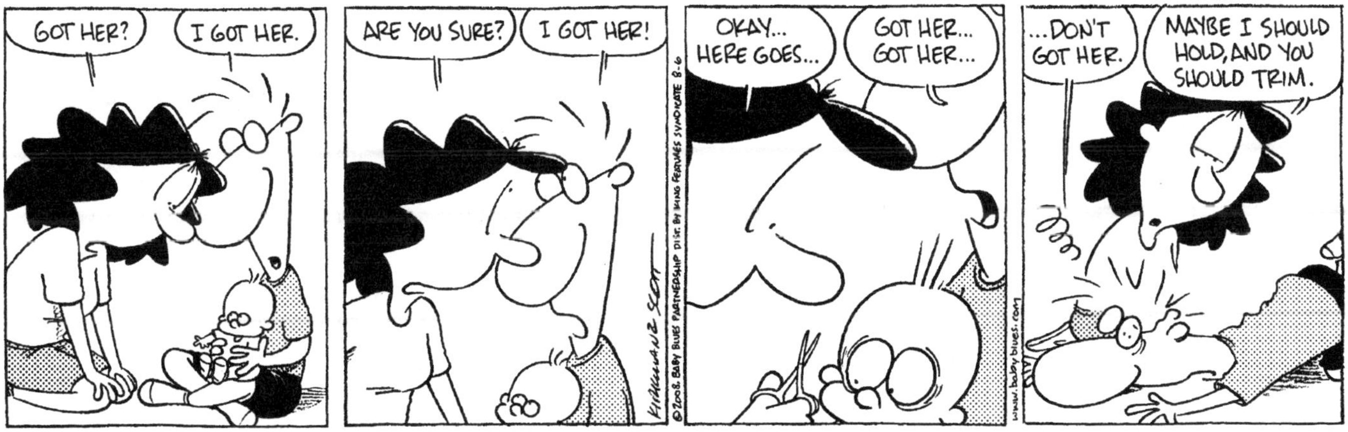
GOT HER?
I GOT HER.
ARE YOU SURE?
I GOT HER!
KIRKMAN & SCOTT
© 2008, Baby Blues Partnership Dist. by King Features Syndicate 8-6
OKAY... HERE GOES...
GOT HER... GOT HER...
...DON'T GOT HER.
MAYBE I SHOULD HOLD, AND YOU SHOULD TRIM.
www.babyblues.com

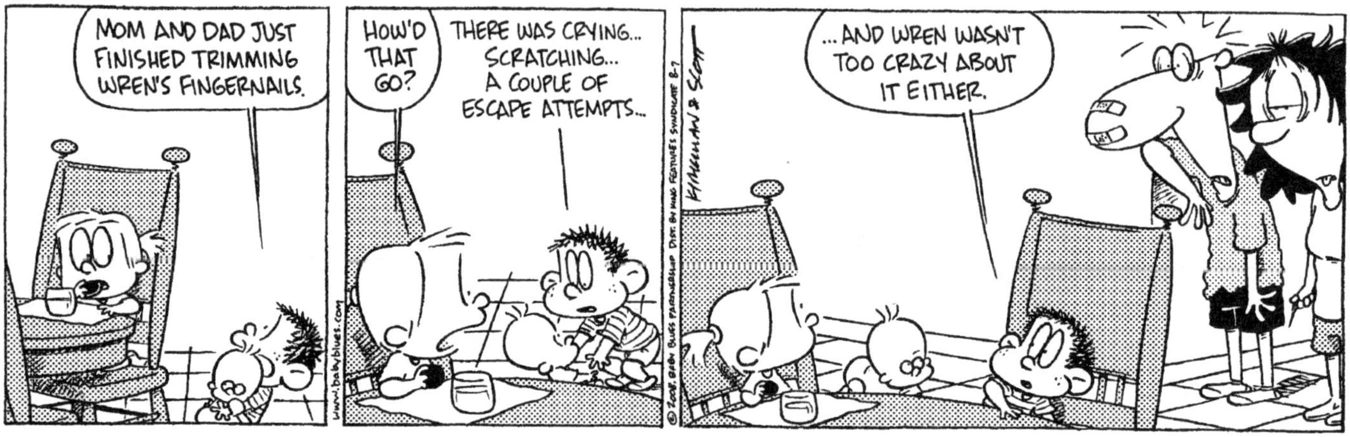
MOM AND DAD JUST FINISHED TRIMMING WREN'S FINGERNAILS.
HOW'D THAT GO?
THERE WAS CRYING... SCRATCHING... A COUPLE OF ESCAPE ATTEMPTS...
...AND WREN WASN'T TOO CRAZY ABOUT IT EITHER.
www.babyblues.com
©2008, Baby Blues Partnership Dist. by King Features Syndicate 8-7
KIRKMAN & SCOTT

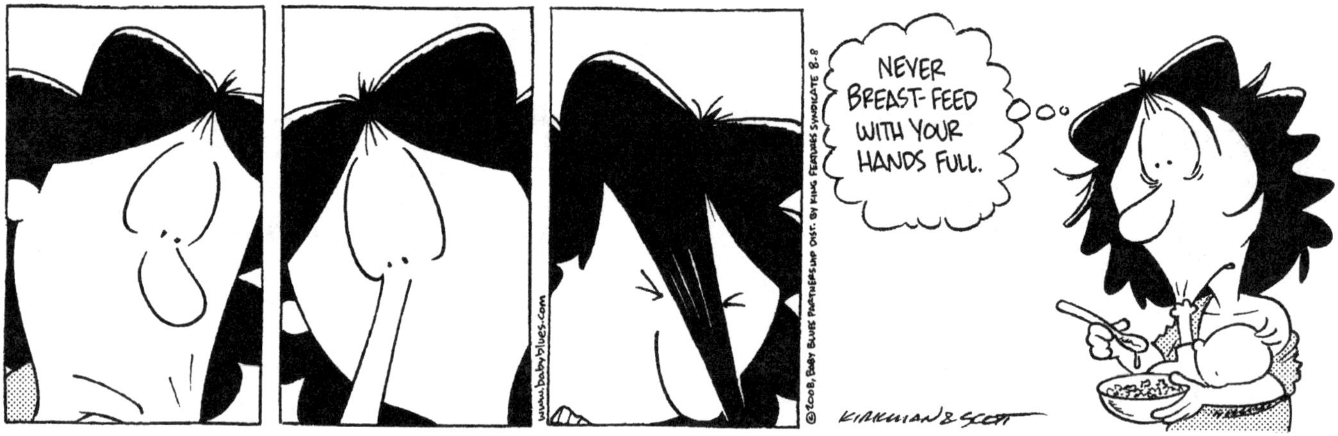
www.babyblues.com
©2008, Baby Blues Partnership Dist. by King Features Syndicate 8-8
NEVER BREAST-FEED WITH YOUR HANDS FULL.
KIRKMAN & SCOTT

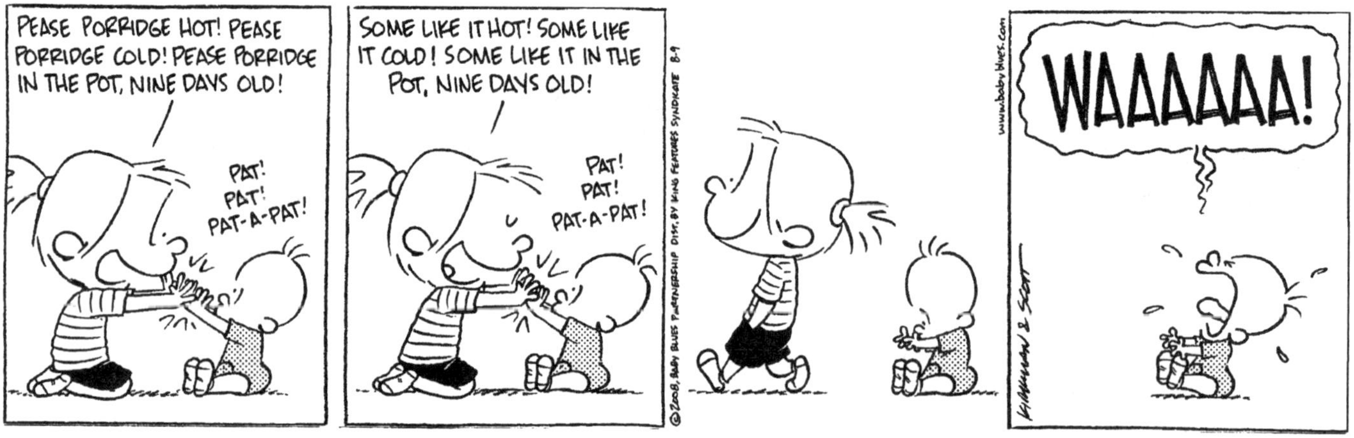
PEASE PORRIDGE HOT! PEASE PORRIDGE COLD! PEASE PORRIDGE IN THE POT, NINE DAYS OLD!
PAT! PAT! PAT-A-PAT!
SOME LIKE IT HOT! SOME LIKE IT COLD! SOME LIKE IT IN THE POT, NINE DAYS OLD!
PAT! PAT! PAT-A-PAT!
©2008, Baby Blues Partnership Dist. by King Features Syndicate 8-9
www.babyblues.com
WAAAAAA!
KIRKMAN & SCOTT

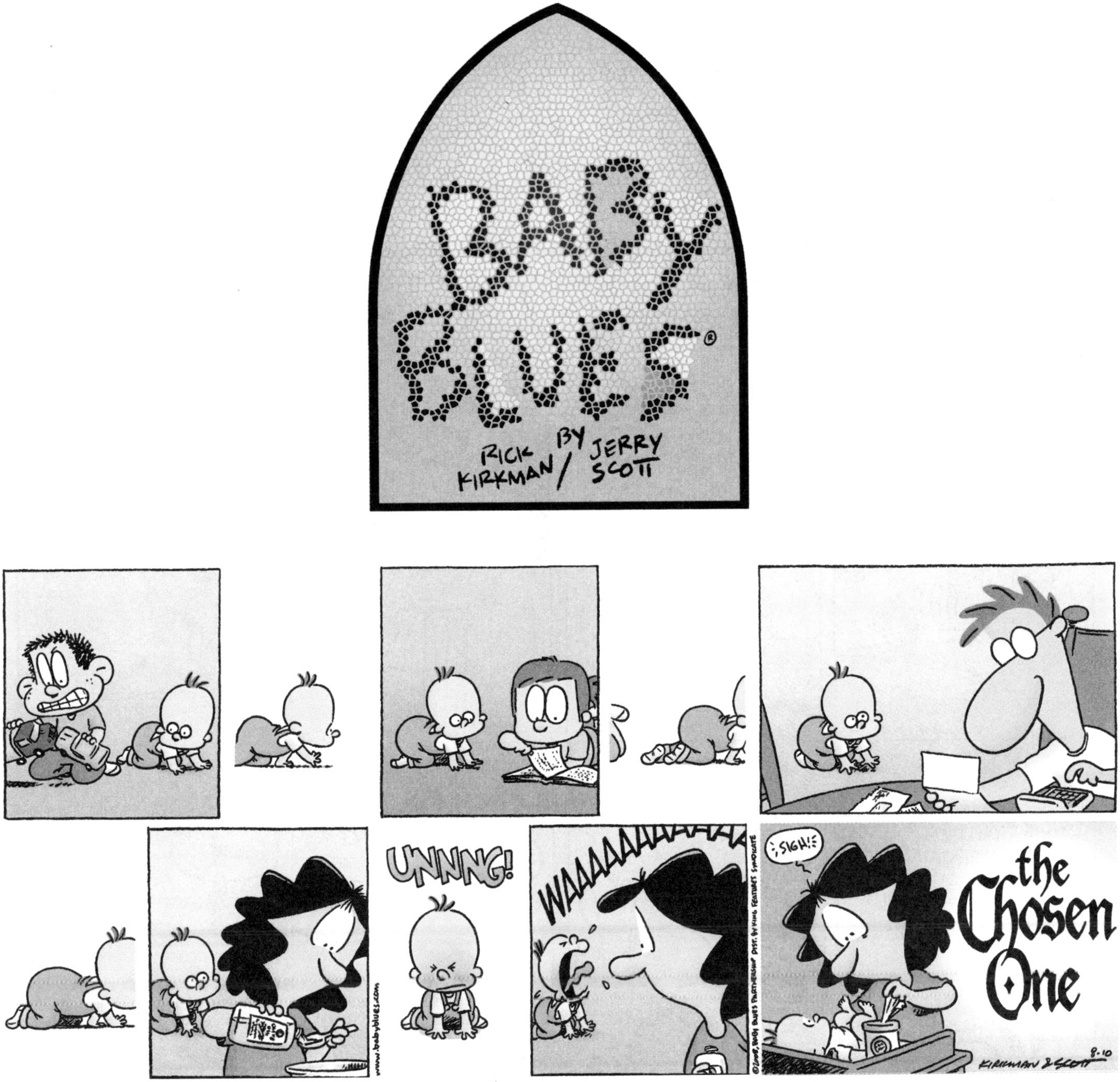
BABY BLUES®
BY RICK KIRKMAN / JERRY SCOTT
www.babyblues.com
UNNNG!
WAAAAAAAAAAA
©2008, BABY BLUES PARTNERSHIP DIST. BY KING FEATURES SYNDICATE
SIGH!
the Chosen One
8-10
KIRKMAN & SCOTT

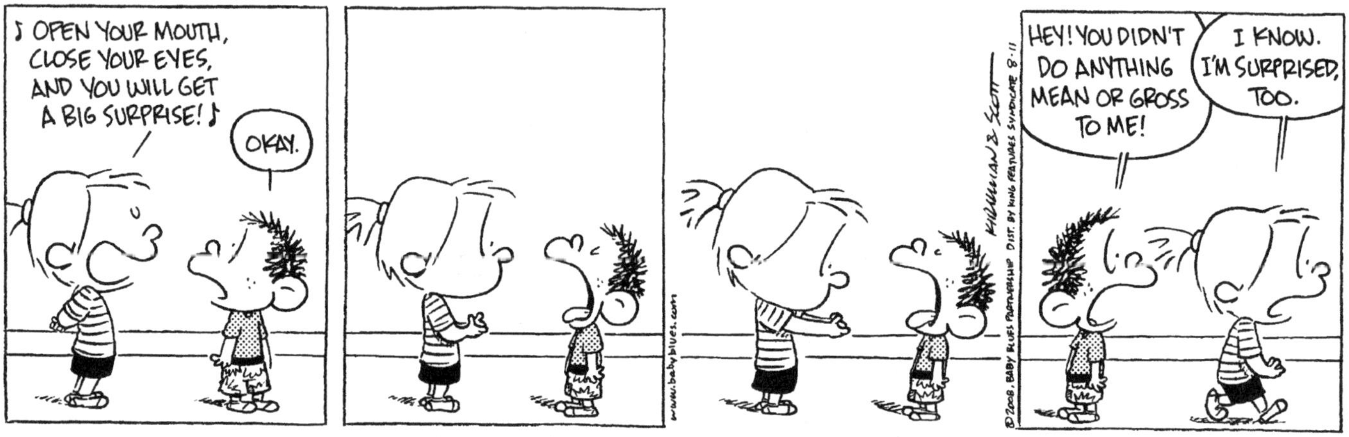
♪ OPEN YOUR MOUTH, CLOSE YOUR EYES, AND YOU WILL GET A BIG SURPRISE! ♪
OKAY.
www.babyblues.com
KIRKMAN & SCOTT
© 2008, BABY BLUES PARTNERSHIP DIST. BY KING FEATURES SYNDICATE 8-11
HEY! YOU DIDN'T DO ANYTHING MEAN OR GROSS TO ME!
I KNOW. I'M SURPRISED, TOO.

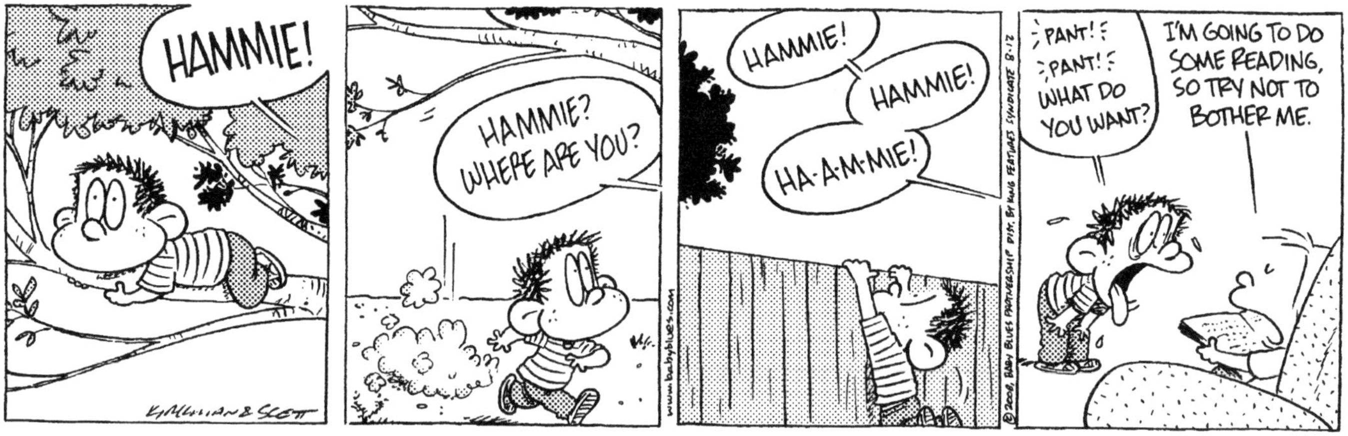
HAMMIE!
KIRKMAN & SCOTT
HAMMIE? WHERE ARE YOU?
www.babyblues.com
HAMMIE!
HAMMIE!
HA-A-M-MIE!
© 2008, BABY BLUES PARTNERSHIP DIST. BY KING FEATURES SYNDICATE 8-12
PANT! PANT! WHAT DO YOU WANT?
I'M GOING TO DO SOME READING, SO TRY NOT TO BOTHER ME.

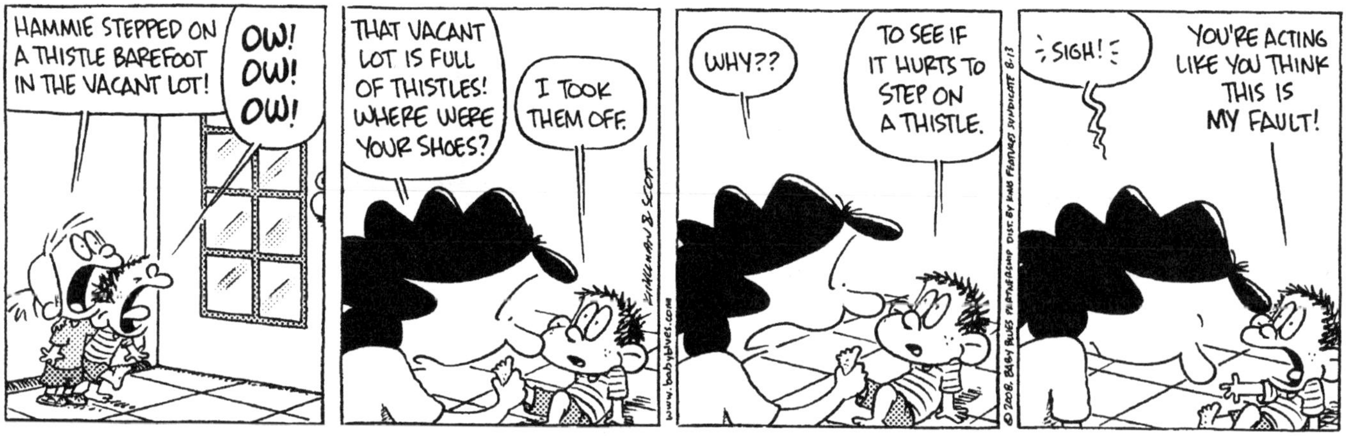
HAMMIE STEPPED ON A THISTLE BAREFOOT IN THE VACANT LOT!
OW! OW! OW!
THAT VACANT LOT IS FULL OF THISTLES! WHERE WERE YOUR SHOES?
I TOOK THEM OFF.
KIRKMAN & SCOTT
www.babyblues.com
WHY??
TO SEE IF IT HURTS TO STEP ON A THISTLE.
© 2008, BABY BLUES PARTNERSHIP DIST. BY KING FEATURES SYNDICATE 8-13
SIGH!
YOU'RE ACTING LIKE YOU THINK THIS IS MY FAULT!

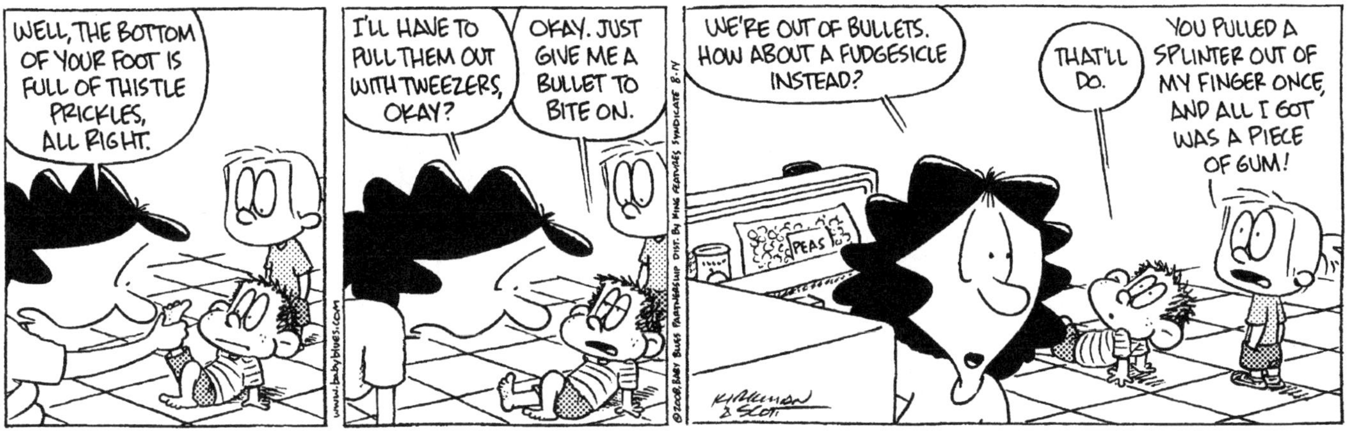
WELL, THE BOTTOM OF YOUR FOOT IS FULL OF THISTLE PRICKLES, ALL RIGHT.
www.babyblues.com
I'LL HAVE TO PULL THEM OUT WITH TWEEZERS, OKAY?
OKAY. JUST GIVE ME A BULLET TO BITE ON.
©2008, BABY BLUES PARTNERSHIP DIST. BY KING FEATURES SYNDICATE 8-14
WE'RE OUT OF BULLETS. HOW ABOUT A FUDGESICLE INSTEAD?
PEAS
THAT'LL DO.
YOU PULLED A SPLINTER OUT OF MY FINGER ONCE, AND ALL I GOT WAS A PIECE OF GUM!
KIRKMAN & SCOTT

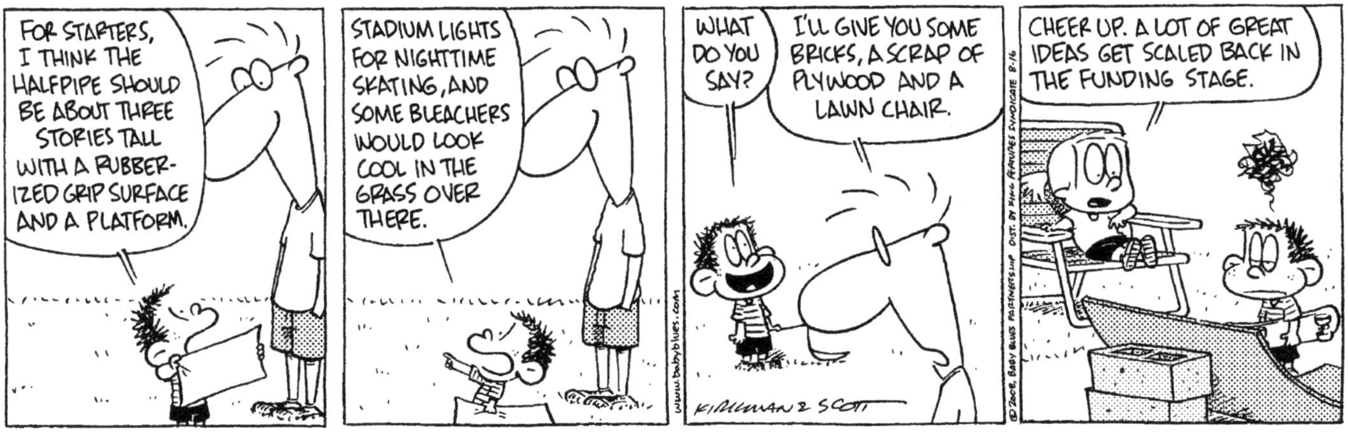
FOR STARTERS, I THINK THE HALFPIPE SHOULD BE ABOUT THREE STORIES TALL WITH A RUBBERIZED GRIP SURFACE AND A PLATFORM.
STADIUM LIGHTS FOR NIGHTTIME SKATING, AND SOME BLEACHERS WOULD LOOK COOL IN THE GRASS OVER THERE.
www.babyblues.com
WHAT DO YOU SAY?
I'LL GIVE YOU SOME BRICKS, A SCRAP OF PLYWOOD AND A LAWN CHAIR.
KIRKMAN & SCOTT
©2008, BABY BLUES PARTNERSHIP DIST. BY KING FEATURES SYNDICATE 8-16
CHEER UP. A LOT OF GREAT IDEAS GET SCALED BACK IN THE FUNDING STAGE.

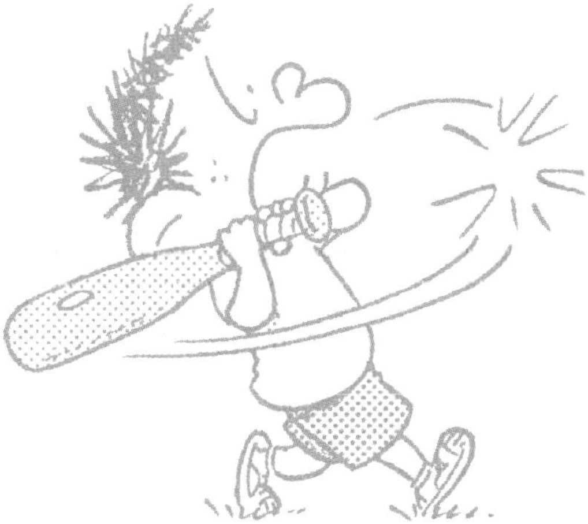

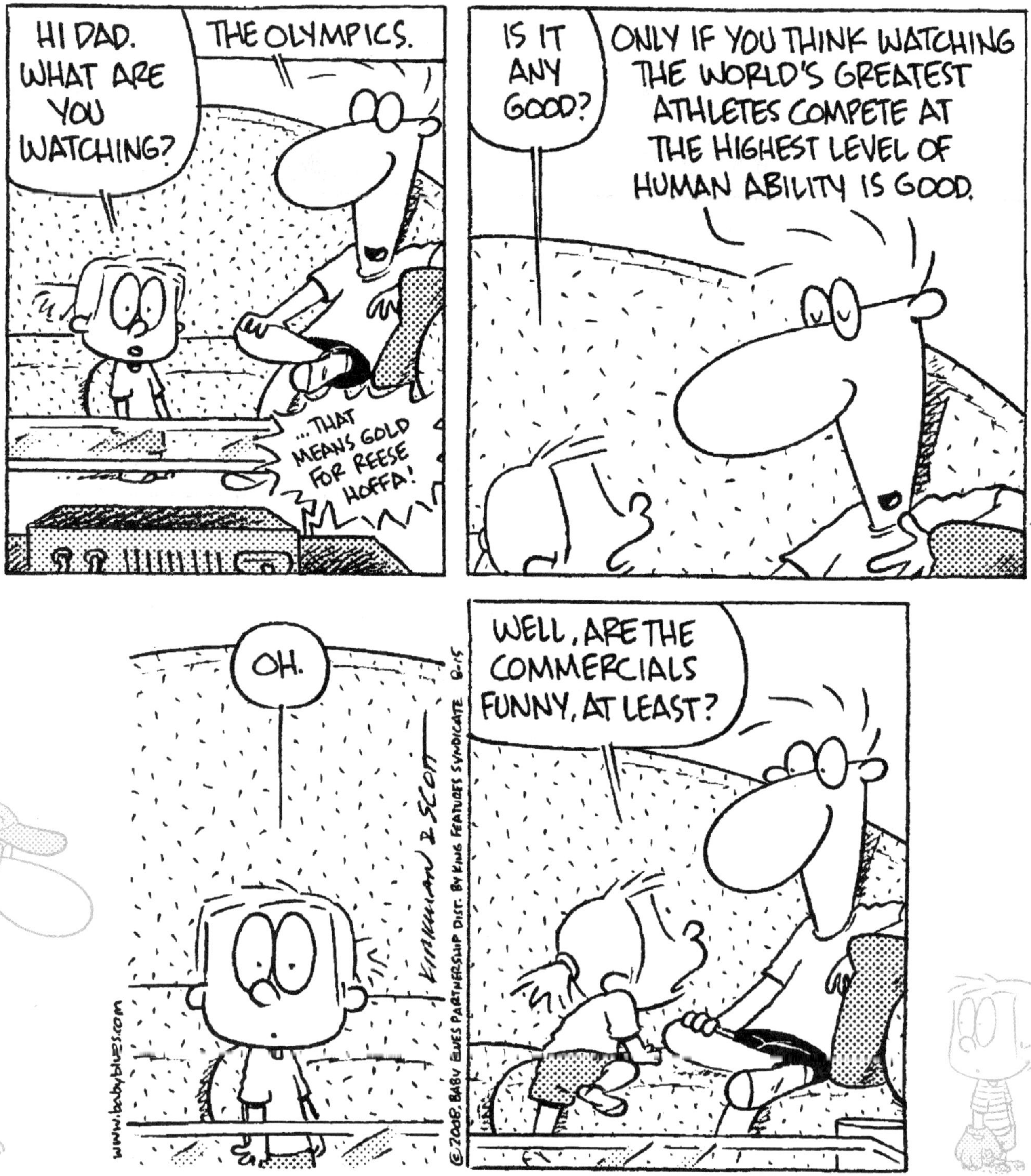
HI DAD. WHAT ARE YOU WATCHING?
THE OLYMPICS.
...THAT MEANS GOLD FOR REESE HOFFA!
IS IT ANY GOOD?
ONLY IF YOU THINK WATCHING THE WORLD'S GREATEST ATHLETES COMPETE AT THE HIGHEST LEVEL OF HUMAN ABILITY IS GOOD.
OH.
WELL, ARE THE COMMERCIALS FUNNY, AT LEAST?
KIRKMAN & SCOTT
©2008, BABY BLUES PARTNERSHIP DIST. BY KING FEATURES SYNDICATE 8-15
www.babyblues.com

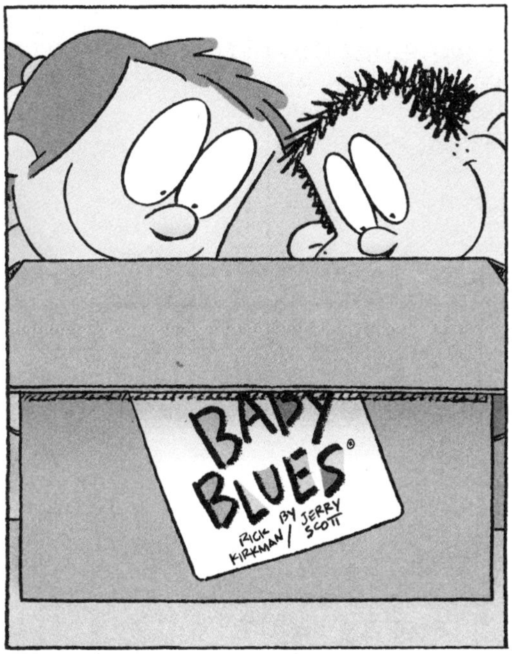
BABY BLUES®
RICK KIRKMAN / BY JERRY SCOTT

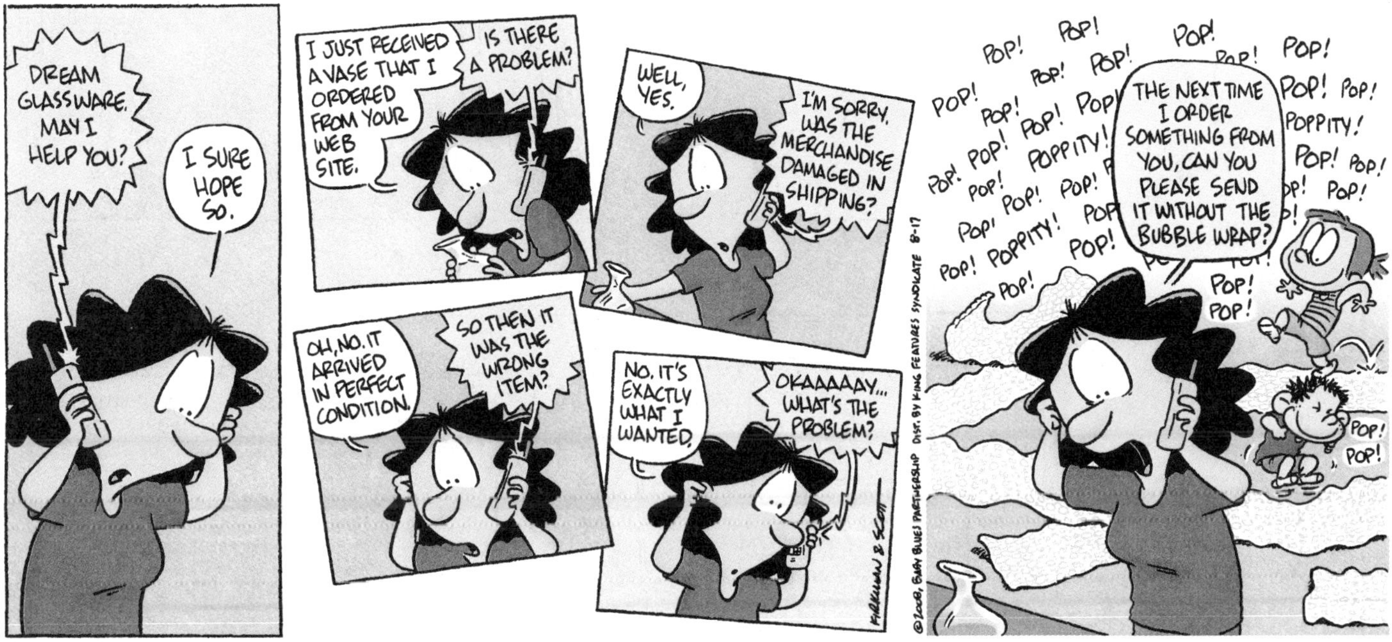
DREAM GLASSWARE. MAY I HELP YOU?
I SURE HOPE SO.
I JUST RECEIVED A VASE THAT I ORDERED FROM YOUR WEB SITE.
IS THERE A PROBLEM?
WELL, YES.
I'M SORRY. WAS THE MERCHANDISE DAMAGED IN SHIPPING?
OH, NO. IT ARRIVED IN PERFECT CONDITION.
SO THEN IT WAS THE WRONG ITEM?
NO, IT'S EXACTLY WHAT I WANTED.
OKAAAAAY... WHAT'S THE PROBLEM?
KIRKMAN & SCOTT
©2008, BABY BLUES PARTNERSHIP DIST. BY KING FEATURES SYNDICATE 8-17
POP! POP! POP! POP! POP! POPPITY!
THE NEXT TIME I ORDER SOMETHING FROM YOU, CAN YOU PLEASE SEND IT WITHOUT THE BUBBLE WRAP?
POP! POP!

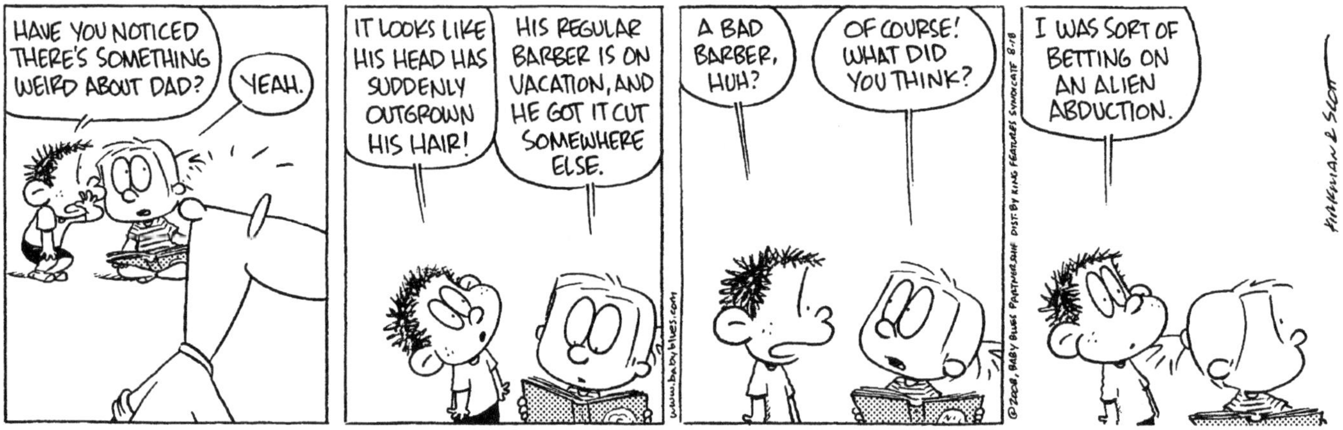
HAVE YOU NOTICED THERE'S SOMETHING WEIRD ABOUT DAD?
YEAH.
IT LOOKS LIKE HIS HEAD HAS SUDDENLY OUTGROWN HIS HAIR!
HIS REGULAR BARBER IS ON VACATION, AND HE GOT IT CUT SOMEWHERE ELSE.
www.babyblues.com
A BAD BARBER, HUH?
OF COURSE! WHAT DID YOU THINK?
©2008, BABY BLUES PARTNERSHIP DIST. BY KING FEATURES SYNDICATE 8-18
I WAS SORT OF BETTING ON AN ALIEN ABDUCTION.
KIRKMAN & SCOTT

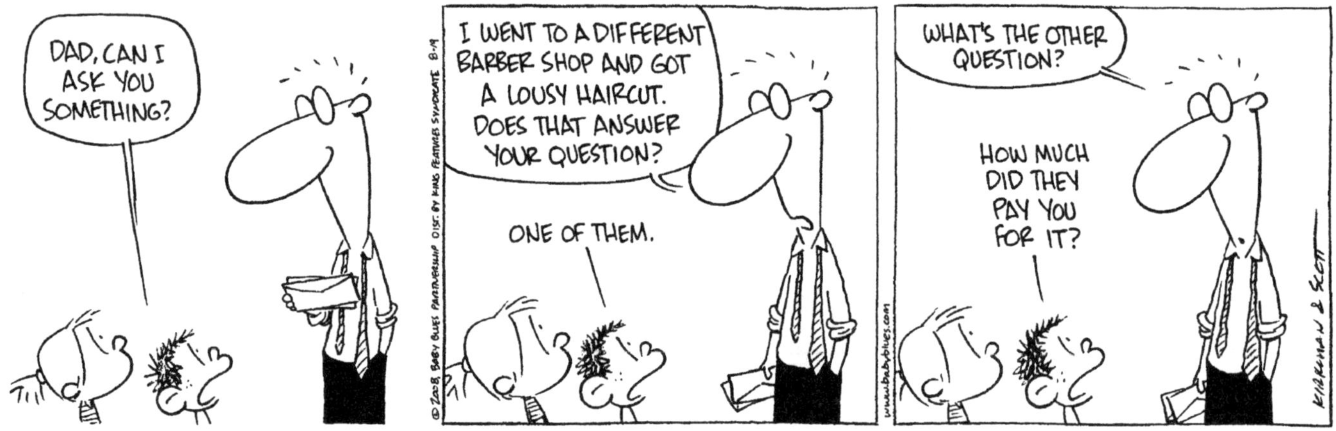
DAD, CAN I ASK YOU SOMETHING?
©2008, BABY BLUES PARTNERSHIP DIST. BY KING FEATURES SYNDICATE 8-19
I WENT TO A DIFFERENT BARBER SHOP AND GOT A LOUSY HAIRCUT. DOES THAT ANSWER YOUR QUESTION?
ONE OF THEM.
www.babyblues.com
WHAT'S THE OTHER QUESTION?
HOW MUCH DID THEY PAY YOU FOR IT?
KIRKMAN & SCOTT

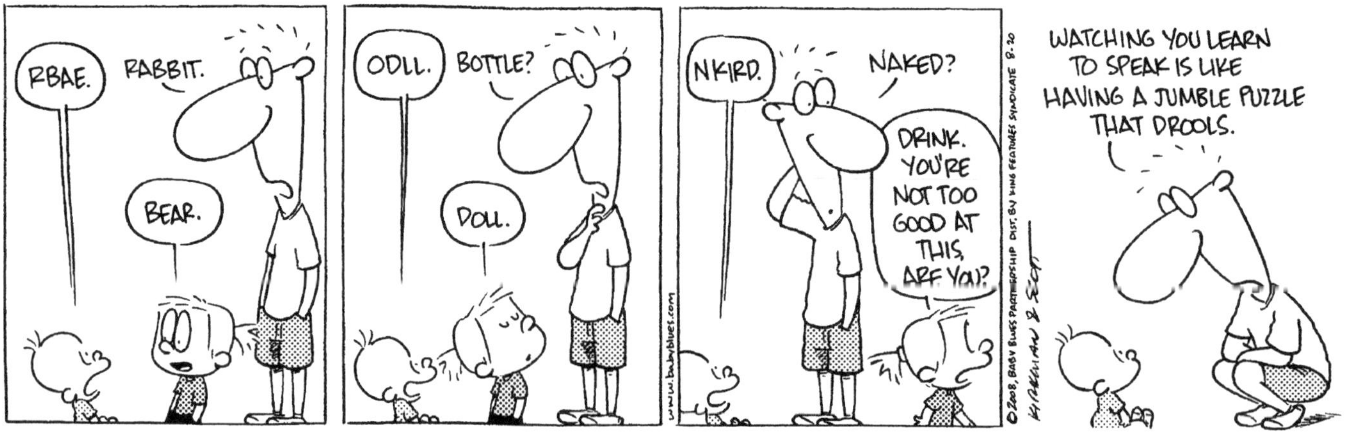
RBAE.
RABBIT.
BEAR.
ODLL.
BOTTLE?
DOLL.
www.babyblues.com
NKIRD.
NAKED?
DRINK. YOU'RE NOT TOO GOOD AT THIS, ARE YOU?
©2008, BABY BLUES PARTNERSHIP DIST. BY KING FEATURES SYNDICATE 8-20
KIRKMAN & SCOTT
WATCHING YOU LEARN TO SPEAK IS LIKE HAVING A JUMBLE PUZZLE THAT DROOLS.

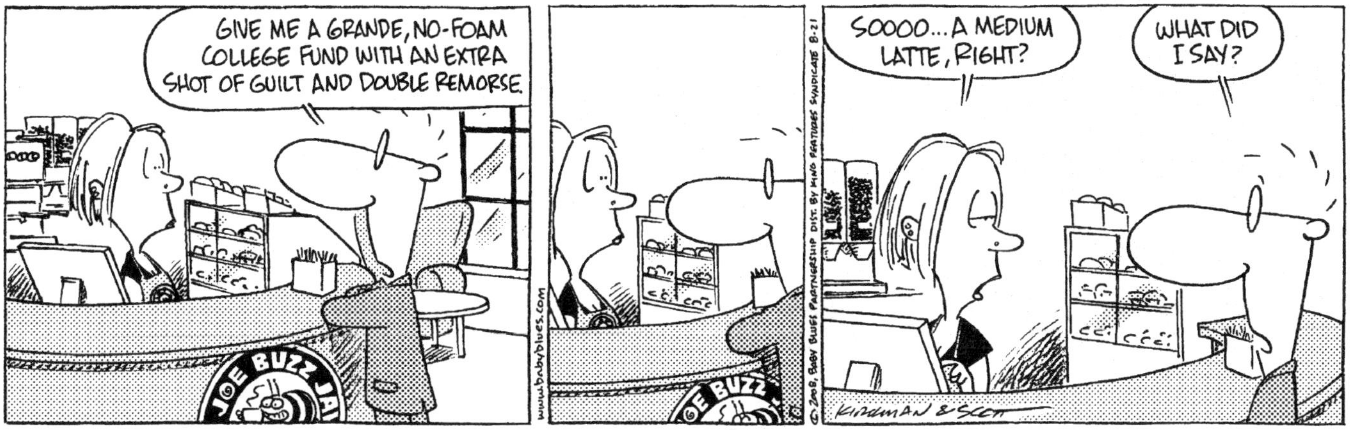
GIVE ME A GRANDE, NO-FOAM COLLEGE FUND WITH AN EXTRA SHOT OF GUILT AND DOUBLE REMORSE.
JOE BUZZ
www.babyblues.com
© 2008, BABY BLUES PARTNERSHIP DIST. BY KING FEATURES SYNDICATE 8-21
SOOOO... A MEDIUM LATTE, RIGHT?
WHAT DID I SAY?
KIRKMAN & SCOTT

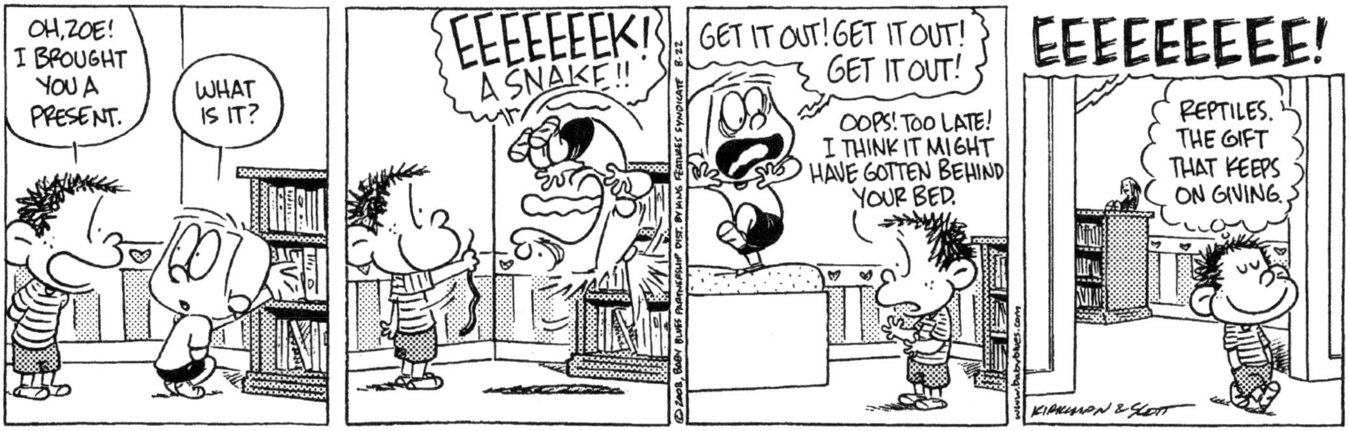
OH, ZOE! I BROUGHT YOU A PRESENT.
WHAT IS IT?
EEEEEEEK! A SNAKE!!
© 2008, BABY BLUES PARTNERSHIP DIST. BY KING FEATURES SYNDICATE 8-22
GET IT OUT! GET IT OUT! GET IT OUT!
OOPS! TOO LATE! I THINK IT MIGHT HAVE GOTTEN BEHIND YOUR BED.
www.babyblues.com
EEEEEEEEE!
REPTILES. THE GIFT THAT KEEPS ON GIVING.
KIRKMAN & SCOTT

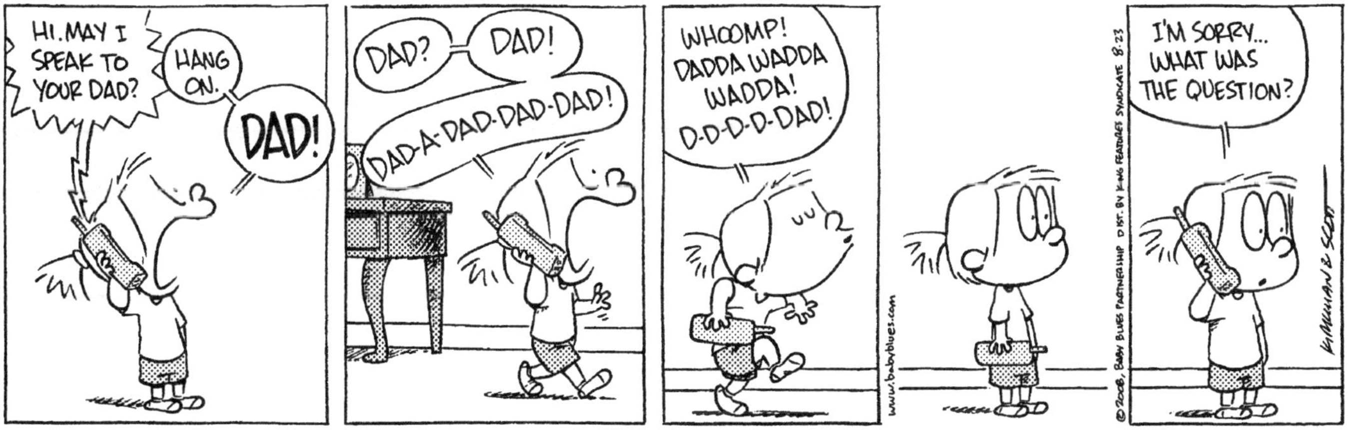
HI. MAY I SPEAK TO YOUR DAD?
HANG ON.
DAD!
DAD?
DAD!
DAD-A-DAD-DAD-DAD!
WHOOMP! DADDA WADDA WADDA! D-D-D-D-DAD!
www.babyblues.com
© 2008, BABY BLUES PARTNERSHIP DIST. BY KING FEATURES SYNDICATE 8-23
I'M SORRY... WHAT WAS THE QUESTION?
KIRKMAN & SCOTT

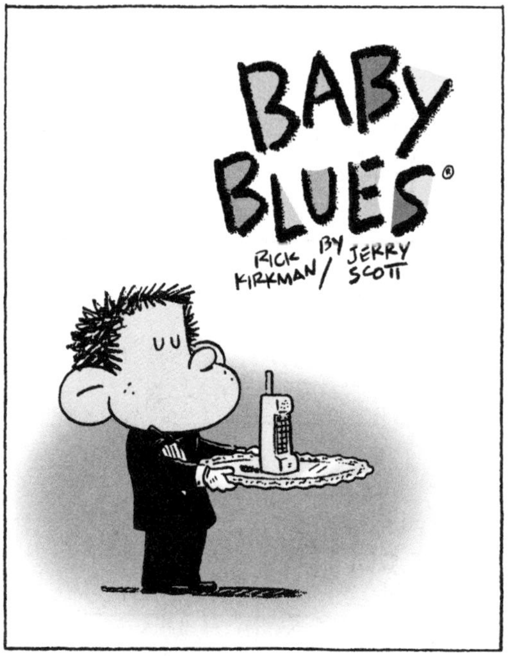
BABY BLUES®
RICK KIRKMAN / BY JERRY SCOTT

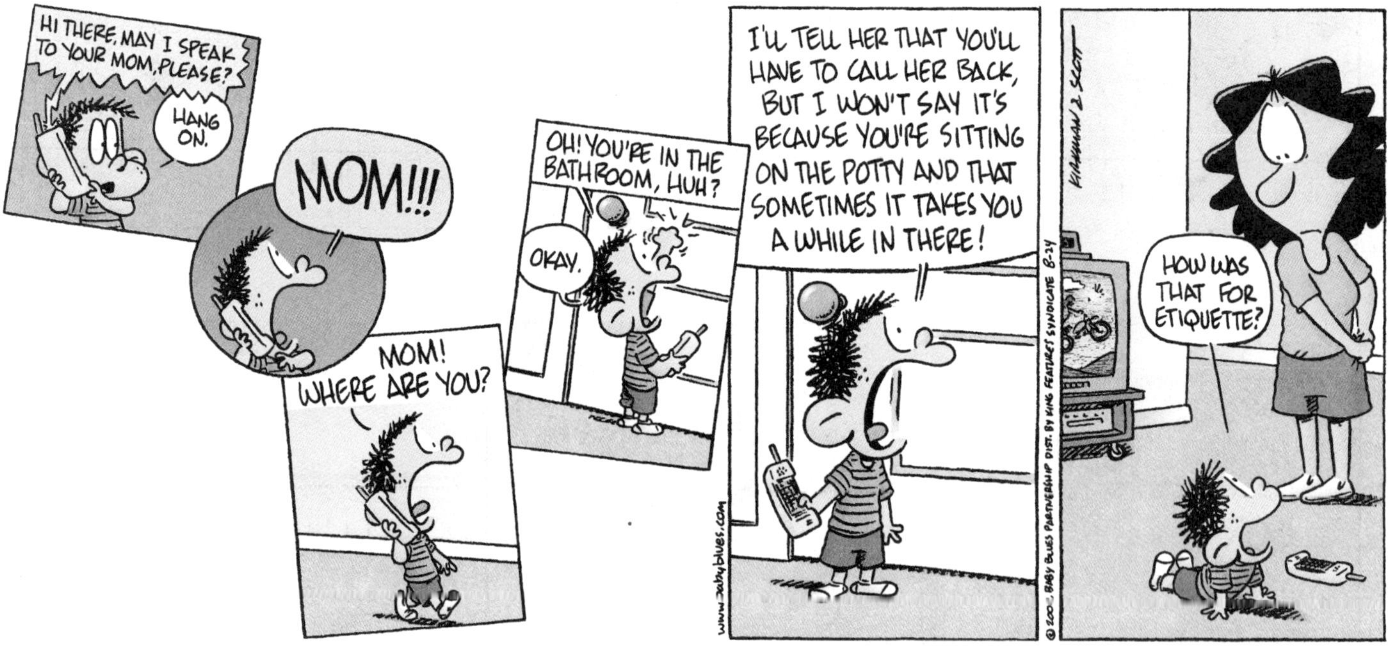
HI THERE. MAY I SPEAK TO YOUR MOM, PLEASE?
HANG ON.
MOM!!!
MOM! WHERE ARE YOU?
OH! YOU'RE IN THE BATHROOM, HUH?
OKAY.
I'LL TELL HER THAT YOU'LL HAVE TO CALL HER BACK, BUT I WON'T SAY IT'S BECAUSE YOU'RE SITTING ON THE POTTY AND THAT SOMETIMES IT TAKES YOU A WHILE IN THERE!
HOW WAS THAT FOR ETIQUETTE?
www.babyblues.com
BABY BLUES PARTNERSHIP DIST. BY KING FEATURES SYNDICATE 8-24
KIRKMAN & SCOTT

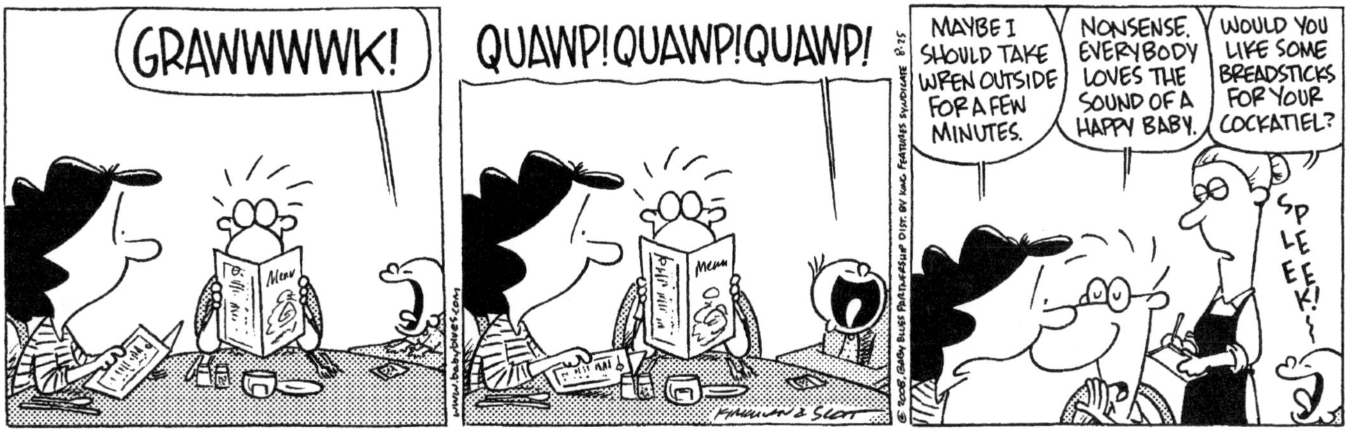
GRAWWWWK!
QUAWP! QUAWP! QUAWP!
MAYBE I SHOULD TAKE WREN OUTSIDE FOR A FEW MINUTES.
NONSENSE. EVERYBODY LOVES THE SOUND OF A HAPPY BABY.
WOULD YOU LIKE SOME BREADSTICKS FOR YOUR COCKATIEL?
SPLEEEK!
www.babyblues.com
KIRKMAN & SCOTT
© 2008, BABY BLUES PARTNERSHIP DIST. BY KING FEATURES SYNDICATE 8-25

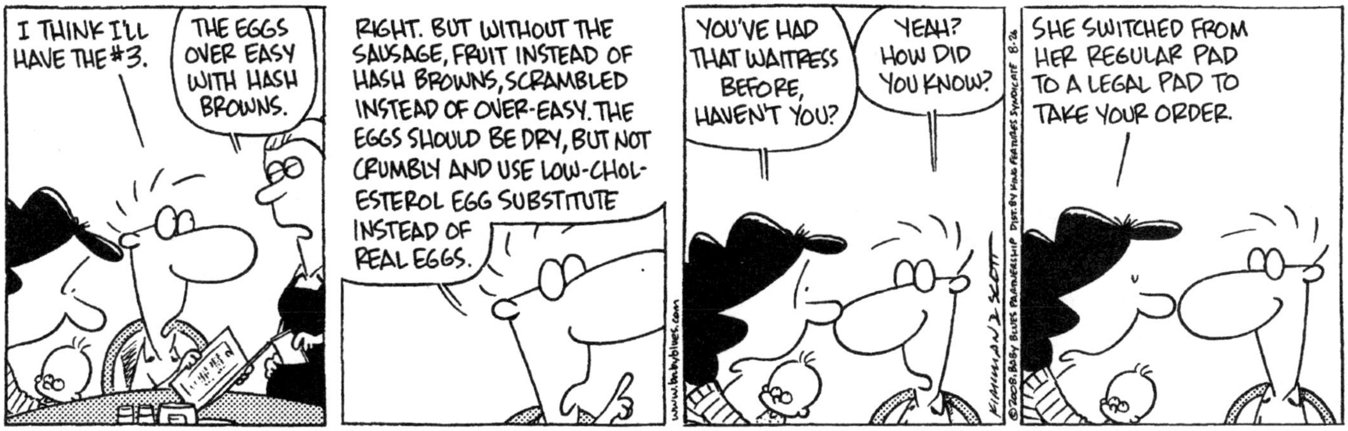
I THINK I'LL HAVE THE #3.
THE EGGS OVER EASY WITH HASH BROWNS.
RIGHT. BUT WITHOUT THE SAUSAGE, FRUIT INSTEAD OF HASH BROWNS, SCRAMBLED INSTEAD OF OVER-EASY. THE EGGS SHOULD BE DRY, BUT NOT CRUMBLY AND USE LOW-CHOLESTEROL EGG SUBSTITUTE INSTEAD OF REAL EGGS.
YOU'VE HAD THAT WAITRESS BEFORE, HAVEN'T YOU?
YEAH? HOW DID YOU KNOW?
SHE SWITCHED FROM HER REGULAR PAD TO A LEGAL PAD TO TAKE YOUR ORDER.
www.babyblues.com
KIRKMAN & SCOTT
© 2008, BABY BLUES PARTNERSHIP DIST. BY KING FEATURES SYNDICATE 8-26

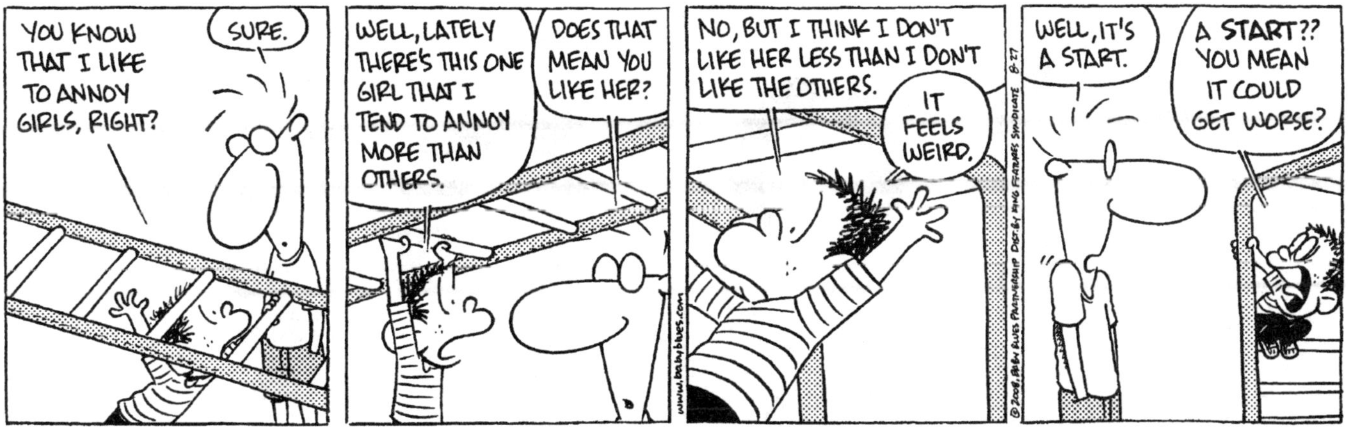
YOU KNOW THAT I LIKE TO ANNOY GIRLS, RIGHT?
SURE.
WELL, LATELY THERE'S THIS ONE GIRL THAT I TEND TO ANNOY MORE THAN OTHERS.
DOES THAT MEAN YOU LIKE HER?
NO, BUT I THINK I DON'T LIKE HER LESS THAN I DON'T LIKE THE OTHERS.
IT FEELS WEIRD.
WELL, IT'S A START.
A START?? YOU MEAN IT COULD GET WORSE?
www.babyblues.com
© 2008, BABY BLUES PARTNERSHIP DIST. BY KING FEATURES SYNDICATE 8-27

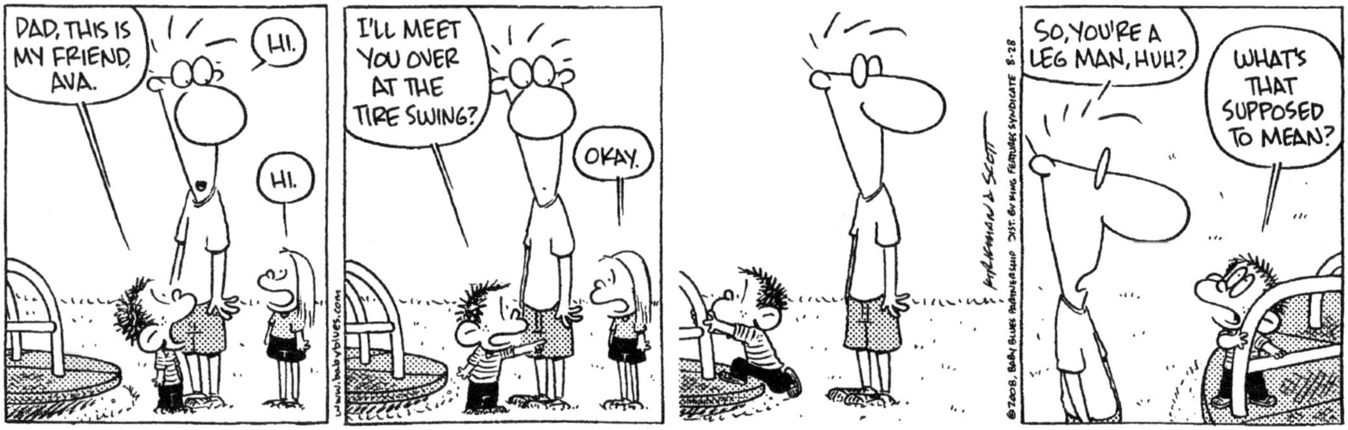
DAD, THIS IS MY FRIEND AVA.
HI.
HI.
I'LL MEET YOU OVER AT THE TIRE SWING?
OKAY.
SO, YOU'RE A LEG MAN, HUH?
WHAT'S THAT SUPPOSED TO MEAN?

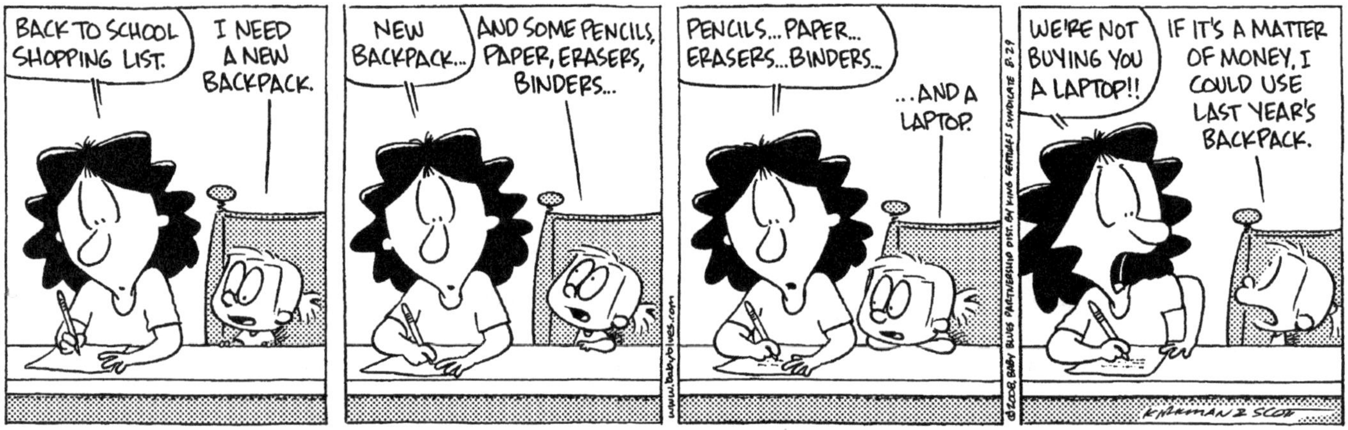
BACK TO SCHOOL SHOPPING LIST.
I NEED A NEW BACKPACK.
NEW BACKPACK...
AND SOME PENCILS, PAPER, ERASERS, BINDERS...
PENCILS... PAPER... ERASERS... BINDERS...
...AND A LAPTOP.
WE'RE NOT BUYING YOU A LAPTOP!!
IF IT'S A MATTER OF MONEY, I COULD USE LAST YEAR'S BACKPACK.

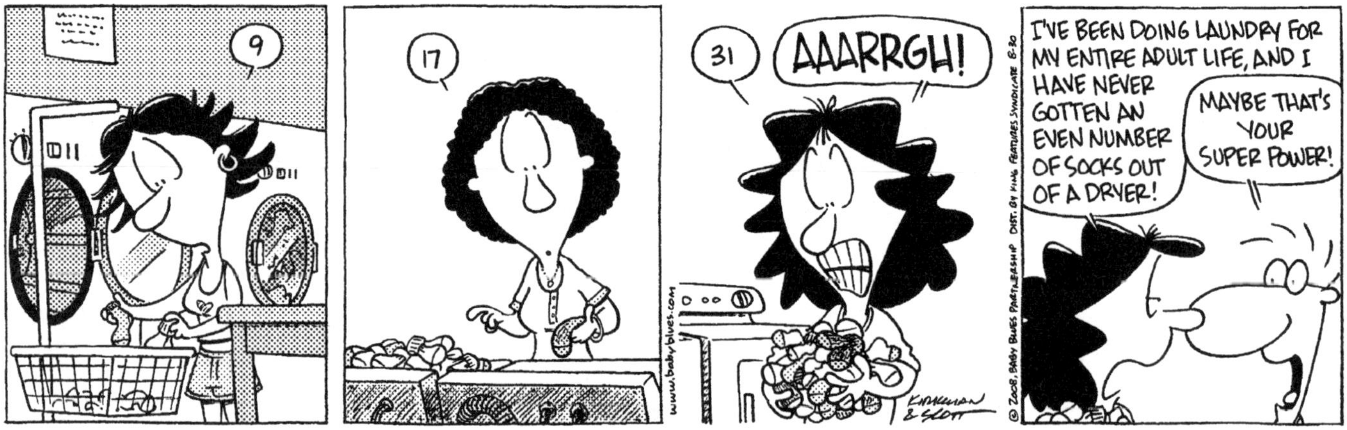
9
17
31
AAARRGH!
I'VE BEEN DOING LAUNDRY FOR MY ENTIRE ADULT LIFE, AND I HAVE NEVER GOTTEN AN EVEN NUMBER OF SOCKS OUT OF A DRYER!
MAYBE THAT'S YOUR SUPER POWER!

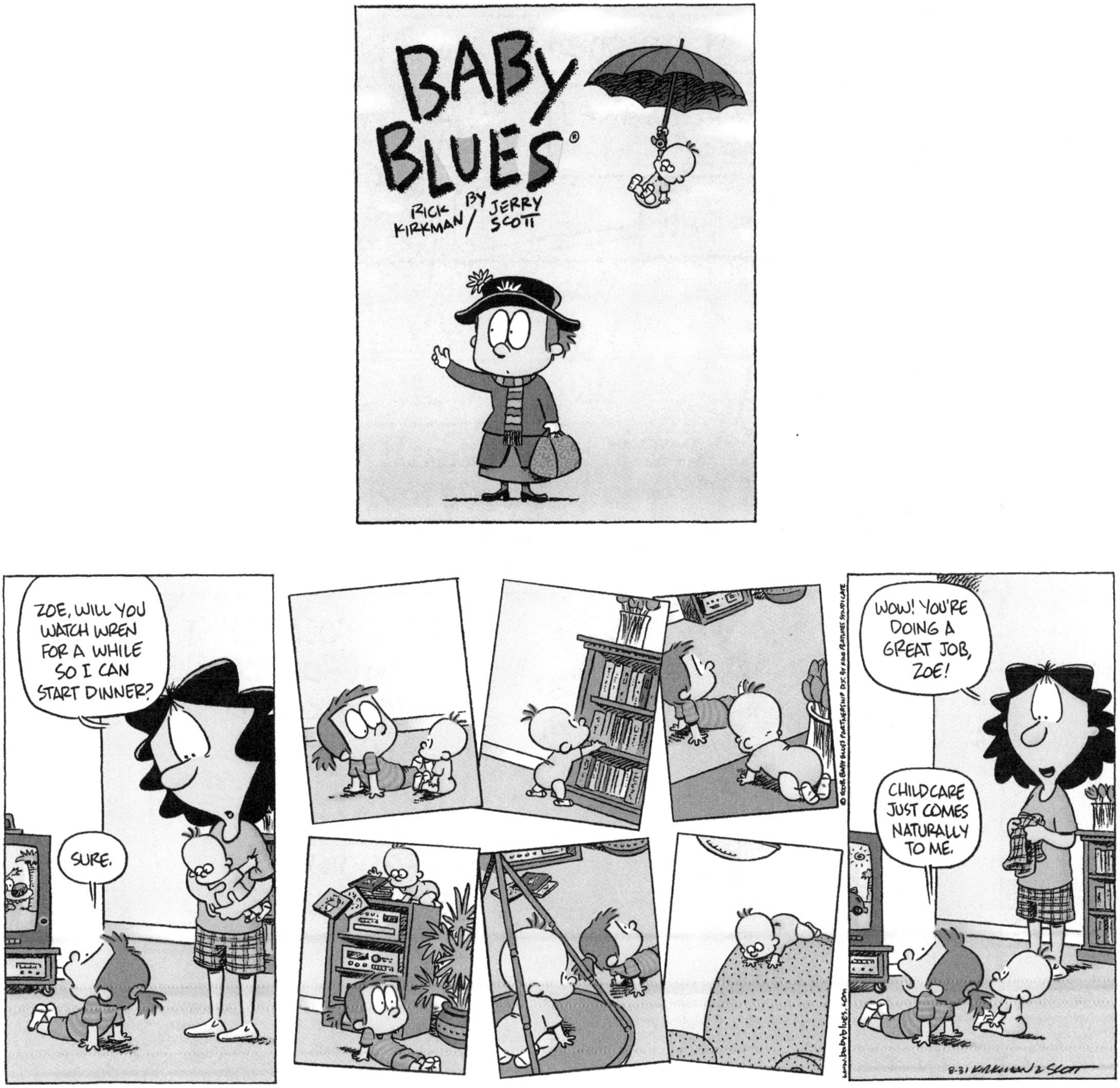
BABY BLUES®
BY RICK KIRKMAN / JERRY SCOTT
ZOE, WILL YOU WATCH WREN FOR A WHILE SO I CAN START DINNER?
SURE.
WOW! YOU'RE DOING A GREAT JOB, ZOE!
CHILDCARE JUST COMES NATURALLY TO ME.
8-31 KIRKMAN & SCOTT

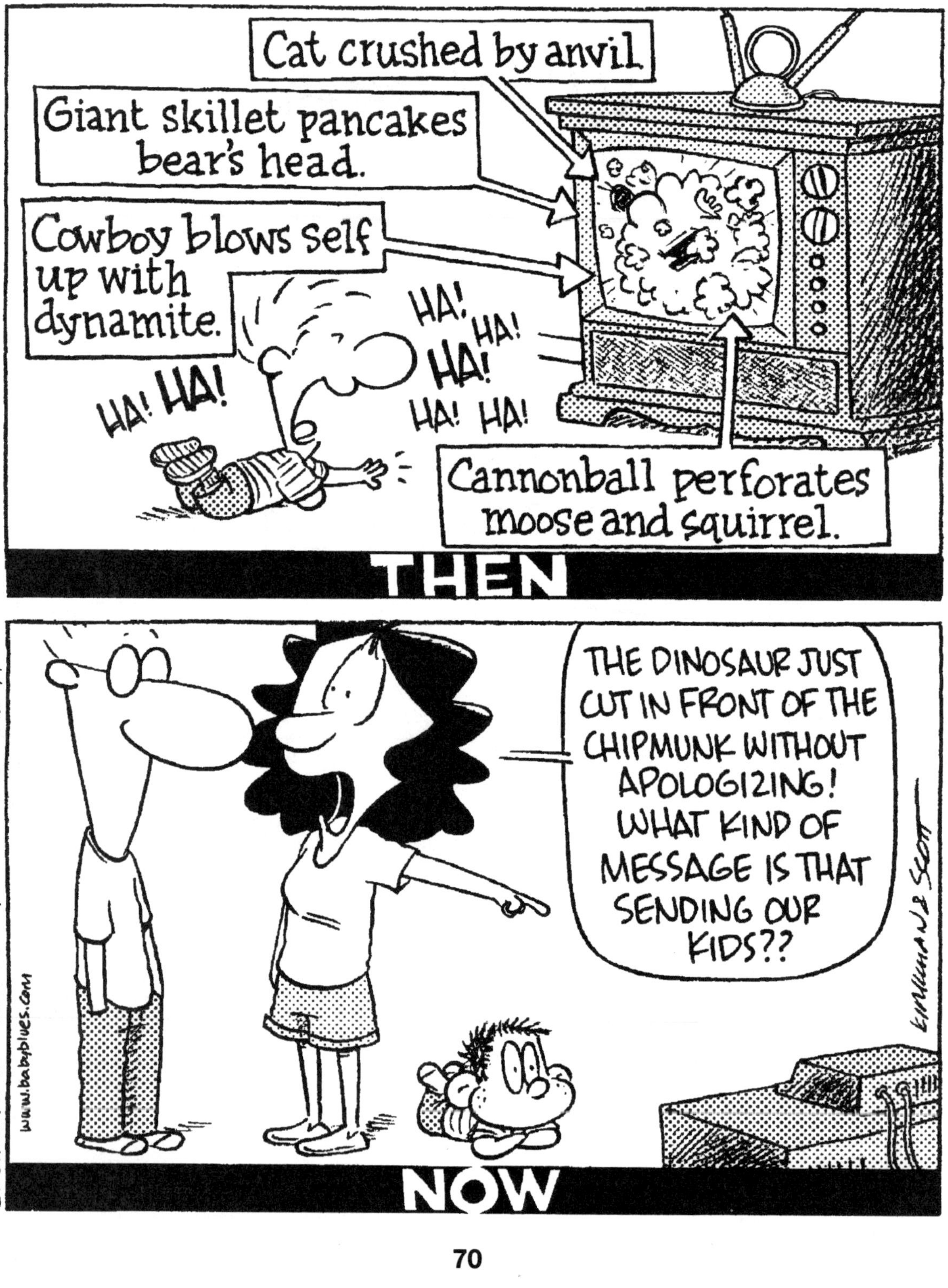

Cat crushed by anvil.
Giant skillet pancakes bear's head.
Cowboy blows self up with dynamite.
HA! HA! HA! HA! HA! HA! HA!
Cannonball perforates moose and squirrel.
THEN
THE DINOSAUR JUST CUT IN FRONT OF THE CHIPMUNK WITHOUT APOLOGIZING! WHAT KIND OF MESSAGE IS THAT SENDING OUR KIDS??
NOW
©2008, BABY BLUES PARTNERSHIP DIST. BY KING FEATURES SYNDICATE 9-1
www.babyblues.com
KIRKMAN & SCOTT

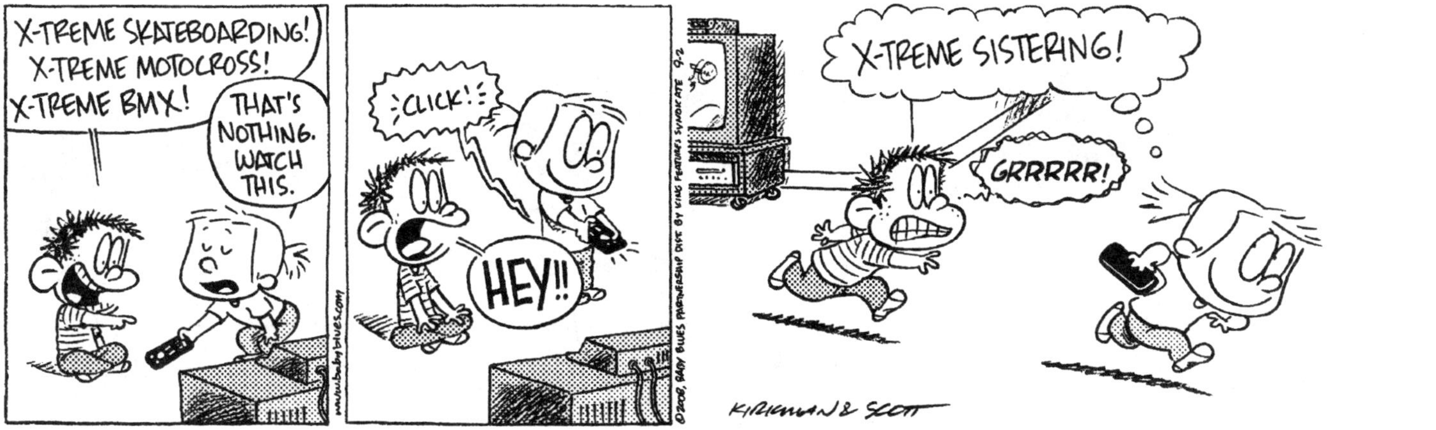
X-TREME SKATEBOARDING! X-TREME MOTOCROSS! X-TREME BMX!
THAT'S NOTHING. WATCH THIS.
CLICK!
HEY!!
X-TREME SISTERING!
GRRRRR!
KIRKMAN & SCOTT

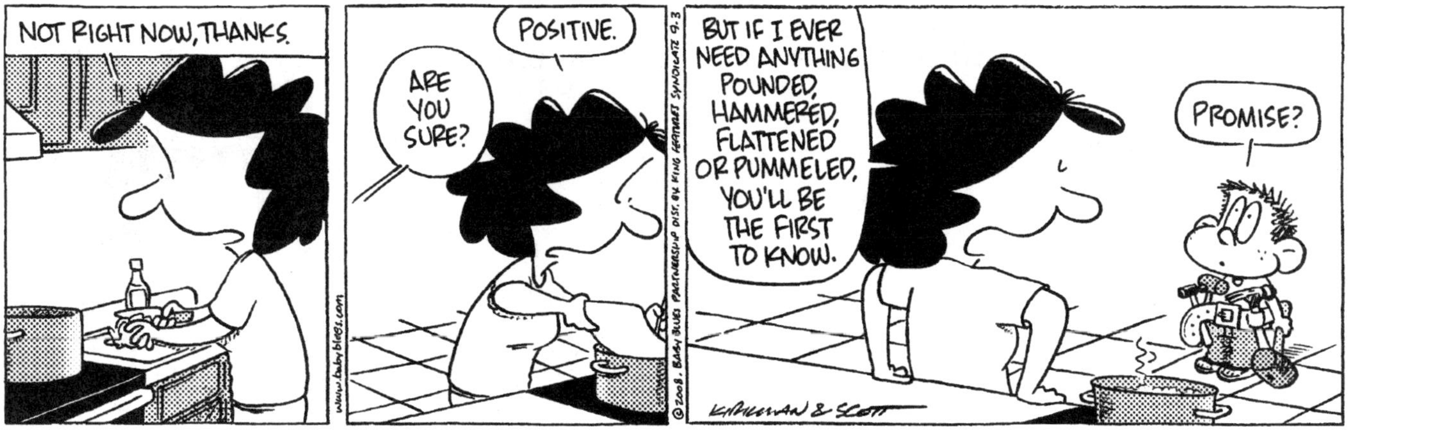
NOT RIGHT NOW, THANKS.
ARE YOU SURE?
POSITIVE.
BUT IF I EVER NEED ANYTHING POUNDED, HAMMERED, FLATTENED OR PUMMELED, YOU'LL BE THE FIRST TO KNOW.
PROMISE?
KIRKMAN & SCOTT

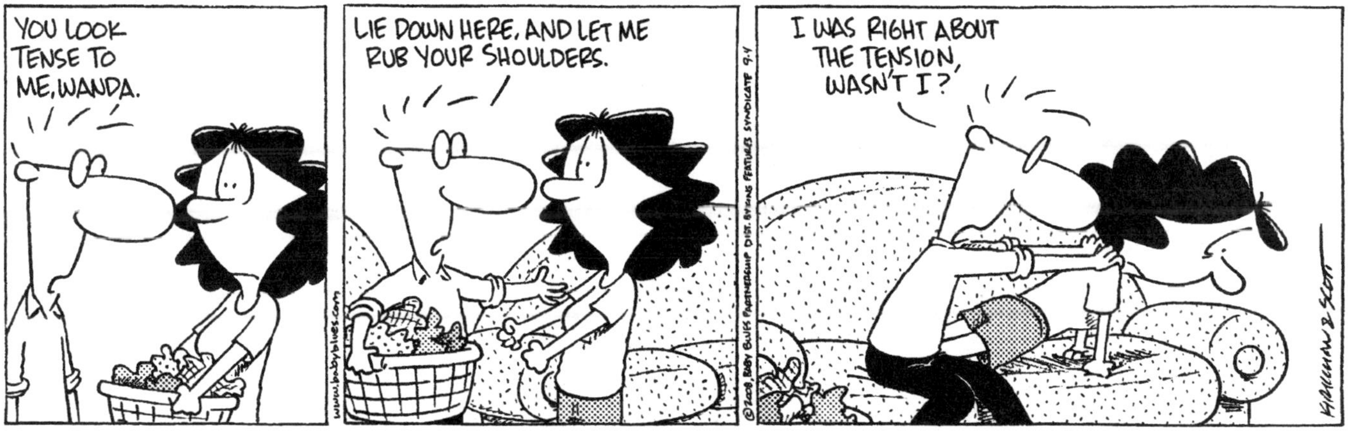
YOU LOOK TENSE TO ME, WANDA.
LIE DOWN HERE, AND LET ME RUB YOUR SHOULDERS.
I WAS RIGHT ABOUT THE TENSION, WASN'T I?
KIRKMAN & SCOTT

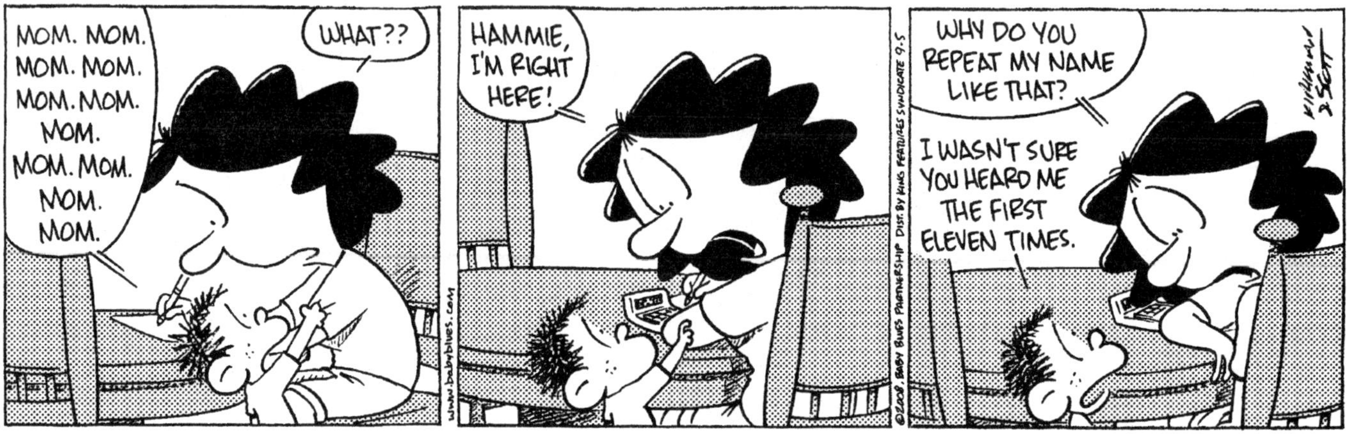
MOM. MOM. MOM. MOM. MOM. MOM. MOM. MOM. MOM. MOM. MOM.
WHAT??
www.babyblues.com
HAMMIE, I'M RIGHT HERE!
©2008, BABY BLUES PARTNERSHIP DIST. BY KING FEATURES SYNDICATE 9-5
WHY DO YOU REPEAT MY NAME LIKE THAT?
I WASN'T SURE YOU HEARD ME THE FIRST ELEVEN TIMES.
KIRKMAN & SCOTT

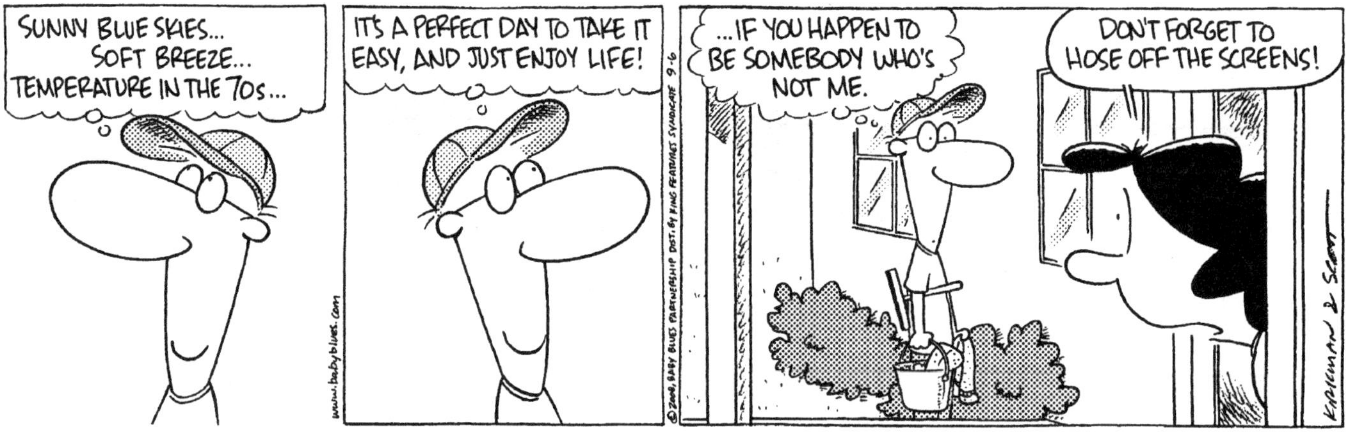
SUNNY BLUE SKIES... SOFT BREEZE... TEMPERATURE IN THE 70s...
www.babyblues.com
IT'S A PERFECT DAY TO TAKE IT EASY, AND JUST ENJOY LIFE!
©2008, BABY BLUES PARTNERSHIP DIST. BY KING FEATURES SYNDICATE 9-6
...IF YOU HAPPEN TO BE SOMEBODY WHO'S NOT ME.
DON'T FORGET TO HOSE OFF THE SCREENS!
KIRKMAN & SCOTT

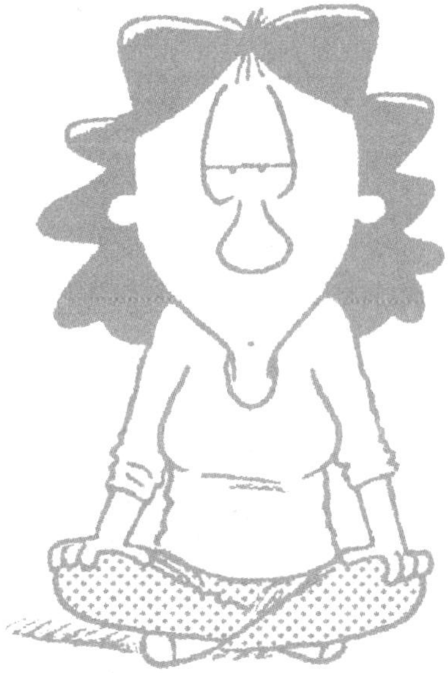

BABY BLUES®
BY
RICK KIRKMAN / JERRY SCOTT

MOM, CAN I ASK YOU SOMETHING?
SURE, H.
DO YOU REMEMBER THE BIGGEST MESS ZOE AND I EVER MADE?
HMMM...
WAS IT THE TIME YOU DECIDED TO COLOR EASTER EGGS IN THE LIVING ROOM?
RIGHT!
WELL, I'M NOT MAKING ANY PROMISES, BUT TODAY MAY BE THE DAY WE SET A BRAND NEW RECORD!
WELL, I PUT A POSITIVE SPIN ON IT. THE REST IS UP TO FATE.
©2008, BABY BLUES PARTNERSHIP DIST. BY KING FEATURES SYNDICATE
www.babyblues.com
KIRKMAN & SCOTT 9-7

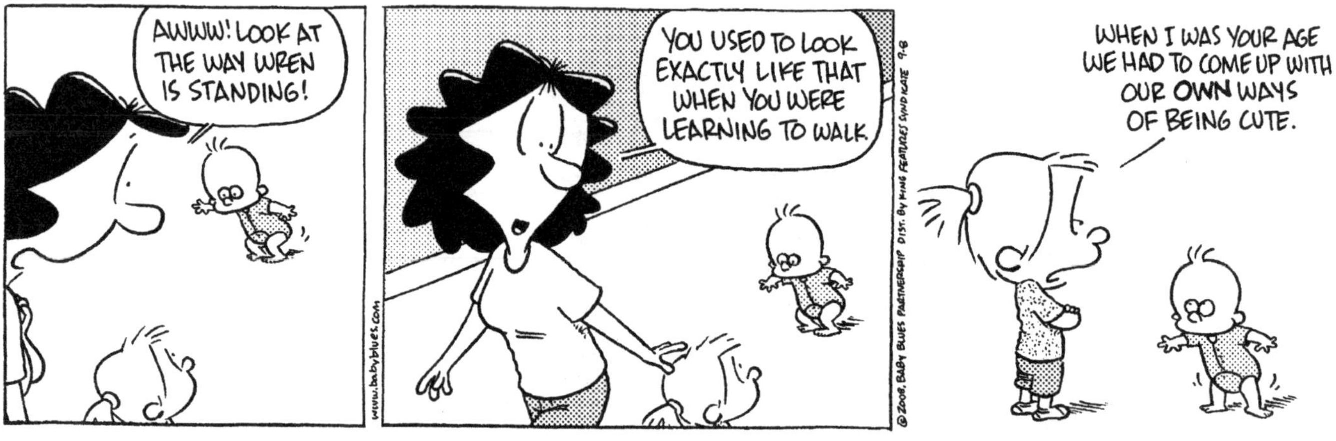
AWWW! LOOK AT THE WAY WREN IS STANDING!
www.babyblues.com
YOU USED TO LOOK EXACTLY LIKE THAT WHEN YOU WERE LEARNING TO WALK.
© 2008, BABY BLUES PARTNERSHIP DIST. BY KING FEATURES SYNDICATE 9-8
WHEN I WAS YOUR AGE WE HAD TO COME UP WITH OUR **OWN** WAYS OF BEING CUTE.

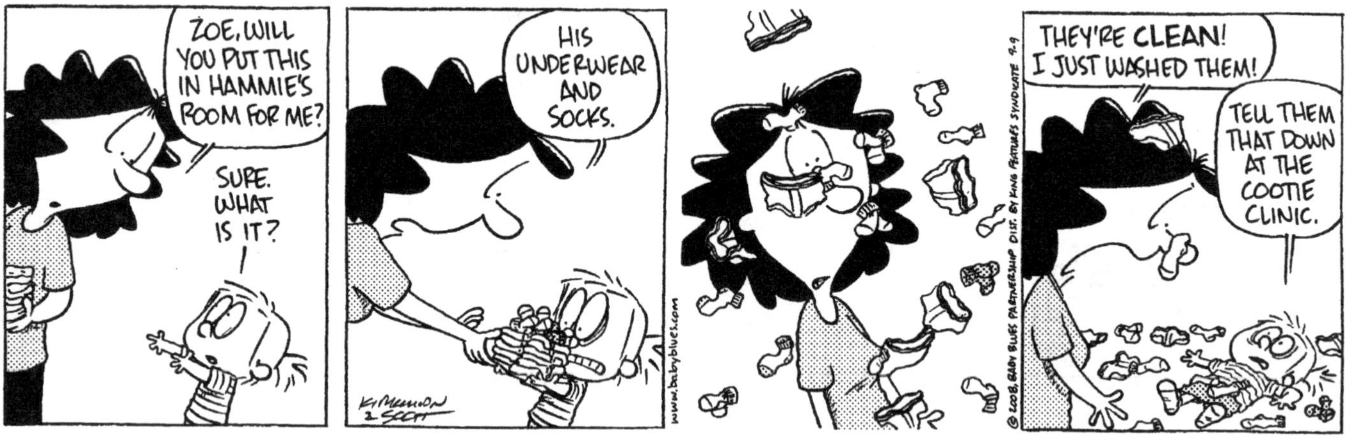
ZOE, WILL YOU PUT THIS IN HAMMIE'S ROOM FOR ME?
SURE. WHAT IS IT?
HIS UNDERWEAR AND SOCKS.
KIRKMAN & SCOTT
www.babyblues.com
© 2008, BABY BLUES PARTNERSHIP DIST. BY KING FEATURES SYNDICATE 9-9
THEY'RE **CLEAN**! I JUST WASHED THEM!
TELL THEM THAT DOWN AT THE COOTIE CLINIC.

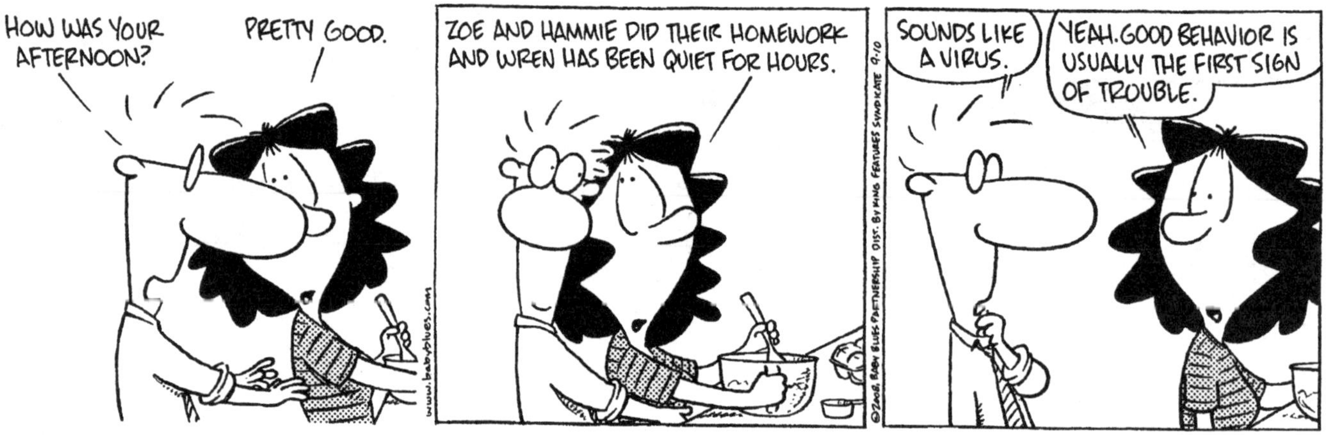
HOW WAS YOUR AFTERNOON?
PRETTY GOOD.
www.babyblues.com
ZOE AND HAMMIE DID THEIR HOMEWORK AND WREN HAS BEEN QUIET FOR HOURS.
© 2008, BABY BLUES PARTNERSHIP DIST. BY KING FEATURES SYNDICATE 9-10
SOUNDS LIKE A VIRUS.
YEAH. GOOD BEHAVIOR IS USUALLY THE FIRST SIGN OF TROUBLE.

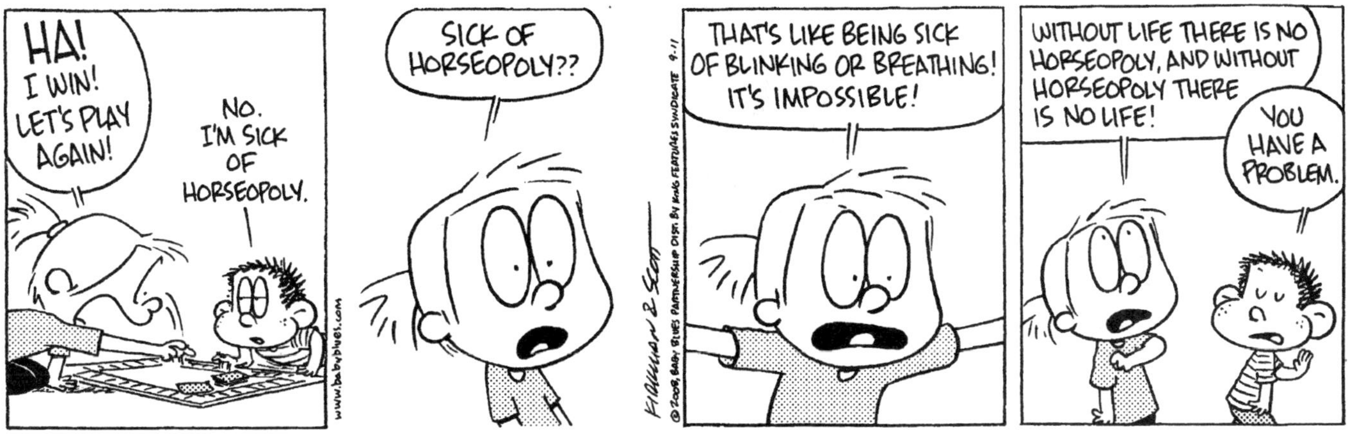
HA! I WIN! LET'S PLAY AGAIN!
NO. I'M SICK OF HORSEOPOLY.
www.babyblues.com
SICK OF HORSEOPOLY??
KIRKMAN & SCOTT
© 2008, BABY BLUES PARTNERSHIP DIST. BY KING FEATURES SYNDICATE 9.11
THAT'S LIKE BEING SICK OF BLINKING OR BREATHING! IT'S IMPOSSIBLE!
WITHOUT LIFE THERE IS NO HORSEOPOLY, AND WITHOUT HORSEOPOLY THERE IS NO LIFE!
YOU HAVE A PROBLEM.

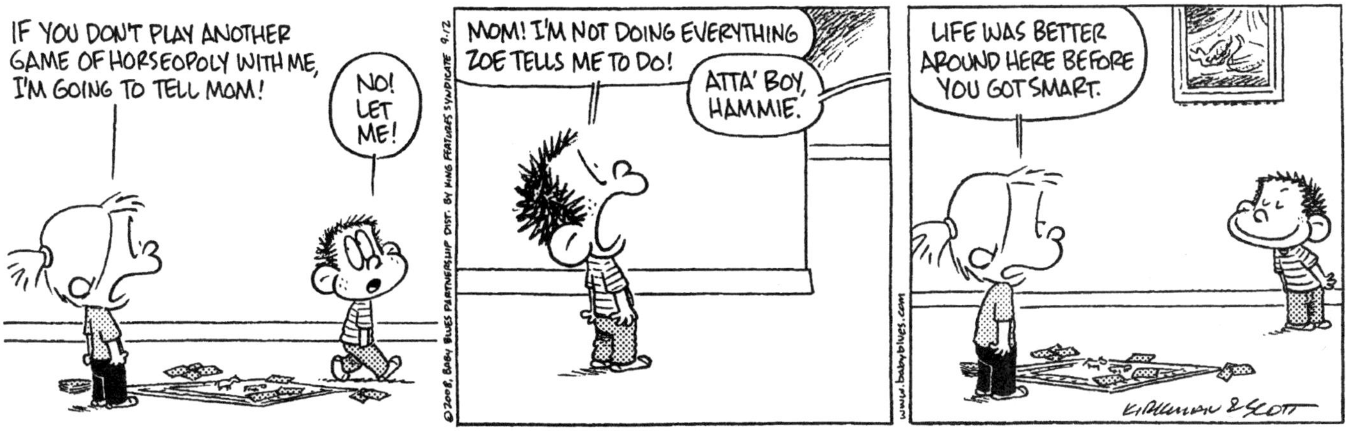
IF YOU DON'T PLAY ANOTHER GAME OF HORSEOPOLY WITH ME, I'M GOING TO TELL MOM!
NO! LET ME!
© 2008, BABY BLUES PARTNERSHIP DIST. BY KING FEATURES SYNDICATE 9.12
MOM! I'M NOT DOING EVERYTHING ZOE TELLS ME TO DO!
ATTA' BOY, HAMMIE.
www.babyblues.com
LIFE WAS BETTER AROUND HERE BEFORE YOU GOT SMART.
KIRKMAN & SCOTT

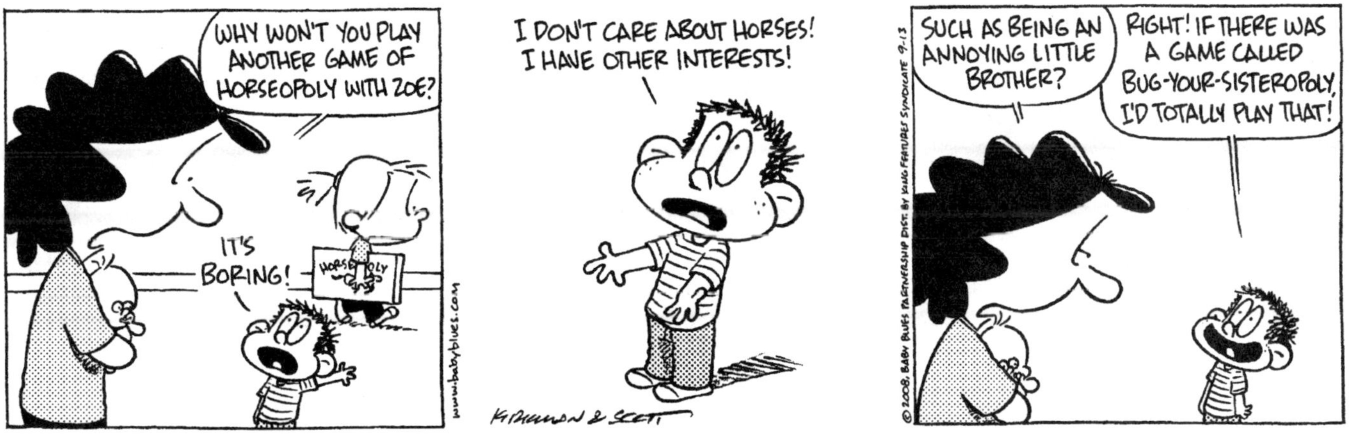
WHY WON'T YOU PLAY ANOTHER GAME OF HORSEOPOLY WITH ZOE?
IT'S BORING!
HORSEOPOLY
www.babyblues.com
I DON'T CARE ABOUT HORSES! I HAVE OTHER INTERESTS!
KIRKMAN & SCOTT
© 2008, BABY BLUES PARTNERSHIP DIST. BY KING FEATURES SYNDICATE 9.13
SUCH AS BEING AN ANNOYING LITTLE BROTHER?
RIGHT! IF THERE WAS A GAME CALLED BUG-YOUR-SISTEROPOLY, I'D TOTALLY PLAY THAT!

BABY BLUES®
BY RICK KIRKMAN / JERRY SCOTT

UNH! UNH!
NO WREN!
UNH! NEEEEE!
NO! ICE CREAM ISN'T GOOD FOR BABIES!
STOP!
WAAAAA!
OH, OKAY...
HERE YOU GO.
LICK!
www.babyblues.com
9-14
KIRKMAN & SCOTT
©2008 BABY BLUES PARTNERSHIP DIST. BY KING FEATURES SYNDICATE
HAMMIE, I SAID YOU COULD HAVE ONE ICE CREAM BAR TODAY.
BUT I HAD TO SHARE MY LAST ONE WITH WREN!

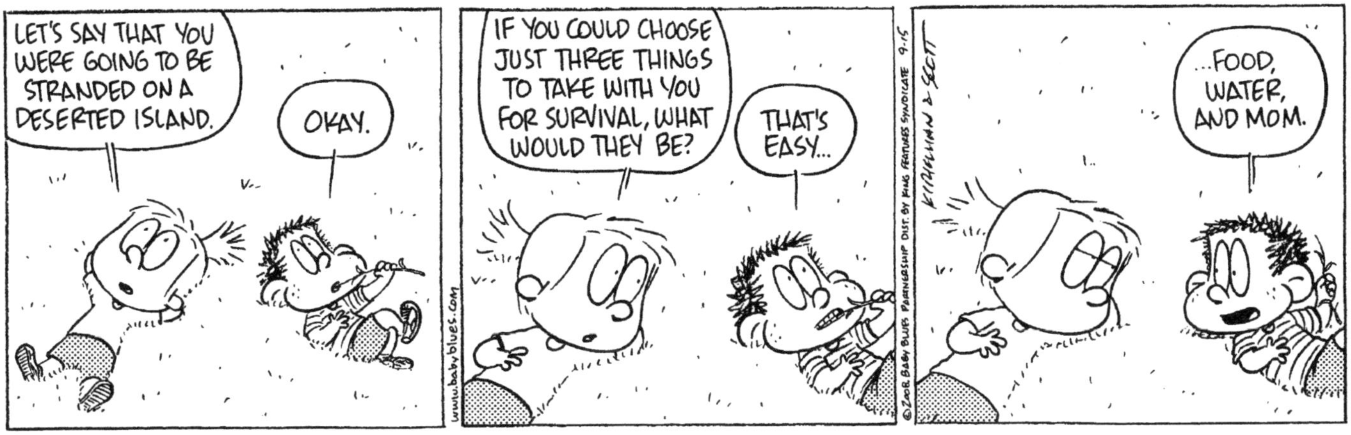
LET'S SAY THAT YOU WERE GOING TO BE STRANDED ON A DESERTED ISLAND.
OKAY.
www.babyblues.com
IF YOU COULD CHOOSE JUST THREE THINGS TO TAKE WITH YOU FOR SURVIVAL, WHAT WOULD THEY BE?
THAT'S EASY...
©2008 BABY BLUES PARTNERSHIP DIST. BY KING FEATURES SYNDICATE 9-15
KIRKMAN & SCOTT
...FOOD, WATER, AND MOM.

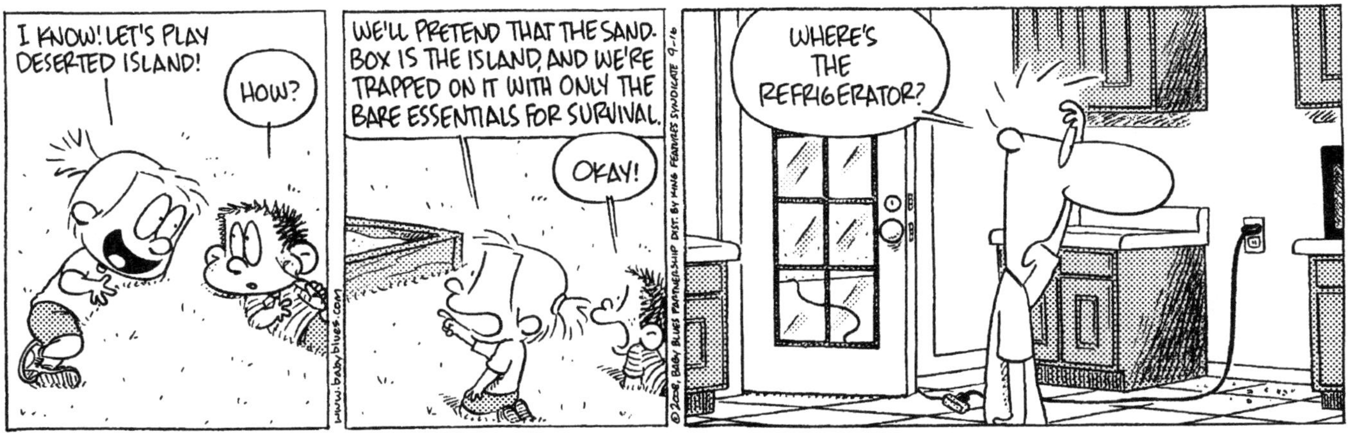
I KNOW! LET'S PLAY DESERTED ISLAND!
HOW?
www.babyblues.com
WE'LL PRETEND THAT THE SANDBOX IS THE ISLAND, AND WE'RE TRAPPED ON IT WITH ONLY THE BARE ESSENTIALS FOR SURVIVAL.
OKAY!
©2008 BABY BLUES PARTNERSHIP DIST. BY KING FEATURES SYNDICATE 9-16
WHERE'S THE REFRIGERATOR?

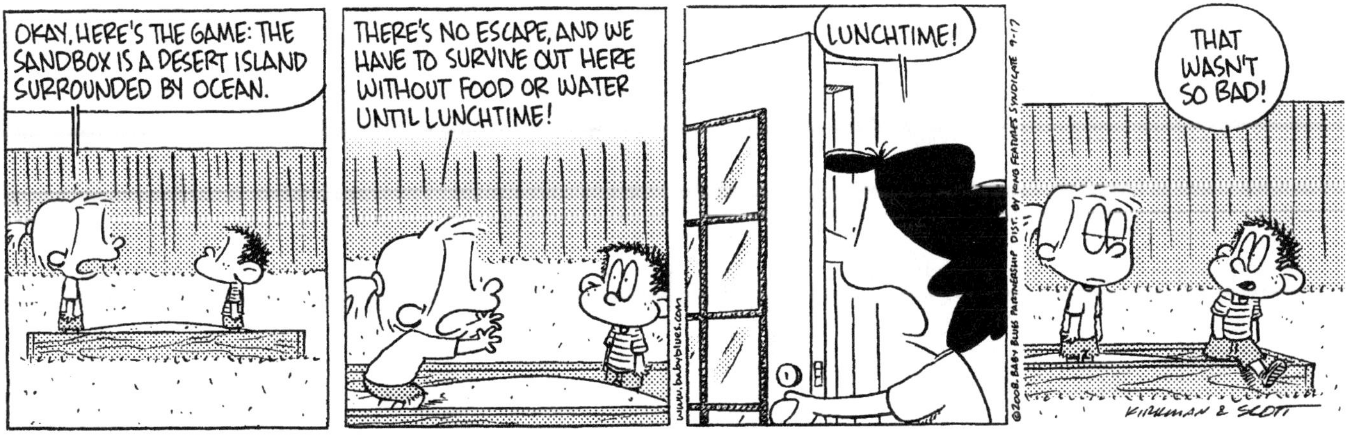
OKAY, HERE'S THE GAME: THE SANDBOX IS A DESERT ISLAND SURROUNDED BY OCEAN.
THERE'S NO ESCAPE, AND WE HAVE TO SURVIVE OUT HERE WITHOUT FOOD OR WATER UNTIL LUNCHTIME!
www.babyblues.com
LUNCHTIME!
©2008 BABY BLUES PARTNERSHIP DIST. BY KING FEATURES SYNDICATE 9-17
THAT WASN'T SO BAD!
KIRKMAN & SCOTT

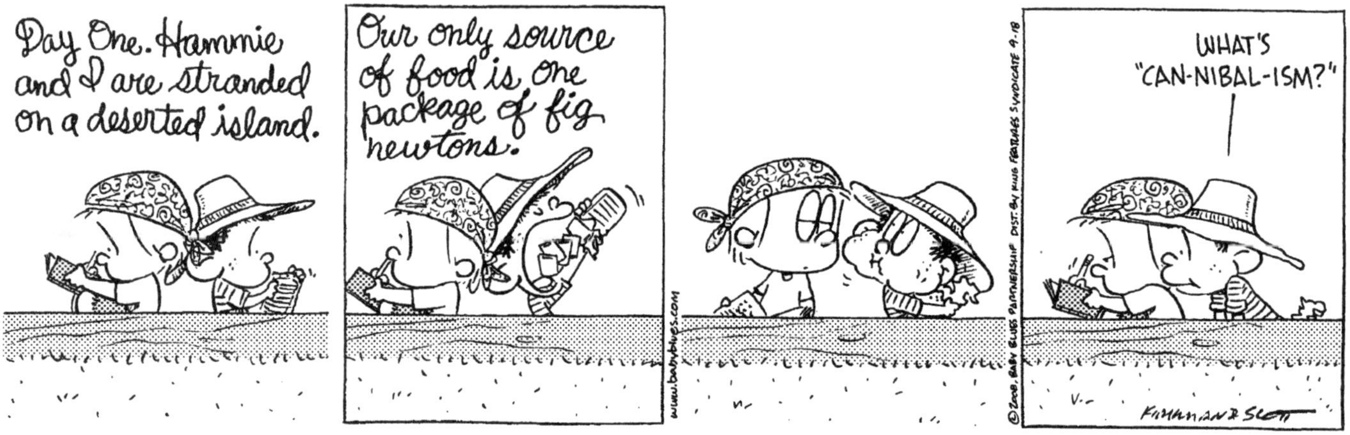
Day One. Hammie and I are stranded on a deserted island.
Our only source of food is one package of fig newtons.
www.babyblues.com
© 2008, Baby Blues Partnership Dist. by King Features Syndicate 9-18
WHAT'S "CAN-NIBAL-ISM?"
Kirkman & Scott

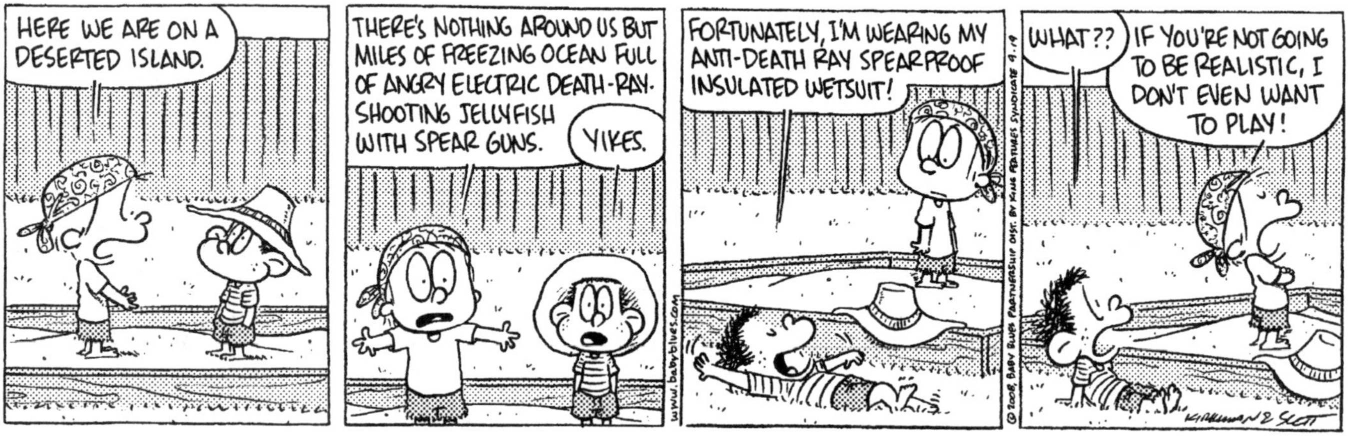
HERE WE ARE ON A DESERTED ISLAND.
THERE'S NOTHING AROUND US BUT MILES OF FREEZING OCEAN FULL OF ANGRY ELECTRIC DEATH-RAY-SHOOTING JELLYFISH WITH SPEAR GUNS.
YIKES.
www.babyblues.com
FORTUNATELY, I'M WEARING MY ANTI-DEATH RAY SPEARPROOF INSULATED WETSUIT!
© 2008, Baby Blues Partnership Dist. by King Features Syndicate 9-19
WHAT??
IF YOU'RE NOT GOING TO BE REALISTIC, I DON'T EVEN WANT TO PLAY!
Kirkman & Scott

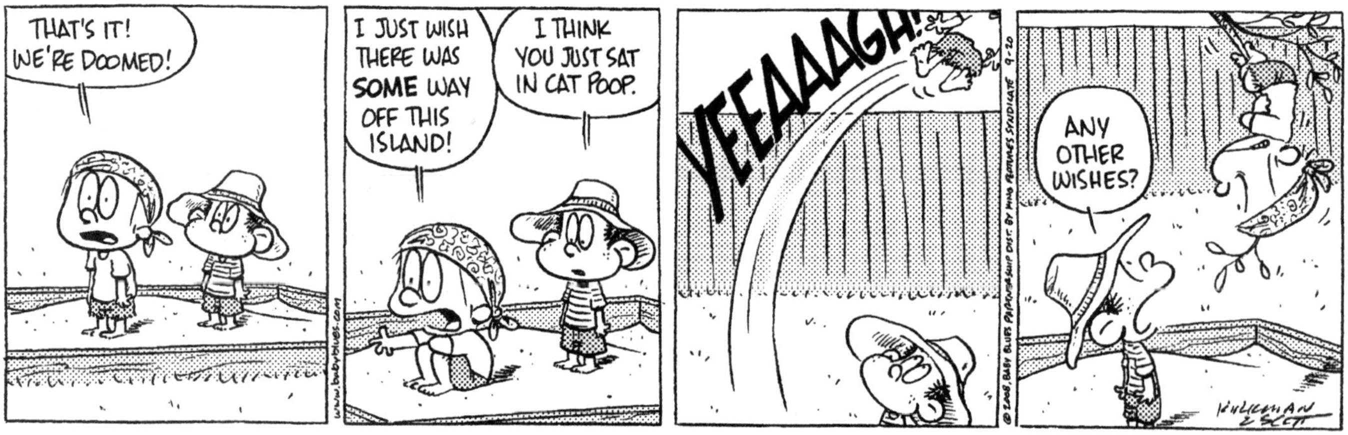
THAT'S IT! WE'RE DOOMED!
www.babyblues.com
I JUST WISH THERE WAS **SOME** WAY OFF THIS ISLAND!
I THINK YOU JUST SAT IN CAT POOP.
YEEAAAGH!
© 2008, Baby Blues Partnership Dist. by King Features Syndicate 9-20
ANY OTHER WISHES?
Kirkman & Scott

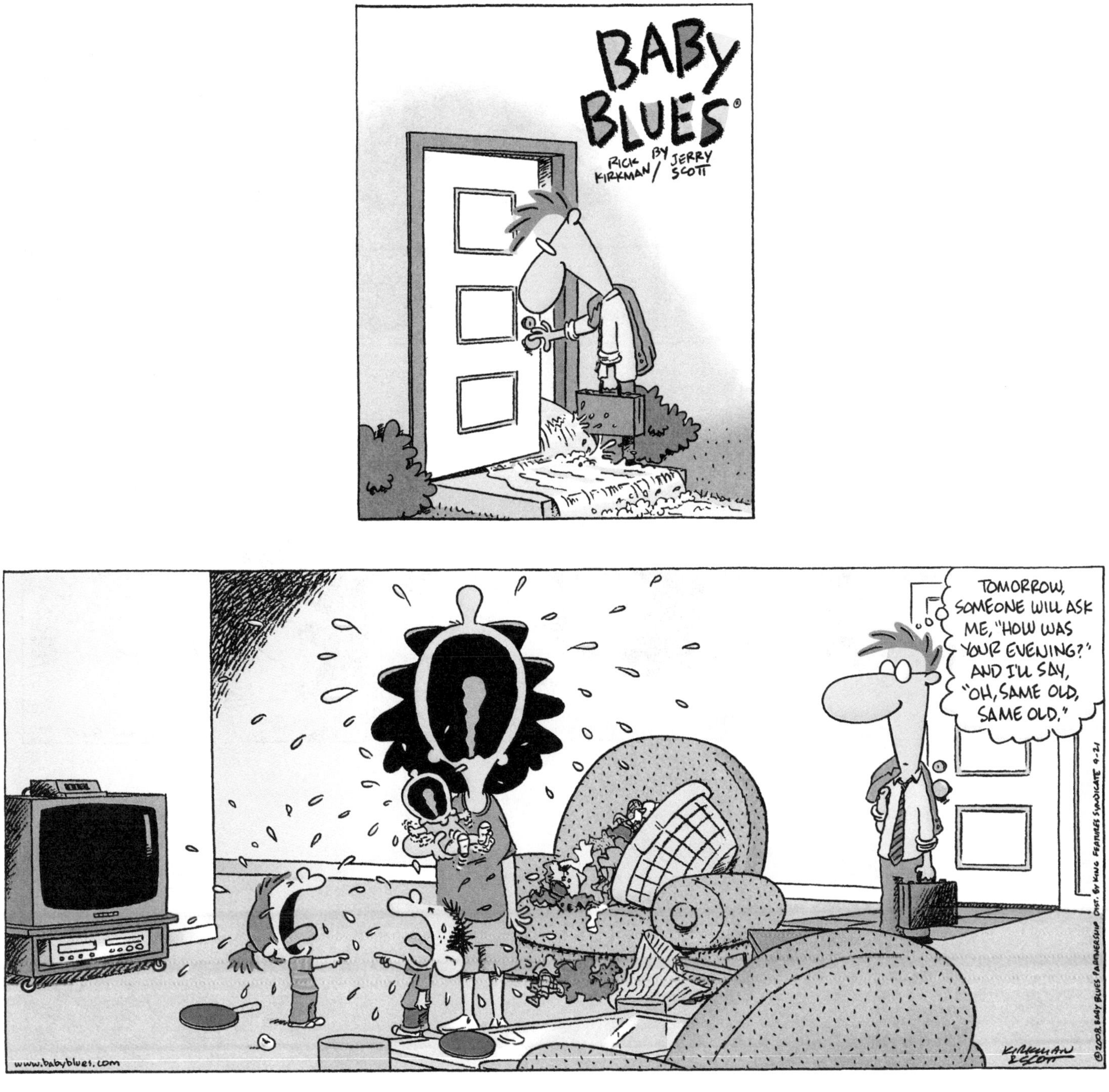
BABY BLUES®
RICK KIRKMAN / BY JERRY SCOTT
TOMORROW, SOMEONE WILL ASK ME, "HOW WAS YOUR EVENING?" AND I'LL SAY, "OH, SAME OLD, SAME OLD."
www.babyblues.com
© 2008 BABY BLUES PARTNERSHIP DIST. BY KING FEATURES SYNDICATE 4-21
KIRKMAN & SCOTT

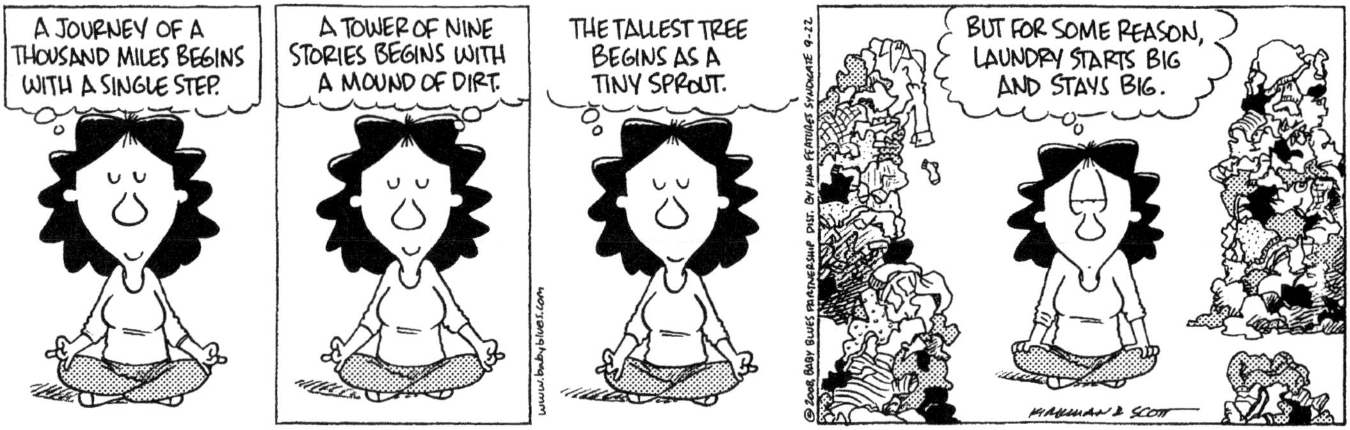
A JOURNEY OF A THOUSAND MILES BEGINS WITH A SINGLE STEP.
A TOWER OF NINE STORIES BEGINS WITH A MOUND OF DIRT.
www.babyblues.com
THE TALLEST TREE BEGINS AS A TINY SPROUT.
© 2008, BABY BLUES PARTNERSHIP DIST. BY KING FEATURES SYNDICATE 9-22
BUT FOR SOME REASON, LAUNDRY STARTS BIG AND STAYS BIG.
KIRKMAN & SCOTT

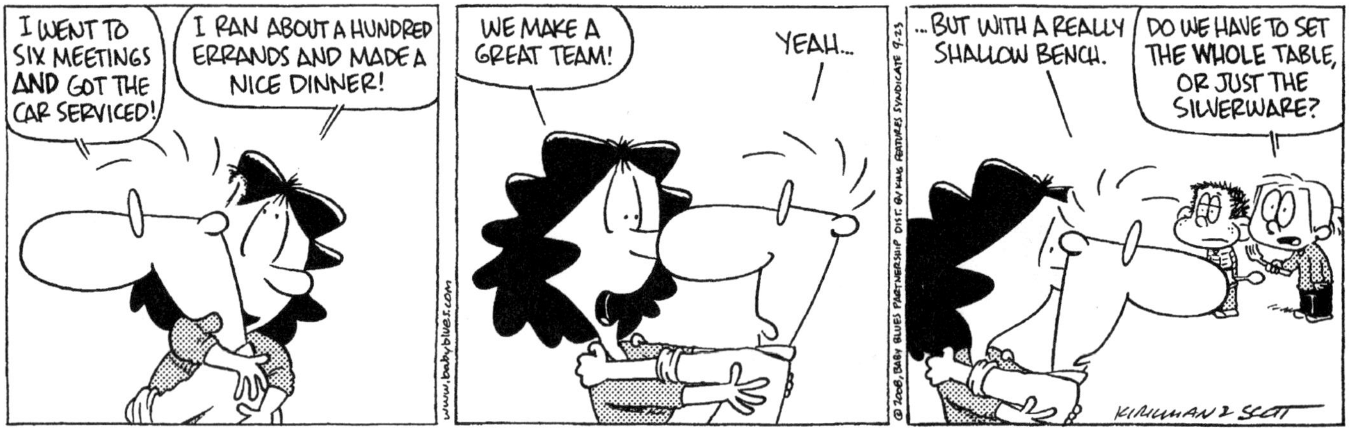
I WENT TO SIX MEETINGS **AND** GOT THE CAR SERVICED!
I RAN ABOUT A HUNDRED ERRANDS AND MADE A NICE DINNER!
www.babyblues.com
WE MAKE A GREAT TEAM!
YEAH...
© 2008, BABY BLUES PARTNERSHIP DIST. BY KING FEATURES SYNDICATE 9-23
...BUT WITH A REALLY SHALLOW BENCH.
DO WE HAVE TO SET THE **WHOLE** TABLE, OR JUST THE SILVERWARE?
KIRKMAN & SCOTT

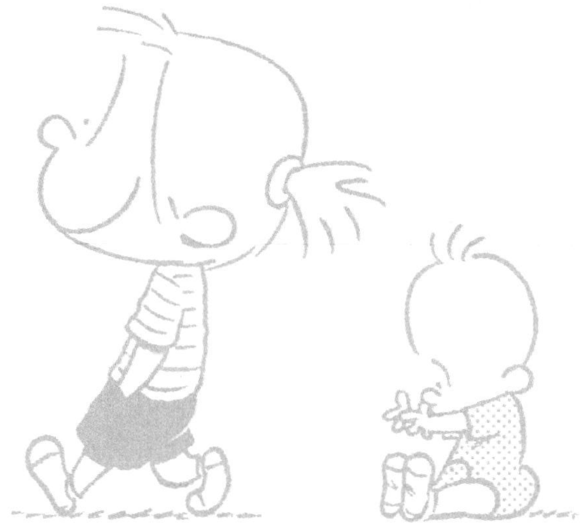

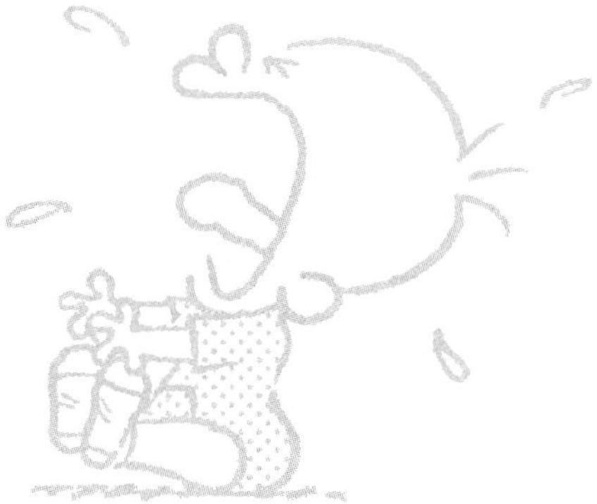

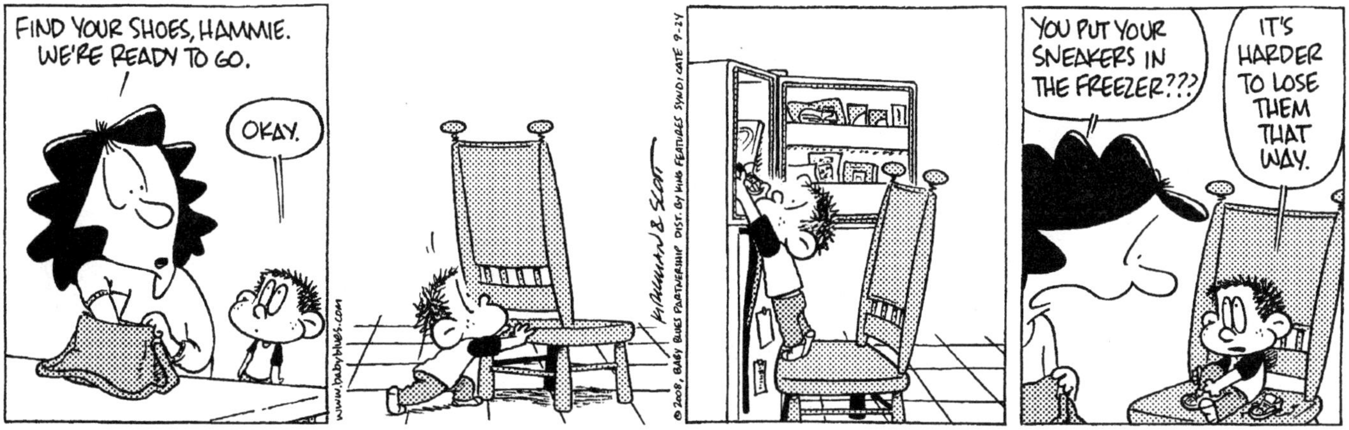
FIND YOUR SHOES, HAMMIE. WE'RE READY TO GO.
OKAY.
YOU PUT YOUR SNEAKERS IN THE FREEZER???
IT'S HARDER TO LOSE THEM THAT WAY.

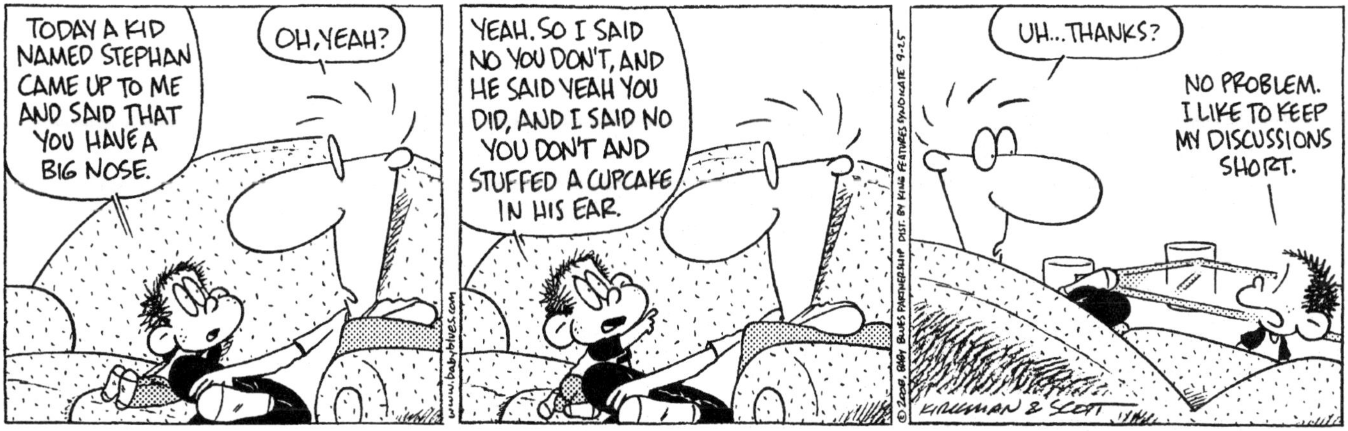
TODAY A KID NAMED STEPHAN CAME UP TO ME AND SAID THAT YOU HAVE A BIG NOSE.
OH, YEAH?
YEAH. SO I SAID NO YOU DON'T, AND HE SAID YEAH YOU DID, AND I SAID NO YOU DON'T AND STUFFED A CUPCAKE IN HIS EAR.
UH...THANKS?
NO PROBLEM. I LIKE TO KEEP MY DISCUSSIONS SHORT.

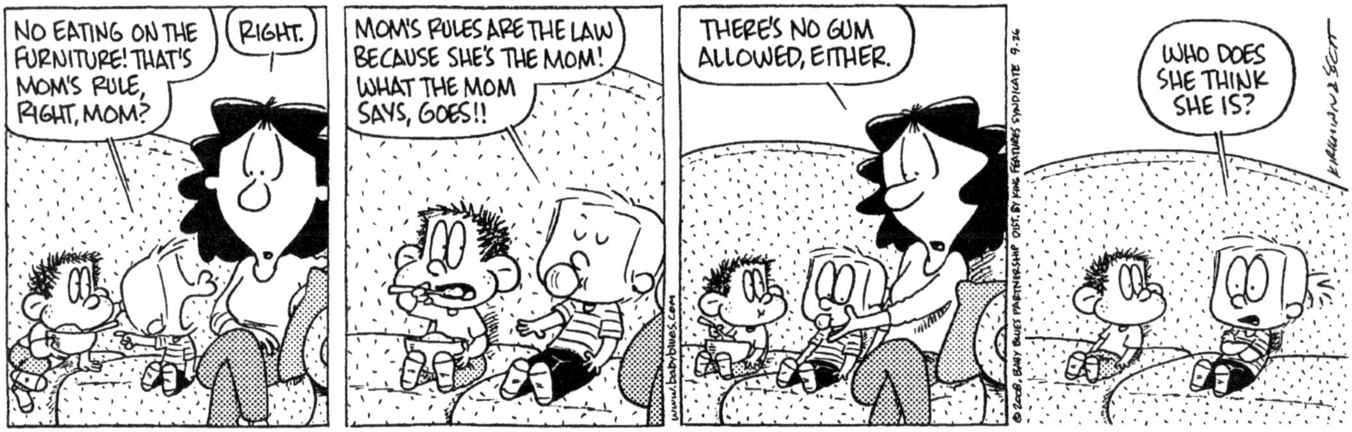
NO EATING ON THE FURNITURE! THAT'S MOM'S RULE, RIGHT, MOM?
RIGHT.
MOM'S RULES ARE THE LAW BECAUSE SHE'S THE MOM! WHAT THE MOM SAYS, GOES!!
www.babyblues.com
THERE'S NO GUM ALLOWED, EITHER.
© 2008, BABY BLUES PARTNERSHIP DIST. BY KING FEATURES SYNDICATE 9-26
WHO DOES SHE THINK SHE IS?
KIRKMAN & SCOTT

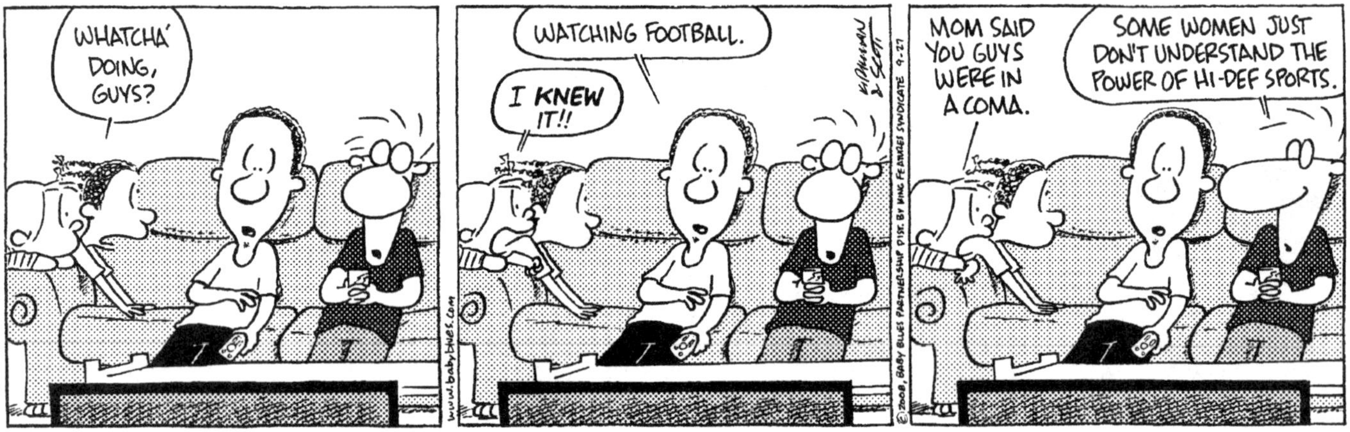
WHATCHA' DOING, GUYS?
www.babyblues.com
WATCHING FOOTBALL.
I KNEW IT!!
KIRKMAN & SCOTT
© 2008, BABY BLUES PARTNERSHIP DIST. BY KING FEATURES SYNDICATE 9-27
MOM SAID YOU GUYS WERE IN A COMA.
SOME WOMEN JUST DON'T UNDERSTAND THE POWER OF HI-DEF SPORTS.

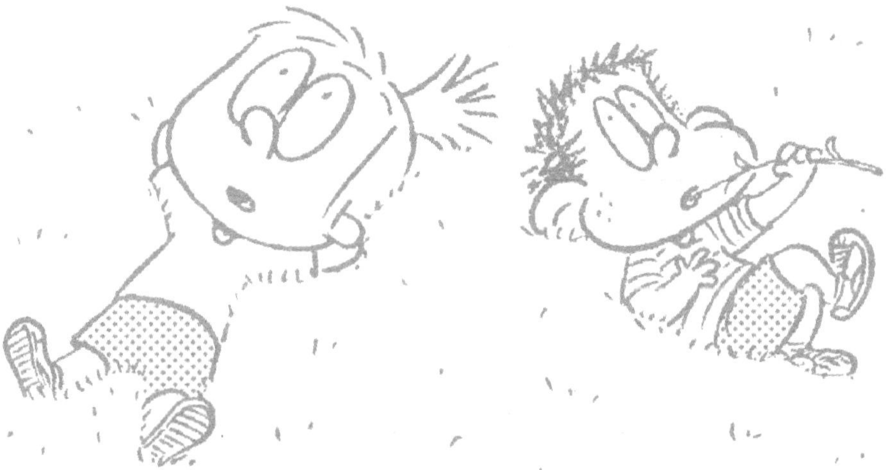

BABY BLUES®
BY RICK KIRKMAN / JERRY SCOTT

ZOE, DID YOU PUT YOUR WATER GLASS IN THE DISHWASHER?
LET ME THINK...
AFTER I FINISHED DRINKING THE WATER, I SET THE GLASS ON THE COFFEE TABLE AND WENT TO USE THE BATHROOM.
THEN I HEARD HAMMIE CALLING ME, SO I WENT IN AND HELPED HIM GLUE A DUCK FEATHER ONTO HIS SHOE...
©2008, BABY BLUES PARTNERSHIP DIST. BY KING FEATURES SYNDICATE 9-28
OH! THEN I REMEMBERED THAT THE TOWEL HAD FALLEN ONTO THE BATHROOM FLOOR AFTER I WASHED MY HANDS, SO I WENT BACK AND HUNG IT UP NICE AND NEATLY.
A-A-AND, I ALSO WIPED THE WATER SPOTS OFF THE MIRROR, JUST LIKE YOU SHOWED ME!
ARE YOU PROUD OF ME, OR WHAT?
YOU BET!
www.babyblues.com
BUT WHAT ABOUT THE WATER GLASS?
WHAT WATER GLASS?
KIRKMAN & SCOTT

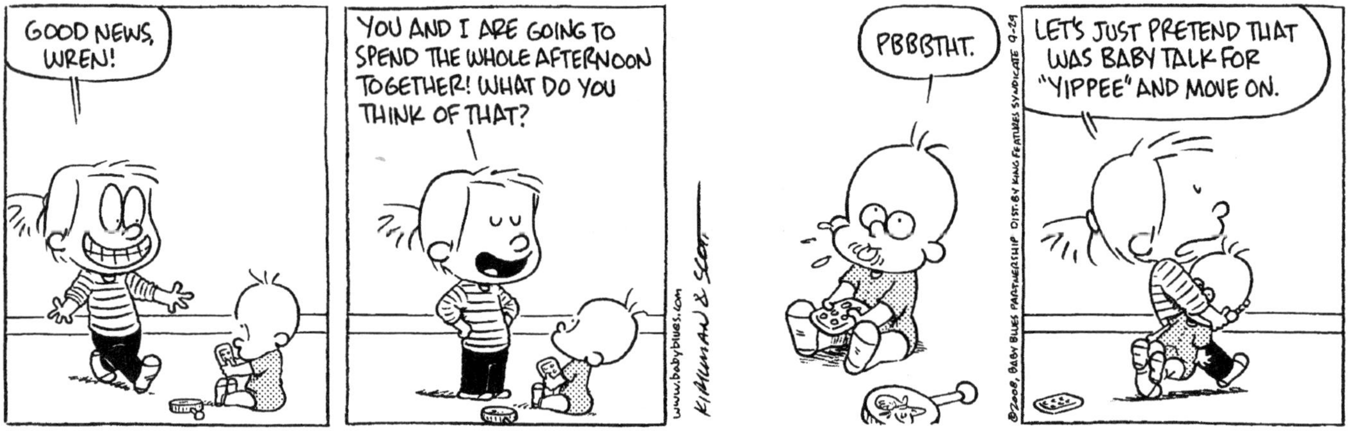
GOOD NEWS, WREN!
YOU AND I ARE GOING TO SPEND THE WHOLE AFTERNOON TOGETHER! WHAT DO YOU THINK OF THAT?
PBBBTHT.
LET'S JUST PRETEND THAT WAS BABY TALK FOR "YIPPEE" AND MOVE ON.

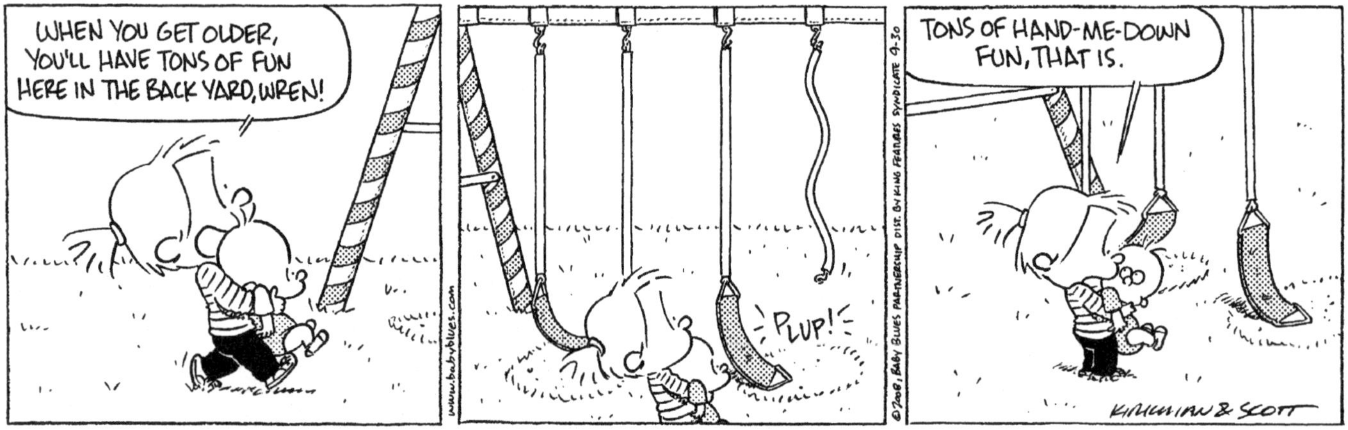
WHEN YOU GET OLDER, YOU'LL HAVE TONS OF FUN HERE IN THE BACK YARD, WREN!
PLUP!
TONS OF HAND-ME-DOWN FUN, THAT IS.

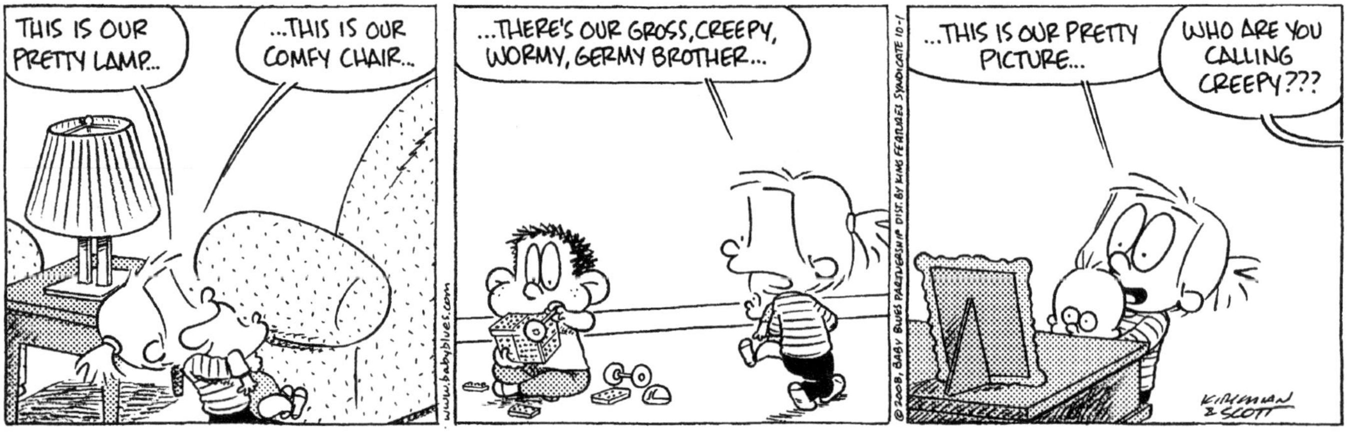
THIS IS OUR PRETTY LAMP...
...THIS IS OUR COMFY CHAIR...
...THERE'S OUR GROSS, CREEPY, WORMY, GERMY BROTHER...
...THIS IS OUR PRETTY PICTURE...
WHO ARE YOU CALLING CREEPY???

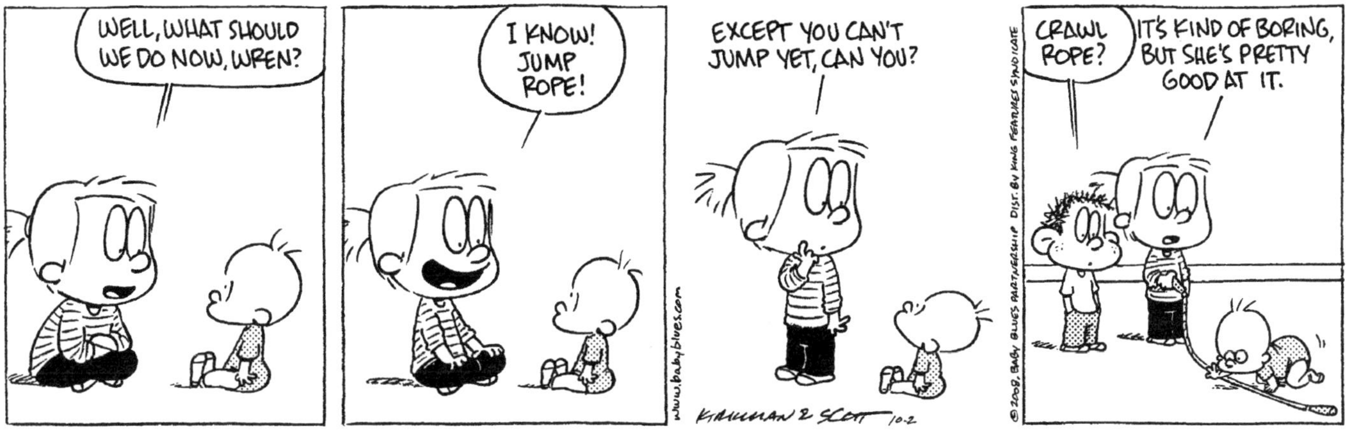
WELL, WHAT SHOULD WE DO NOW, WREN?
I KNOW! JUMP ROPE!
EXCEPT YOU CAN'T JUMP YET, CAN YOU?
CRAWL ROPE?
IT'S KIND OF BORING, BUT SHE'S PRETTY GOOD AT IT.
www.babyblues.com
KIRKMAN & SCOTT 10-2
© 2008, BABY BLUES PARTNERSHIP DIST. BY KING FEATURES SYNDICATE

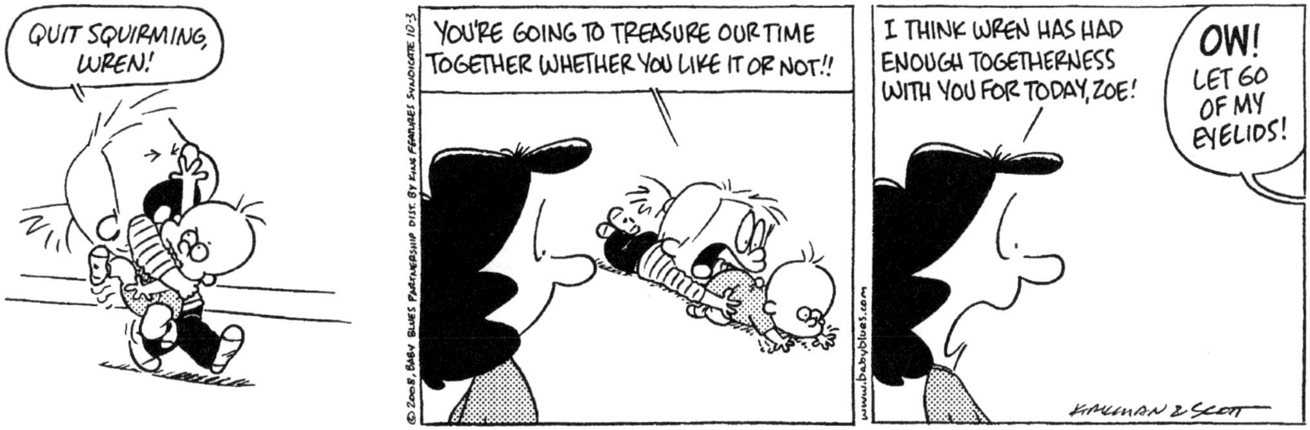
QUIT SQUIRMING, WREN!
YOU'RE GOING TO TREASURE OUR TIME TOGETHER WHETHER YOU LIKE IT OR NOT!!
© 2008, BABY BLUES PARTNERSHIP DIST. BY KING FEATURES SYNDICATE 10-3
I THINK WREN HAS HAD ENOUGH TOGETHERNESS WITH YOU FOR TODAY, ZOE!
OW! LET GO OF MY EYELIDS!
www.babyblues.com
KIRKMAN & SCOTT

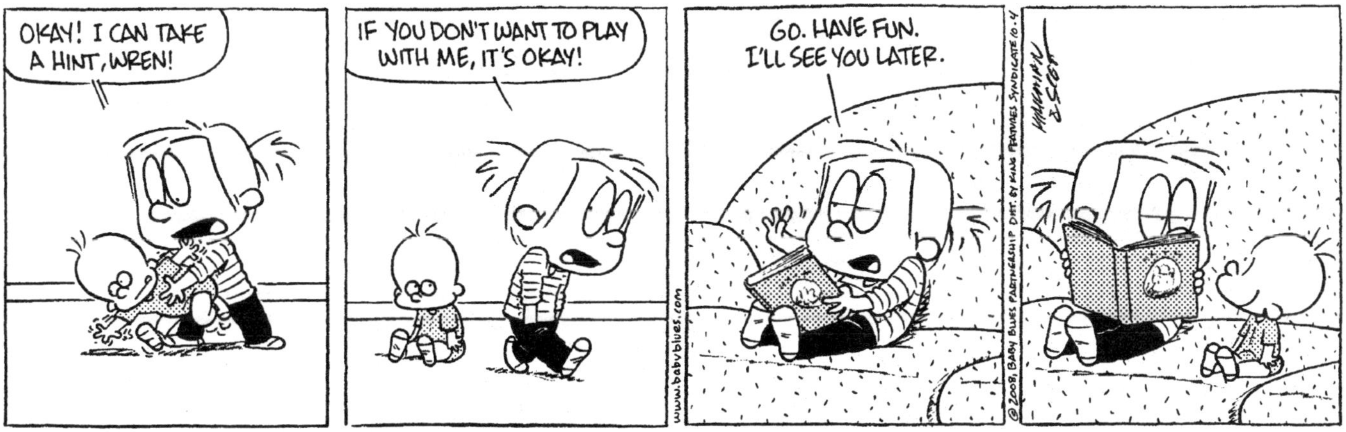
OKAY! I CAN TAKE A HINT, WREN!
IF YOU DON'T WANT TO PLAY WITH ME, IT'S OKAY!
www.babyblues.com
GO. HAVE FUN. I'LL SEE YOU LATER.
© 2008, BABY BLUES PARTNERSHIP DIST. BY KING FEATURES SYNDICATE 10-4
KIRKMAN & SCOTT

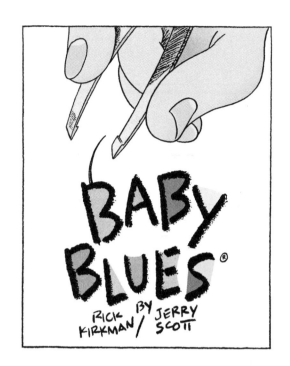

BABY BLUES®

BY RICK KIRKMAN / JERRY SCOTT

GASP! I HAVE A CHIN HAIR!

YOU MEAN CHINNY?

WAIT...

...YOU KNEW I HAD A CHIN HAIR, AND YOU NAMED IT?

I DIDN'T. ZOE DID.

WE EVEN MADE UP A SONG ABOUT HIM. WANNA' HEAR IT?

NO! I DON'T WANT TO HEAR A SONG YOU WROTE ABOUT MY CHIN HAIR!

ARE YOU SURE? IT'S TO THE TUNE OF "ROW, ROW, ROW YOUR BOAT."

WHERE ARE MY TWEEZERS?

10-5

GOT IT!

POINK!

www.babyblues.com

SIGH! BYE, CHINNY.

AND GOOD RIDDANCE!

©2006 BABY BLUES PARTNERSHIP DIST BY KING FEATURES SYNDICATE

SHOULDN'T WE NOTIFY HIS NEXT OF KIN?

KIRKMAN & SCOTT

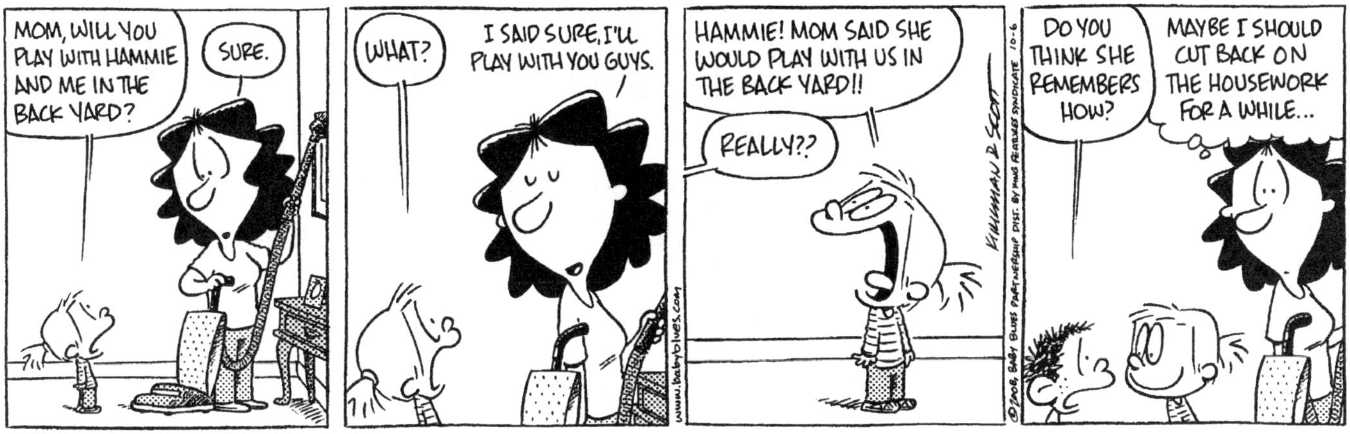
MOM, WILL YOU PLAY WITH HAMMIE AND ME IN THE BACK YARD?
SURE.
WHAT?
I SAID SURE, I'LL PLAY WITH YOU GUYS.
HAMMIE! MOM SAID SHE WOULD PLAY WITH US IN THE BACK YARD!!
REALLY??
DO YOU THINK SHE REMEMBERS HOW?
MAYBE I SHOULD CUT BACK ON THE HOUSEWORK FOR A WHILE...

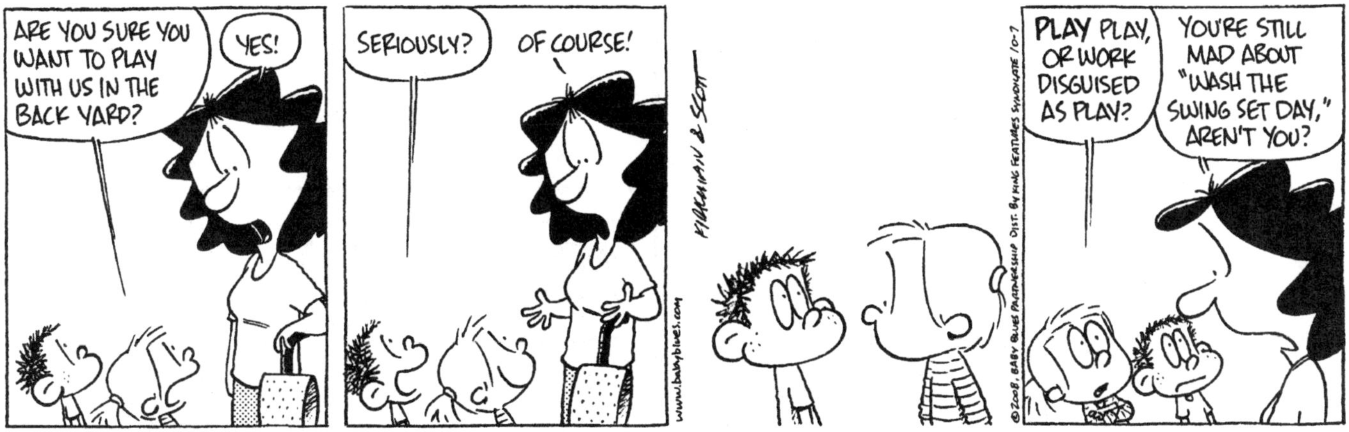
ARE YOU SURE YOU WANT TO PLAY WITH US IN THE BACK YARD?
YES!
SERIOUSLY?
OF COURSE!
PLAY PLAY, OR WORK DISGUISED AS PLAY?
YOU'RE STILL MAD ABOUT "WASH THE SWING SET DAY," AREN'T YOU?

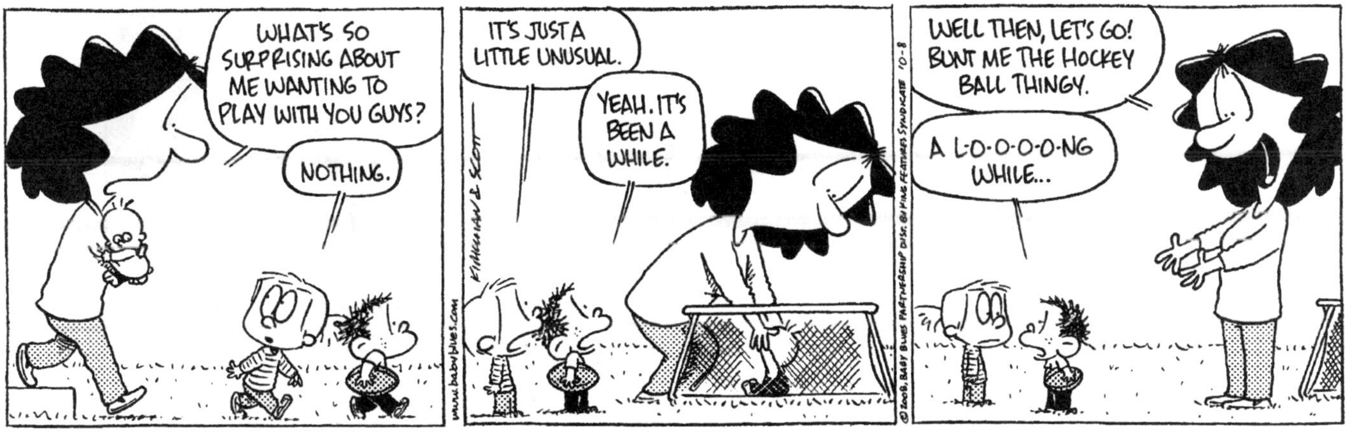
WHAT'S SO SURPRISING ABOUT ME WANTING TO PLAY WITH YOU GUYS?
NOTHING.
IT'S JUST A LITTLE UNUSUAL.
YEAH. IT'S BEEN A WHILE.
WELL THEN, LET'S GO! BUNT ME THE HOCKEY BALL THINGY.
A L-O-O-O-O-NG WHILE...

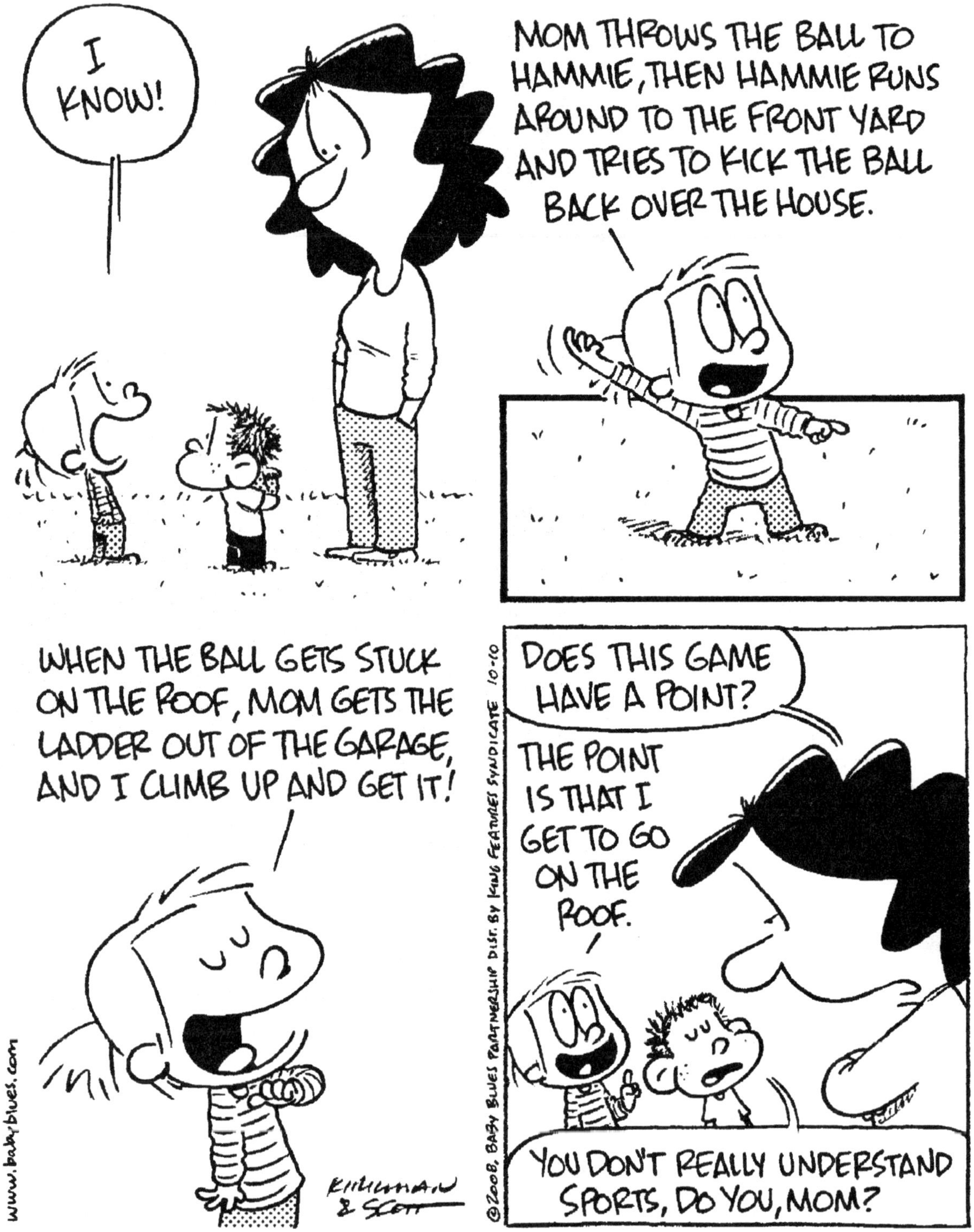
I KNOW!
MOM THROWS THE BALL TO HAMMIE, THEN HAMMIE RUNS AROUND TO THE FRONT YARD AND TRIES TO KICK THE BALL BACK OVER THE HOUSE.
WHEN THE BALL GETS STUCK ON THE ROOF, MOM GETS THE LADDER OUT OF THE GARAGE, AND I CLIMB UP AND GET IT!
DOES THIS GAME HAVE A POINT?
THE POINT IS THAT I GET TO GO ON THE ROOF.
YOU DON'T REALLY UNDERSTAND SPORTS, DO YOU, MOM?
KIRKMAN & SCOTT
www.babyblues.com
©2008, BABY BLUES PARTNERSHIP DIST. BY KING FEATURES SYNDICATE 10-10

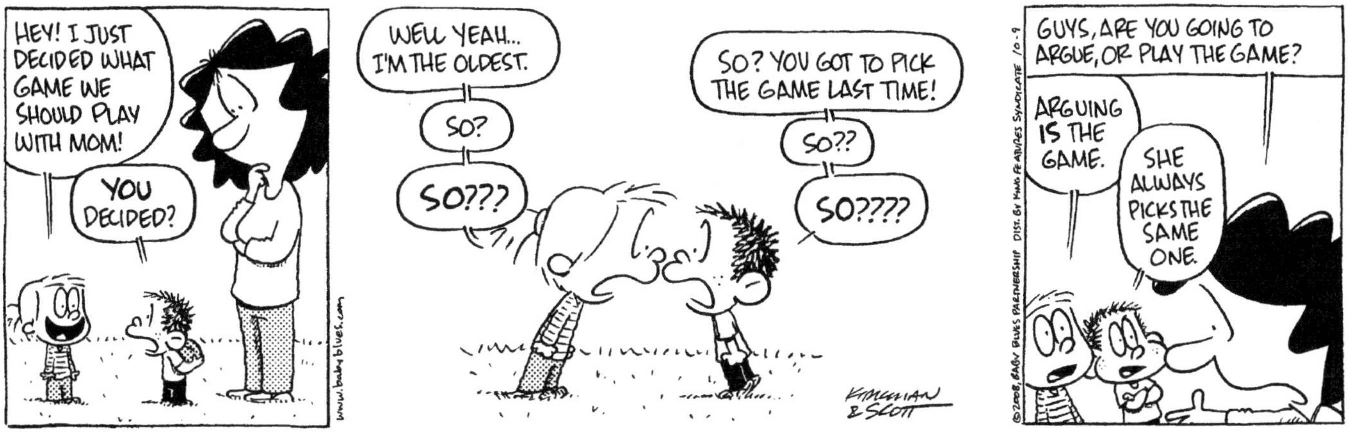
HEY! I JUST DECIDED WHAT GAME WE SHOULD PLAY WITH MOM!
YOU DECIDED?
www.babyblues.com
WELL YEAH... I'M THE OLDEST.
SO?
SO???
SO? YOU GOT TO PICK THE GAME LAST TIME!
SO??
SO????
KIRKMAN & SCOTT
© 2008, BABY BLUES PARTNERSHIP DIST. BY KING FEATURES SYNDICATE 10-9
GUYS, ARE YOU GOING TO ARGUE, OR PLAY THE GAME?
ARGUING IS THE GAME.
SHE ALWAYS PICKS THE SAME ONE.

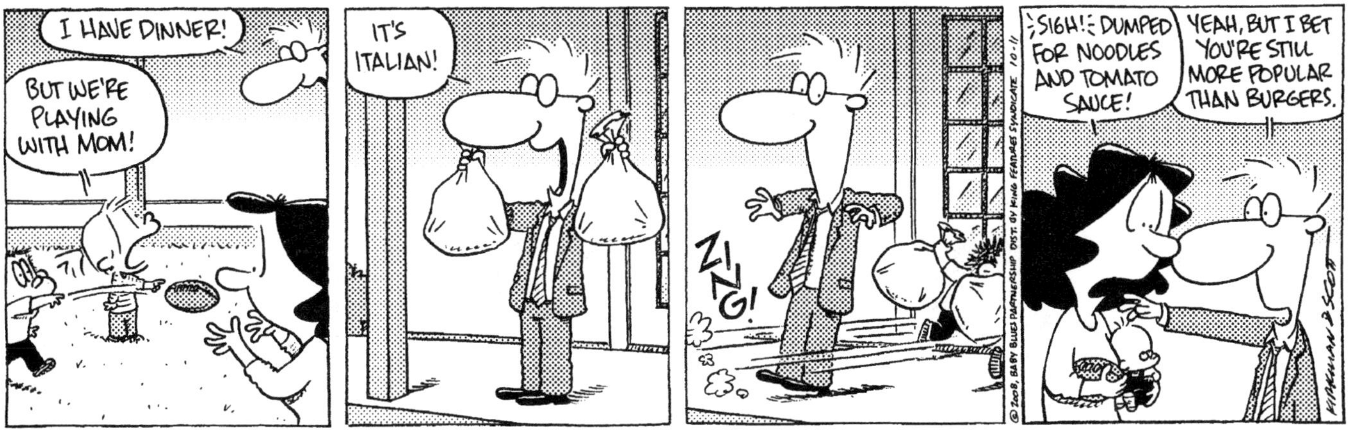
I HAVE DINNER!
BUT WE'RE PLAYING WITH MOM!
IT'S ITALIAN!
ZING!
© 2008, BABY BLUES PARTNERSHIP DIST. BY KING FEATURES SYNDICATE 10-11
SIGH! DUMPED FOR NOODLES AND TOMATO SAUCE!
YEAH, BUT I BET YOU'RE STILL MORE POPULAR THAN BURGERS.
KIRKMAN & SCOTT

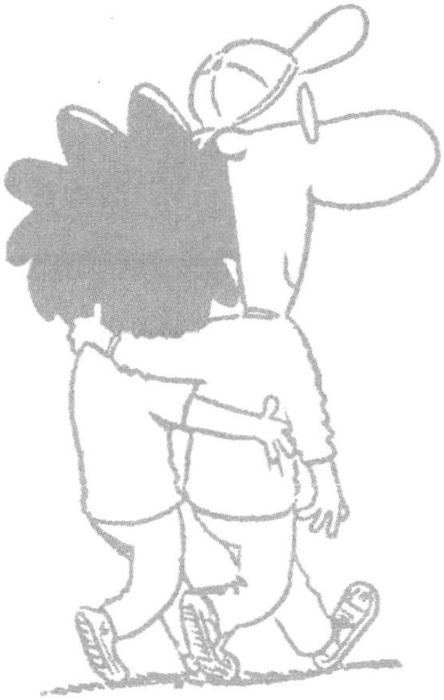

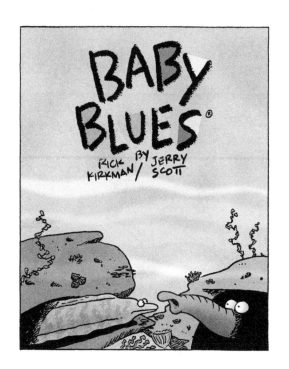

LOOK WHAT I PAINTED IN ART CLASS.

WHAT IS IT?

CAN'T YOU TELL?

WELL, IT KIND OF LOOKS LIKE AN EEL...

ZOE! TELL MOM WHAT IT IS!

MOM'S RIGHT. I THINK IT'S AN EEL, TOO.

I CAN'T BELIEVE THIS!

BELIEVE WHAT?

10-12

DAD, WILL YOU TELL THESE TWO AMATEURS WHAT I PAINTED HERE?

IT'S AN ELEPHANT.

www.babyblues.com

THANK YOU! AT LEAST SOMEBODY AROUND HERE APPRECIATES QUALITY ART!

HOW DID YOU KNOW WHAT IT WAS??

ALL OF HIS ELEPHANTS LOOK LIKE EELS.

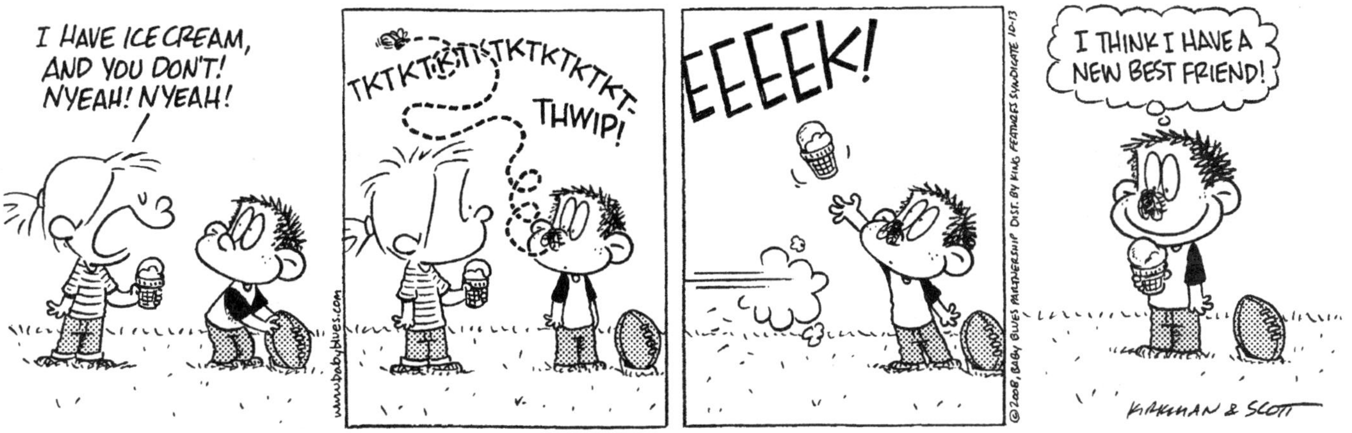
I HAVE ICE CREAM, AND YOU DON'T! NYEAH! NYEAH!
www.babyblues.com
TKTKTKTKTKTKTKTKTKTKT-
THWIP!
EEEEK!
© 2008, BABY BLUES PARTNERSHIP DIST. BY KING FEATURES SYNDICATE 10-13
I THINK I HAVE A NEW BEST FRIEND!
KIRKMAN & SCOTT

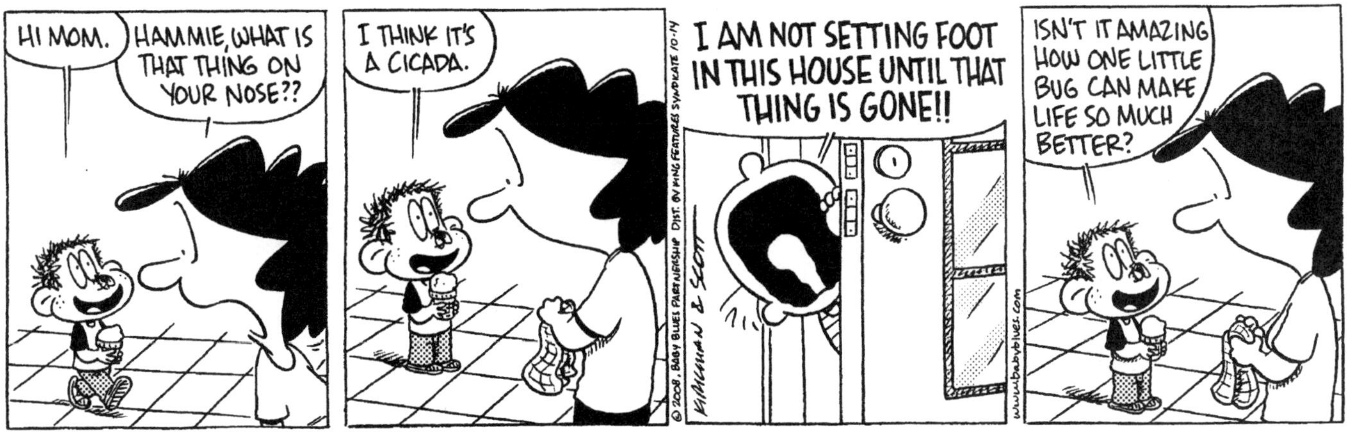
HI MOM.
HAMMIE, WHAT IS THAT THING ON YOUR NOSE??
I THINK IT'S A CICADA.
© 2008, BABY BLUES PARTNERSHIP DIST. BY KING FEATURES SYNDICATE 10-14
KIRKMAN & SCOTT
I AM NOT SETTING FOOT IN THIS HOUSE UNTIL THAT THING IS GONE!!
www.babyblues.com
ISN'T IT AMAZING HOW ONE LITTLE BUG CAN MAKE LIFE SO MUCH BETTER?

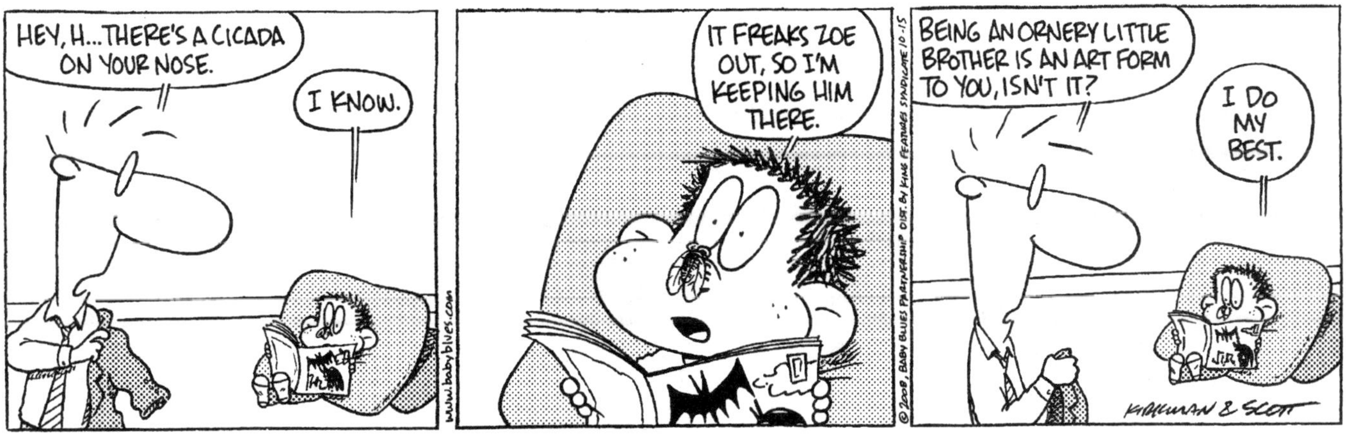
HEY, H...THERE'S A CICADA ON YOUR NOSE.
I KNOW.
www.babyblues.com
IT FREAKS ZOE OUT, SO I'M KEEPING HIM THERE.
© 2008, BABY BLUES PARTNERSHIP DIST. BY KING FEATURES SYNDICATE 10-15
BEING AN ORNERY LITTLE BROTHER IS AN ART FORM TO YOU, ISN'T IT?
I DO MY BEST.
KIRKMAN & SCOTT

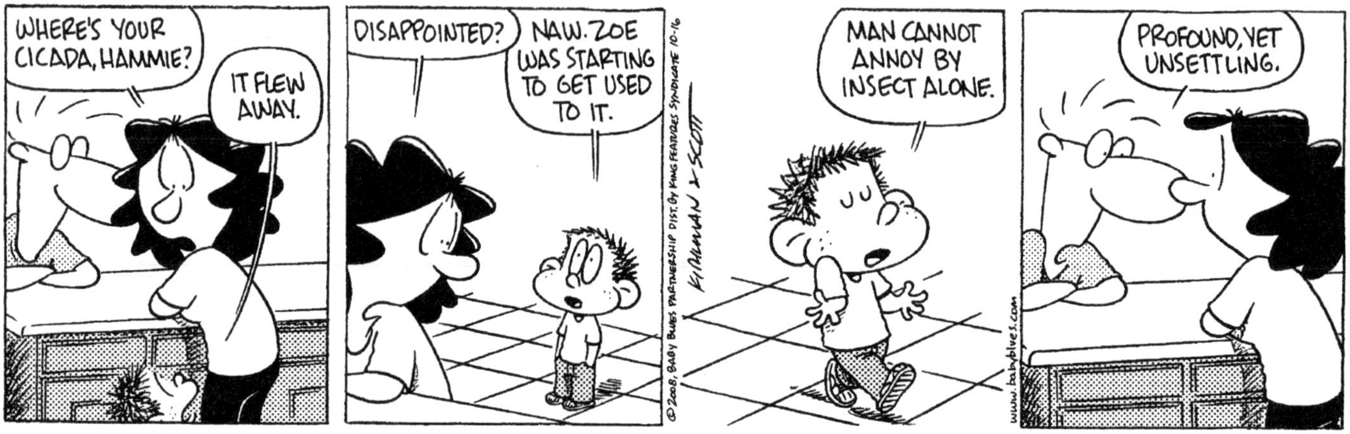
WHERE'S YOUR CICADA, HAMMIE?
IT FLEW AWAY.
DISAPPOINTED?
NAW. ZOE WAS STARTING TO GET USED TO IT.
© 2008, BABY BLUES PARTNERSHIP DIST. BY KING FEATURES SYNDICATE 10-16
KIRKMAN & SCOTT
MAN CANNOT ANNOY BY INSECT ALONE.
www.babyblues.com
PROFOUND, YET UNSETTLING.

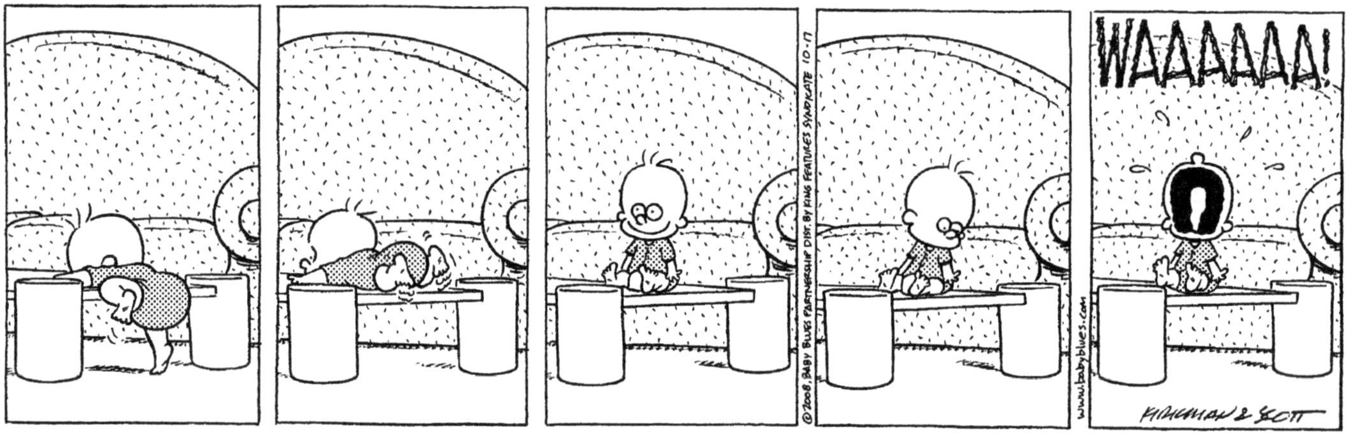
© 2008, BABY BLUES PARTNERSHIP DIST. BY KING FEATURES SYNDICATE 10-17
www.babyblues.com
WAAAAAA!
KIRKMAN & SCOTT

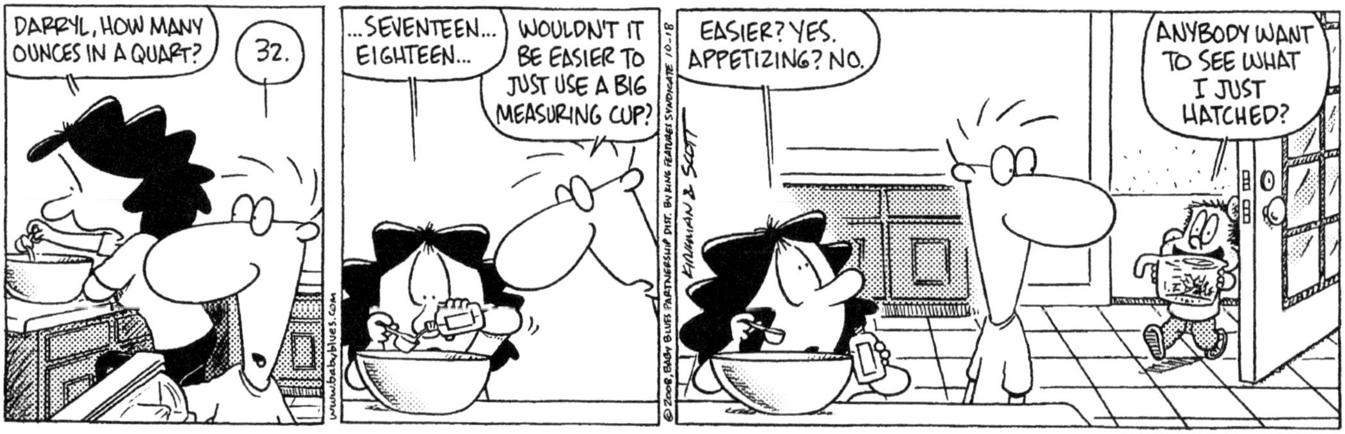
DARRYL, HOW MANY OUNCES IN A QUART?
32.
www.babyblues.com
...SEVENTEEN... EIGHTEEN...
WOULDN'T IT BE EASIER TO JUST USE A BIG MEASURING CUP?
© 2008, BABY BLUES PARTNERSHIP DIST. BY KING FEATURES SYNDICATE 10-18
KIRKMAN & SCOTT
EASIER? YES. APPETIZING? NO.
ANYBODY WANT TO SEE WHAT I JUST HATCHED?

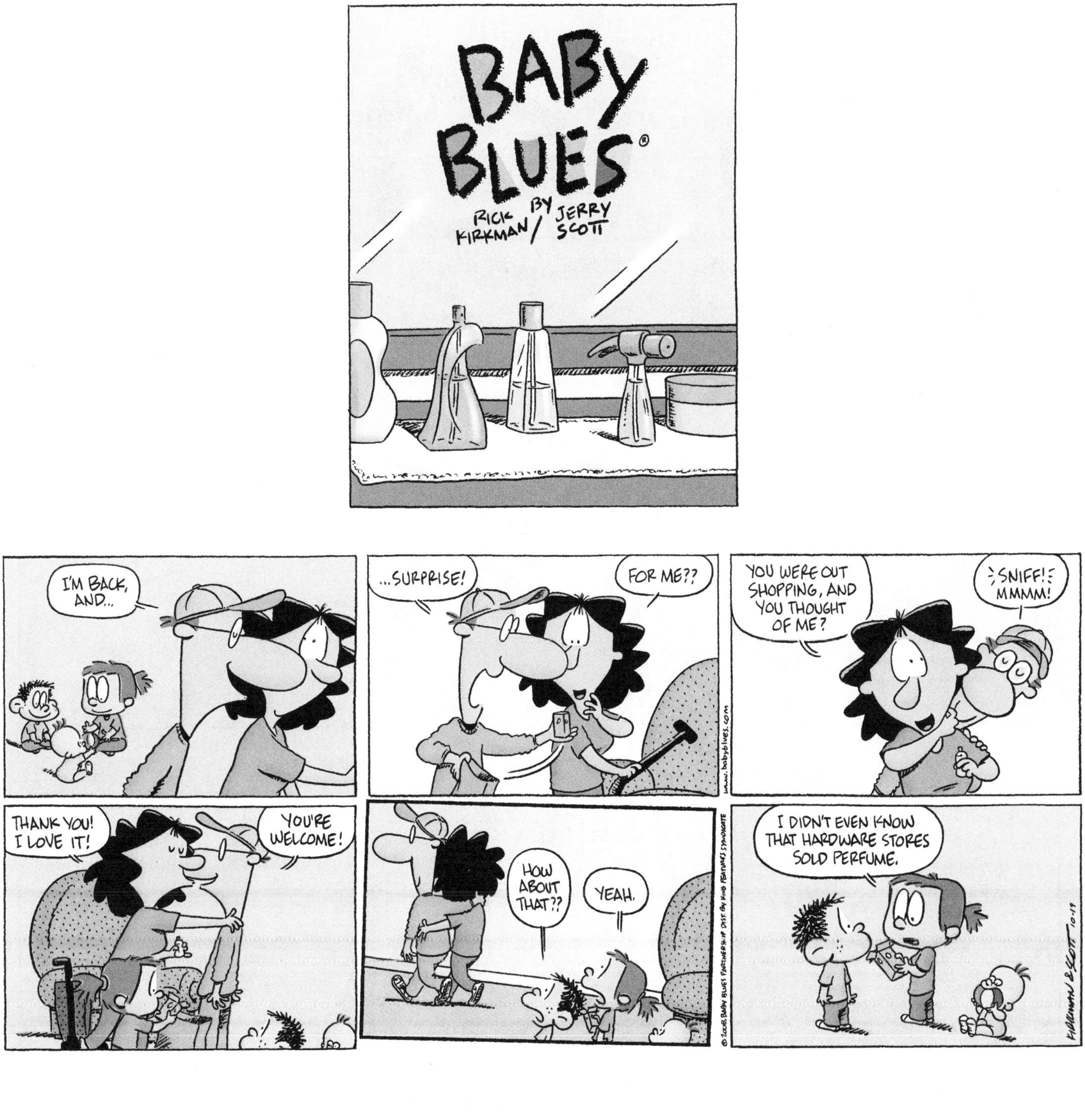
BABY BLUES®
BY RICK KIRKMAN / JERRY SCOTT
I'M BACK, AND...
...SURPRISE!
FOR ME??
YOU WERE OUT SHOPPING, AND YOU THOUGHT OF ME?
SNIFF! MMMM!
www.babyblues.com
THANK YOU! I LOVE IT!
YOU'RE WELCOME!
HOW ABOUT THAT??
YEAH.
© 2008, BABY BLUES PARTNERSHIP DIST. BY KING FEATURES SYNDICATE
I DIDN'T EVEN KNOW THAT HARDWARE STORES SOLD PERFUME.
KIRKMAN & SCOTT 10-19

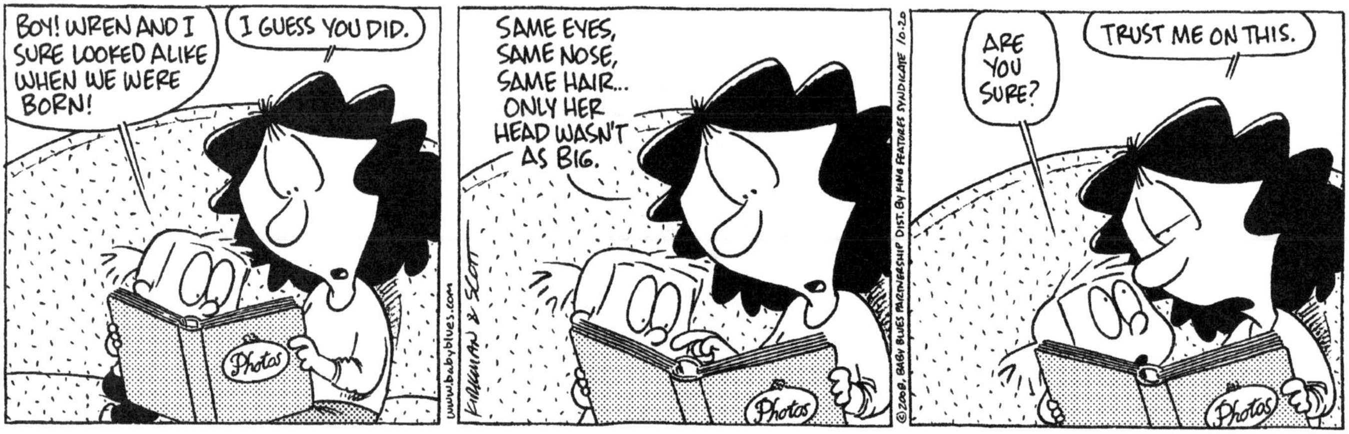
BOY! WREN AND I SURE LOOKED ALIKE WHEN WE WERE BORN!
I GUESS YOU DID.
www.babyblues.com
KIRKMAN & SCOTT
SAME EYES, SAME NOSE, SAME HAIR... ONLY HER HEAD WASN'T AS BIG.
© 2008, BABY BLUES PARTNERSHIP DIST. BY KING FEATURES SYNDICATE 10-20
ARE YOU SURE?
TRUST ME ON THIS.

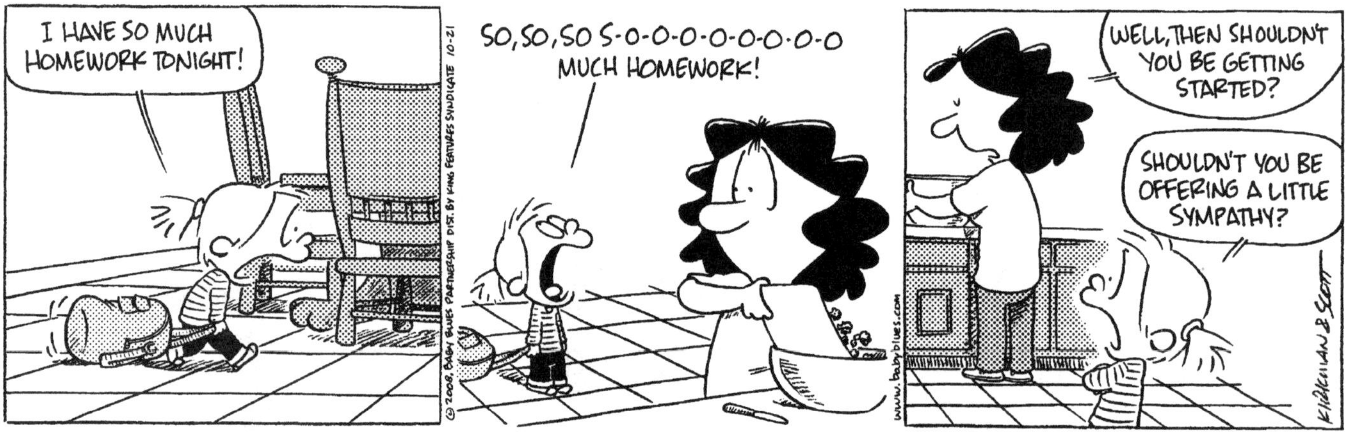
I HAVE SO MUCH HOMEWORK TONIGHT!
© 2008, BABY BLUES PARTNERSHIP DIST. BY KING FEATURES SYNDICATE 10-21
SO, SO, SO S-O-O-O-O-O-O-O-O-O MUCH HOMEWORK!
www.babyblues.com
WELL, THEN SHOULDN'T YOU BE GETTING STARTED?
SHOULDN'T YOU BE OFFERING A LITTLE SYMPATHY?
KIRKMAN & SCOTT

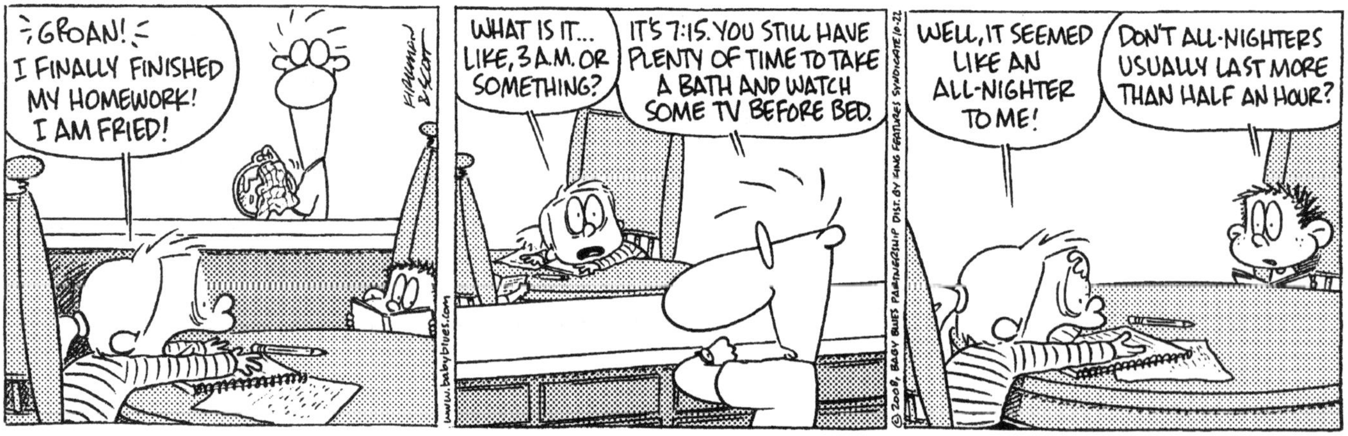
GROAN!
I FINALLY FINISHED MY HOMEWORK! I AM FRIED!
KIRKMAN & SCOTT
www.babyblues.com
WHAT IS IT... LIKE, 3 A.M. OR SOMETHING?
IT'S 7:15. YOU STILL HAVE PLENTY OF TIME TO TAKE A BATH AND WATCH SOME TV BEFORE BED.
© 2008, BABY BLUES PARTNERSHIP DIST. BY KING FEATURES SYNDICATE 10-22
WELL, IT SEEMED LIKE AN ALL-NIGHTER TO ME!
DON'T ALL-NIGHTERS USUALLY LAST MORE THAN HALF AN HOUR?

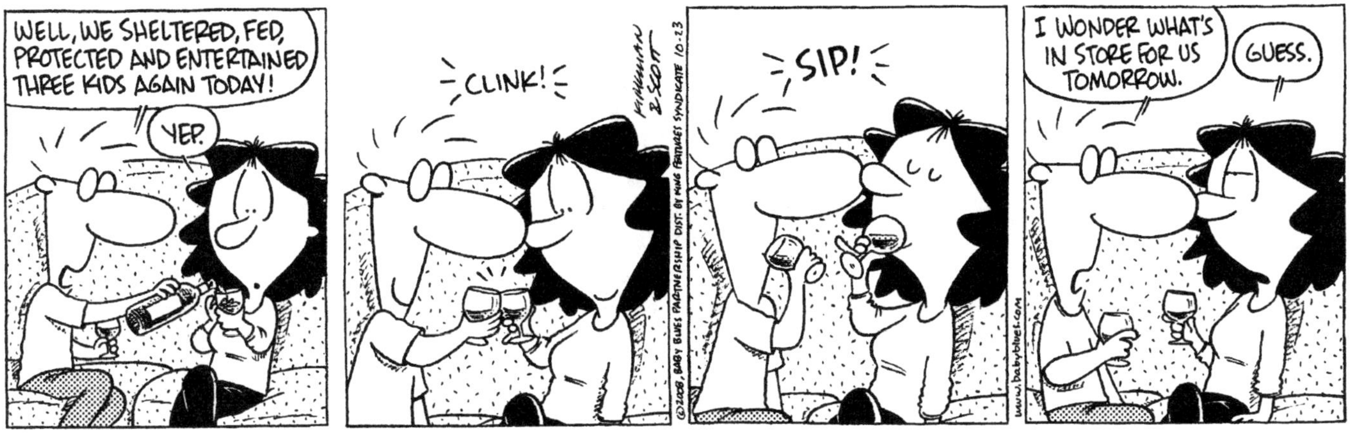
WELL, WE SHELTERED, FED, PROTECTED AND ENTERTAINED THREE KIDS AGAIN TODAY!
YEP.
CLINK!
KIRKMAN & SCOTT 10-23
©2008, BABY BLUES PARTNERSHIP DIST. BY KING FEATURES SYNDICATE
SIP!
www.babyblues.com
I WONDER WHAT'S IN STORE FOR US TOMORROW.
GUESS.

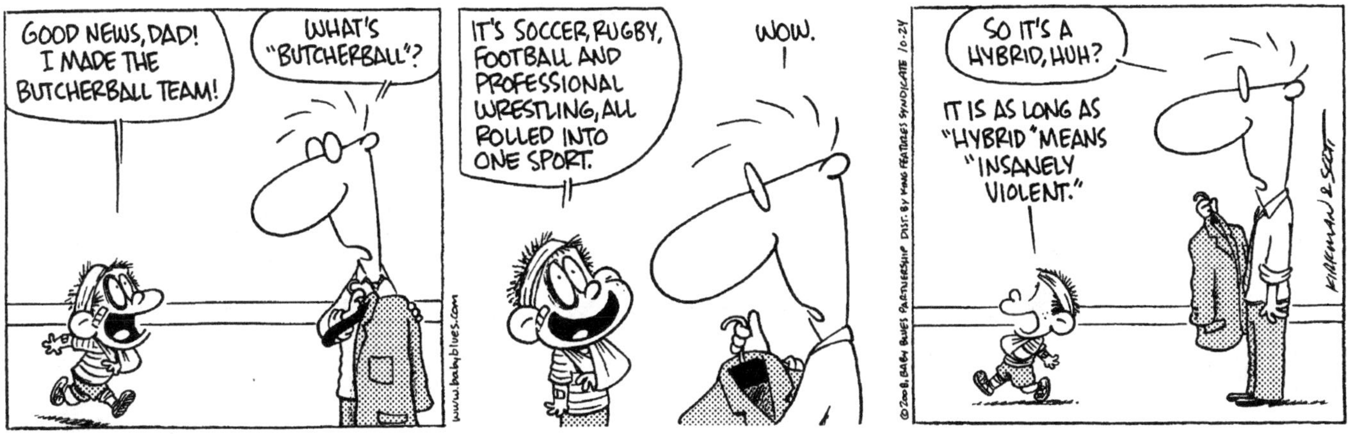
GOOD NEWS, DAD! I MADE THE BUTCHERBALL TEAM!
WHAT'S "BUTCHERBALL"?
www.babyblues.com
IT'S SOCCER, RUGBY, FOOTBALL AND PROFESSIONAL WRESTLING, ALL ROLLED INTO ONE SPORT.
WOW.
©2008, BABY BLUES PARTNERSHIP DIST. BY KING FEATURES SYNDICATE 10-24
SO IT'S A HYBRID, HUH?
IT IS AS LONG AS "HYBRID" MEANS "INSANELY VIOLENT."
KIRKMAN & SCOTT

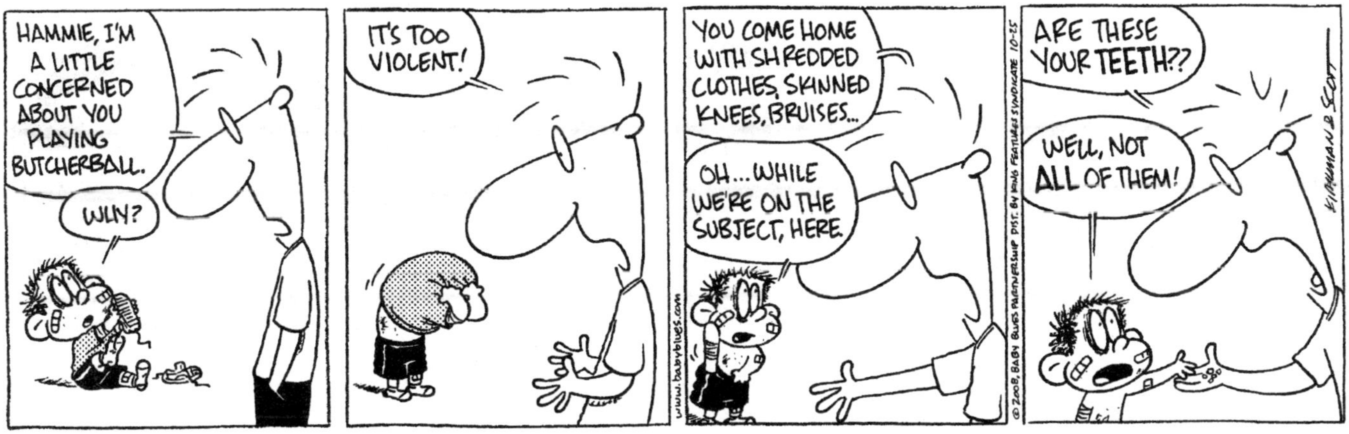
HAMMIE, I'M A LITTLE CONCERNED ABOUT YOU PLAYING BUTCHERBALL.
WHY?
IT'S TOO VIOLENT!
www.babyblues.com
YOU COME HOME WITH SHREDDED CLOTHES, SKINNED KNEES, BRUISES...
OH... WHILE WE'RE ON THE SUBJECT, HERE.
©2008, BABY BLUES PARTNERSHIP DIST. BY KING FEATURES SYNDICATE 10-25
ARE THESE YOUR TEETH??
WELL, NOT ALL OF THEM!
KIRKMAN & SCOTT

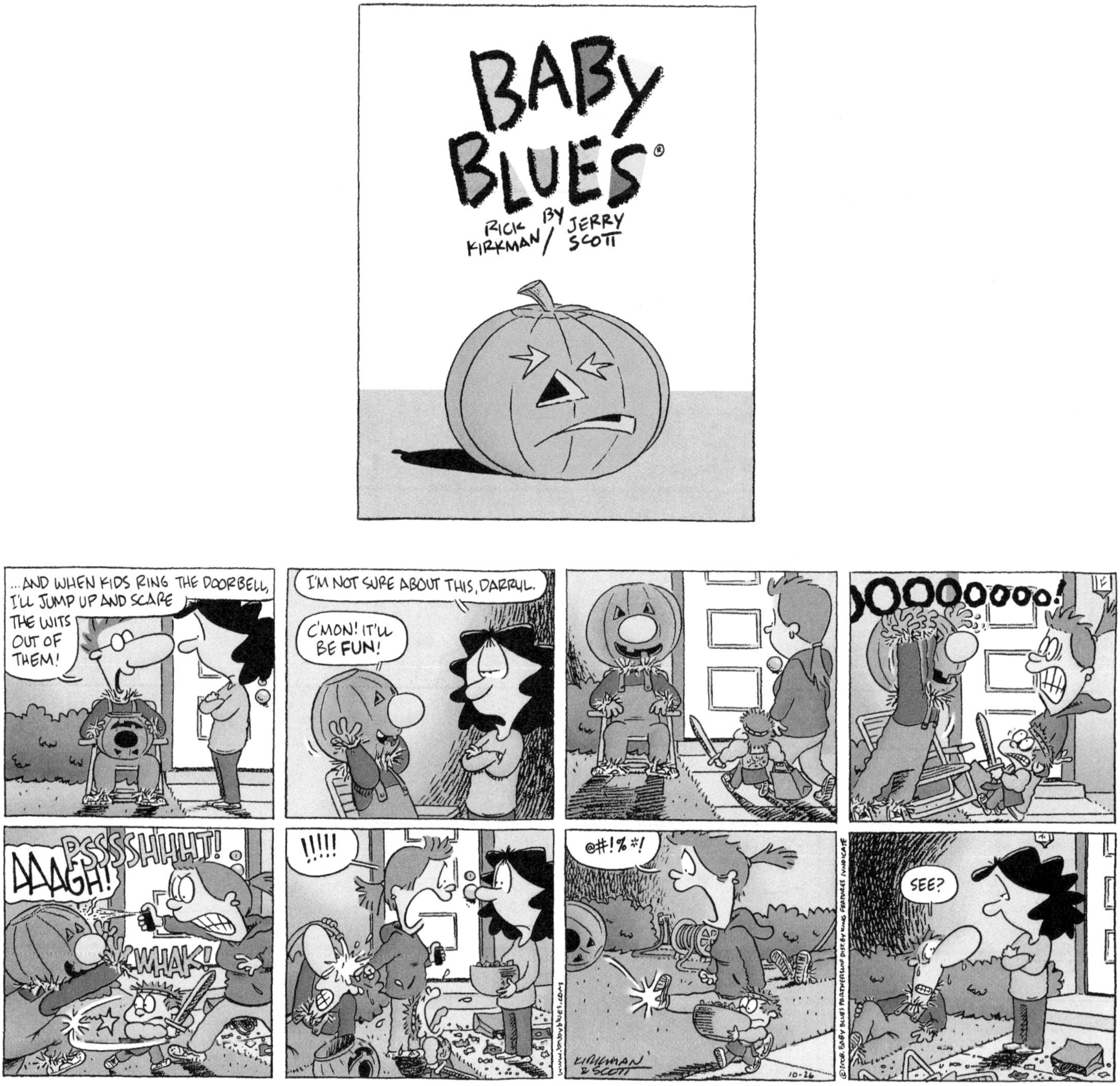
BABY BLUES®
BY RICK KIRKMAN / JERRY SCOTT
...AND WHEN KIDS RING THE DOORBELL, I'LL JUMP UP AND SCARE THE WITS OUT OF THEM!
I'M NOT SURE ABOUT THIS, DARRYL.
C'MON! IT'LL BE FUN!
OOOOOOOO!
AAAGH!
PSSSSHHHT!
WHAK!
!!!!!
@#!%*!
KIRKMAN & SCOTT
10-26
SEE?

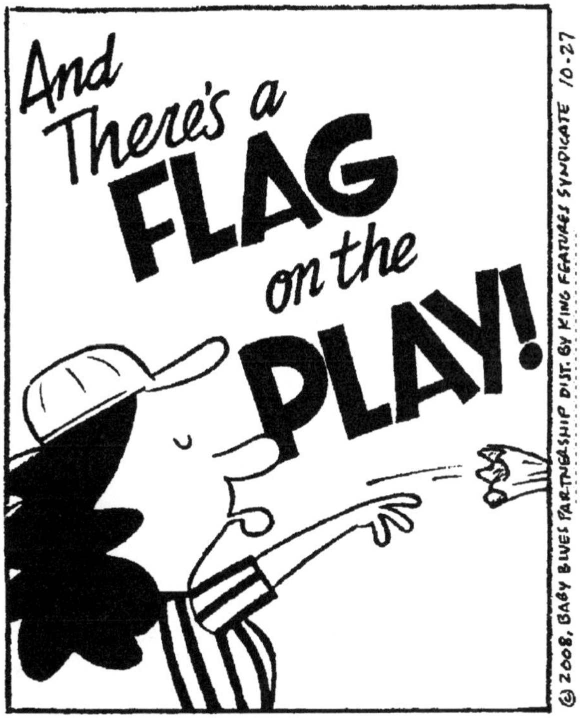
And There's a FLAG on the PLAY!
© 2008, BABY BLUES PARTNERSHIP DIST. BY KING FEATURES SYNDICATE 10-27

Clipping

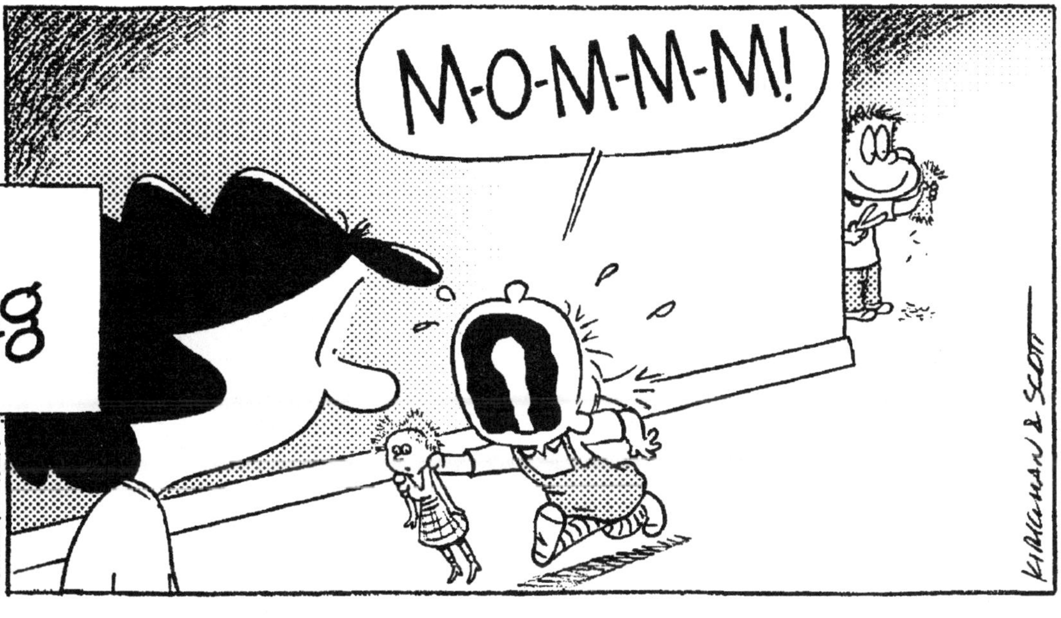
M-O-M-M-M!
www.babyblues.com
KIRKMAN & SCOTT

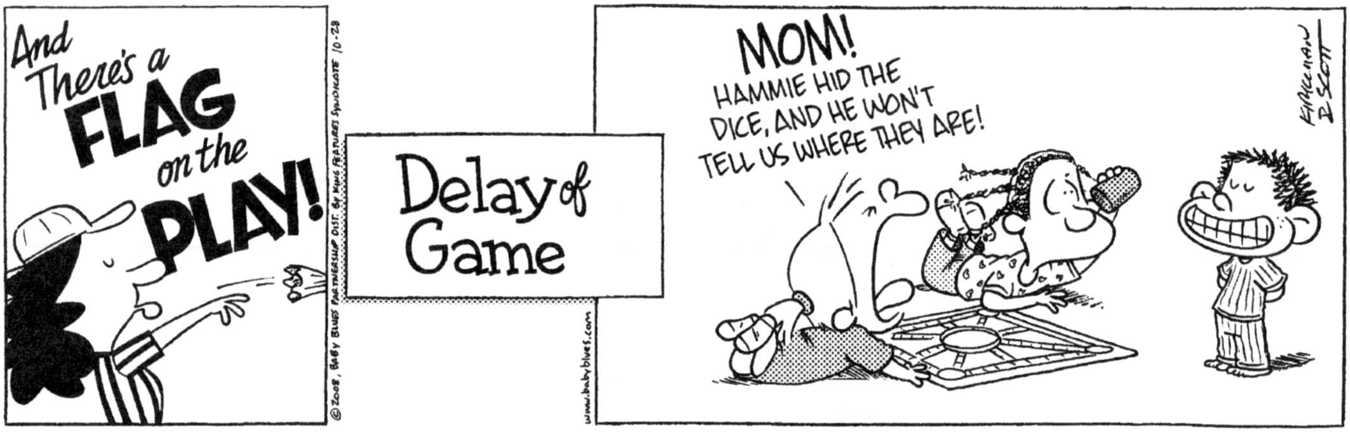
And There's a FLAG on the PLAY!
© 2008, Baby Blues Partnership Dist. by King Features Syndicate 10-28
Delay of Game
www.babyblues.com
MOM!
HAMMIE HID THE DICE, AND HE WON'T TELL US WHERE THEY ARE!
KIRKMAN & SCOTT

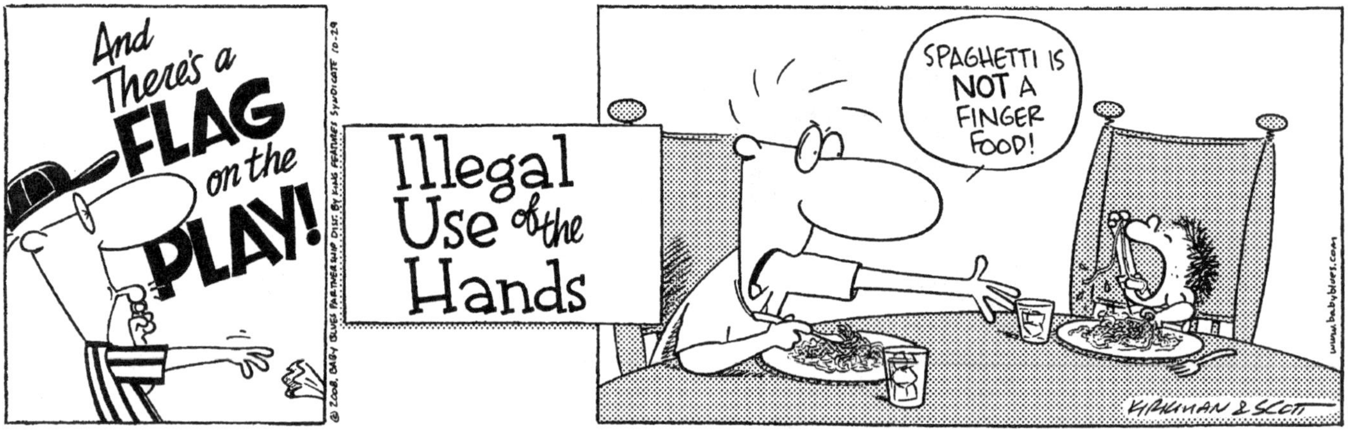
And There's a FLAG on the PLAY!
© 2008, Baby Blues Partnership Dist. by King Features Syndicate 10-29
Illegal Use of the Hands
SPAGHETTI IS NOT A FINGER FOOD!
www.babyblues.com
KIRKMAN & SCOTT

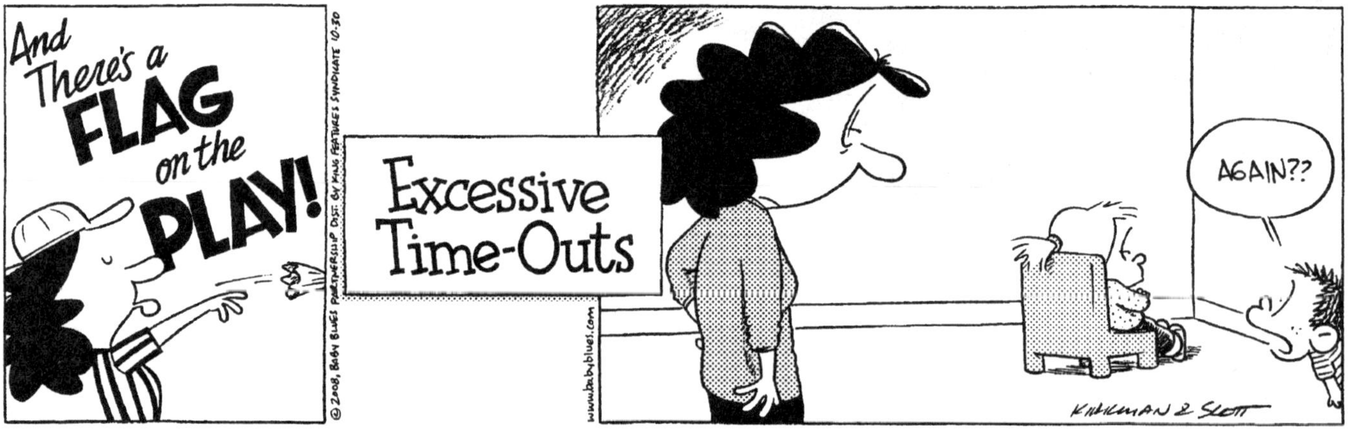
And There's a FLAG on the PLAY!
© 2008, Baby Blues Partnership Dist. by King Features Syndicate 10-30
Excessive Time-Outs
www.babyblues.com
AGAIN??
KIRKMAN & SCOTT

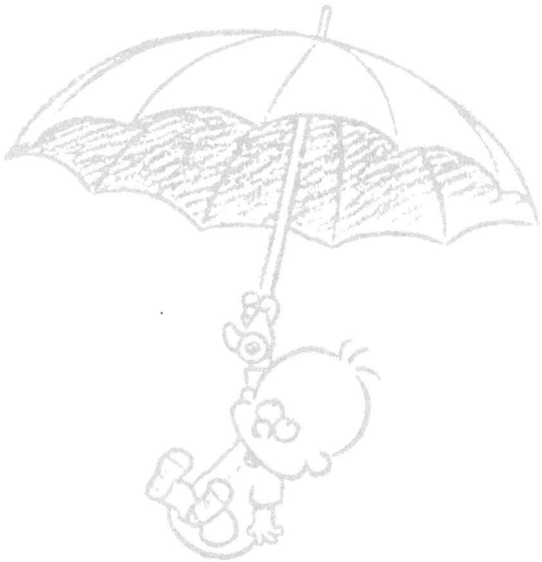

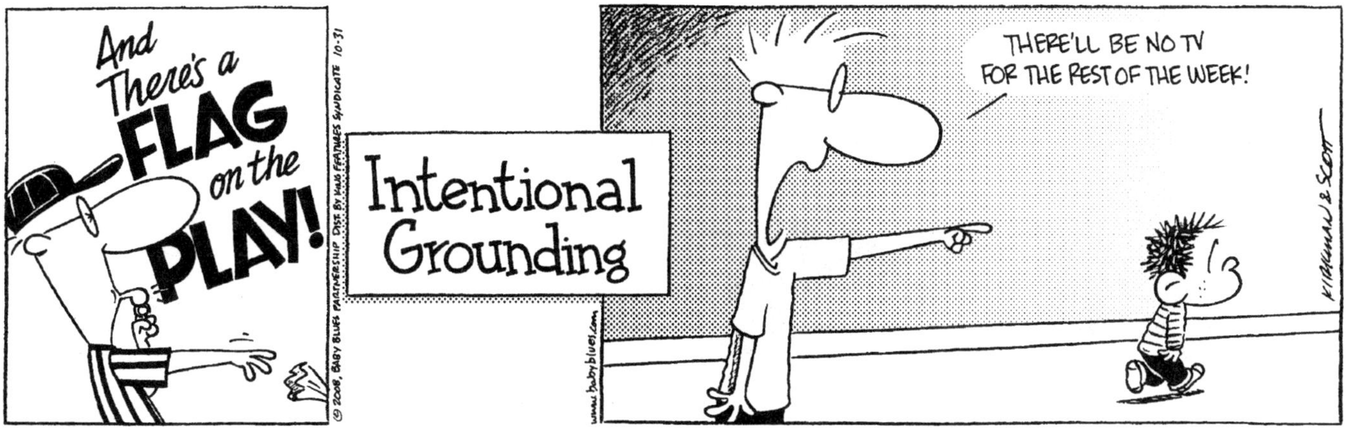
And There's a FLAG on the PLAY!
Intentional Grounding
THERE'LL BE NO TV FOR THE REST OF THE WEEK!
© 2008, BABY BLUES PARTNERSHIP DIST. BY KING FEATURES SYNDICATE 10-31
www.babyblues.com
KIRKMAN & SCOTT

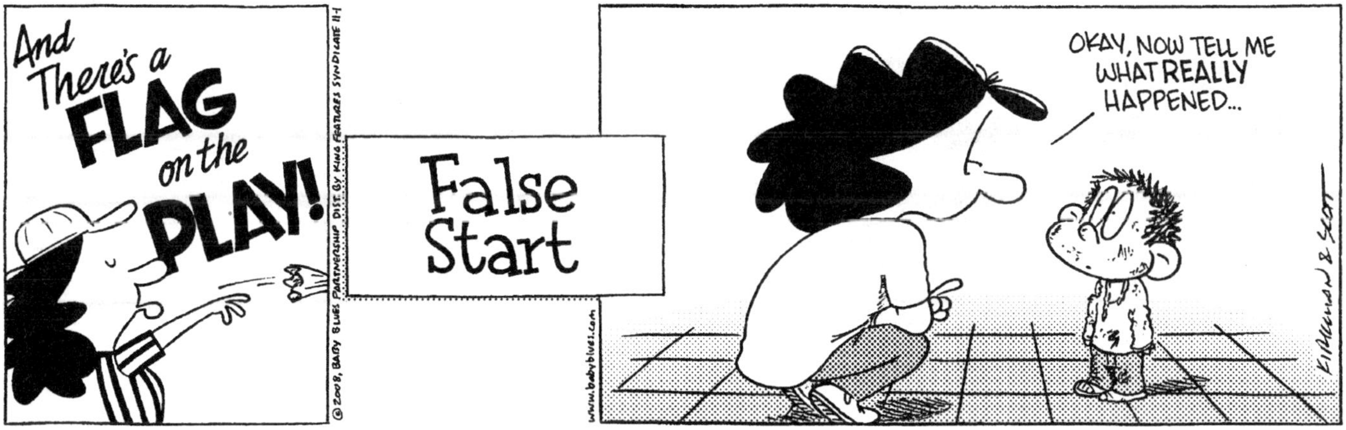
And There's a FLAG on the PLAY!
False Start
OKAY, NOW TELL ME WHAT REALLY HAPPENED...
© 2008, BABY BLUES PARTNERSHIP DIST. BY KING FEATURES SYNDICATE 11-1
www.babyblues.com
KIRKMAN & SCOTT

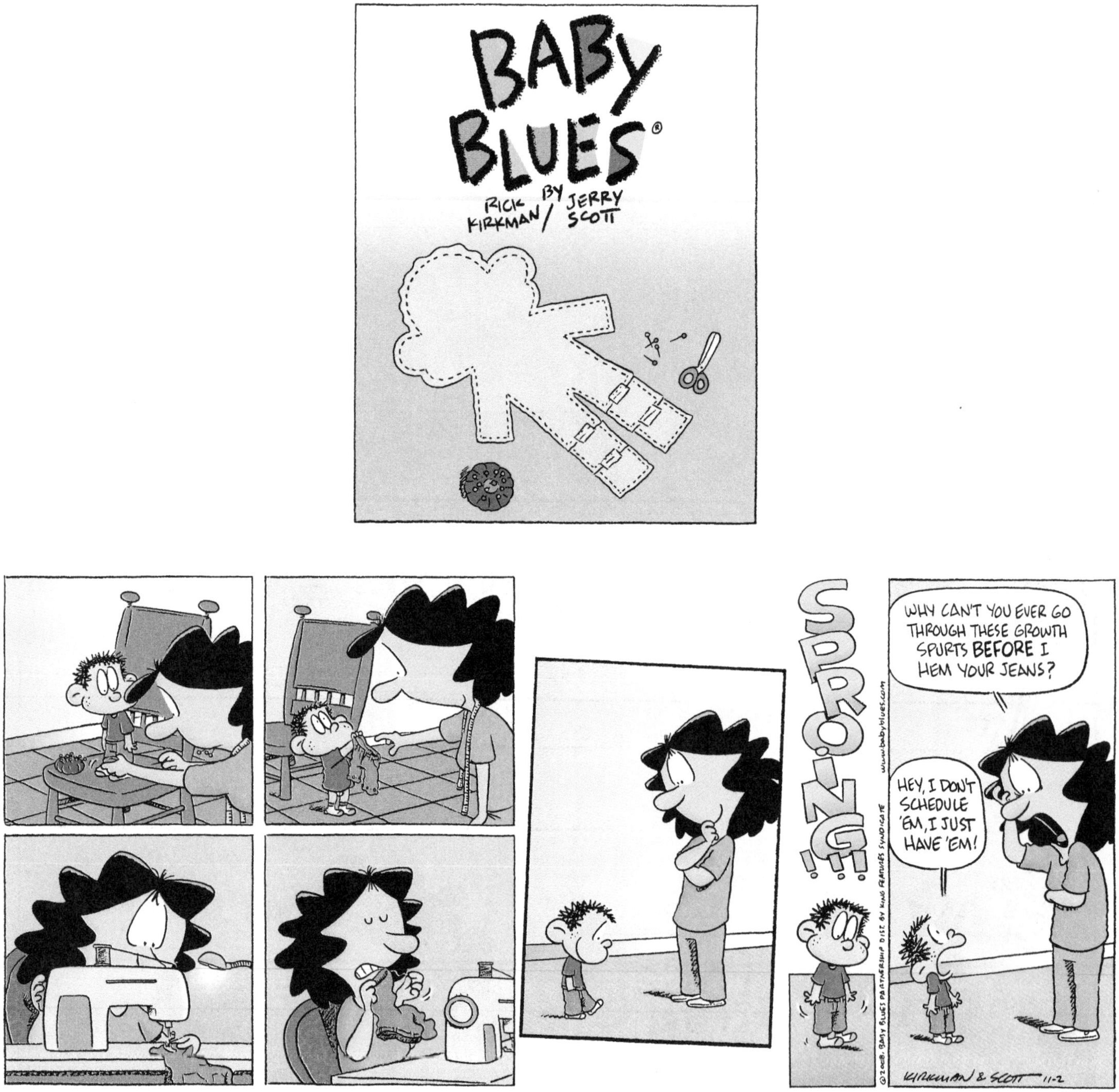
BABY BLUES®
BY RICK KIRKMAN / JERRY SCOTT
SPROING!!!
WHY CAN'T YOU EVER GO THROUGH THESE GROWTH SPURTS BEFORE I HEM YOUR JEANS?
HEY, I DON'T SCHEDULE 'EM, I JUST HAVE 'EM!
©2008, BABY BLUES PARTNERSHIP DIST. BY KING FEATURES SYNDICATE
www.babyblues.com
KIRKMAN & SCOTT 11-2

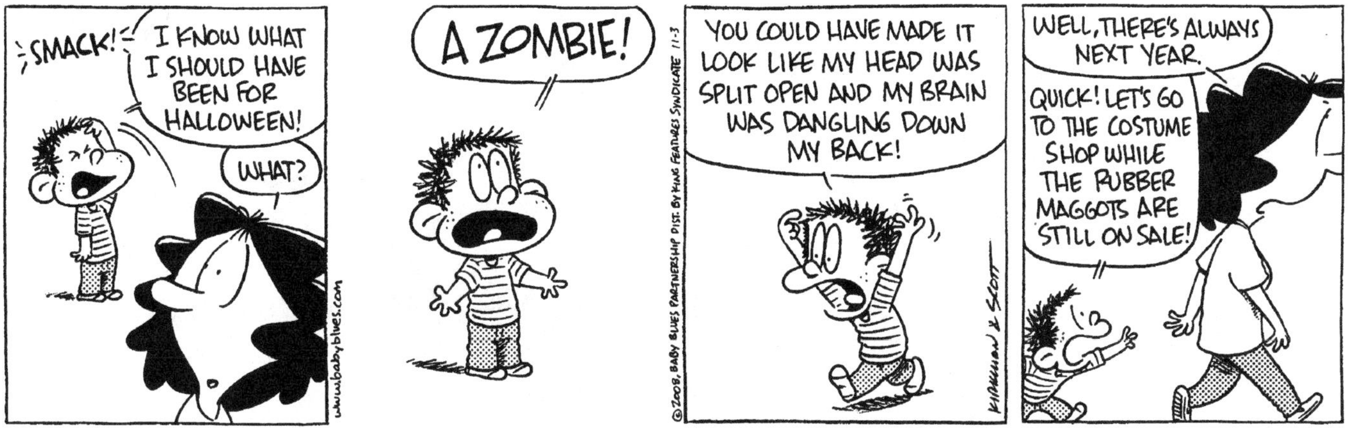
SMACK!
I KNOW WHAT I SHOULD HAVE BEEN FOR HALLOWEEN!
WHAT?
www.babyblues.com
A ZOMBIE!
©2008, BABY BLUES PARTNERSHIP DIST. BY KING FEATURES SYNDICATE 11-3
YOU COULD HAVE MADE IT LOOK LIKE MY HEAD WAS SPLIT OPEN AND MY BRAIN WAS DANGLING DOWN MY BACK!
KIRKMAN & SCOTT
WELL, THERE'S ALWAYS NEXT YEAR.
QUICK! LET'S GO TO THE COSTUME SHOP WHILE THE RUBBER MAGGOTS ARE STILL ON SALE!

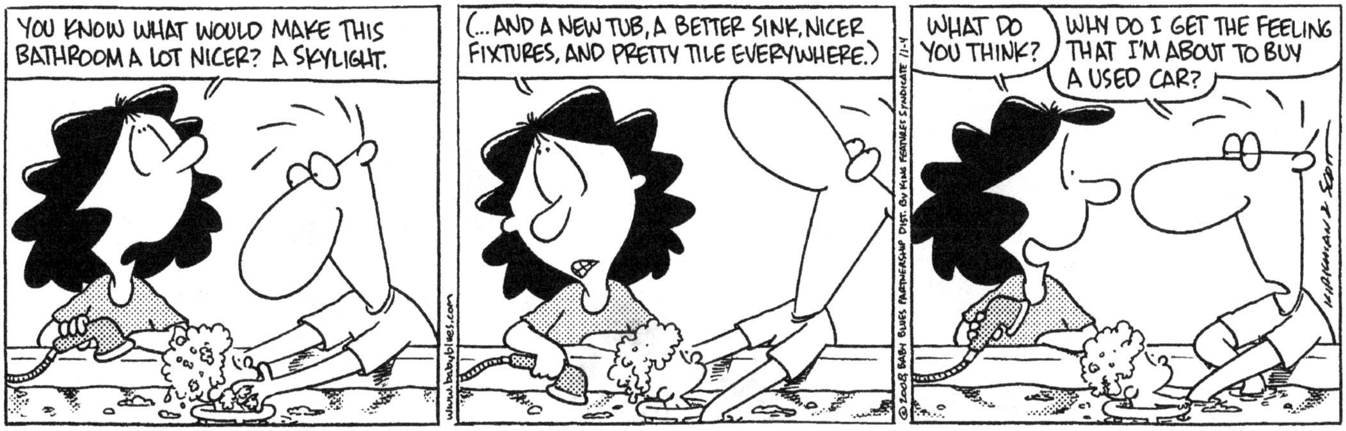
YOU KNOW WHAT WOULD MAKE THIS BATHROOM A LOT NICER? A SKYLIGHT.
www.babyblues.com
(...AND A NEW TUB, A BETTER SINK, NICER FIXTURES, AND PRETTY TILE EVERYWHERE.)
©2008, BABY BLUES PARTNERSHIP DIST. BY KING FEATURES SYNDICATE 11-4
WHAT DO YOU THINK?
WHY DO I GET THE FEELING THAT I'M ABOUT TO BUY A USED CAR?
KIRKMAN & SCOTT

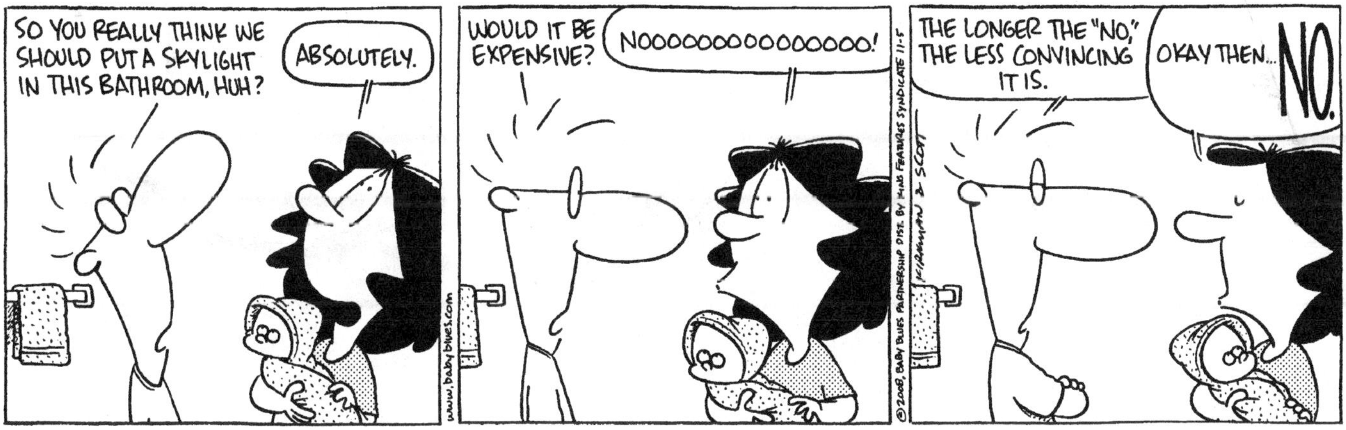
SO YOU REALLY THINK WE SHOULD PUT A SKYLIGHT IN THIS BATHROOM, HUH?
ABSOLUTELY.
www.babyblues.com
WOULD IT BE EXPENSIVE?
NOOOOOOOOOOOOOOO!
©2008, BABY BLUES PARTNERSHIP DIST. BY KING FEATURES SYNDICATE 11-5
KIRKMAN & SCOTT
THE LONGER THE "NO," THE LESS CONVINCING IT IS.
OKAY THEN... NO.

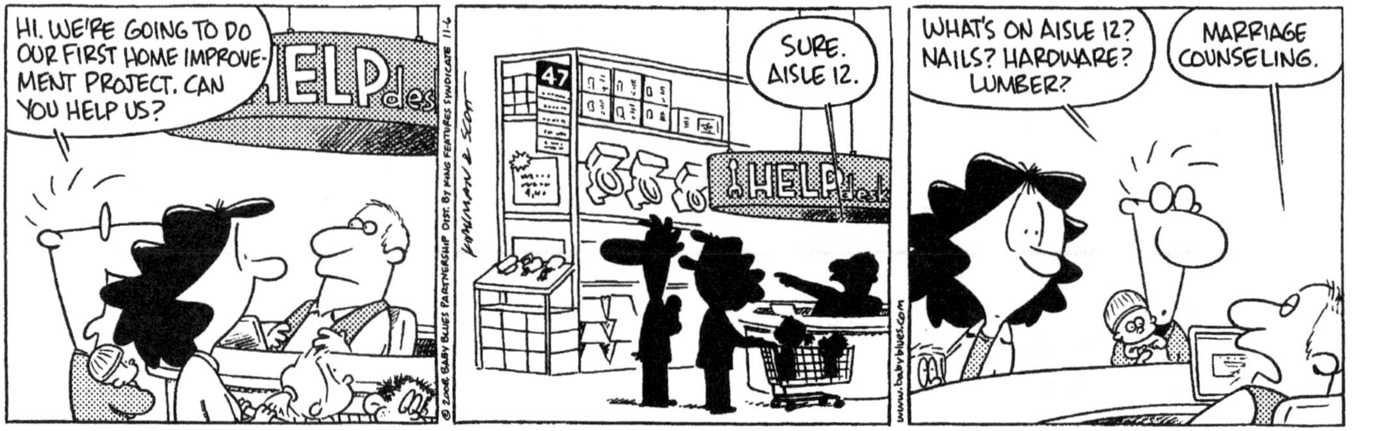
HI. WE'RE GOING TO DO OUR FIRST HOME IMPROVEMENT PROJECT. CAN YOU HELP US?
HELP desk
© 2008 BABY BLUES PARTNERSHIP DIST. BY KING FEATURES SYNDICATE 11-6
KIRKMAN & SCOTT
47
SURE. AISLE 12.
www.babyblues.com
WHAT'S ON AISLE 12? NAILS? HARDWARE? LUMBER?
MARRIAGE COUNSELING.

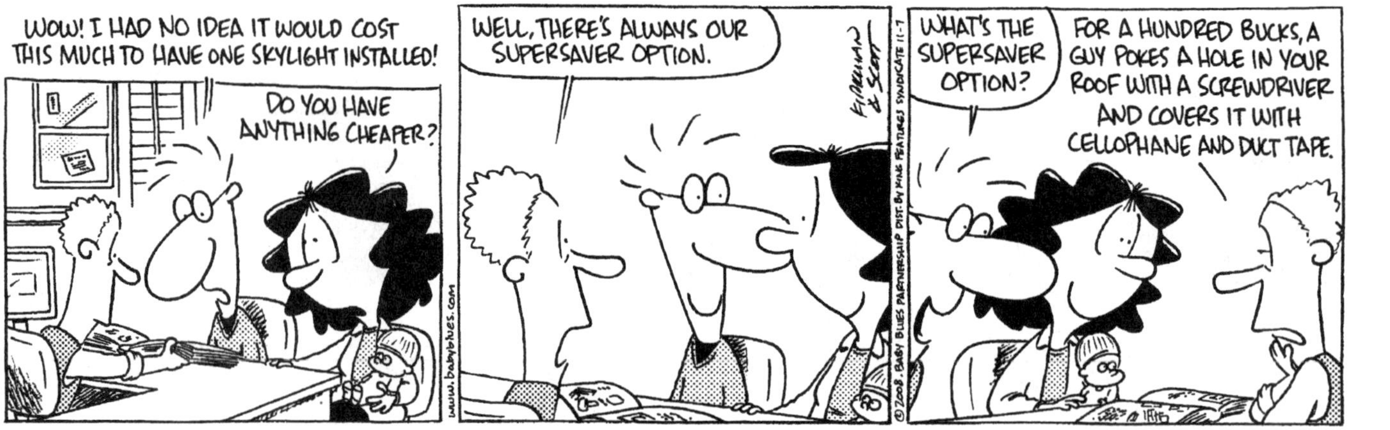
WOW! I HAD NO IDEA IT WOULD COST THIS MUCH TO HAVE ONE SKYLIGHT INSTALLED!
DO YOU HAVE ANYTHING CHEAPER?
www.babyblues.com
WELL, THERE'S ALWAYS OUR SUPERSAVER OPTION.
KIRKMAN & SCOTT
© 2008 BABY BLUES PARTNERSHIP DIST. BY KING FEATURES SYNDICATE 11-7
WHAT'S THE SUPERSAVER OPTION?
FOR A HUNDRED BUCKS, A GUY POKES A HOLE IN YOUR ROOF WITH A SCREWDRIVER AND COVERS IT WITH CELLOPHANE AND DUCT TAPE.

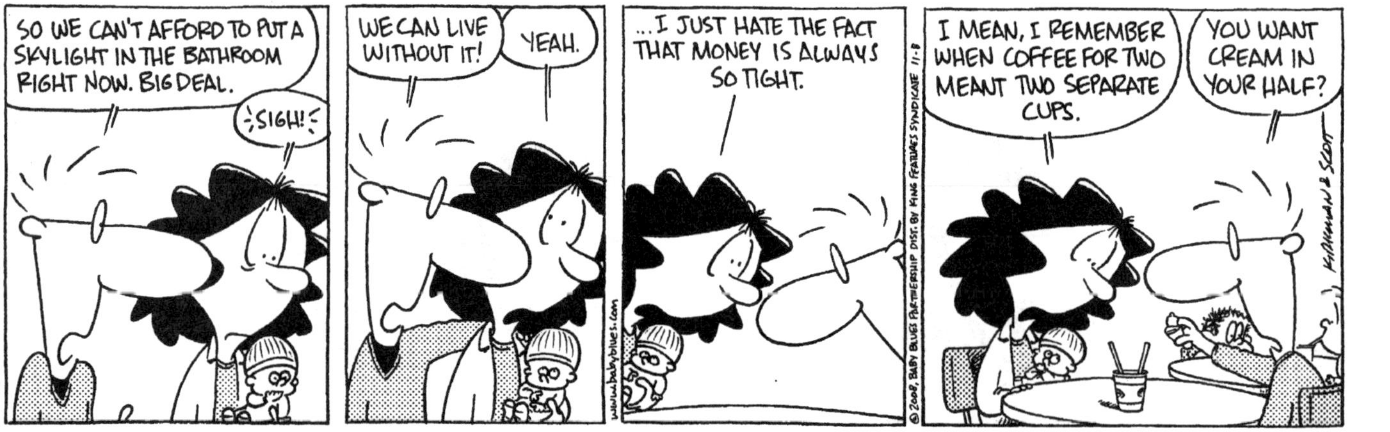
SO WE CAN'T AFFORD TO PUT A SKYLIGHT IN THE BATHROOM RIGHT NOW. BIG DEAL.
SIGH!
WE CAN LIVE WITHOUT IT!
YEAH.
www.babyblues.com
...I JUST HATE THE FACT THAT MONEY IS ALWAYS SO TIGHT.
© 2008 BABY BLUES PARTNERSHIP DIST. BY KING FEATURES SYNDICATE 11-8
I MEAN, I REMEMBER WHEN COFFEE FOR TWO MEANT TWO SEPARATE CUPS.
YOU WANT CREAM IN YOUR HALF?
KIRKMAN & SCOTT

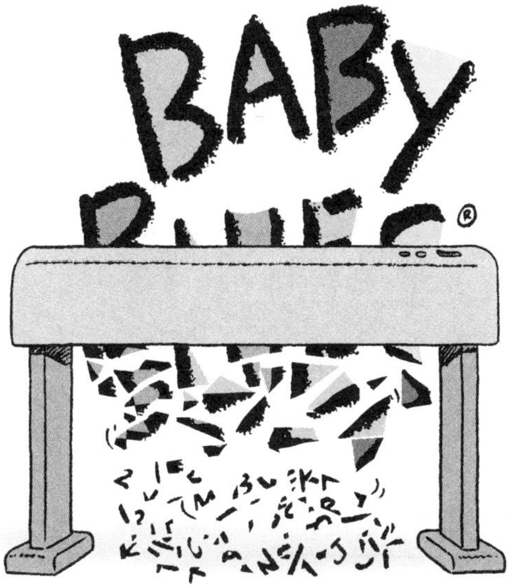
BABY BLUES®

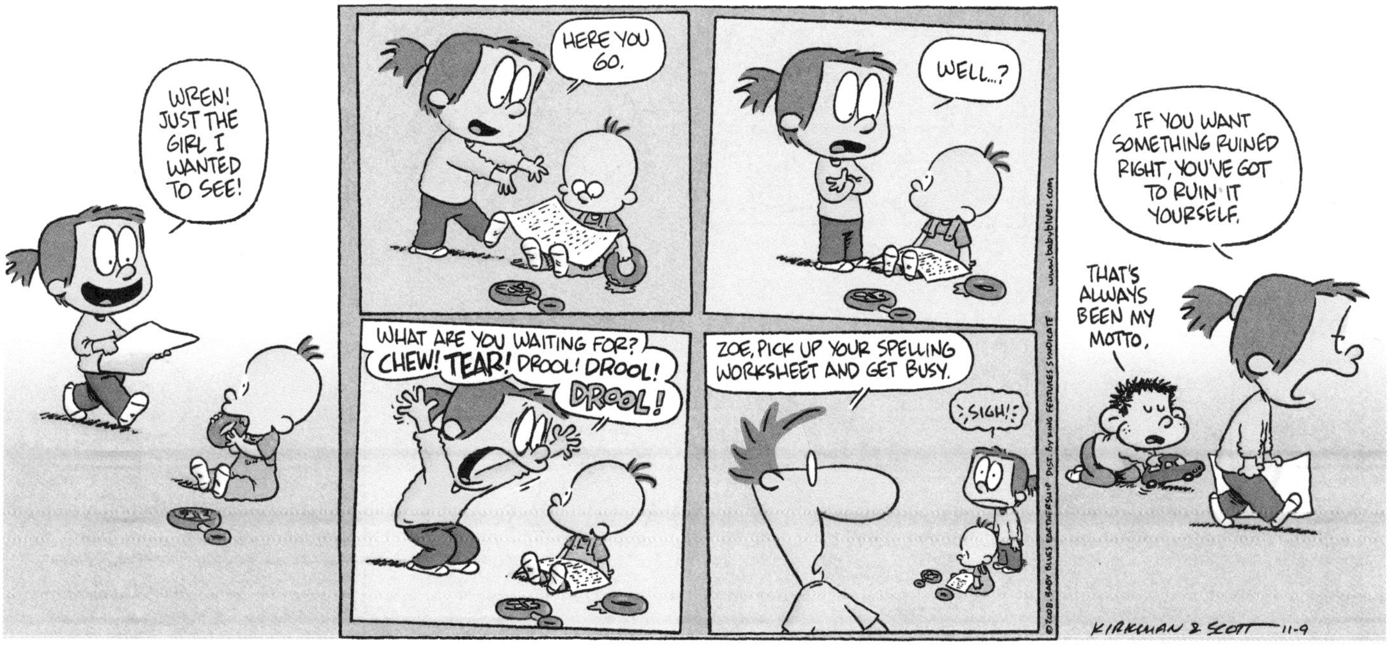
WREN! JUST THE GIRL I WANTED TO SEE!
HERE YOU GO.
WELL...?
WHAT ARE YOU WAITING FOR? CHEW! TEAR! DROOL! DROOL! DROOL!
ZOE, PICK UP YOUR SPELLING WORKSHEET AND GET BUSY.
SIGH!
IF YOU WANT SOMETHING RUINED RIGHT, YOU'VE GOT TO RUIN IT YOURSELF.
THAT'S ALWAYS BEEN MY MOTTO.
www.babyblues.com
©2008 BABY BLUES PARTNERSHIP DIST. BY KING FEATURES SYNDICATE
KIRKMAN & SCOTT 11-9

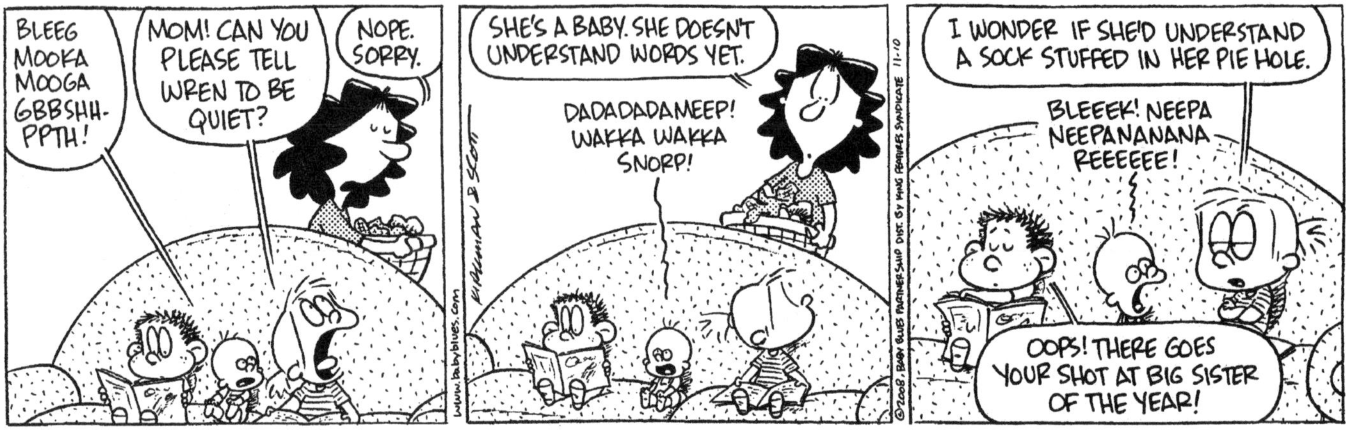
BLEEG MOOKA MOOGA GBBSHH-PPTH!
MOM! CAN YOU PLEASE TELL WREN TO BE QUIET?
NOPE. SORRY.
KIRKMAN & SCOTT
www.babyblues.com
SHE'S A BABY. SHE DOESN'T UNDERSTAND WORDS YET.
DADADADAMEEP! WAKKA WAKKA SNORP!
© 2008, BABY BLUES PARTNERSHIP DIST. BY KING FEATURES SYNDICATE 11-10
I WONDER IF SHE'D UNDERSTAND A SOCK STUFFED IN HER PIE HOLE.
BLEEEK! NEEPA NEEPANANANA REEEEEE!
OOPS! THERE GOES YOUR SHOT AT BIG SISTER OF THE YEAR!

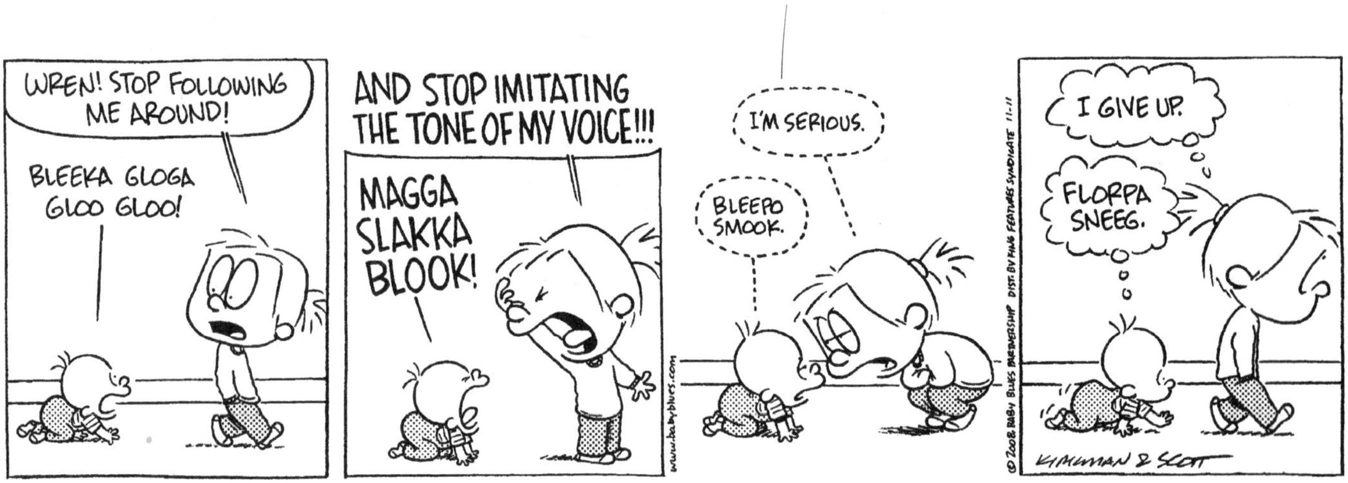
WREN! STOP FOLLOWING ME AROUND!
BLEEKA GLOGA GLOO GLOO!
AND STOP IMITATING THE TONE OF MY VOICE!!!
MAGGA SLAKKA BLOOK!
www.babyblues.com
I'M SERIOUS.
BLEEPO SMOOK.
© 2008, BABY BLUES PARTNERSHIP DIST. BY KING FEATURES SYNDICATE 11-11
I GIVE UP.
FLORPA SNEEG.
KIRKMAN & SCOTT

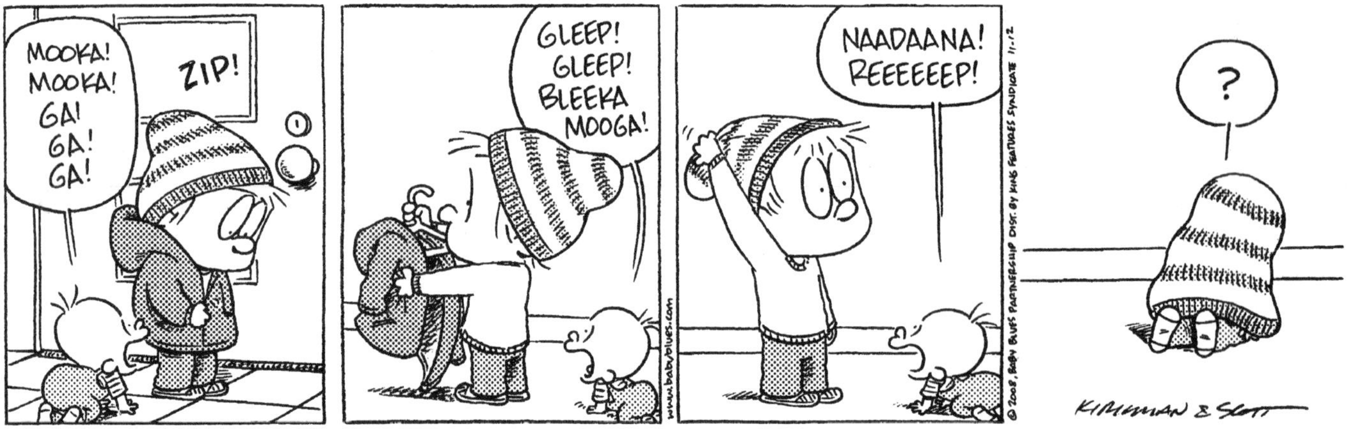
MOOKA! MOOKA! GA! GA! GA!
ZIP!
GLEEP! GLEEP! BLEEKA MOOGA!
www.babyblues.com
NAADAANA! REEEEEEP!
© 2008, BABY BLUES PARTNERSHIP DIST. BY KING FEATURES SYNDICATE 11-12
?
KIRKMAN & SCOTT

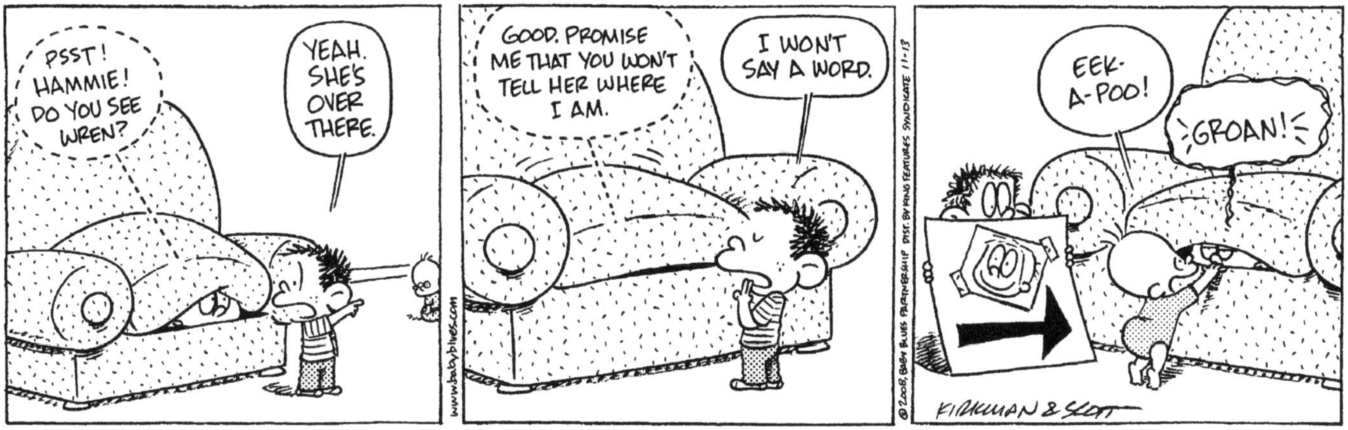
PSST! HAMMIE! DO YOU SEE WREN?
YEAH. SHE'S OVER THERE.
GOOD. PROMISE ME THAT YOU WON'T TELL HER WHERE I AM.
I WON'T SAY A WORD.
EEK-A-POO!
GROAN!
www.babyblues.com
©2008, BABY BLUES PARTNERSHIP DIST. BY KING FEATURES SYNDICATE 11-13
KIRKMAN & SCOTT

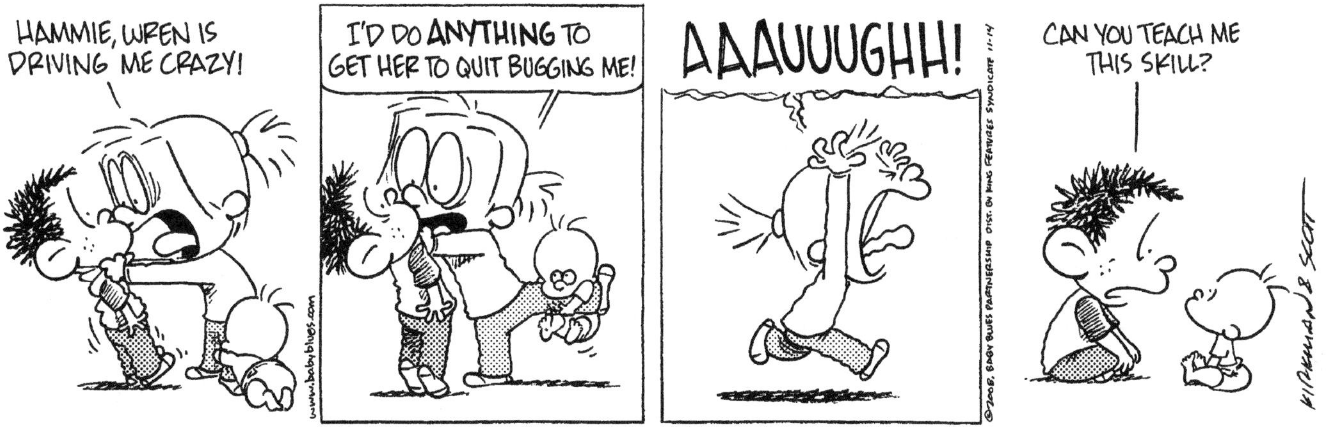
HAMMIE, WREN IS DRIVING ME CRAZY!
I'D DO ANYTHING TO GET HER TO QUIT BUGGING ME!
AAAUUUGHH!
CAN YOU TEACH ME THIS SKILL?
www.babyblues.com
©2008, BABY BLUES PARTNERSHIP DIST. BY KING FEATURES SYNDICATE 11-14
KIRKMAN & SCOTT

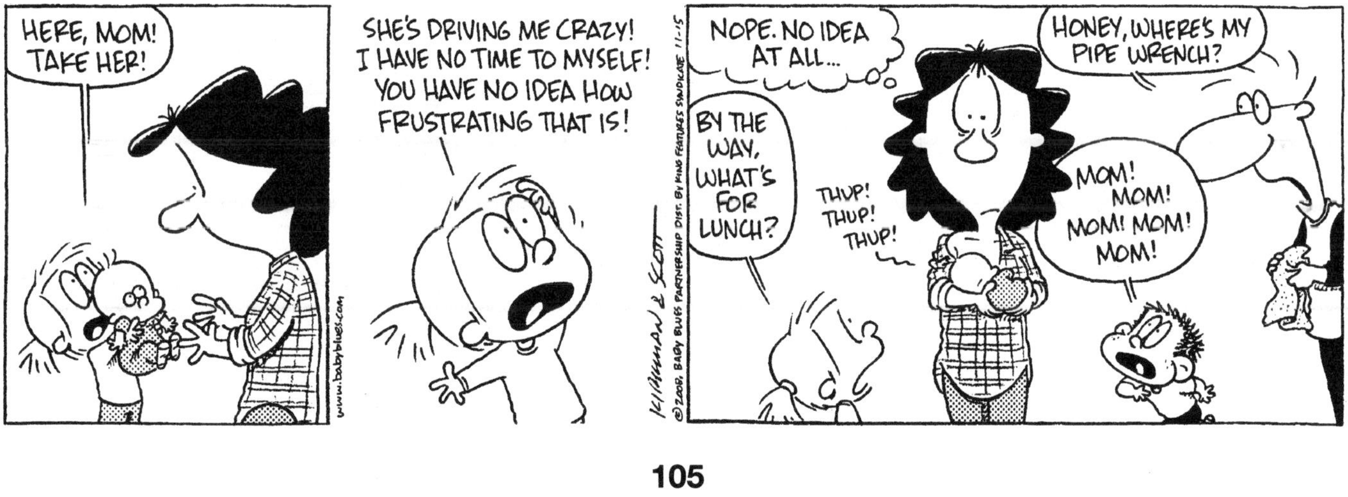
HERE, MOM! TAKE HER!
SHE'S DRIVING ME CRAZY! I HAVE NO TIME TO MYSELF! YOU HAVE NO IDEA HOW FRUSTRATING THAT IS!
NOPE. NO IDEA AT ALL...
HONEY, WHERE'S MY PIPE WRENCH?
BY THE WAY, WHAT'S FOR LUNCH?
THUP! THUP! THUP!
MOM! MOM! MOM! MOM! MOM!
www.babyblues.com
©2008, BABY BLUES PARTNERSHIP DIST. BY KING FEATURES SYNDICATE 11-15
KIRKMAN & SCOTT

BABY BLUES®

BIP! BIP! BIP! BIP! BIP! BIP! BIP! BIP! BIP! BIP! BIP!
11-16
BIP!
www.babyblues.com
BIP!
© 2008 BABY BLUES PARTNERSHIP DIST. BY KING FEATURES SYNDICATE
SHE REALLY, REALLY LIKES THE SWEATER.
APPARENTLY.
BIP!
BIP!
KIRKMAN & SCOTT

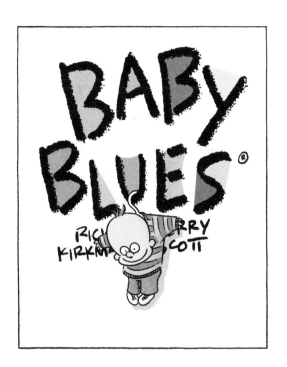

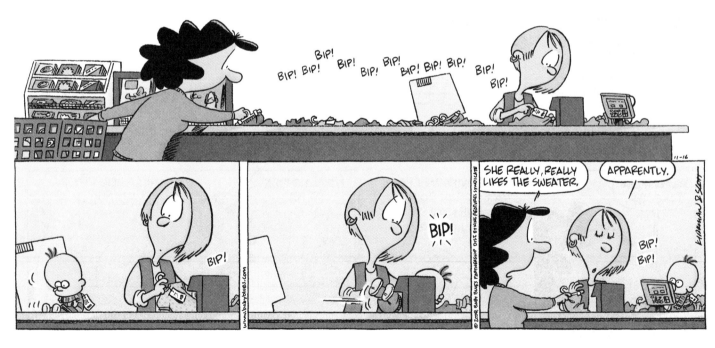

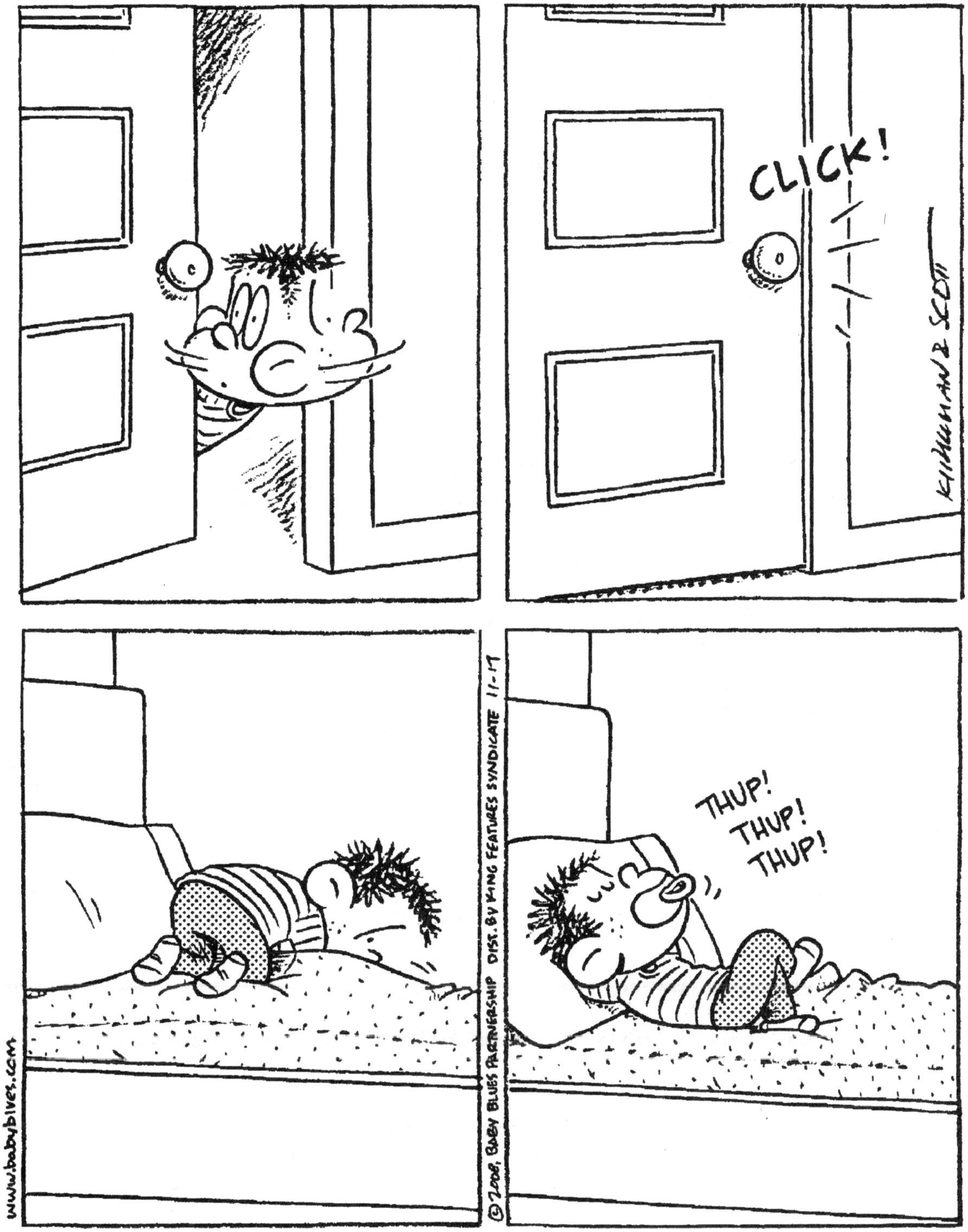
CLICK!
KIRKMAN & SCOTT
THUP!
THUP!
THUP!
© 2008, BABY BLUES PARTNERSHIP DIST. BY KING FEATURES SYNDICATE 11-17
www.babyblues.com

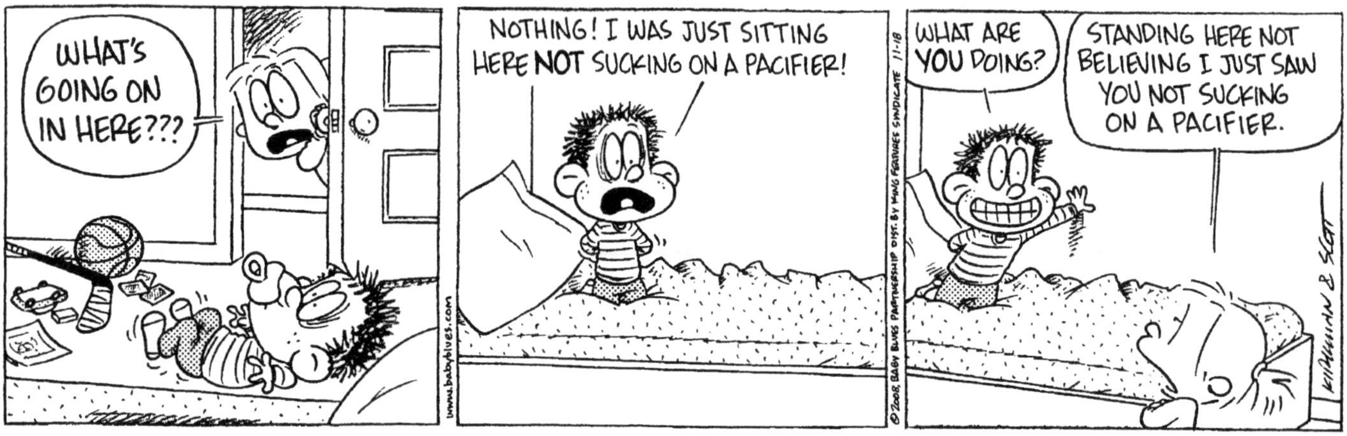
WHAT'S GOING ON IN HERE???
NOTHING! I WAS JUST SITTING HERE **NOT** SUCKING ON A PACIFIER!
WHAT ARE **YOU** DOING?
STANDING HERE NOT BELIEVING I JUST SAW YOU NOT SUCKING ON A PACIFIER.

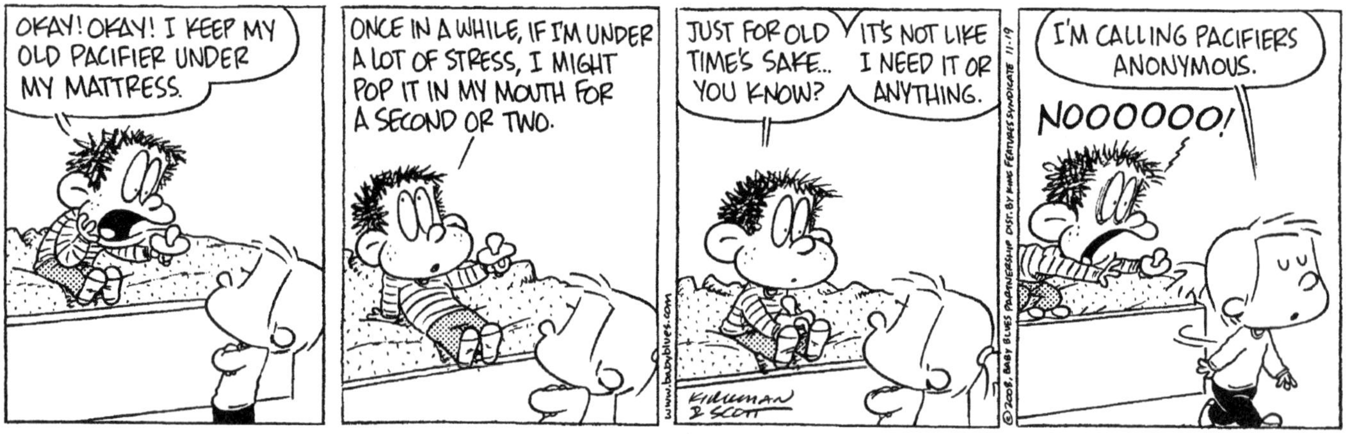
OKAY! OKAY! I KEEP MY OLD PACIFIER UNDER MY MATTRESS.
ONCE IN A WHILE, IF I'M UNDER A LOT OF STRESS, I MIGHT POP IT IN MY MOUTH FOR A SECOND OR TWO.
JUST FOR OLD TIME'S SAKE... YOU KNOW?
IT'S NOT LIKE I NEED IT OR ANYTHING.
I'M CALLING PACIFIERS ANONYMOUS.
NOOOOOO!

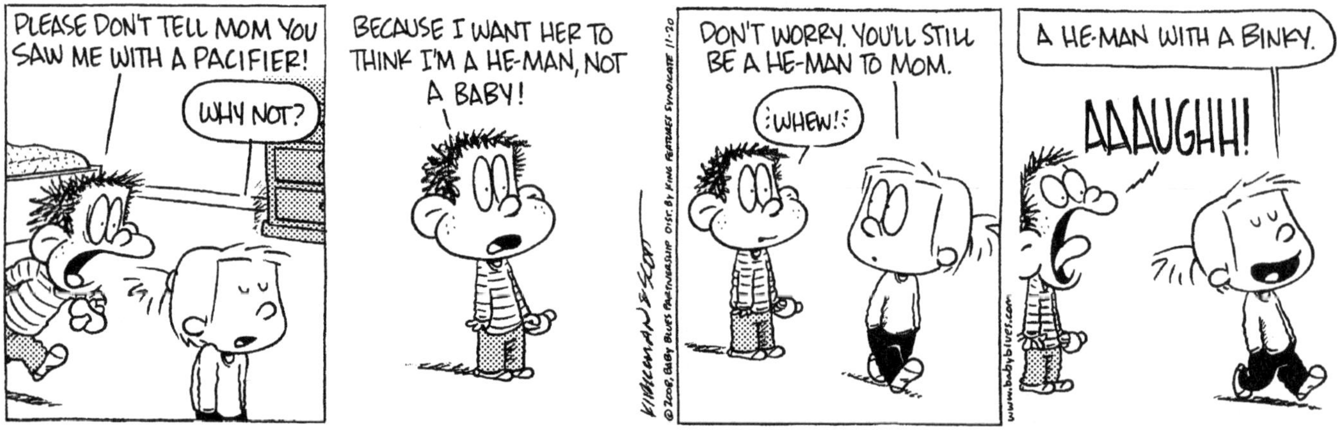
PLEASE DON'T TELL MOM YOU SAW ME WITH A PACIFIER!
WHY NOT?
BECAUSE I WANT HER TO THINK I'M A HE-MAN, NOT A BABY!
DON'T WORRY. YOU'LL STILL BE A HE-MAN TO MOM.
WHEW!
A HE-MAN WITH A BINKY.
AAAUGHH!

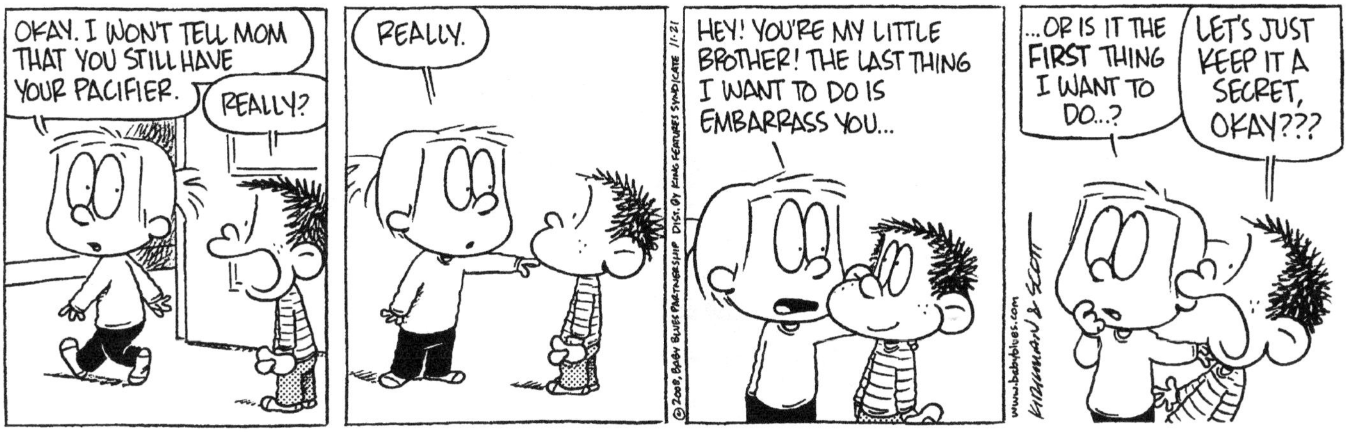
OKAY. I WON'T TELL MOM THAT YOU STILL HAVE YOUR PACIFIER.
REALLY?
REALLY.
© 2008, BABY BLUES PARTNERSHIP DIST. BY KING FEATURES SYNDICATE 11-21
HEY! YOU'RE MY LITTLE BROTHER! THE LAST THING I WANT TO DO IS EMBARRASS YOU...
www.babyblues.com
KIRKMAN & SCOTT
...OR IS IT THE FIRST THING I WANT TO DO...?
LET'S JUST KEEP IT A SECRET, OKAY???

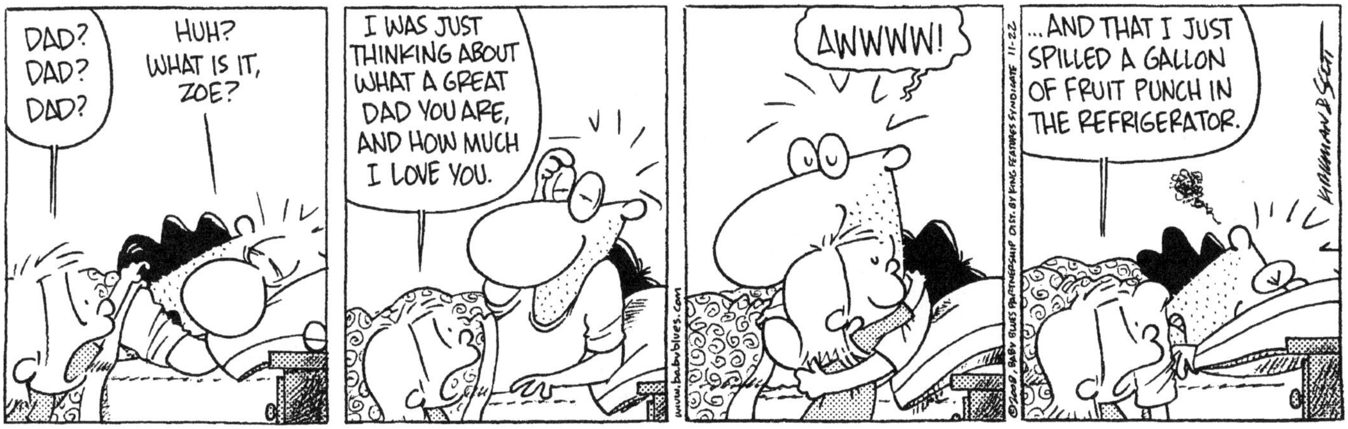
DAD? DAD? DAD?
HUH? WHAT IS IT, ZOE?
I WAS JUST THINKING ABOUT WHAT A GREAT DAD YOU ARE, AND HOW MUCH I LOVE YOU.
www.babyblues.com
AWWWW!
© 2008, BABY BLUES PARTNERSHIP DIST. BY KING FEATURES SYNDICATE 11-22
...AND THAT I JUST SPILLED A GALLON OF FRUIT PUNCH IN THE REFRIGERATOR.
KIRKMAN & SCOTT

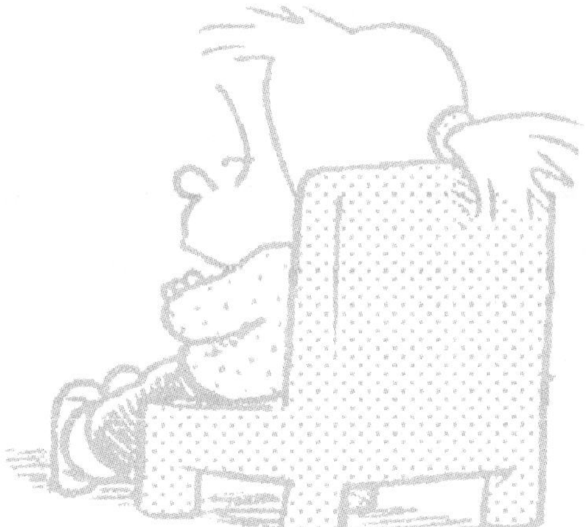

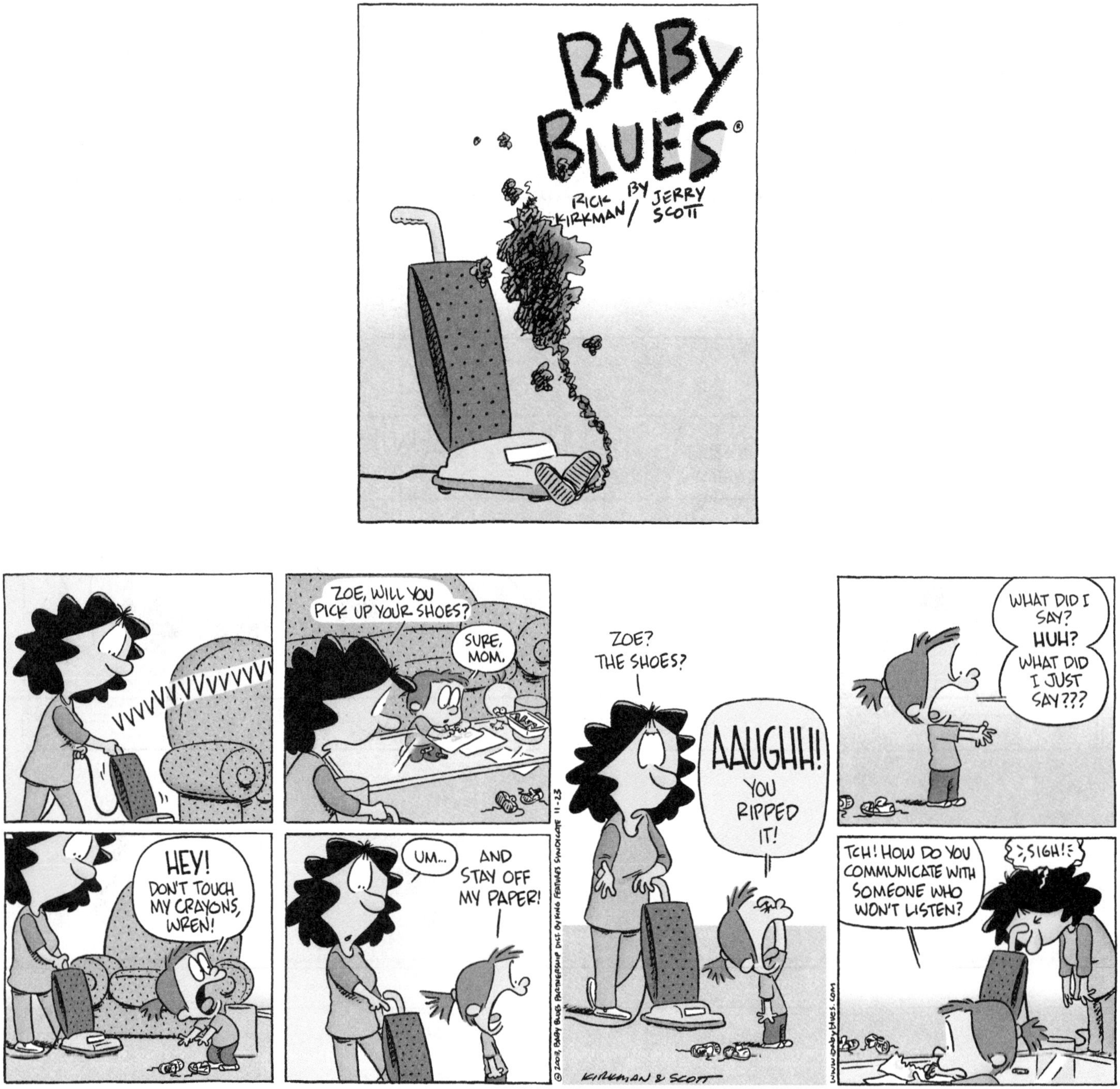

BABY BLUES®
BY RICK KIRKMAN / JERRY SCOTT
VVVVVVVVVVVVVVVV
ZOE, WILL YOU PICK UP YOUR SHOES?
SURE, MOM.
HEY! DON'T TOUCH MY CRAYONS, WREN!
UM...
AND STAY OFF MY PAPER!
ZOE? THE SHOES?
AAUGHH! YOU RIPPED IT!
© 2003, BABY BLUES PARTNERSHIP DIST. BY KING FEATURES SYNDICATE 11-23
KIRKMAN & SCOTT
WHAT DID I SAY? HUH? WHAT DID I JUST SAY???
TCH! HOW DO YOU COMMUNICATE WITH SOMEONE WHO WON'T LISTEN?
SIGH!
www.babyblues.com

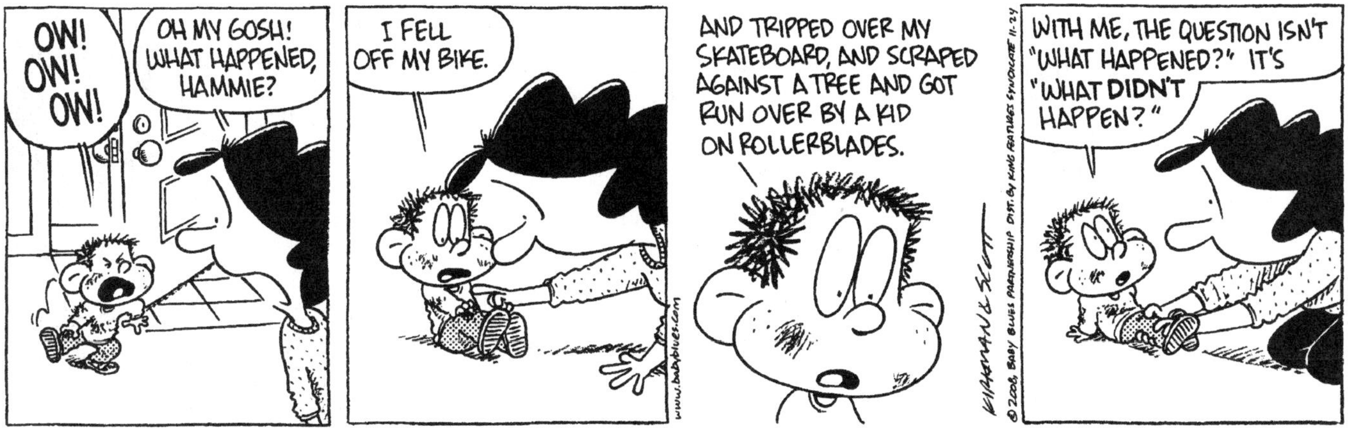
OW! OW! OW!
OH MY GOSH! WHAT HAPPENED, HAMMIE?
I FELL OFF MY BIKE.
www.babyblues.com
AND TRIPPED OVER MY SKATEBOARD, AND SCRAPED AGAINST A TREE AND GOT RUN OVER BY A KID ON ROLLERBLADES.
KIRKMAN & SCOTT
© 2008, BABY BLUES PARTNERSHIP DIST. BY KING FEATURES SYNDICATE 11-24
WITH ME, THE QUESTION ISN'T "WHAT HAPPENED?" IT'S "WHAT DIDN'T HAPPEN?"

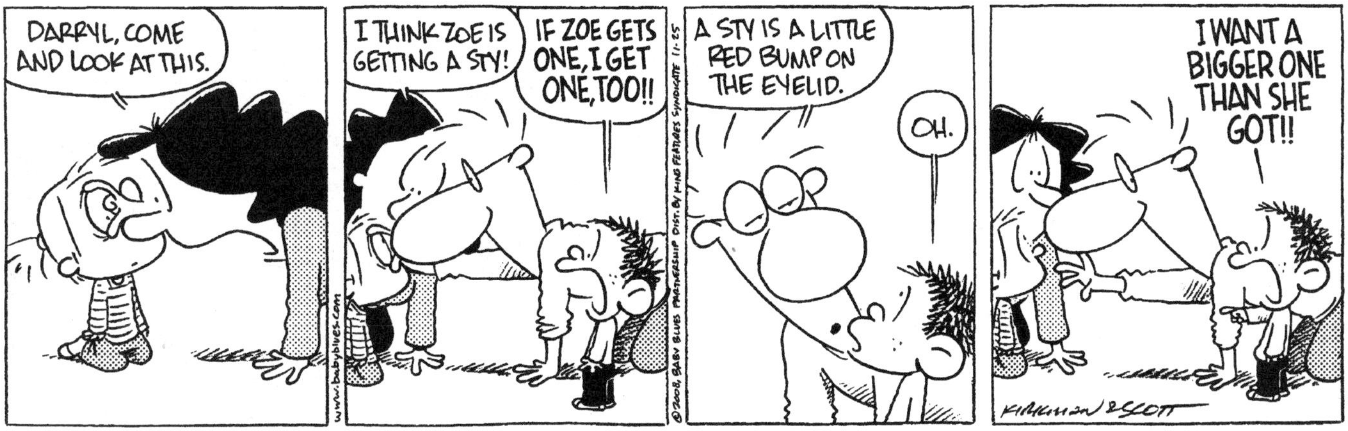
DARRYL, COME AND LOOK AT THIS.
www.babyblues.com
I THINK ZOE IS GETTING A STY!
IF ZOE GETS ONE, I GET ONE, TOO!!
© 2008, BABY BLUES PARTNERSHIP DIST. BY KING FEATURES SYNDICATE 11-25
A STY IS A LITTLE RED BUMP ON THE EYELID.
OH.
I WANT A BIGGER ONE THAN SHE GOT!!
KIRKMAN & SCOTT

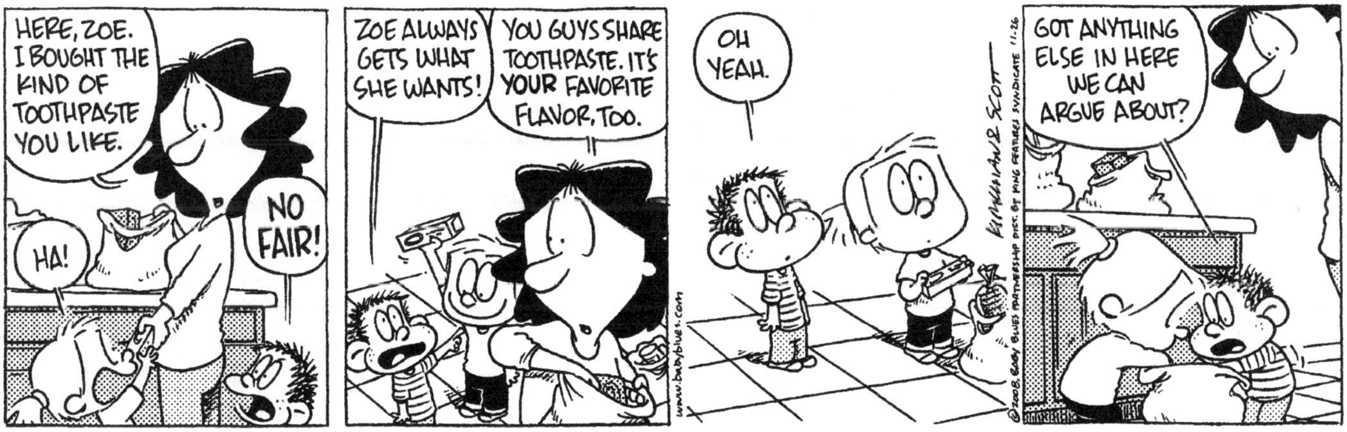
HERE, ZOE. I BOUGHT THE KIND OF TOOTHPASTE YOU LIKE.
HA!
NO FAIR!
www.babyblues.com
ZOE ALWAYS GETS WHAT SHE WANTS!
YOU GUYS SHARE TOOTHPASTE. IT'S YOUR FAVORITE FLAVOR, TOO.
OH YEAH.
KIRKMAN & SCOTT
© 2008, BABY BLUES PARTNERSHIP DIST. BY KING FEATURES SYNDICATE 11-26
GOT ANYTHING ELSE IN HERE WE CAN ARGUE ABOUT?

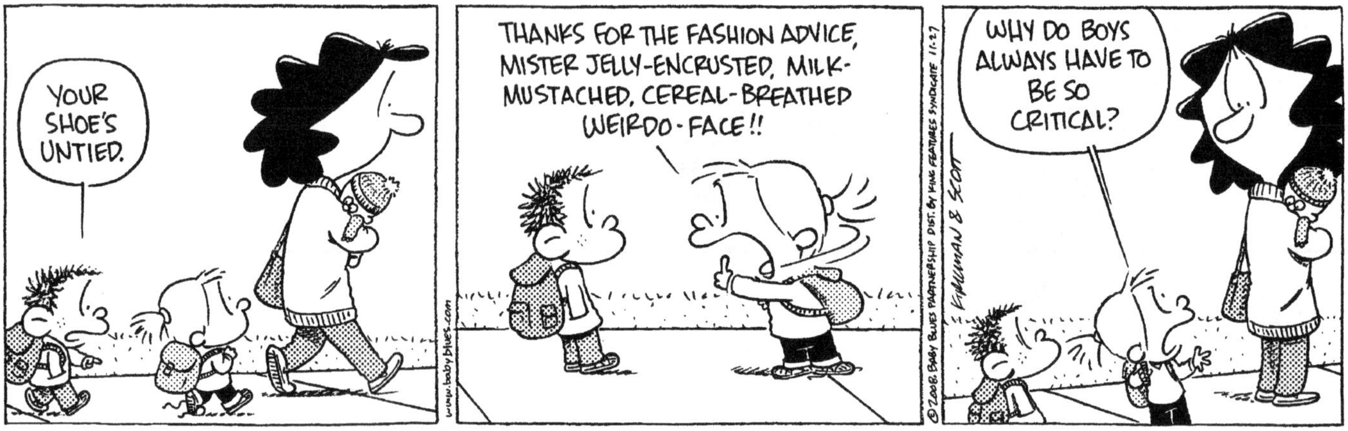
YOUR SHOE'S UNTIED.
THANKS FOR THE FASHION ADVICE, MISTER JELLY-ENCRUSTED, MILK-MUSTACHED, CEREAL-BREATHED WEIRDO-FACE!!
WHY DO BOYS ALWAYS HAVE TO BE SO CRITICAL?
www.babyblues.com
© 2008, BABY BLUES PARTNERSHIP DIST. BY KING FEATURES SYNDICATE 11-27
KIRKMAN & SCOTT

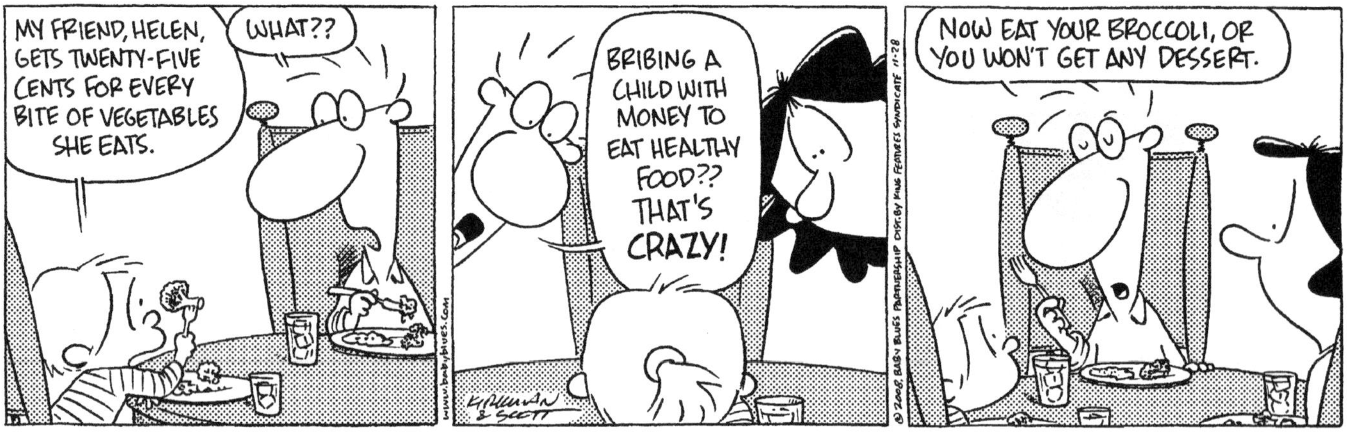
MY FRIEND, HELEN, GETS TWENTY-FIVE CENTS FOR EVERY BITE OF VEGETABLES SHE EATS.
WHAT??
BRIBING A CHILD WITH MONEY TO EAT HEALTHY FOOD?? THAT'S CRAZY!
NOW EAT YOUR BROCCOLI, OR YOU WON'T GET ANY DESSERT.
www.babyblues.com
KIRKMAN & SCOTT
© 2008, BABY BLUES PARTNERSHIP DIST. BY KING FEATURES SYNDICATE 11-28

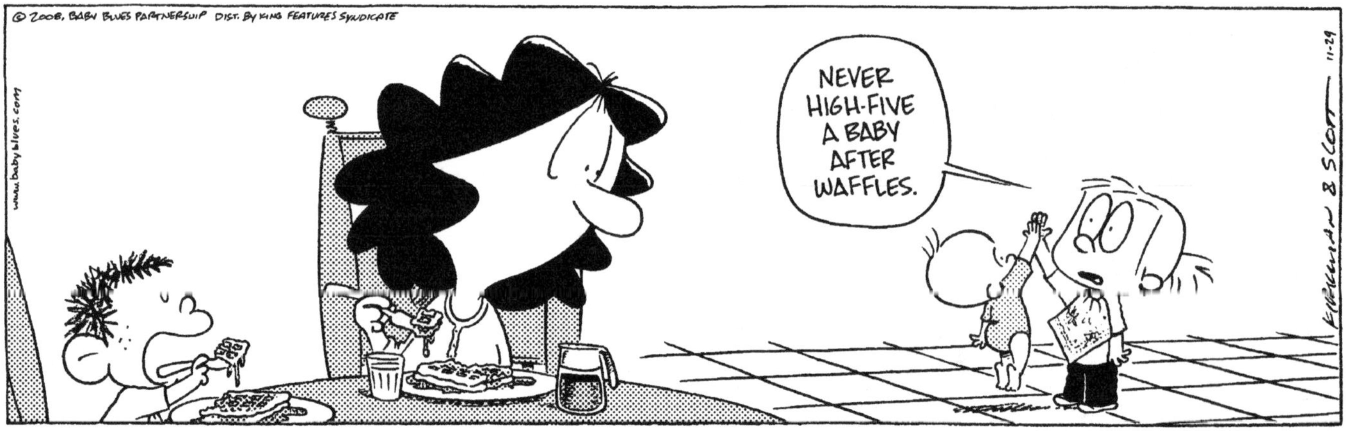
© 2008, BABY BLUES PARTNERSHIP DIST. BY KING FEATURES SYNDICATE
www.babyblues.com
NEVER HIGH-FIVE A BABY AFTER WAFFLES.
KIRKMAN & SCOTT 11-29

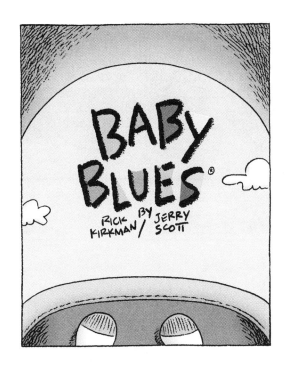

BABY BLUES®
BY
RICK KIRKMAN / JERRY SCOTT

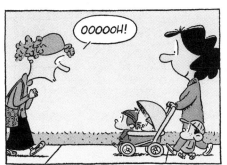

OOOOOH!
WOOK AT YOOUUUUUU!
AREN'T YOU JUST THE CUTEST THING THERE IS? YES YOU ARE!
WIGGA! WIGGA! WIGGA!
BLADDLE-ADDL-ADDL! BYE-BYEEEEE!!
www.babyblues.com
SIGH!
©2008 BABY BLUES PARTNERSHIP DIST BY KING FEATURES SYNDICATE
GROWNUPS ARE WEIRD.
IF I DID THAT TO WREN, I'D BE GROUNDED 'TIL I WAS IN HIGH SCHOOL.
KIRKMAN & SCOTT
11-30

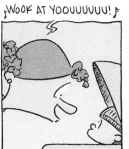

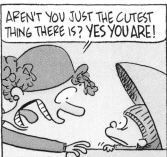

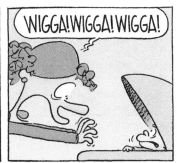

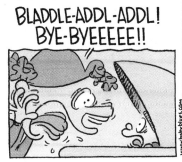

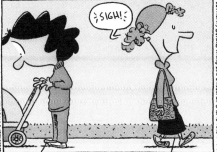

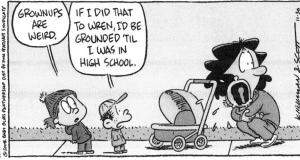

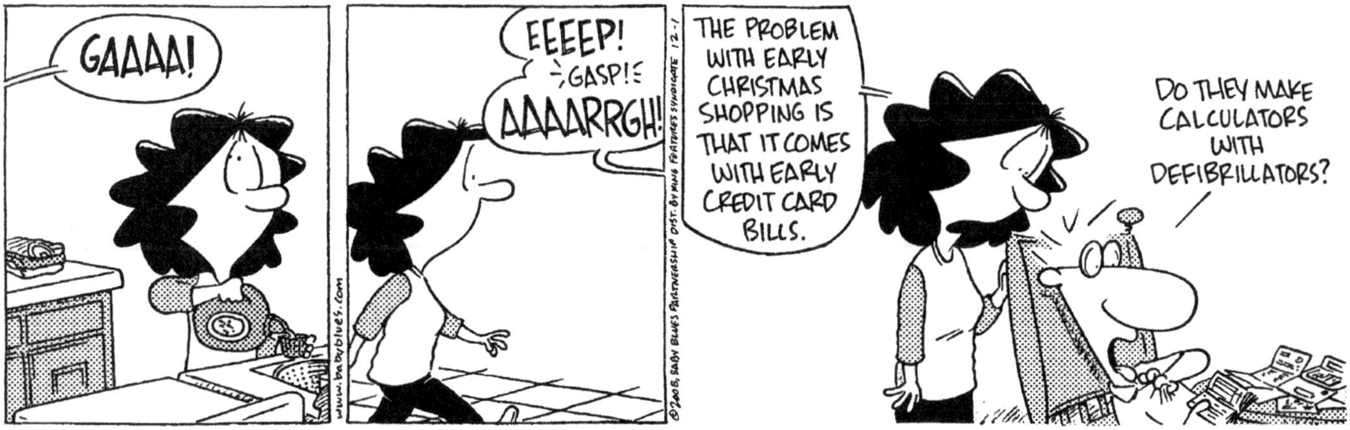
GAAAA!
www.babyblues.com
EEEEP!
GASP!
AAAARRGH!
©2008, Baby Blues Partnership Dist. by King Features Syndicate 12-1
THE PROBLEM WITH EARLY CHRISTMAS SHOPPING IS THAT IT COMES WITH EARLY CREDIT CARD BILLS.
DO THEY MAKE CALCULATORS WITH DEFIBRILLATORS?

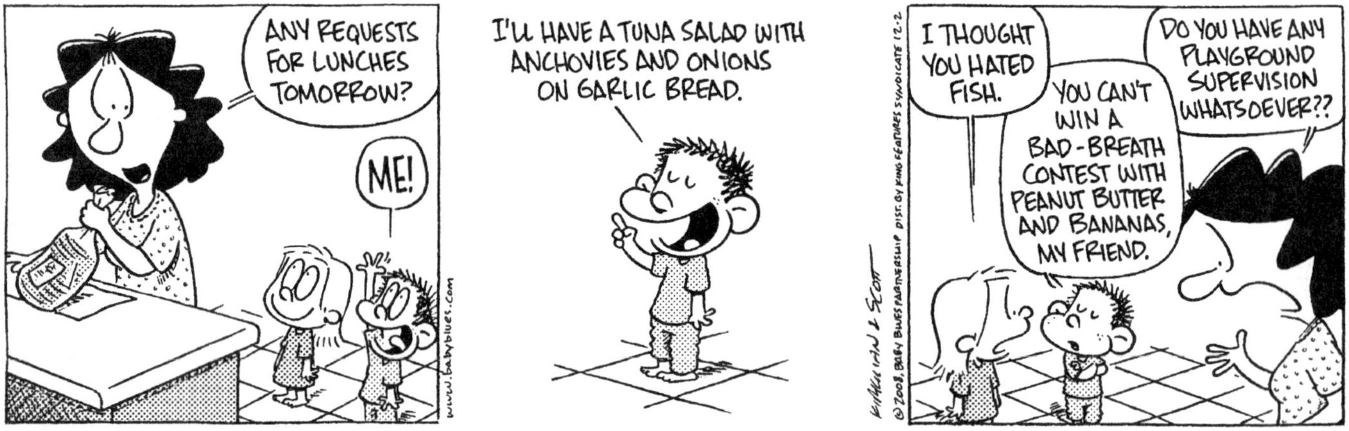
ANY REQUESTS FOR LUNCHES TOMORROW?
ME!
www.babyblues.com
I'LL HAVE A TUNA SALAD WITH ANCHOVIES AND ONIONS ON GARLIC BREAD.
KIRKMAN & SCOTT
©2008, Baby Blues Partnership Dist. by King Features Syndicate 12-2
I THOUGHT YOU HATED FISH.
YOU CAN'T WIN A BAD-BREATH CONTEST WITH PEANUT BUTTER AND BANANAS, MY FRIEND.
DO YOU HAVE ANY PLAYGROUND SUPERVISION WHATSOEVER??

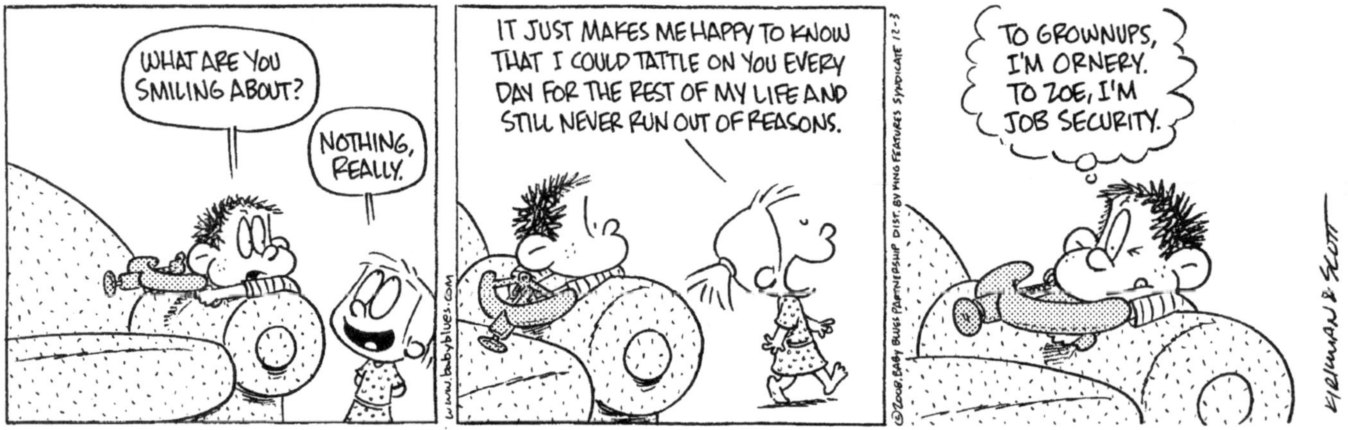
WHAT ARE YOU SMILING ABOUT?
NOTHING, REALLY.
www.babyblues.com
IT JUST MAKES ME HAPPY TO KNOW THAT I COULD TATTLE ON YOU EVERY DAY FOR THE REST OF MY LIFE AND STILL NEVER RUN OUT OF REASONS.
©2008, Baby Blues Partnership Dist. by King Features Syndicate 12-3
TO GROWNUPS, I'M ORNERY. TO ZOE, I'M JOB SECURITY.
KIRKMAN & SCOTT

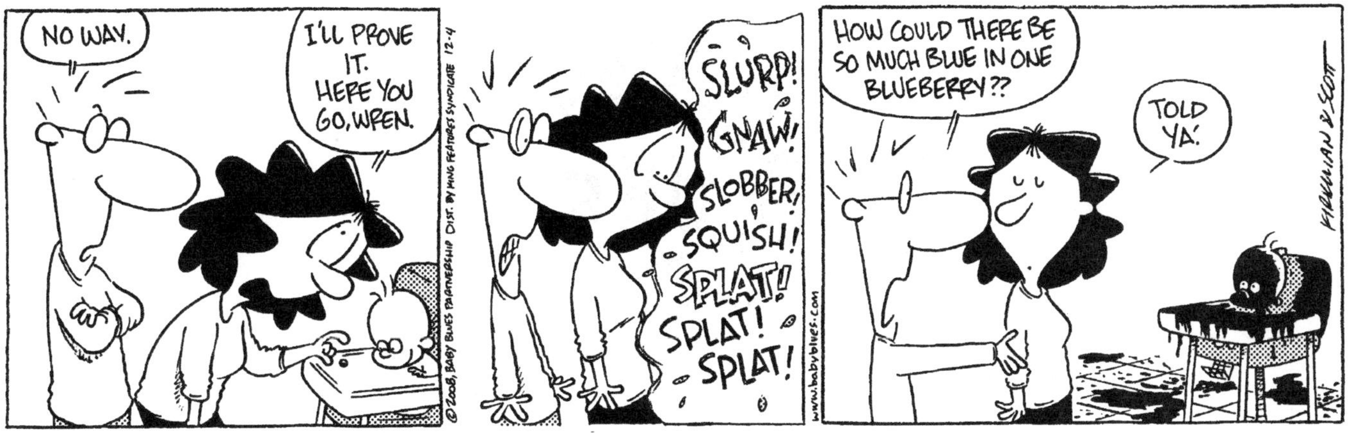
NO WAY.
I'LL PROVE IT. HERE YOU GO, WREN.
© 2008, Baby Blues Partnership Dist. by King Features Syndicate 12-4
SLURP!
GNAW!
SLOBBER!
SQUISH!
SPLAT!
SPLAT!
SPLAT!
www.babyblues.com
HOW COULD THERE BE SO MUCH BLUE IN ONE BLUEBERRY??
TOLD YA.
KIRKMAN & SCOTT

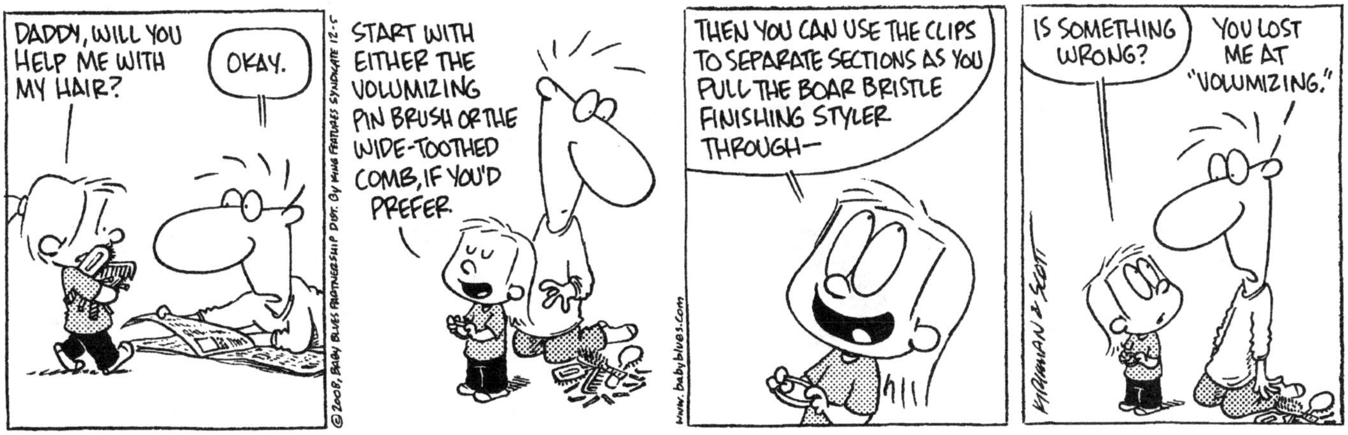
DADDY, WILL YOU HELP ME WITH MY HAIR?
OKAY.
© 2008, Baby Blues Partnership Dist. by King Features Syndicate 12-5
START WITH EITHER THE VOLUMIZING PIN BRUSH OR THE WIDE-TOOTHED COMB, IF YOU'D PREFER.
www.babyblues.com
THEN YOU CAN USE THE CLIPS TO SEPARATE SECTIONS AS YOU PULL THE BOAR BRISTLE FINISHING STYLER THROUGH—
IS SOMETHING WRONG?
YOU LOST ME AT "VOLUMIZING."
KIRKMAN & SCOTT

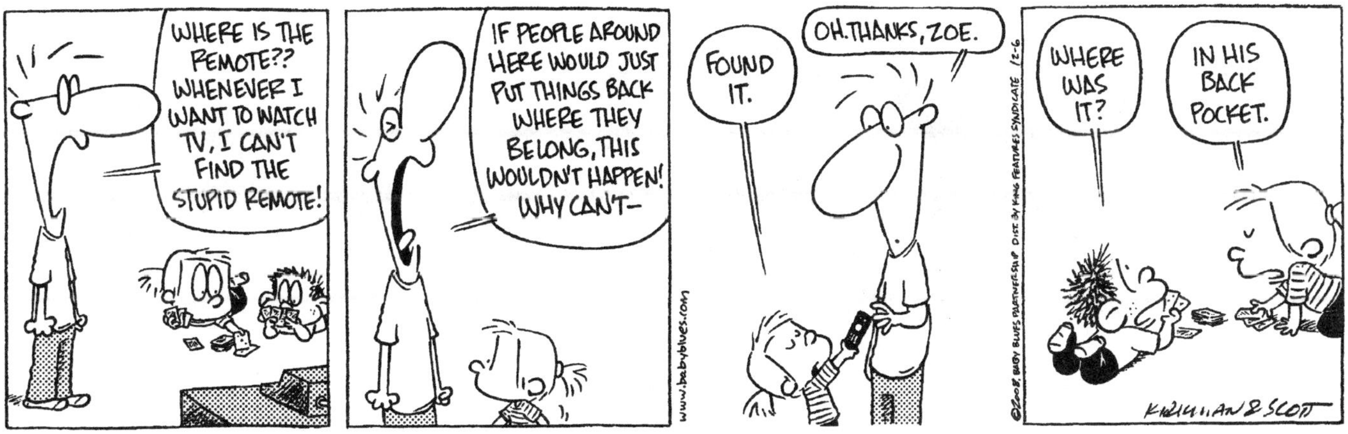
WHERE IS THE REMOTE?? WHENEVER I WANT TO WATCH TV, I CAN'T FIND THE STUPID REMOTE!
IF PEOPLE AROUND HERE WOULD JUST PUT THINGS BACK WHERE THEY BELONG, THIS WOULDN'T HAPPEN! WHY CAN'T—
www.babyblues.com
FOUND IT.
OH. THANKS, ZOE.
© 2008, Baby Blues Partnership Dist. by King Features Syndicate 12-6
WHERE WAS IT?
IN HIS BACK POCKET.
KIRKMAN & SCOTT

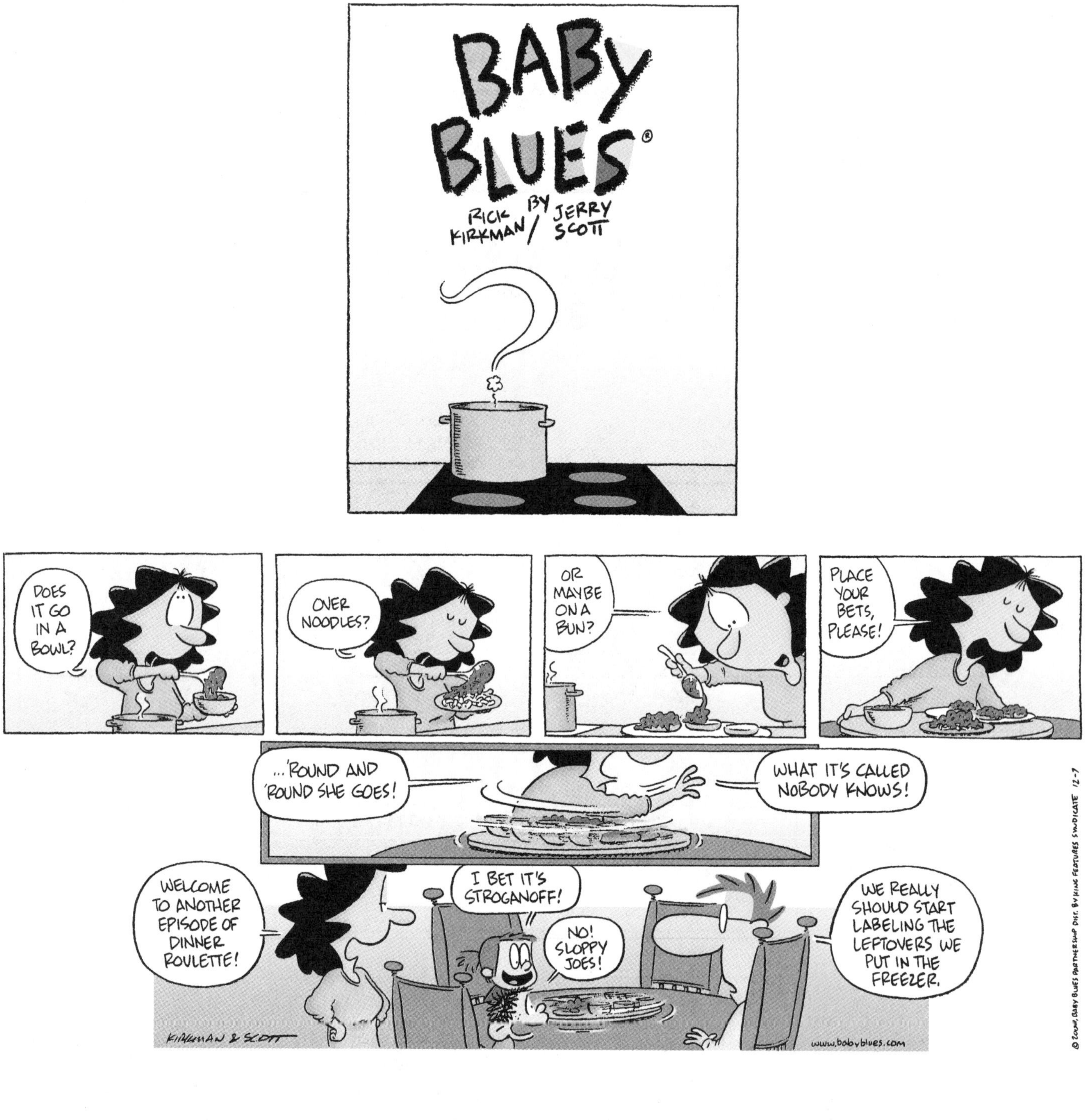
BABY BLUES®
BY RICK KIRKMAN / JERRY SCOTT
DOES IT GO IN A BOWL?
OVER NOODLES?
OR MAYBE ON A BUN?
PLACE YOUR BETS, PLEASE!
...'ROUND AND 'ROUND SHE GOES!
WHAT IT'S CALLED NOBODY KNOWS!
WELCOME TO ANOTHER EPISODE OF DINNER ROULETTE!
I BET IT'S STROGANOFF!
NO! SLOPPY JOES!
WE REALLY SHOULD START LABELING THE LEFTOVERS WE PUT IN THE FREEZER.
KIRKMAN & SCOTT
www.babyblues.com
© 2007, BABY BLUES PARTNERSHIP DIST. BY KING FEATURES SYNDICATE 12-7

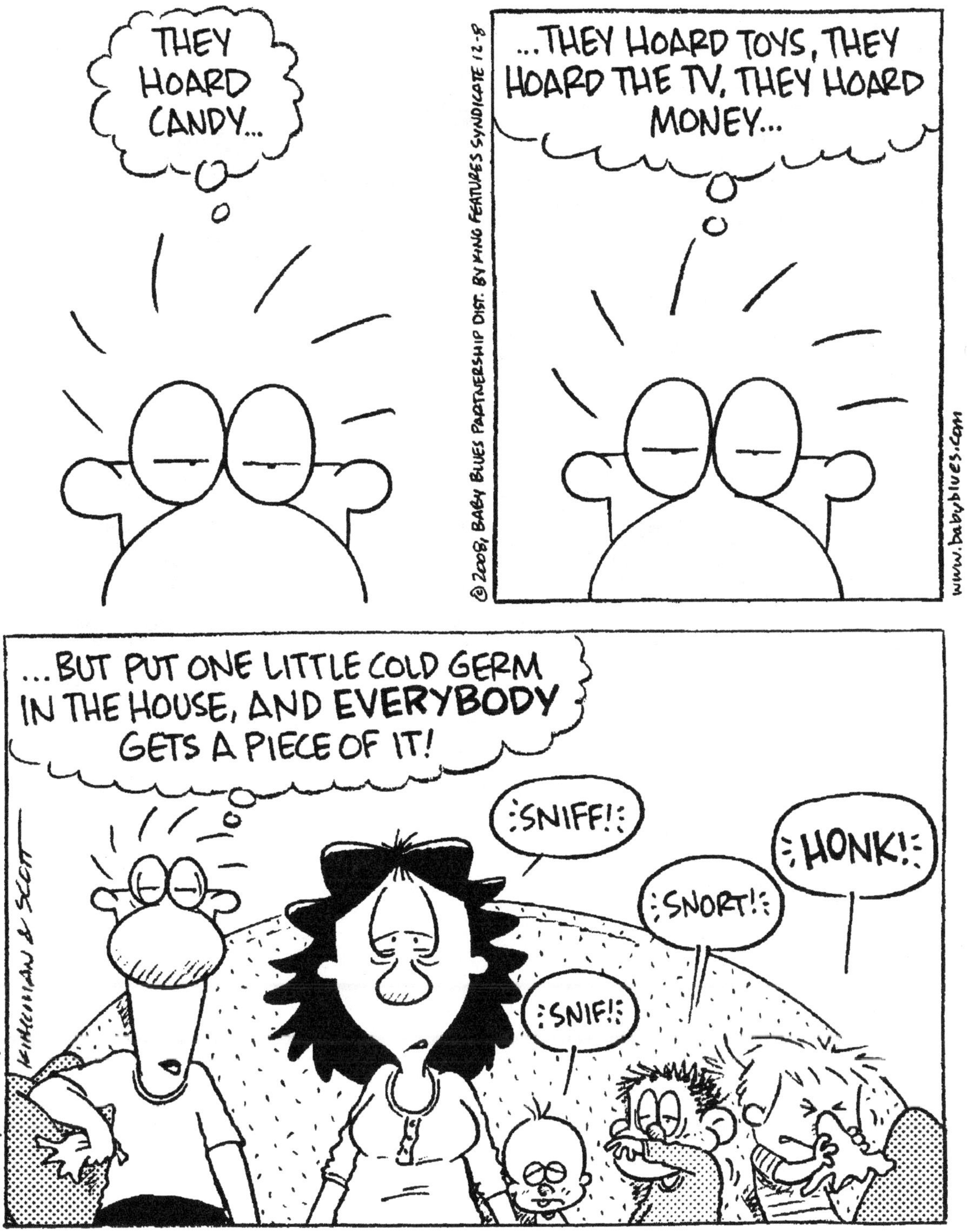
THEY HOARD CANDY...
© 2008, BABY BLUES PARTNERSHIP DIST. BY KING FEATURES SYNDICATE 12-8
...THEY HOARD TOYS, THEY HOARD THE TV, THEY HOARD MONEY...
www.babyblues.com
...BUT PUT ONE LITTLE COLD GERM IN THE HOUSE, AND EVERYBODY GETS A PIECE OF IT!
KIRKMAN & SCOTT
SNIFF!
SNIF!
SNORT!
HONK!

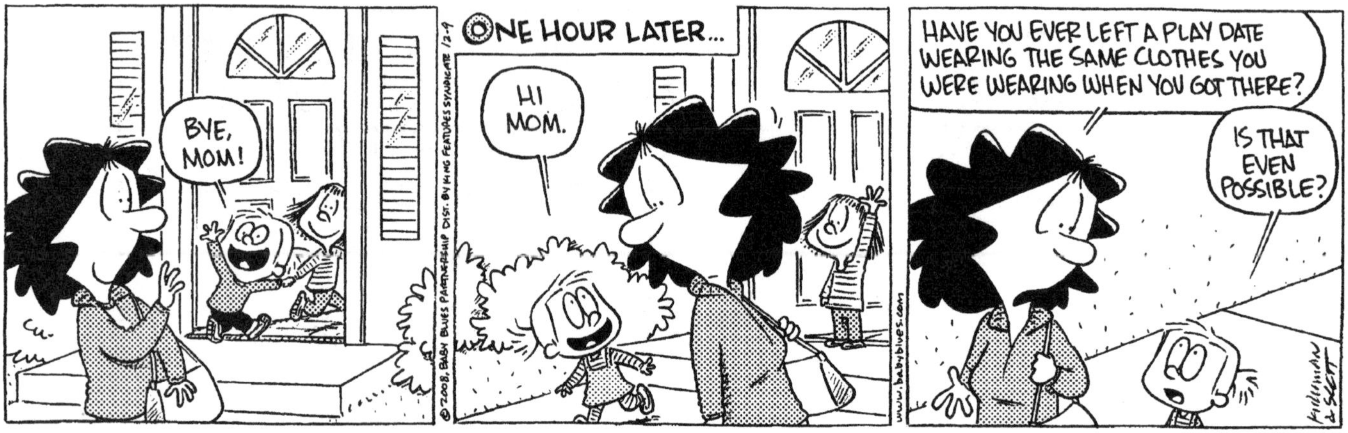
BYE, MOM!
©2008, BABY BLUES PARTNERSHIP DIST. BY KING FEATURES SYNDICATE 12-9
ONE HOUR LATER...
HI MOM.
www.babyblues.com
HAVE YOU EVER LEFT A PLAY DATE WEARING THE SAME CLOTHES YOU WERE WEARING WHEN YOU GOT THERE?
IS THAT EVEN POSSIBLE?
KIRKMAN & SCOTT

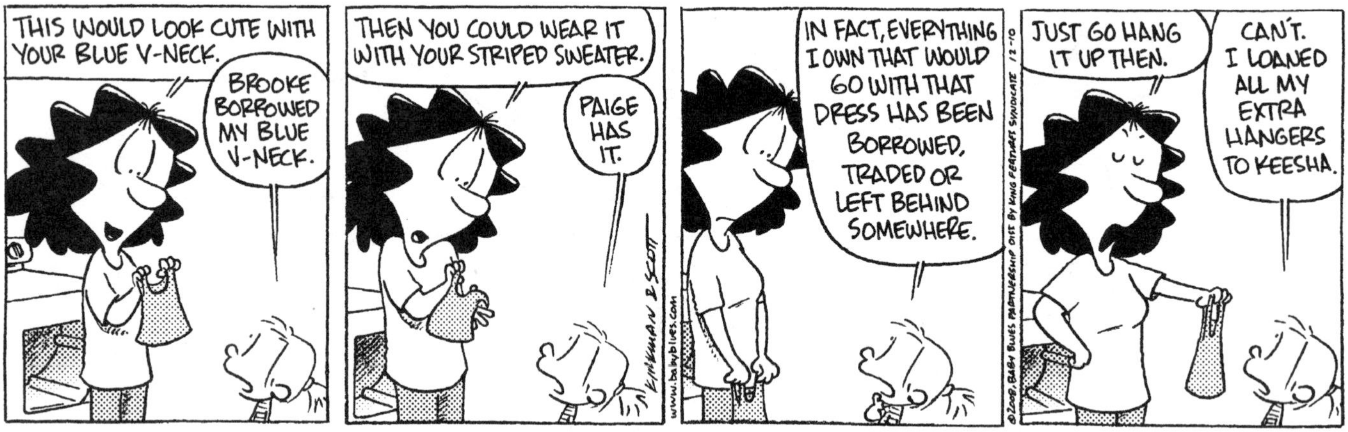
THIS WOULD LOOK CUTE WITH YOUR BLUE V-NECK.
BROOKE BORROWED MY BLUE V-NECK.
THEN YOU COULD WEAR IT WITH YOUR STRIPED SWEATER.
PAIGE HAS IT.
KIRKMAN & SCOTT
www.babyblues.com
IN FACT, EVERYTHING I OWN THAT WOULD GO WITH THAT DRESS HAS BEEN BORROWED, TRADED OR LEFT BEHIND SOMEWHERE.
©2008, BABY BLUES PARTNERSHIP DIST. BY KING FEATURES SYNDICATE 12-10
JUST GO HANG IT UP THEN.
CAN'T. I LOANED ALL MY EXTRA HANGERS TO KEESHA.

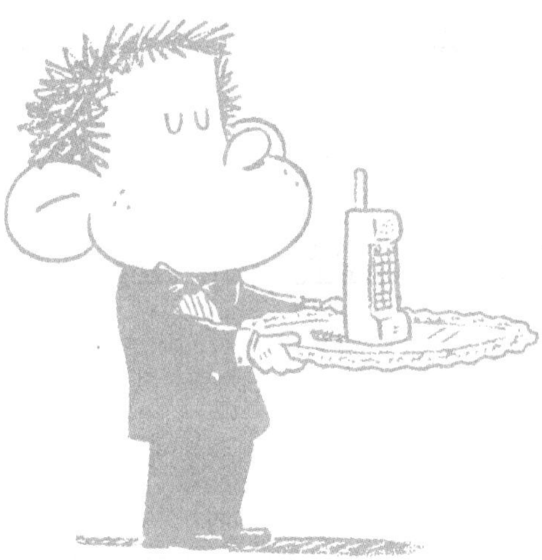

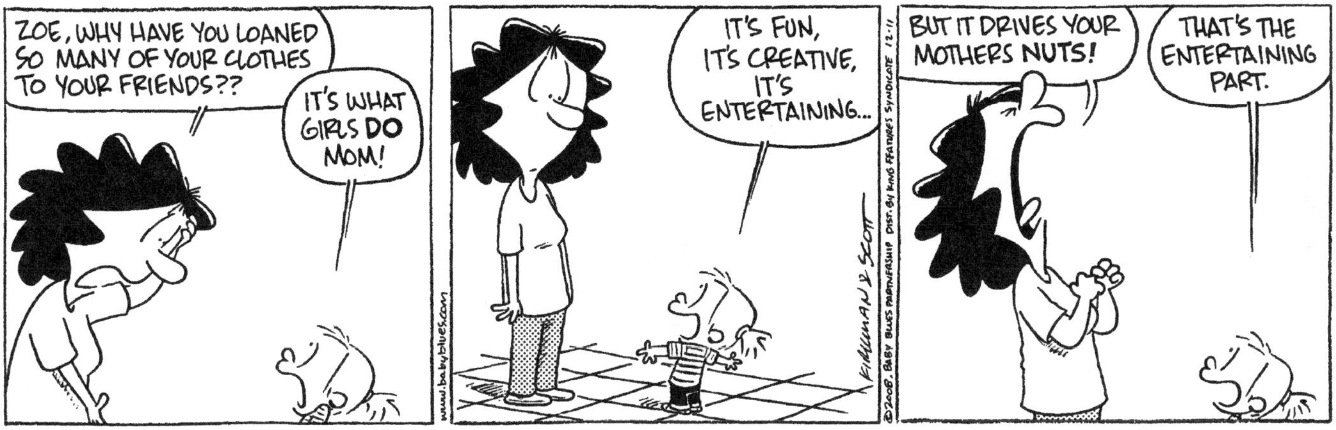
ZOE, WHY HAVE YOU LOANED SO MANY OF YOUR CLOTHES TO YOUR FRIENDS??
IT'S WHAT GIRLS **DO** MOM!
www.babyblues.com
IT'S FUN, IT'S CREATIVE, IT'S ENTERTAINING...
KIRKMAN & SCOTT
© 2008, BABY BLUES PARTNERSHIP DIST. BY KING FEATURES SYNDICATE 12-11
BUT IT DRIVES YOUR MOTHERS **NUTS!**
THAT'S THE ENTERTAINING PART.

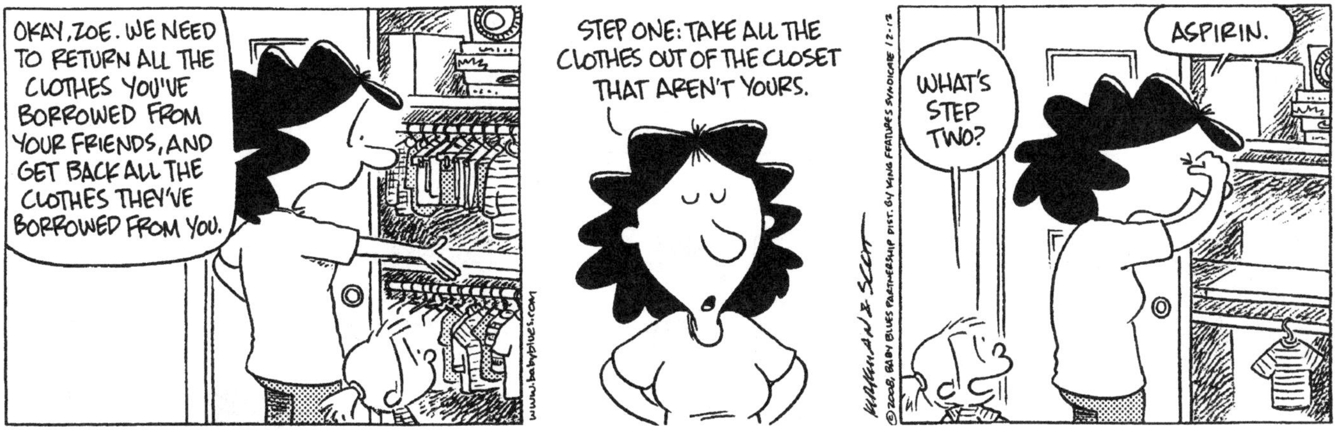
OKAY, ZOE. WE NEED TO RETURN ALL THE CLOTHES YOU'VE BORROWED FROM YOUR FRIENDS, AND GET BACK ALL THE CLOTHES THEY'VE BORROWED FROM YOU.
www.babyblues.com
STEP ONE: TAKE ALL THE CLOTHES OUT OF THE CLOSET THAT AREN'T YOURS.
KIRKMAN & SCOTT
© 2008, BABY BLUES PARTNERSHIP DIST. BY KING FEATURES SYNDICATE 12-12
WHAT'S STEP TWO?
ASPIRIN.

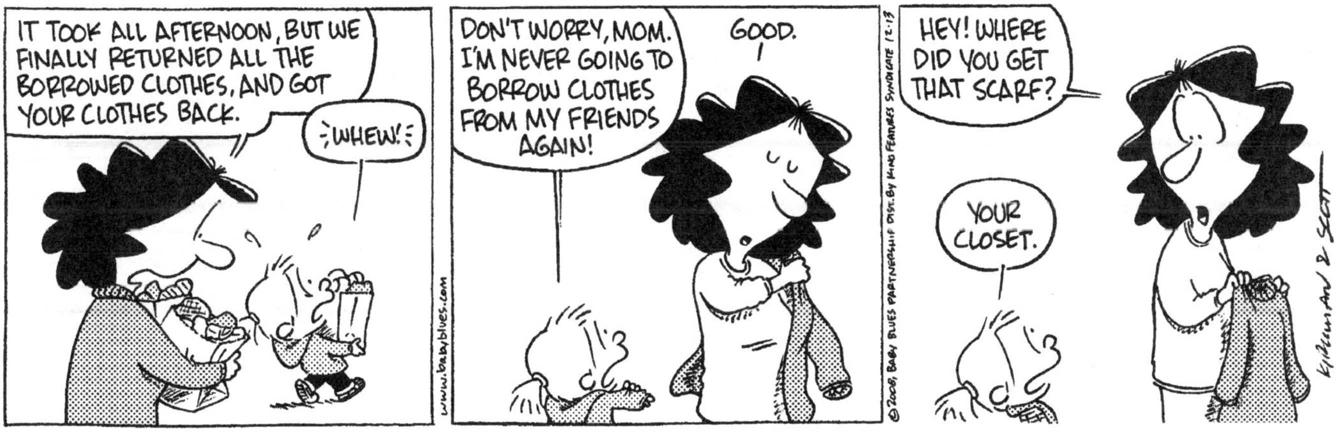
IT TOOK ALL AFTERNOON, BUT WE FINALLY RETURNED ALL THE BORROWED CLOTHES, AND GOT YOUR CLOTHES BACK.
WHEW!
www.babyblues.com
DON'T WORRY, MOM. I'M NEVER GOING TO BORROW CLOTHES FROM MY FRIENDS AGAIN!
GOOD.
© 2008, BABY BLUES PARTNERSHIP DIST. BY KING FEATURES SYNDICATE 12-13
HEY! WHERE DID YOU GET THAT SCARF?
YOUR CLOSET.
KIRKMAN & SCOTT

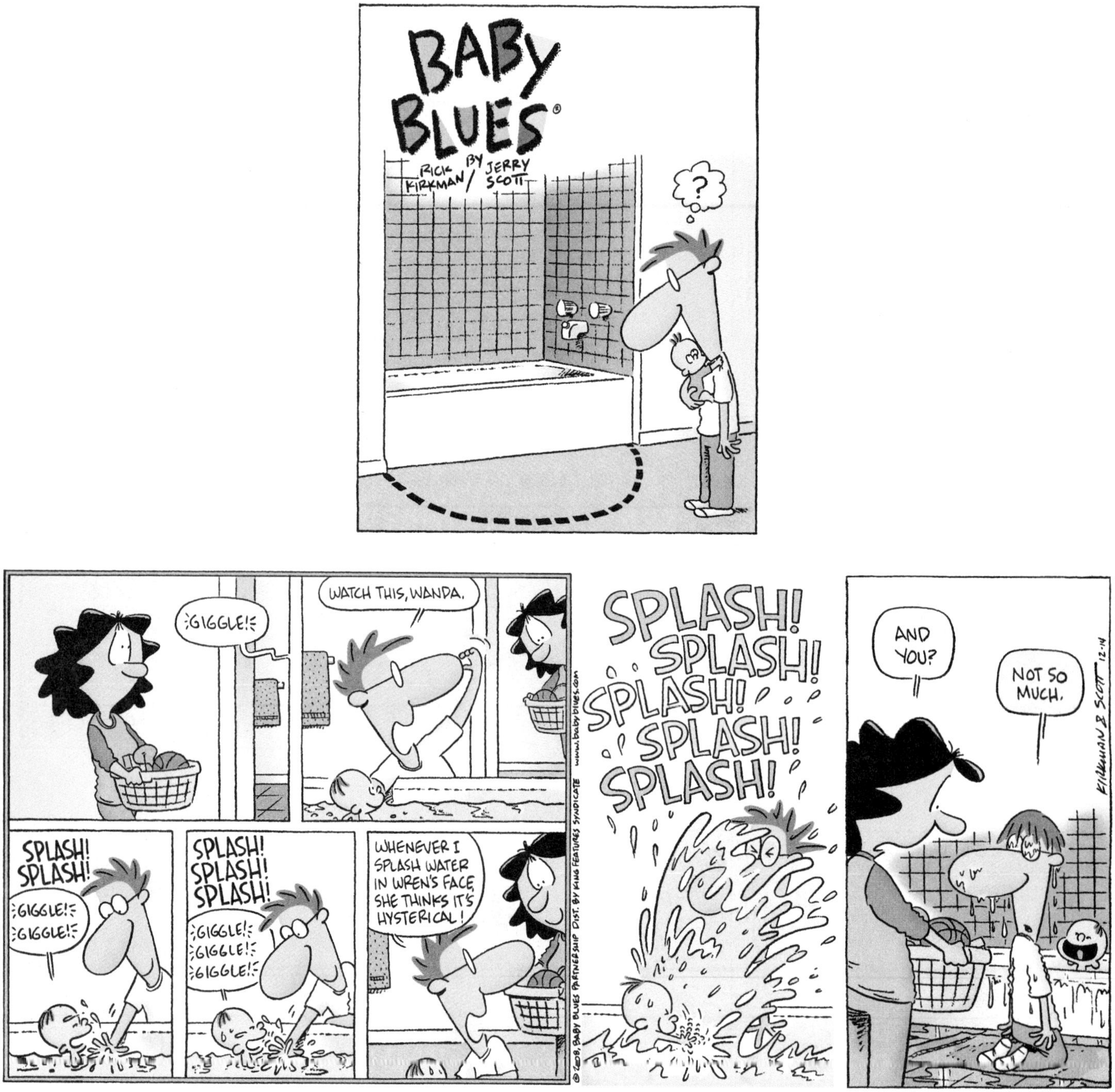
BABY BLUES®
RICK KIRKMAN / JERRY SCOTT
?
GIGGLE!
WATCH THIS, WANDA.
SPLASH! SPLASH!
GIGGLE! GIGGLE!
SPLASH! SPLASH! SPLASH!
GIGGLE! GIGGLE! GIGGLE!
WHENEVER I SPLASH WATER IN WREN'S FACE, SHE THINKS IT'S HYSTERICAL!
SPLASH! SPLASH! SPLASH! SPLASH! SPLASH!
AND YOU?
NOT SO MUCH.
© 2008, BABY BLUES PARTNERSHIP DIST. BY KING FEATURES SYNDICATE www.babyblues.com
KIRKMAN & SCOTT 12-14

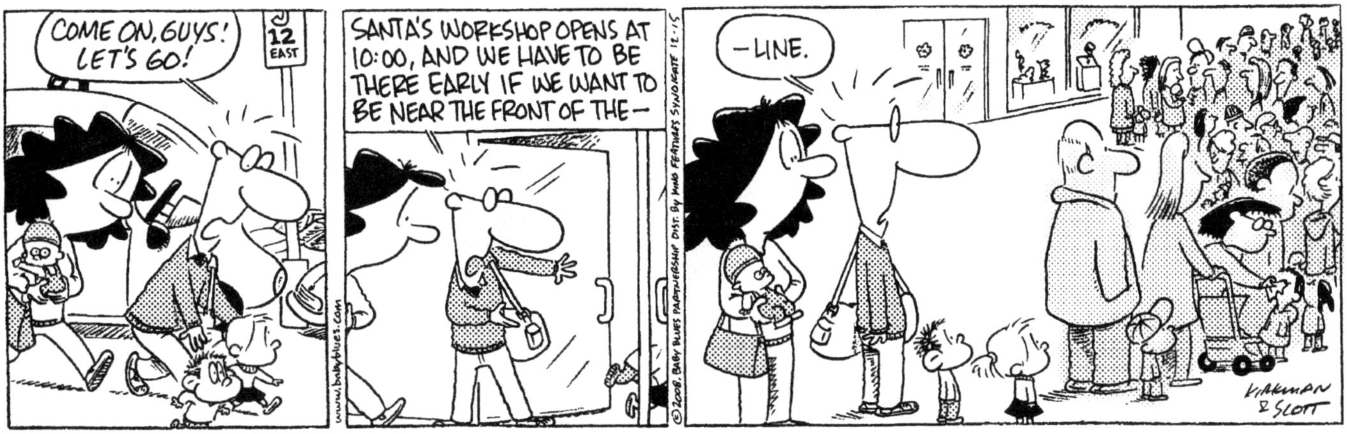
COME ON, GUYS! LET'S GO!
12 EAST
SANTA'S WORKSHOP OPENS AT 10:00, AND WE HAVE TO BE THERE EARLY IF WE WANT TO BE NEAR THE FRONT OF THE—
—LINE.
www.babyblues.com
© 2008, Baby Blues Partnership Dist. by King Features Syndicate 12-15
Kirkman & Scott

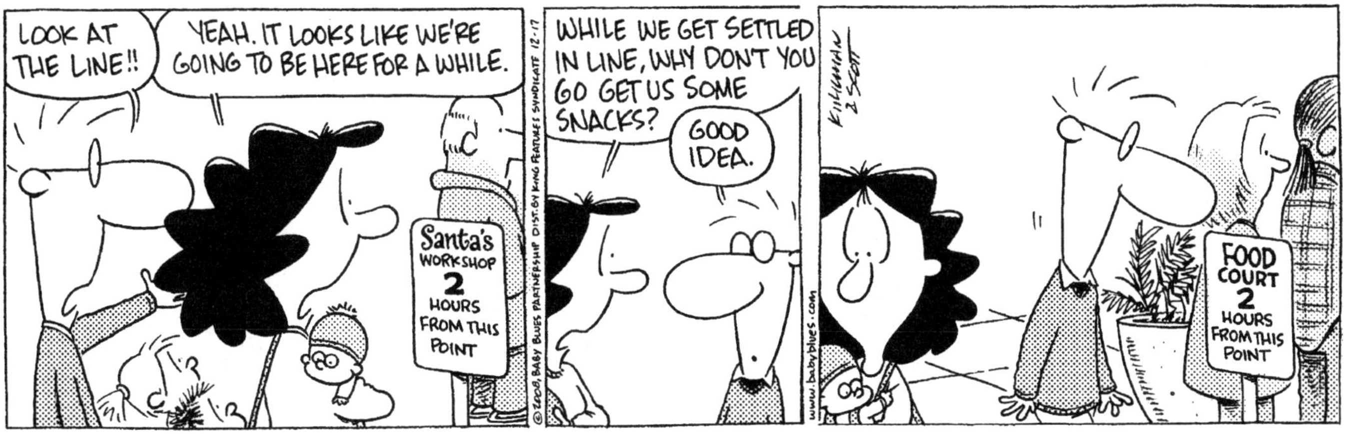
LOOK AT THE LINE!!
YEAH. IT LOOKS LIKE WE'RE GOING TO BE HERE FOR A WHILE.
Santa's WORKSHOP 2 HOURS FROM THIS POINT
© 2008, Baby Blues Partnership Dist. by King Features Syndicate 12-17
WHILE WE GET SETTLED IN LINE, WHY DON'T YOU GO GET US SOME SNACKS?
GOOD IDEA.
Kirkman & Scott
www.babyblues.com
FOOD COURT 2 HOURS FROM THIS POINT

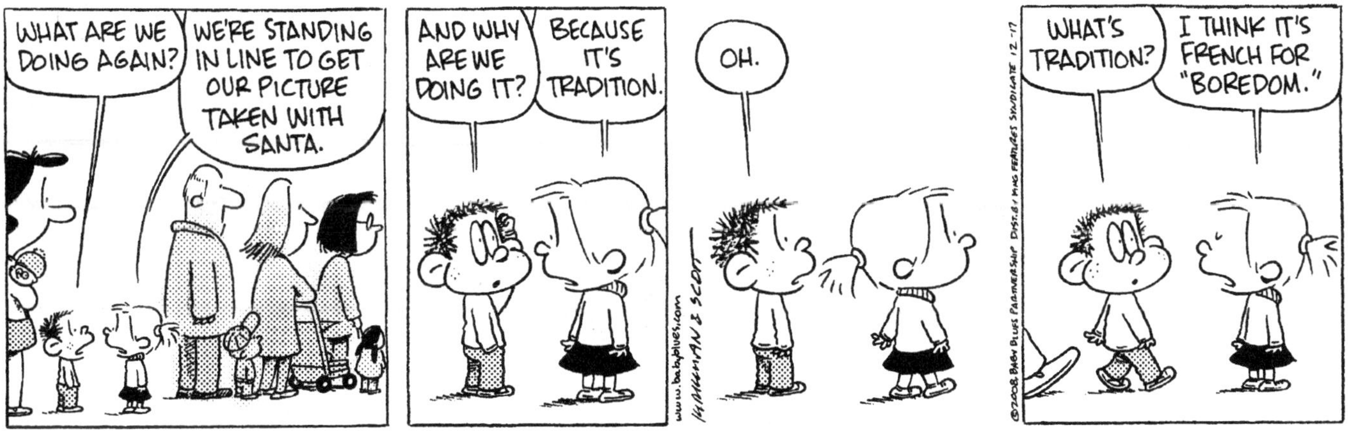
WHAT ARE WE DOING AGAIN?
WE'RE STANDING IN LINE TO GET OUR PICTURE TAKEN WITH SANTA.
AND WHY ARE WE DOING IT?
BECAUSE IT'S TRADITION.
www.babyblues.com
Kirkman & Scott
OH.
© 2008, Baby Blues Partnership Dist. by King Features Syndicate 12-17
WHAT'S TRADITION?
I THINK IT'S FRENCH FOR "BOREDOM."

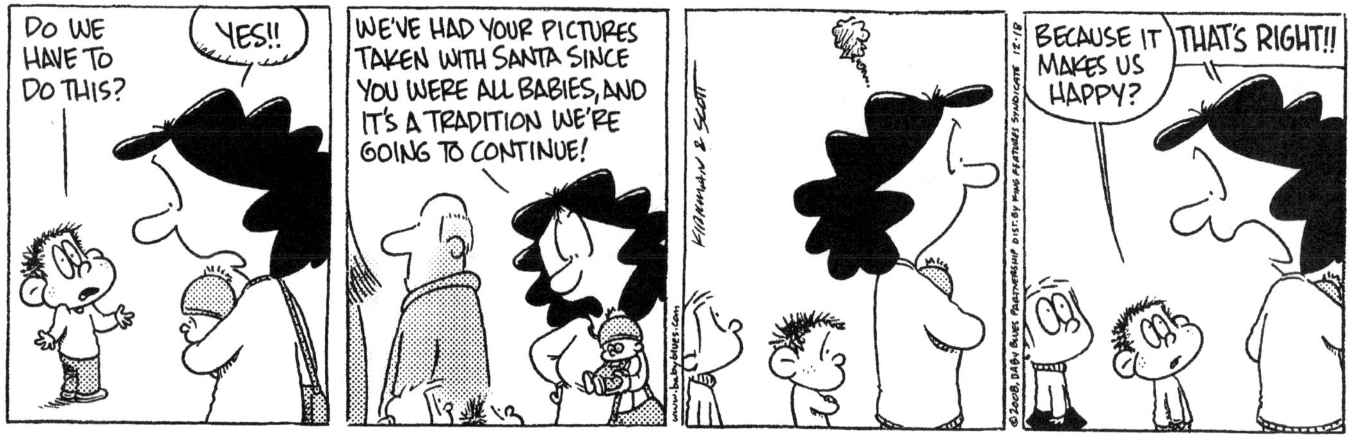
DO WE HAVE TO DO THIS?
YES!!
WE'VE HAD YOUR PICTURES TAKEN WITH SANTA SINCE YOU WERE ALL BABIES, AND IT'S A TRADITION WE'RE GOING TO CONTINUE!
KIRKMAN & SCOTT
www.babyblues.com
BECAUSE IT MAKES US HAPPY?
THAT'S RIGHT!!
©2008, BABY BLUES PARTNERSHIP DIST. BY KING FEATURES SYNDICATE 12-18

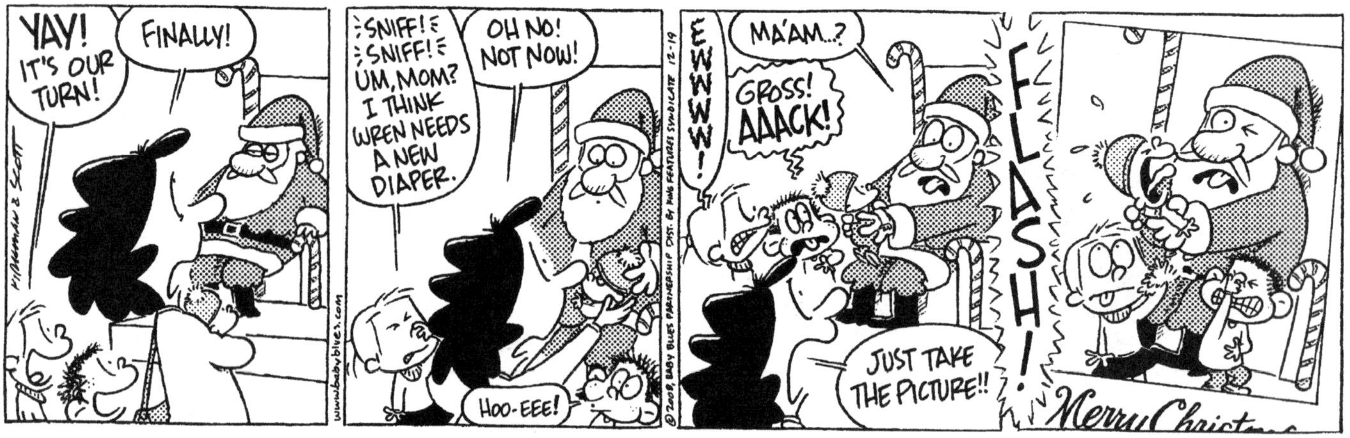
YAY! IT'S OUR TURN!
FINALLY!
KIRKMAN & SCOTT
www.babyblues.com
SNIFF! SNIFF! UM, MOM? I THINK WREN NEEDS A NEW DIAPER.
OH NO! NOT NOW!
HOO-EEE!
©2008, BABY BLUES PARTNERSHIP DIST. BY KING FEATURES SYNDICATE 12-19
EWWWW!
MA'AM...?
GROSS! AAACK!
JUST TAKE THE PICTURE!!
FLASH!
Merry Christmas

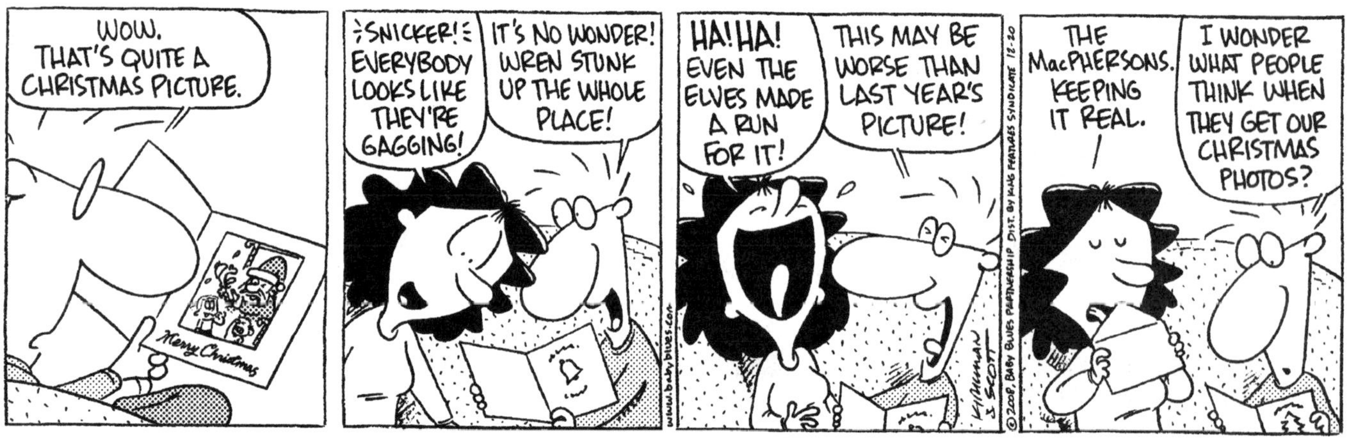
WOW. THAT'S QUITE A CHRISTMAS PICTURE.
Merry Christmas
SNICKER! EVERYBODY LOOKS LIKE THEY'RE GAGGING!
IT'S NO WONDER! WREN STUNK UP THE WHOLE PLACE!
www.babyblues.com
HA! HA! EVEN THE ELVES MADE A RUN FOR IT!
THIS MAY BE WORSE THAN LAST YEAR'S PICTURE!
KIRKMAN & SCOTT
THE MacPHERSONS. KEEPING IT REAL.
I WONDER WHAT PEOPLE THINK WHEN THEY GET OUR CHRISTMAS PHOTOS?
©2008, BABY BLUES PARTNERSHIP DIST. BY KING FEATURES SYNDICATE 12-20

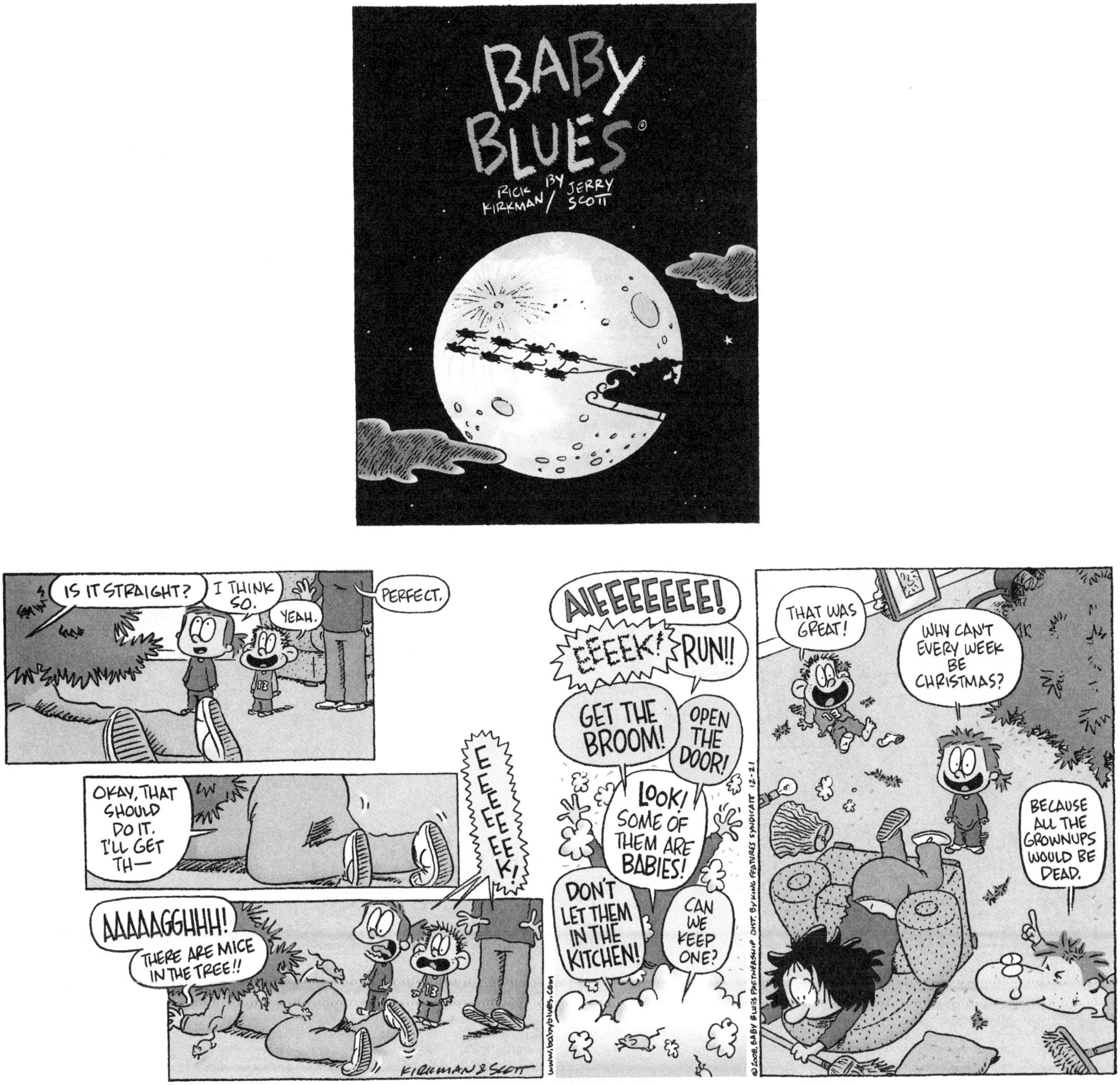
BABY BLUES®
BY RICK KIRKMAN / JERRY SCOTT
IS IT STRAIGHT?
I THINK SO.
YEAH.
PERFECT.
OKAY, THAT SHOULD DO IT. I'LL GET TH—
EEEEEEEK!
AAAAAGGHHH!
THERE ARE MICE IN THE TREE!!
KIRKMAN & SCOTT
www.babyblues.com
AIEEEEEEEE!
EEEEK!
RUN!!
GET THE BROOM!
OPEN THE DOOR!
LOOK! SOME OF THEM ARE BABIES!
DON'T LET THEM IN THE KITCHEN!
CAN WE KEEP ONE?
©2008, BABY BLUES PARTNERSHIP DIST. BY KING FEATURES SYNDICATE 12-21
THAT WAS GREAT!
WHY CAN'T EVERY WEEK BE CHRISTMAS?
BECAUSE ALL THE GROWNUPS WOULD BE DEAD.

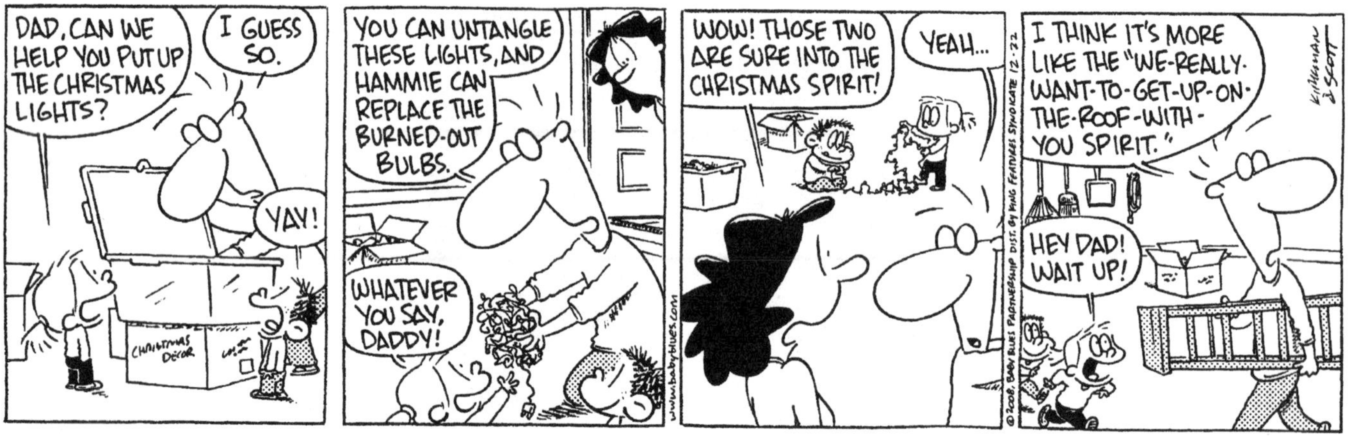
DAD, CAN WE HELP YOU PUT UP THE CHRISTMAS LIGHTS?
I GUESS SO.
YAY!
CHRISTMAS DECOR
YOU CAN UNTANGLE THESE LIGHTS, AND HAMMIE CAN REPLACE THE BURNED-OUT BULBS.
WHATEVER YOU SAY, DADDY!
www.babyblues.com
WOW! THOSE TWO ARE SURE INTO THE CHRISTMAS SPIRIT!
YEAH...
© 2008, BABY BLUES PARTNERSHIP DIST. BY KING FEATURES SYNDICATE 12-22
I THINK IT'S MORE LIKE THE "WE-REALLY-WANT-TO-GET-UP-ON-THE-ROOF-WITH-YOU SPIRIT."
HEY DAD! WAIT UP!
KIRKMAN & SCOTT

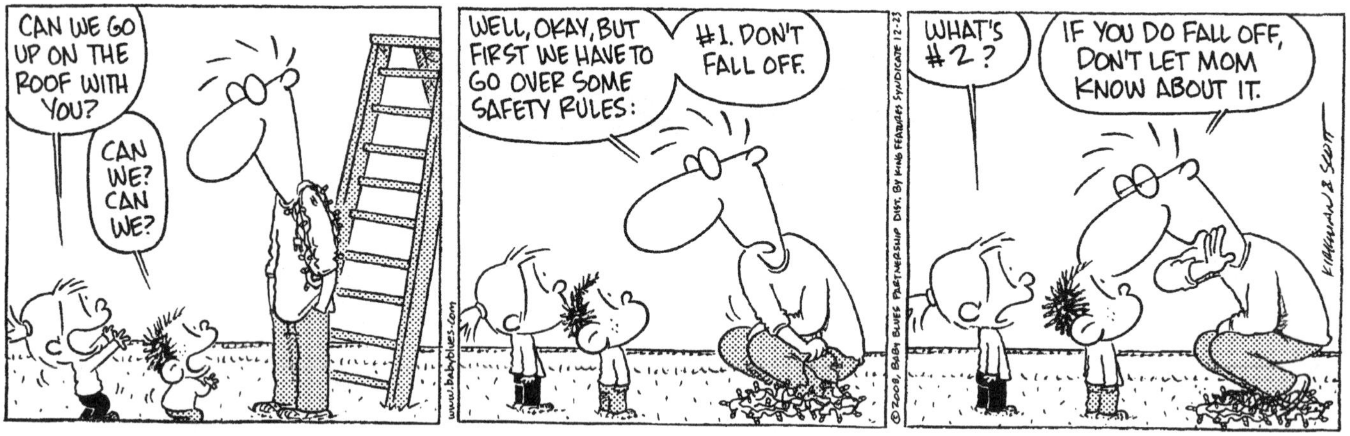
CAN WE GO UP ON THE ROOF WITH YOU?
CAN WE? CAN WE?
www.babyblues.com
WELL, OKAY, BUT FIRST WE HAVE TO GO OVER SOME SAFETY RULES:
#1. DON'T FALL OFF.
© 2008, BABY BLUES PARTNERSHIP DIST. BY KING FEATURES SYNDICATE 12-23
WHAT'S #2?
IF YOU DO FALL OFF, DON'T LET MOM KNOW ABOUT IT.
KIRKMAN & SCOTT

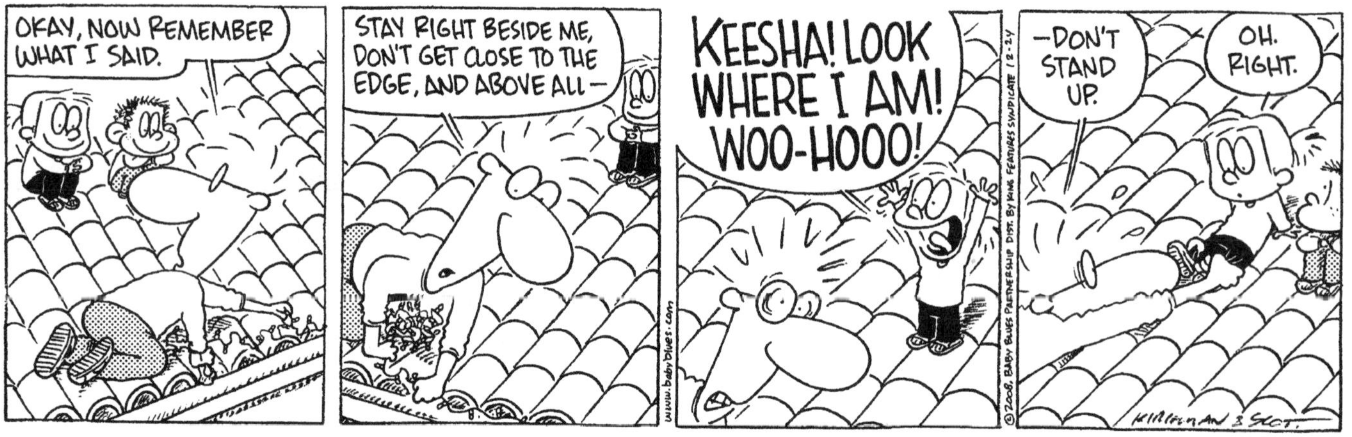
OKAY, NOW REMEMBER WHAT I SAID.
STAY RIGHT BESIDE ME, DON'T GET CLOSE TO THE EDGE, AND ABOVE ALL—
www.babyblues.com
KEESHA! LOOK WHERE I AM! WOO-HOOO!
© 2008, BABY BLUES PARTNERSHIP DIST. BY KING FEATURES SYNDICATE 12-24
—DON'T STAND UP.
OH. RIGHT.
KIRKMAN & SCOTT

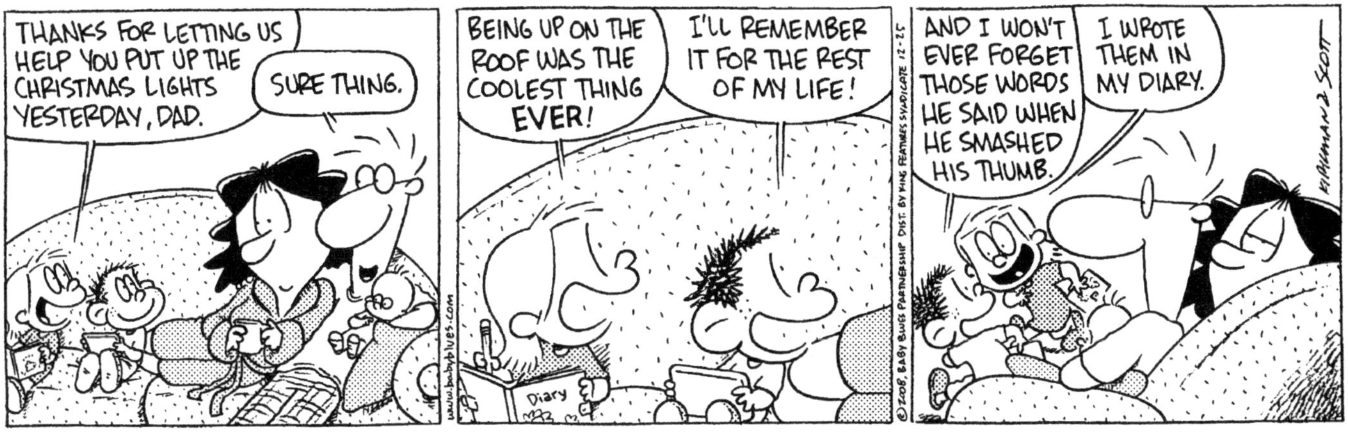
THANKS FOR LETTING US HELP YOU PUT UP THE CHRISTMAS LIGHTS YESTERDAY, DAD.
SURE THING.
www.babyblues.com
BEING UP ON THE ROOF WAS THE COOLEST THING EVER!
I'LL REMEMBER IT FOR THE REST OF MY LIFE!
Diary
©2008, BABY BLUES PARTNERSHIP DIST. BY KING FEATURES SYNDICATE 12-25
AND I WON'T EVER FORGET THOSE WORDS HE SAID WHEN HE SMASHED HIS THUMB.
I WROTE THEM IN MY DIARY.
KIRKMAN & SCOTT

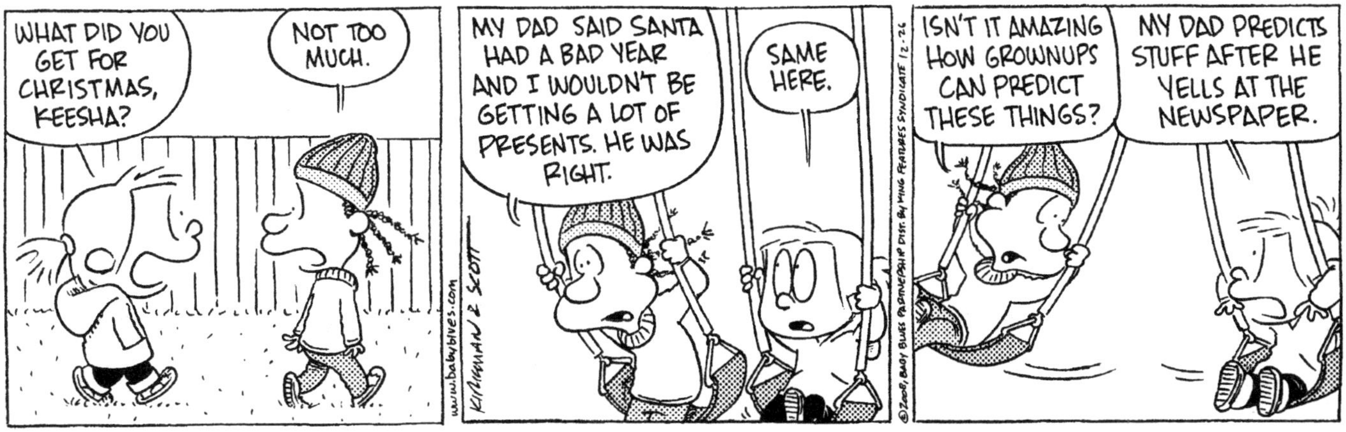
WHAT DID YOU GET FOR CHRISTMAS, KEESHA?
NOT TOO MUCH.
www.babyblues.com
KIRKMAN & SCOTT
MY DAD SAID SANTA HAD A BAD YEAR AND I WOULDN'T BE GETTING A LOT OF PRESENTS. HE WAS RIGHT.
SAME HERE.
©2008, BABY BLUES PARTNERSHIP DIST. BY KING FEATURES SYNDICATE 12-26
ISN'T IT AMAZING HOW GROWNUPS CAN PREDICT THESE THINGS?
MY DAD PREDICTS STUFF AFTER HE YELLS AT THE NEWSPAPER.

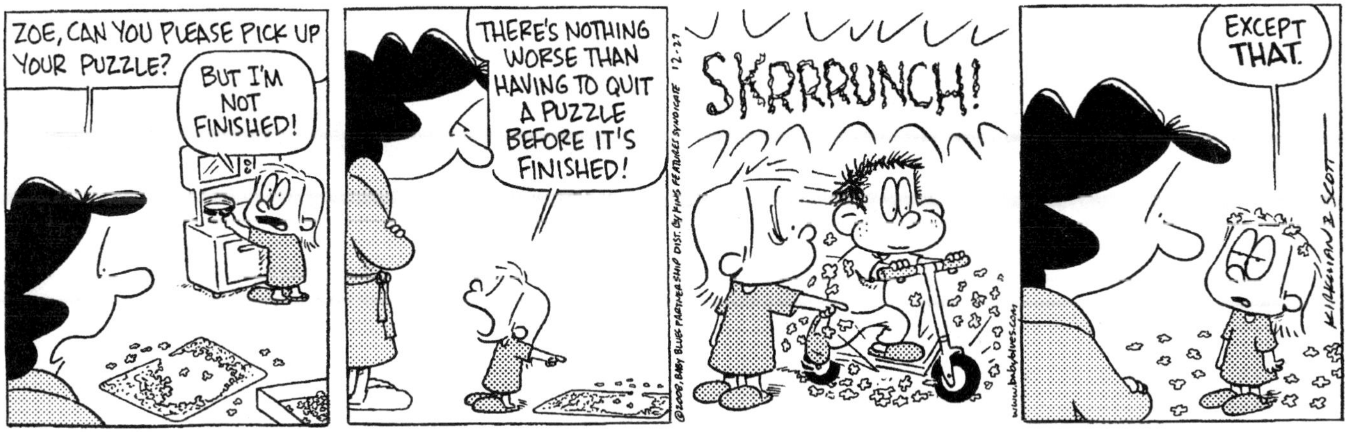
ZOE, CAN YOU PLEASE PICK UP YOUR PUZZLE?
BUT I'M NOT FINISHED!
THERE'S NOTHING WORSE THAN HAVING TO QUIT A PUZZLE BEFORE IT'S FINISHED!
©2008, BABY BLUES PARTNERSHIP DIST. BY KING FEATURES SYNDICATE 12-27
SKRRRUNCH!
www.babyblues.com
EXCEPT THAT.
KIRKMAN & SCOTT

BABY BLUES®
BY
RICK KIRKMAN / JERRY SCOTT

OKAY, I'M READY.
WOW!
HUH?
THAT SWEATER LOOKS GREAT ON YOU, HAMMIE!
I LOVE THE PATTERN, IT FITS BEAUTIFULLY, AND THE COLOR MAKES YOUR EYES LOOK AMAZING!
YOU'RE A TOTAL BABE-MAGNET NOW!
12-28
KIRKMAN & SCOTT
www.babyblues.com
© 2008 BABY BLUES PARTNERSHIP DIST. BY KING FEATURES SYNDICATE
WHY IS YOUR SWEATER ON INSIDE-OUT?
I'M REVERSING MY POLARITY.

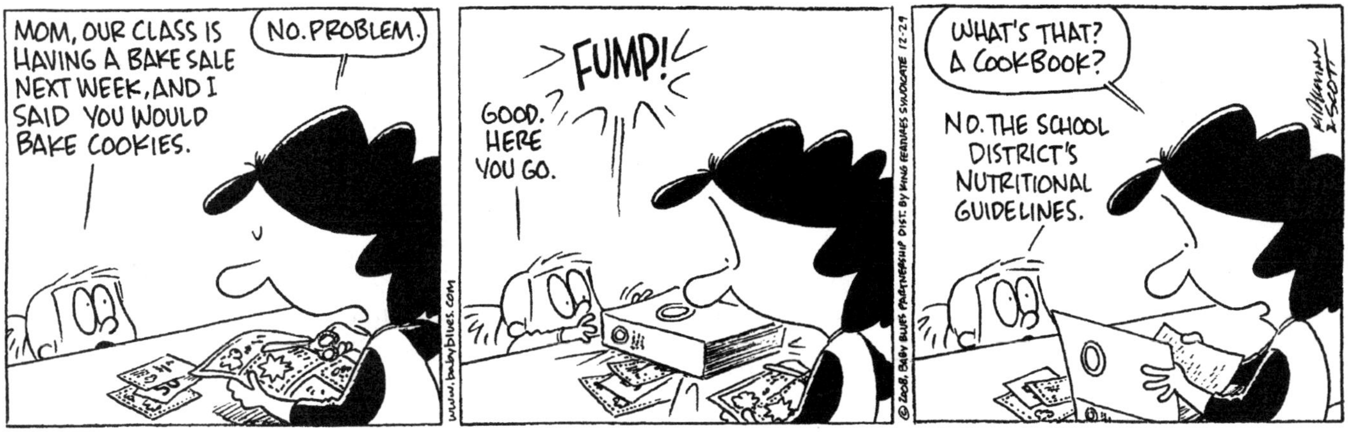
MOM, OUR CLASS IS HAVING A BAKE SALE NEXT WEEK, AND I SAID YOU WOULD BAKE COOKIES.
NO. PROBLEM.
www.babyblues.com
FUMP!
GOOD. HERE YOU GO.
© 2008, BABY BLUES PARTNERSHIP DIST. BY KING FEATURES SYNDICATE 12-29
WHAT'S THAT? A COOKBOOK?
NO. THE SCHOOL DISTRICT'S NUTRITIONAL GUIDELINES.
KIRKMAN & SCOTT

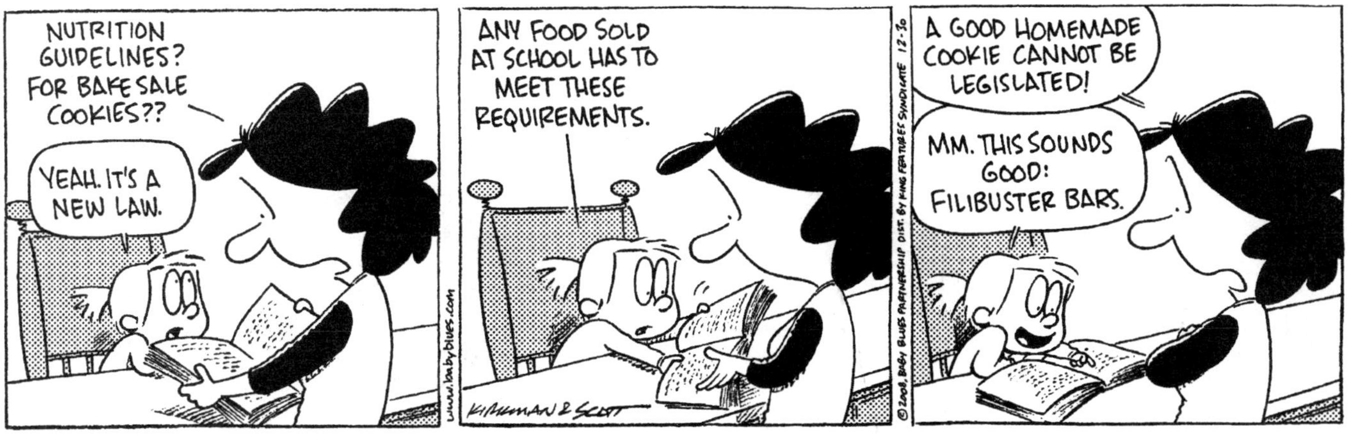
NUTRITION GUIDELINES? FOR BAKE SALE COOKIES??
YEAH. IT'S A NEW LAW.
www.babyblues.com
ANY FOOD SOLD AT SCHOOL HAS TO MEET THESE REQUIREMENTS.
KIRKMAN & SCOTT
© 2008, BABY BLUES PARTNERSHIP DIST. BY KING FEATURES SYNDICATE 12-30
A GOOD HOMEMADE COOKIE CANNOT BE LEGISLATED!
MM. THIS SOUNDS GOOD: FILIBUSTER BARS.

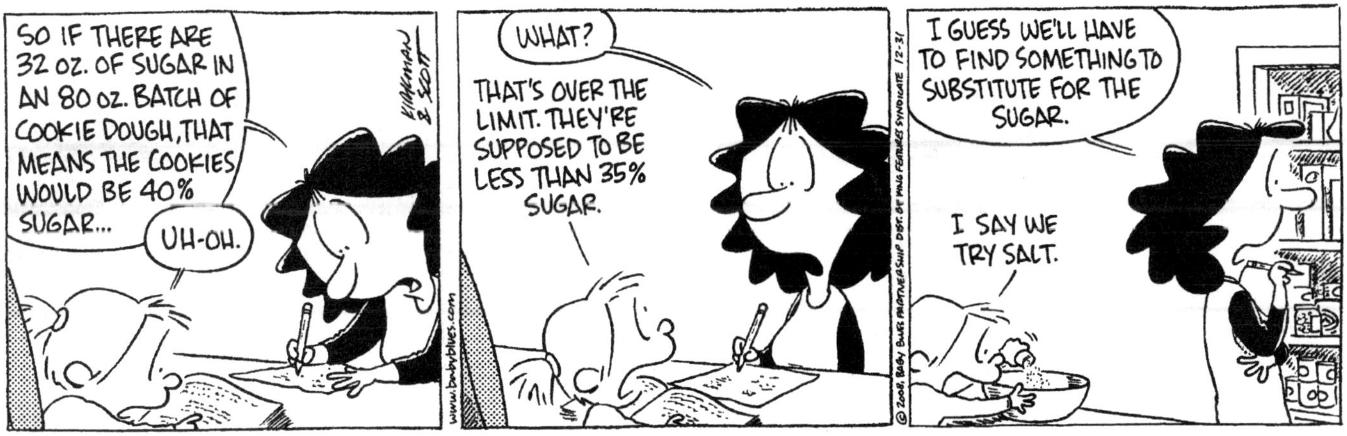
SO IF THERE ARE 32 OZ. OF SUGAR IN AN 80 OZ. BATCH OF COOKIE DOUGH, THAT MEANS THE COOKIES WOULD BE 40% SUGAR...
UH-OH.
KIRKMAN & SCOTT
www.babyblues.com
WHAT?
THAT'S OVER THE LIMIT. THEY'RE SUPPOSED TO BE LESS THAN 35% SUGAR.
© 2008, BABY BLUES PARTNERSHIP DIST. BY KING FEATURES SYNDICATE 12-31
I GUESS WE'LL HAVE TO FIND SOMETHING TO SUBSTITUTE FOR THE SUGAR.
I SAY WE TRY SALT.

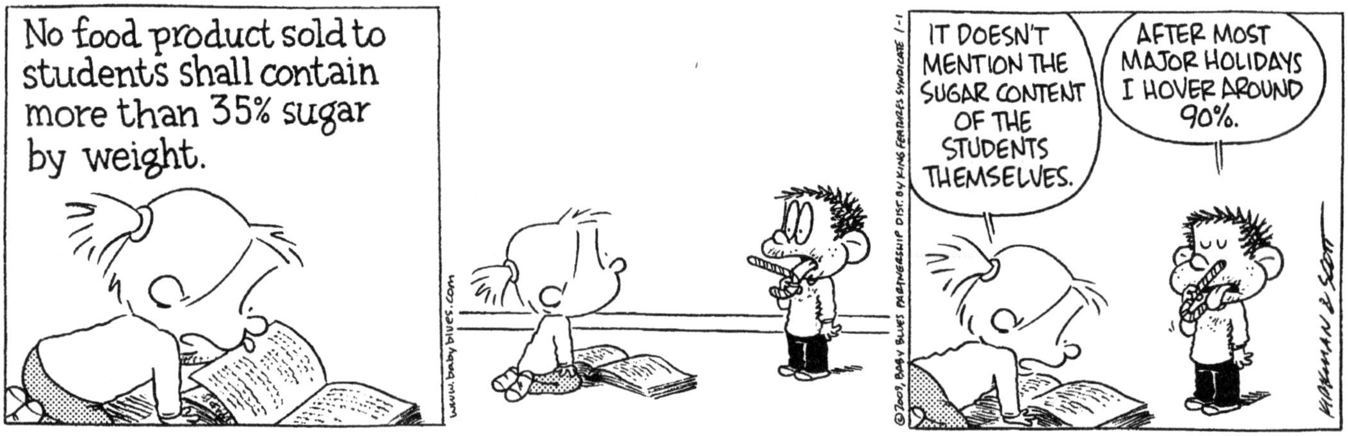
No food product sold to students shall contain more than 35% sugar by weight.
www.babyblues.com
IT DOESN'T MENTION THE SUGAR CONTENT OF THE STUDENTS THEMSELVES.
AFTER MOST MAJOR HOLIDAYS I HOVER AROUND 90%.
© 2009, BABY BLUES PARTNERSHIP DIST. BY KING FEATURES SYNDICATE 1-1
KIRKMAN & SCOTT

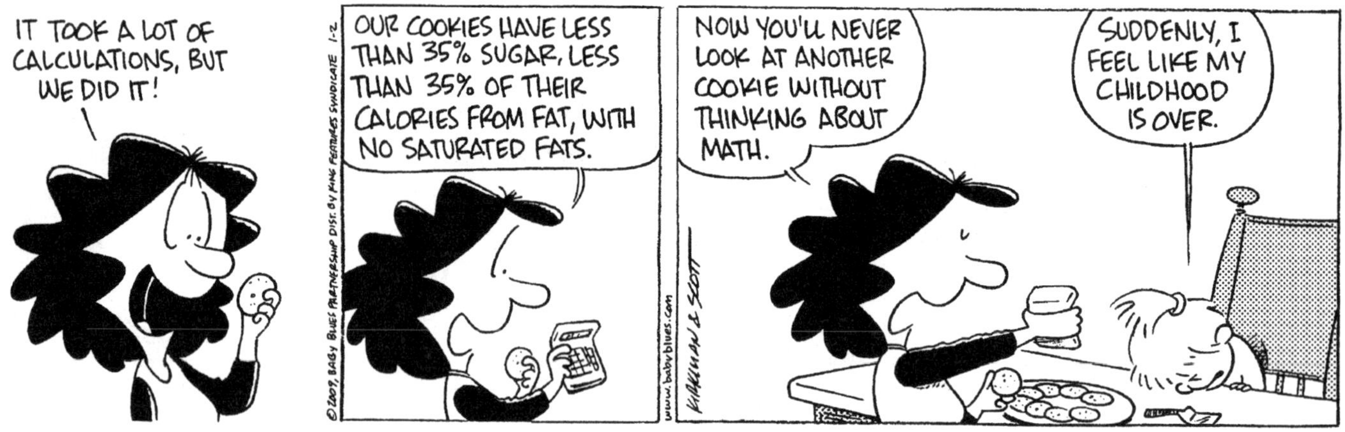
IT TOOK A LOT OF CALCULATIONS, BUT WE DID IT!
OUR COOKIES HAVE LESS THAN 35% SUGAR, LESS THAN 35% OF THEIR CALORIES FROM FAT, WITH NO SATURATED FATS.
© 2009, BABY BLUES PARTNERSHIP DIST. BY KING FEATURES SYNDICATE 1-2
www.babyblues.com
KIRKMAN & SCOTT
NOW YOU'LL NEVER LOOK AT ANOTHER COOKIE WITHOUT THINKING ABOUT MATH.
SUDDENLY, I FEEL LIKE MY CHILDHOOD IS OVER.

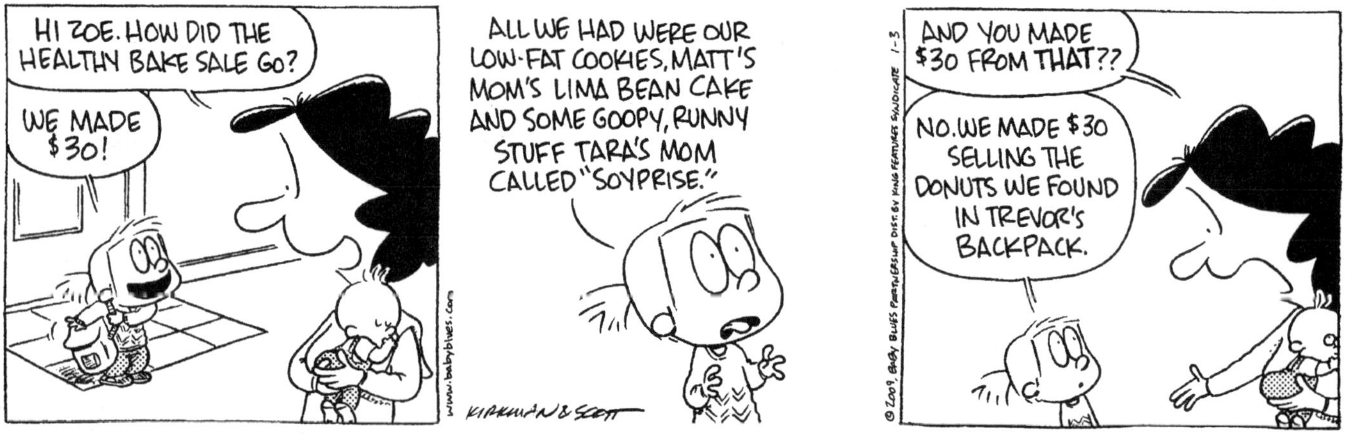
HI ZOE. HOW DID THE HEALTHY BAKE SALE GO?
WE MADE $30!
www.babyblues.com
ALL WE HAD WERE OUR LOW-FAT COOKIES, MATT'S MOM'S LIMA BEAN CAKE AND SOME GOOPY, RUNNY STUFF TARA'S MOM CALLED "SOYPRISE."
KIRKMAN & SCOTT
AND YOU MADE $30 FROM THAT??
NO. WE MADE $30 SELLING THE DONUTS WE FOUND IN TREVOR'S BACKPACK.
© 2009, BABY BLUES PARTNERSHIP DIST. BY KING FEATURES SYNDICATE 1-3